6 50

RAGE AND FIRE

A Life of Louise Colet

Pioneer Feminist,
Literary Star,
Flaubert's Muse

Francine du Plessix Gray

Simon & Schuster
New York • London • Toronto • Sydney • Tokyo • Singapore

SIMON & SCHUSTER
ROCKEFELLER CENTER
1230 AVENUE OF THE AMERICAS
NEW YORK, NEW YORK 10020

DESIGNED BY LEVAVI & LEVAVI
MANUFACTURED IN THE UNITED STATES OF AMERICA

1   3   5   7   9   10   8   6   4   2

LIBRARY OF CONGRESS CATALOGING IN PUBLICATION DATA

GRAY, FRANCINE DU PLESSIX.
RAGE AND FIRE: A LIFE OF LOUISE COLET, PIONEER FEMINIST, LITERARY
STAR, FLAUBERT'S MUSE / FRANCINE DU PLESSIX GRAY.
P.   CM.
INCLUDES BIBLIOGRAPHICAL REFERENCES AND INDEX.
1. COLET, LOUISE, 1810–1876—BIOGRAPHY.   2. FLAUBERT, GUSTAVE,
1821–1880—RELATIONS WITH WOMEN.   3. WOMEN AND LITERATURE—FRANCE—
HISTORY—19TH CENTURY.   4. WOMEN AUTHORS, FRENCH—19TH CENTURY—
BIOGRAPHY.   5. FEMINISTS—FRANCE—BIOGRAPHY.   I. TITLE.
PQ2209.C6Z66   1994
848'.709—DC20   ISBN: 0-671-74238-8   [B]   93-41216 CIP

PHOTO CREDITS

1 Courtesy of Bibliothèque Ceccano, Avignon.
2, 5, 12, 20, 30 Cliché des Musées Nationaux, Paris.
3, 4 Photographs by Francine Gray.
6, 7, 21 Courtesy of Musée Calvet, Avignon.
8, 11, 13, 15, 16, 17, 19, 22, 24, 29 Bibliothèque Nationale, Paris.
9 © 1994 ARS, New York/SPADEM, Paris.
10 Musée Granet, Aix-en-Provence.
14 Micheline Bood. *L'Indomptable Louise Colet.* © Pierre Horay Publishers, Paris.
18 Courtesy of Musée Flaubert, Rouen.
23 The Mansell Collection, London.
25 The Metropolitan Museum of Art, Bequest of Mrs. H.O. Havemeyer, 1929. The H.O. Havemeyer
   Collection. (29.100.59).
26 Musée du Vieil Aix, Aix-en-Provence.
27, 28 Nicole Priollaud, ed. *La Femme au 19e Siècle.* © Editions Liana Levi, Paris.

Acknowledgments

My first and greatest debt is to my cherished editor of the past two decades, Alice Mayhew. From the outset of this venture she offered me the greatest gift I could have received—her trust in the possibility that the life of a heretofore obscure nineteenth-century woman could be material for an exciting book. Beyond this initial leap of faith, and the enthusiasm and affectionate support she always offers me during my writer's doldrums, I'm grateful for the more than habitual rigor with which she edited this text. This time round, she was aided in this operation by her young colleague Elizabeth Stein, whose own acumen and editorial skills are downright uncanny for someone only a few years out of college. Much gratitude, Liz, for the patience and cheer with which you calmed my yowls during the more painful moments of prose surgery.

My next debt of gratitude is to my dearest friend and mentor, Ethel Woodward de Croisset, my perennial hostess in Paris, who for the umpteenth time sheltered, fed, and consoled me during my research trips to Paris. Often forcing me to rest and eat properly (activities which only she seems able to impose upon me), she continually soothed me during my compulsive working schedules at the Bibliothèque Nationale and other archives. Ethel displayed an ardent curiosity in this particular project, occasionally accompanying me on my forays; her keen insights into women's issues in general, and the plight of nineteenth-century French women in particular, were terrific sources of inspiration.

I am grateful to my treasured friend Claude Nabokoff, who brought her remarkable expertise as an art historian and pictorial researcher to the problem of finding images pertinent to Colet's life and career, and without whose collaboration I could have spent months floundering in the Byzantine procedures of the Bibliothèque Nationale's Cabinet d'Estampes. And my loving thanks to three other Paris chums—Gabrielle Van Zuylen, Mary Sargent d'Anglejan, and Micheline Fried—who kept my spirits buoyed by their enthusiasm for this undertaking, and also helped to keep me sane, cheered, and splendidly fed during my research trips to France.

I'm particularly grateful for the pioneering work done in Flaubert studies by Francis Steegmuller, by Professor Jean Bruneau, and by Professor Lucette Czyba of the Université de Besancon. It is a third rereading of Steegmuller's splendid book *Flaubert and Madame Bovary* that initially incited me to write a biography of Louise Colet. The dazzling Pléiade edition of Flaubert's *Correspondance* executed by Professor Bruneau has been a gold mine for my research, as it is bound to be to all Flaubertistes for generations to come, and the time Professor Bruneau generously granted me to share his impressions of the Colet-Flaubert relationship was of inestimable value. Equally precious were my conversations with Professor Czyba, whose remarkable book *La Femme dans les Romans de Flaubert* will remain a milestone in nineteenth-century Women's Studies.

Of the families in France who helped me to document this book, I owe particular gratitude to Maurice Hendrik Bood, who gave me access to the family archives leagued decades ago to his wife, the late Micheline Bood. The spirit of trust and generous hospitality with which M. Bood allowed me to use the facilities of his office, and of his photocopying machines, was memorable.

Neither can I forget the graciousness with which M. Paul Révoil, Louise Colet's great-great-grandnephew and the present owner of her childhood home in Provence, received me at their ancestral dwelling, the "Hostellerie de Servanes." M. Révoil and his wife allowed me to share whatever family archives they possessed, and also invited me to sample the charm of one of the most enchanting country inns I've come across in southern France.

The most rewarding research for this book was done at the remarkable

Bibliothèque Municipale d'Avignon, (denoted on Avignon street maps as "Médiathèque Ceccano"), which houses a Colet archive of some 6,000 folio pages, the Fonds Louise Colet. My thanks to its ever cordial and competent staff, and to its director, Mlle. Francoise de Forbin, for all their help. I am also indebted to the staff of the Musée Calvet in Avignon, and of its generous director, Madame Marie-Pierre Foissy-Aufrère, for enabling me to view their collection of Colet memorabilia during the years their institution was closed to the public and undergoing an intensive renovation.

Deep gratitude to those of my friends who read my book in early manuscript form and pointed out the many passages that needed to be neatened or shortened: my beloved comrades of forty-five years and perennial first readers—Joanna Rose, Leo Lerman, and Gray Foy; my friends Dodie Kazanjian and Mary "Bab" Huvelle, whose laser-sharp vision for graceful diction and rightness of tone helped me inestimably during the first months of the honing process; and Professor Janet Beizer of the University of Virginia, a star in the field of nineteenth-century French studies, who, beyond her formidable proficiency in that area of scholarship, showed sisterly support in the meticulousness with which she read my manuscript.

Finally, I extend my heartfelt thanks to the wonderful young women who helped me with my research on Louise Colet, and without whose skillful assistance this book might have been delayed by many months: Rosario Manalo, who aided me in the first stages of my investigations; Kay Abella, who saved my sanity in the last phases of correcting proofs; Sahar Amer and Catherine Dana of Yale University, whose dedication to my enterprise has been beyond the call of duty, and whom I look forward impatiently to collaborating with in the course of writing my next book.

And—"World without End"—infinite gratitude to my cherished friends and agents, Anne and Georges Borchardt, who remain, as ever, invaluable sources of wisdom, cheer, astute advice, and rock-solid support.

With deep gratitude to
the John Simon Guggenheim Memorial Foundation
for their support

Again, to Cleve Gray
with passion and wonder

Contents

Prologue

❦

RAGE AND FIRE

Opening images:

A rainy night in May of 1854. A man and a woman who have been lovers for many years sit across from each other in a Paris flat, arguing.

The woman is a celebrated writer, hostess of one of the city's most eminent literary salons. In her mid-forties, she is statuesque, still beautiful, her hair falling to her shoulders in a cascade of golden ringlets. Sitting by her fireplace, her legs crossed, she swings her foot emphatically as she hurls accusations at her visitor.

Her foot occasionally strikes the man's own leg as she voices her outrage.

The man is thirty-three years old, eleven years younger than she, an obscure provincial who aspires to a literary career. He is of massive build, balding prematurely, his mouth somewhat blackened by the mercury treatments he takes for syphilis.

He winces each time the woman's leg hits his.

For nearly eight years they have poured their ambitions, their sorrows, their love and lust, into several thousand pages of correspondence.

She has a Mediterranean temperament, is extroverted, gregarious, quick-tempered, incapable of subterfuge. He is secretive, a loner, a master of self-control, dedicated only to the glory of his art.

Known in Paris as "the Muse," she is a friend of Victor Hugo, Alfred de Musset, and Alfred de Vigny, has published a score of books, and has won the Académie Française poetry prize three times in a row, more often than any other woman in French history.

The young man has not yet published a word. The woman sitting with him by the fire was the first to recognize and encourage his genius.

Over the course of these eight years, their relationship has foundered on a host of differences; yet he has been the love of her life, and she of his.

The woman is Louise Colet. The man is Gustave Flaubert.

This evening Gustave and Louise have agreed to meet at nine o'clock at her flat on the Rue de Sèvres (now the site of the Hotel Lutétia). Gustave arrives at nine-fifteen.

"You're late because you've been out with those whores again!" she cries. "You're always with those women. I've always known you preferred that filth to me!"

She goes on. He has betrayed every promise he made her in the past year, he is a fickle good-for-nothing, he has no heart.

Gustave stares at the fire in Louise's grate. The walls of Louise's living room—sky blue like her eyes—are hung with souvenirs of her youth in Provence: portraits of her mother and her maternal grandfather, a bust of her hero Mirabeau, the greatest orator of the 1789 revolution.

As she continues to cry out her grievances, Louise's leg hits Gustave's once more, and his thoughts turn to violence.

He measures the distance between the fireplace and her forehead.

He imagines himself quickly reaching into the fire . . .

Taking up a burning log . . .

Swiftly striking her with it, setting fire to her golden hair and azure dress, smashing her head over and over until she falls into a ring of cleansing, quieting fire . . .

"I was really quite ready to kill her," Gustave would report years later to his friends.

"Killing her . . . yes, it was the only way out. The fantasy lasted a good long while."

"I'd have done it," he would explain, "but suddenly I was caught by a vision—the vision of a courtroom, of being surrounded by police."

"Perhaps I was a coward!" he would add, with his booming laugh.

"Here's what held me back: I imagined those hard, ice-cold courtroom seats crackling under my thighs . . . *that*'s what kept me from it. So instead of killing her, I rose from my chair and left."

Gustave and Louise never saw each other again.

It is now October of 1879, a quarter of a century later. Louise Colet has been dead for three years. After the success of his novel *Madame Bovary,* for which Louise was a model and a consultant, Gustave Flaubert published the popular *Salammbô;* the controversial *Sentimental Education;* the much-acclaimed *Three Tales.* He now corresponds with admirers from all over Europe, has been decorated with the Legion of Honor and feted by France's royal family.

Gustave has grown very portly, is almost totally bald, and has only one tooth left in a mouth now totally blackened by mercury medications. On this October night at his home in Croisset, a few miles from Rouen, where he has lived since the age of twenty-two, Gustave, now fifty-seven years old, is plagued by thoughts of death. He has invited one of his closest friends for dinner, a young writer he considers to be his chief disciple, Guy de Maupassant.

"Thank you, thank you for coming, dear boy," Gustave says as his guest arrives, embracing Maupassant tenderly. "We're not about to have a cheerful evening; I want to burn most of my old letters, things I don't want anyone to read. And I couldn't face doing it alone. You'll spend the night here, all right? . . . And if I become distraught, we can talk a bit."

The two men stroll for a while by Flaubert's house, which overlooks the Seine, walking down an alley lined with linden trees that still stand today. They go in for dinner, Flaubert has ordered a particularly fine meal, opened the oldest Bordeaux in his cellar. "I've got to be tough tonight," he keeps repeating to Maupassant. "I can't afford one moment of softness."

After dinner they return to Flaubert's study, a large, book-filled room. They sit by the fireplace and smoke a few pipes, the small white ceramic pipes Flaubert brought back decades before from the Near East. Then Flaubert rises from his chair.

"Please help me," he asks Maupassant.

They go into his bedroom, a long, narrow room off his study. They take up the handles of a large suitcase that stands behind a curtain and bring it back into his study, place it in front of the fire roaring in the grate.

Flaubert opens the suitcase. It is full of papers. "Here's my life," Flaubert says. "I want to keep a small part of it and burn the rest. Sit down, friend, read for a while. I'm going to destroy a few things."

The first letters Flaubert opens, the most recent ones, he tosses into the fire with no hesitation. Then he starts unfolding some older ones, lingering over them, sighing. "Here's one from Madame Sand, listen." And he reads a few passages to Maupassant, repeating softly, "Ah, what a great fellow that woman was."

Flaubert reads a few more letters aloud, mostly recent ones from famous people, whose inanities he describes in a booming voice, with great bursts of laughter. He puts them aside, to keep as inspiration for his work in progress, a satiric novel to be called *Bouvard et Pécuchet.* Others he throws brusquely into the fire, barely looking at them as they burst into flame and illuminate the darkest recesses of the room.

The hours pass. Flaubert does not speak anymore as he continues to read. The letters seem to reach further and further into his past, to his youth. From time to time he murmurs a name, sighs, makes the desolate gesture of a mourner at a grave. These more intimate papers he only glances at, burning heaps of them, as if he wishes to destroy most memories and loves.

The large clock off the study rings out four A.M. Flaubert is still burning papers. Suddenly, in the middle of a particularly thick packet of letters, he comes upon a package tied with a narrow ribbon. He opens it very slowly, takes out a small silken shoe; inside it is a faded rose rolled in a woman's handkerchief, its lace yellow with age.

Flaubert kisses these three relics sorrowfully. Then he throws them into the fireplace along with the thick sheaf of letters that surround them, wiping his eyes. Dawn has come, and his bonfire is nearly finished.

I believe that those last missives—the ones bound together with the silk slipper, the withered rose, the faded kerchief—were the many hundreds of letters written to Flaubert by Louise Colet. That is why I have written this book. To reinstate a colleague into the annals of her time. To do her justice. To resurrect yet another woman whose memory has been erased by the caprices of men.

1.

Provence

❧❦❧

The next time you're in Provence, trace your way down a Michelin map thirty kilometers south of Avignon, some eight minutes' drive beyond the towns of Les Baux and Saint-Rémy, and you will easily find Mouriès, the little village neighboring Louise Révoil Colet's ancestral home. Barely changed since her time, the Château de Servanes is less than a mile from the village. It is a rustic ocher-hued mansion surrounded by dovecotes and olive mills, reached through an alley of ancient oaks. Pines, cypresses, venerable elms, groves of olive, fig, and almond trees pervade the faerie landscape of Servanes, which has remained in the possession of Louise Colet's family since the seventeenth century, and where she spent a good part of her first twenty-four years.

The sprawling two-story dwelling, built flat-roofed in the Provençal *mas* style for protection from the dreaded mistral wind, is extended by stables, sheepfolds, granges. Behind the verdant terrain that surrounds it, the same stony dust-pale hills that make Les Baux one of the wonders of Europe stretch out as far as the eye can see. The name Servanes derives from the Provençal word *serba,* "source of water"; and the mossy water basins facing the main house, afloat with water lilies and flanked by antique statuary, still give it the aura of a somnolent oasis.

One is very close here to the great Aurelian Way, which connected Rome to Paris. To this day, shards of Greek pottery, Roman coins, fragments of classical statuary, are found in the fields surrounding Servanes. In this sun-dappled site suffused with the fragrance of thyme and lavender, hovering beneath a bank of brooding mountains, there is as much solitude as there was in Louise's time, and the sense of a glory irretrievably lost. A perfect place, in sum, for a young girl born in 1810 to grow into a Romantic poet, into a woman who was to embody the excesses of Romantic illusions.

Aix-en-Provence, some fifty miles east of Servanes, the city where Louise Révoil Colet was born and where three generations of her ancestors served as members of the Parliament of Provence, played an equal role in shaping her exuberant, stormy nature and the character of the eccentric family that oppressed her throughout her youth.

Aix is a city dominated by the memory of King René, the greatest ruler of medieval Provence. This gentle, idealistic leader, one of the most gifted poets, painters, and musicians of his time, had been king of Jerusalem, Sicily, Aragon, Valencia, Majorca, Sardinia, and Corsica, as well as duke of Anjou and count of Barcelona and of Piedmont. As beloved by the Provençals as Charlemagne is by the northern French, during his decades of rule (1430–1480) he gave Aix equal ranking with Paris as France's leading cultural center, and lulled his people into delusions of perpetual grandeur.

For many centuries, Provence's local parliament, drawn almost exclusively from its aristocracy and landed gentry, enjoyed a greater independence than any other ruling elite in France. In the second half of the seventeenth century, when their pomp and power reached an apogee, the patricians of Aix built the sumptuous palaces that still line the south side of the city's main thoroughfare, Cours Mirabeau, then called "Grand Cours."

The street itself, a stone's throw from where Louise was born and lived for many winters, reflected the high-handedness of the city's ruling class. Until the revolution of 1789, the Grand Cours was reserved exclusively for the use of the nobility. On those Sundays and holidays when the "people" were allowed to use the Cours, they were restricted to the northern, nonresidential side of the street.

Aix-en-Provence's aristocracy personified as few other societies in France the excesses of the *ancien régime*. It was notorious for its rigid class barriers and sexual scandals: courtesans managing houses of prostitution within the walls of convents, noblemen bribing judges to acquit them of charges of murdering their wives, gangs of drunken young squires performing sadistic murder rituals on peasants.

No wonder that in this libertine, self-indulgent environment little effort was made to correct the severe economic crises that began to grip the entire Aix region in the half century that preceded the Revolution. In those decades, the city's modest commerce—embroidery, the bottling of olive oil and candied fruit—was rendered obsolete by the industrial changes transforming the rest of Europe. The restructuring of the entire administrative system of the French provinces following Napoleon's coup d'etat of 1800 further precipitated Aix's decline. The city was demoted from its historic place as capital of Provence to the modest status of sub-prefecture, and Marseilles became the first city of the south of France. In one of her early poems, Louise Révoil Colet expressed the resentment of her fellow Aixois toward this shift of power:

Poor vassal! O despair of a crowned head,
Mother of a kingdom and widow of the great René,
Sleeping on the memory of your royal purple,
You've become the vassal of a new Tyre, the rich Marseilles!

Like a beggar sitting on your own threshold
Yet still maintaining your pride,
You look with patrician disdain
Upon this upstart grown rich in trade.

In 1815, when Louise was four years old, the battle of Waterloo brought an end to Napoleon's brief second reign, the "Hundred Days." The second restoration of the Bourbon monarchy that same year brought twofold elation to Aix-en-Provence's royalist citizenry, for the official title of the sixty-year-old Louis XVIII—Louis XVI's younger brother, an amiable and lazy glutton so fat that he had to be carried by four men up any incline or flight of stairs—was Comte de Provence.

But Louis XVIII's return to the throne did not stop the city's decline. By the 1820s, when Louise Révoil was reaching adolescence, Aix was being called "the mummified city," "the sleeping beauty," "a dead sea," "the antechamber to a cemetery." "The sepulchral city where I was born but where I would not wish to die," Louise herself described it in 1831. "Life is so sad here," one of her contemporaries wrote, citing the renown of Aix's medicinal waters, "that the bathers, while curing their physical ills, might die of boredom."

Visiting the city at mid-century, Émile Zola noted the archaic segrega-
tion that continued to govern the Cours Mirabeau's pedestrian traffic in
the midst of its growing poverty. Decades after the Revolution, the gentry—squires in torn jabots of faded lace, ladies shielding their faces with
fans to draw attention away from their lack of jewels—still walked on the
southern, "palace" side of the Cours; etiquette still restricted the "people" to the north side of the Cours, where fruit and refreshment peddlers
hawked their services in front of cafés and shops. "Six to eight feet separated them," Zola commented, "and they remained a thousand miles
apart."

Few members of the Aix nobility were bold or progressive enough to
defy their caste and walk on the plebeian side of the Cours Mirabeau.
Louise's father, Henri-Antoine Révoil, a very conformist bourgeois born
into the merchant class, who directed Aix-en-Provence's postal system,
might have preferred to enjoy the privilege of the elite into which he had
married, and to walk on the "noble" side of the Cours. It was through the
express wish of Louise's aristocratic mother, Henriette Le Blanc de Servanes Révoil, that her family always walked on the "people's" side.

Indeed, the divergent backgrounds and ideologies of Louise Révoil
Colet's family typify many of the conflicts that divided nineteenth-century
French society.

The domain of Servanes, where Louise's family spent the spring and
summer months, had once belonged to the lords of the neighboring town
of Les Baux-de-Provence and was acquired in the seventeenth century by
Louise's maternal ancestors. The château itself was built in the mid-
eighteenth century by Louise's great-grandfather, Seigneur Louis Le
Blanc de Luveaunes. Like several generations of his forefathers, he was a
member of the Parliament of Provence and the recipient of a military
order reserved for the nobility, the Ordre de Saint-Louis. It was his son
Jean-Baptiste, Louise's ultraliberal, belligerent grandfather, who would
ignite Louise's literary imagination and inspire all of her political impulses.

Unlike earlier members of the Le Blanc family, Jean-Baptiste Le Blanc,
an archetypal freethinker of the Enlightenment era, preferred revolution
and literature to parliamentary intrigues. The library he built at his home
in Servanes included the greatest playwrights, poets, and progressive
thinkers of France, from Ronsard and Corneille to Voltaire and Montesquieu. He had a vile temper and was once suspended from the Parliament
of Aix for assaulting a local notable. Like many of France's progressive
noblemen, including his friend the Aix-born patrician Mirabeau, Jean-

Baptiste Le Blanc was an early partisan of the revolutionary cause. A decade before the Revolution, Jean-Baptiste, who changed the family name from Le Blanc de Luveaunes to Le Blanc de Servanes in honor of his country estate, discarded his coat of arms and campaigned to abolish most of the privileges enjoyed by the Aix aristocracy. Upon the outbreak of the conflict, he joined the most militant faction of the revolutionary forces—the *sans-culottes,* or "trouserless ones"—and dedicated himself to purging his region of royalists. During the Terror he was elected mayor of the town of Les Baux, five miles from Servanes, and went to Paris as Les Baux's deputy to the Revolutionary Convention.

Jean-Baptiste's populist views had already been in evidence in the 1770s, when he shocked the local nobility by marrying a commoner who was the most acclaimed beauty of the nearby city of Arles. Marguerite Rousseau, the daughter of a Rhône boatman, was known as the "Rose of Provence." One stormy summer night in 1793, during the height of the Terror, a young army lieutenant posted in the area of Les Baux, Henri-Antoine Révoil, came to knock at the door of Servanes in quest of shelter. Jean-Baptiste Le Blanc readily offered the young man a room. Within a few weeks, Révoil, the son of a prosperous Lyons merchant who was chief furrier to the King of Naples, fell head over heels in love with his host's daughter, Henriette Le Blanc, who like her mother was well known throughout Provence for her beauty, and asked for her hand in marriage.

The Le Blancs' fortune, and the domain of Servanes, had been devastated by the revolutionary war and by Jean-Baptiste's prodigal, utopian ways. The roof of their château needed replacement, its vineyards had never recovered from the disastrous frosts of 1788, its farm buildings were in shambles. In young Révoil they detected a kind, industrious character and—ever dear to the French—a little fortune, direly needed to repair the damages inflicted on their estate. They happily married their daughter to the stolid young bourgeois. Henri-Antoine and Henriette Révoil had six children, of whom Louise was the youngest.

By 1800 Révoil had become director of the Aix-en-Provence Postal Service. Thus he was spared many of the financial problems that plagued the citizens of Aix. As a government employee he was comfortably provided for; during the winter he lived with his family on town property, on a floor of one of grandest mansions of the Rue de l'Opéra, at the northernmost end of the Cours Mirabeau. Having been enchanted by his father-in-law's country estate from his first glimpse of it, Révoil offered to buy Servanes.

Jean-Baptiste, who had recently been widowed, seemed relieved by his son-in-law's offer. He took his money and ran to Paris. There he spent the last twenty years of his life happily dabbling in progressive politics, protesting the remonarchization of France under Napoleon and Louis XVIII, and exchanging anticlerical views with his freethinking chums.

Jean-Baptiste occasionally traveled back to Provence to visit his daughter's family and admire the restoration of his family domain, which he could never had managed by himself; and he doted on the youngest of the Révoil brood. At the end of each summer visit to Servanes, Louise's grandfather would whisper to her with his parting hug to "remember and love your mother's heritage." Grateful as he was to Henri-Antoine Révoil for taking care of his family and their ancestral home, Jean-Baptiste may well have been vexed by the conformism of his son-in-law, a man of strongly royalist loyalties and a devout Roman Catholic, who led his wife and children to Mass every Sunday of the year.

Louise, born on August 15, 1810, was the youngest and most independent of Henriette Le Blanc's and Henri-Antoine Révoil's six children. And by all accounts she was as impetuous and headstrong as she was lovely. At the age of five she had the china-blue eyes and the long, silken blond curls that would remain her trademark for the next half century. "From the cradle," an early biographer noted, "she was the world's most beautiful child, but untameable, full of willpower and anger. . . . She often indulged in long, violent fits of tears, and grew up besieged by her sisters' enmity."

Louise's mother favored her youngest girl to an extravagant degree, perhaps because she was the only one of her offspring who took after her side of the family, the progressive, idealistic Le Blancs. While her siblings inherited their father's conservative attitudes, Louise had the nonconformist character of her maternal grandfather, his literary inclinations, and his populist views. From the time she was six, for instance, during the family's months in Servanes, Louise had a habit of hiding food from her dinner plate in her pockets, later running into the village of Mouriès to distribute it to less privileged children.

And from an early age Louise was persecuted by her brothers and sisters, not only because they were jealous of their mother's favorite but because of her many odd ways. With the exception of her sister Marie, who was the closest to Louise in age, the older Révoil children constantly derided Louise's thirst for knowledge—her appetite for solitary reading and studying foreign languages, her gift for memorizing poetry.

Adolphe, Joséphine, Jean-Jérome, Auguste—these four siblings, whose spitefulness over the years triggered much of the persecution complex she would suffer from throughout her life—constantly mocked Louise for refusing to take part in such traditional children's games as hide-and-seek or in such conventional girlhood occupations as needlepoint and playing with dolls. This "somber, brooding child"—Louise's own description—was growing up an intellectual tomboy whose uncommon beauty was blended with a masculine independence and resolve and her maternal grandfather's quick temper. Her governess once joined her siblings in forcing her to abandon her reading and take up her knitting needles; little Louise stood on tiptoe and slapped the young woman in the face.

From then on Henriette Le Blanc Révoil allowed her rebellious youngest child to spend all her time browsing among books; during summers at their country home in Servanes, she gave her full access to the library of poetry and history classics collected by Louise's grandfather.

By the age of twelve, Louise was composing several poems a month, and her conflicts with her siblings had grown. At Servanes, she tried to avoid their taunts by locking herself into her bedroom or into the library. Or she escaped to Mouriès, a ten-minute stroll from the family house, where she often visited with her nurse, Reine Picard, to whom she would remain devoted throughout her life. Her books in hand, she took increasingly long walks alone each summer into the miles of olive groves that surround Servanes—eventually, as a teenager, to the heights of the dusty gray Alpilles hills behind the house, to the tormented peaks of nearby Les Baux.

It was harder for Louise to avoid her siblings during the cooler months, in Aix-en-Provence. There Louise took to her room, writing in her diary, memorizing verses from books hoarded for the winter from her grandfather's library at Servanes.

"Louise lived quite apart, composing, in verse or prose, the most romantic little stories, repeating for herself, by the hour, the dramas swarming in her head. And when her brothers and sisters surprised her thus, conversing with her Muse, they oppressed her with their sarcasm and mockery." So Louise later described the solitude of her youth to one of her contemporaries. But even Louise's own room was not sufficient refuge. Pretending to play hide-and-seek, her siblings once invaded her shelter and attacked her with knitting needles. She then took to hiding in a secret corner of the roof, from which she had a view of the entire drowsy town of Aix-en-Provence.

Little sound reached her rooftop perch from King René's once glorious city save church bells, the murmur of crystalline fountains, the occasional street vendors' calls on the "people's" side of the Cours Mirabeau.

From her hideaway she could see rows of thick-shading plane trees, so wide they can be encircled by three men touching their outstretched arms, rustling among cobblestones now overgrown with grass. She could see the broad high tower of the Cathédrale Saint-Sauveur, where she had been baptized and which she often visited to admire a wondrous painting of medieval times, Nicolas Froment's *Burning Bush*. She looked down the Rue de l'Opéra, past the house, a few doors away, where Paul Cézanne would be born several years later, toward the groves of olives and almond trees that still lie below the majestic, breastlike forms of Montagne Sainte-Victoire. She could see a few blocks across town to the Square d'Albertas, named after an eighteenth-century noble who destroyed five acres of private citizens' dwellings and replaced them with a row of ornate facades in order to enjoy a better view from his own palace's windows.

At the age of twenty-two, Louise would compose a fine sonnet to her native town, inspired by those rooftop contemplations:

Oh my old city, I still remember,
When at sunsets bathed in waves of gold,
We arrived to the top
Of an olive-colored hill surmounting you,
My love of native soil sprang toward you:
Toward your walls, your earth, your old marble,
Your tepid fountains, whose undulating sprays
Spring toward the rainbow with a gentle fall.
Then the alley filled with centenary elms,
Shielding you from the sun on August days,
Seemed to reach its green arms from afar
As those of a mother stretch out to her daughter.

The association of "mother" with the proud, poor city Louise so loved in her youth would reappear in her poetry for many years. Louise's passion for her mother was as deep as her mother's for her. In her poetry, Louise idealized Henriette Révoil into an earthy, angelic figure who much recalls Sidonie Landoy, the mother of her compatriot and colleague Colette.

Henriette Le Blanc Révoil was certainly a woman of unusual culture and compassion. At a time when many French citizens denounced Romanticism as subversive, she was a devotee of the movement's earliest prophets, particularly of the great essayist and statesman whom she punningly referred to as "Château-Brilliant." And notwithstanding the anticlerical views she had inherited from her father, Henriette was beloved by the clergy of Aix-en-Provence, for as a young girl during the Terror she had given shelter to scores of clergymen fleeing the violence of revolutionary troops. She had saved the bishop of Aix from the guillotine by hiding him in secret rooms of her family house while her father was in Paris attending the convention; she consoled the outcast by reading aloud to him, prepared his food herself.

Years later, Louise vividly remembered the affection with which the bishop greeted her and her mother when they visited him in his splendid episcopal palace, where Aix's summer music festivals are now held. He would stuff Louise's pockets with sweets and holy-name-day cards and inevitably retain mother and daughter for dinner. One day, as the bishop was gently chiding Henriette Révoil for her anticlerical opinions, he said to her with a wry smile: "I'm not certain that you're a Christian, but I'm convinced that you're a saint."

Perhaps because of her close links to the Le Blanc side of the family, Louise tells us little about her father in her writings. Yet we know that the kind, self-effacing Henri Révoil made his own contribution to his youngest child's education. Often speaking to her in Italian, his second language, he took Louise on his lap and told her stories of his youth in Naples. He sang arias from the operas—Pergolese, Cimarosa—that he had heard at the San Carlo theater. He described the city's raucous street life, imitated the Pinocchio puppet shows performed in the port of Santa Lucia and the raucous cries of fish and lemonade vendors. Louise listened enraptured, staring at the three large oil paintings of Vesuvius, erupting in flames over a blue Mediterranean, that Henri Révoil had brought back from his travels. Her fluency in Italian, her dedication in her later years to Italy's revolutionary movement, the Risorgimento, might certainly be traced to those cherished hours with her father.

With her mother as her principal tutor, and her grandfather's book collection as her only source of study, Louise acquired an education that was remarkable for any woman of her time. By her late teens she was proficient in Italian, Greek, and Latin and had taught herself enough English to translate excerpts of Shakespeare's plays. She had a good grasp of classical and medieval history and was well versed in all periods of French poetry and prose.

This was an outstanding education for a girl of the modest provincial gentry who, unlike her wealthier peers, had no tutor or governess to oversee her studies. In France as in much of Europe, no public schooling was provided for girls until the late nineteenth century. Women's education, in fact, was considered by many to be a grave danger to the fabric of society. The most influential French thinker of the Napoleonic and restoration era, Joseph de Maistre, denied his daughters the right to study Latin and Greek alongside their brothers because it might "undermine their domestic devotions." And Louise Révoil Colet's first biographer, her contemporary Eugène de Mirecourt, commented on her intellectual achievements with the condescension typical of his generation: "We would regret to see the more beautiful half of humankind adopt [Louise's] overly solid and pedantic education."

No wonder, then, that Joséphine, Adolphe, Auguste, and Jean-Jérome—whose characters combined the conservatism of their father's clan with the insolence of the Aixois gentry—thought their youngest sister was a freak.

The Le Blanc family motto—perhaps a pun on the name of their country estate—was *"Servane la Rimembreza,"* Provençal for "Put Your Memory to Use." It was a slogan that Louise would take to heart: until her last days she would not forget, or forgive, her siblings' malice. Her first collection of verse, *Fleurs du Midi,* "Flowers of the South," written in Servanes between her twentieth and twenty-fourth years and published in Paris soon after she arrived there as a young bride, is filled with bitter memories of their contempt.

These plaintive, elegiac poems are each prefaced by a quote from some hero or heroine of the Romantic movement—Saint Augustine, Petrarch, Shakespeare, Wordsworth, Byron, Chateaubriand, Madame de Staël, Edgar Quinet, George Sand, André Chénier, Pierre-Jean de Béranger (then France's most popular poet, jailed for subversive activities by Charles X), Abbé de Lamennais (the radical Paris priest who influenced George Sand and Eugène Delacroix). They express a double alienation, one immediate, the other more symbolic: the alienation of a young woman misunderstood by her own blood kin, and the solitude of the Romantic artist martyred by the world's indifference.

Alone! Without ever reaching the source where I can sate my thirst!
Alone! Without another soul which my own soul could reach!
Alone, always alone!

Louise's complaints about her siblings' rancor are frequently contrasted to her mother's love.

My mother—at that very name
A balm flows upon my burning soul
To my other blood kin I am almost a stranger
I never knew a brother's tenderness, or a sister's love.

And one of her most bitter verses:

False of spirit, narrow in their virtues and their faults,
Egotism and gold are their only idols. . . .
Just as a tree branch withers on its desiccated trunk,
At their side my ardent, forthright soul wasted away.

In 1826, during Louise's fifteenth summer, her father died. The Révoils were suddenly deprived of most sources of income and dispossessed of the handsome city lodgings they had occupied for decades in Aix. Henriette Révoil's four unmarried children accompanied her to Lyons to spend the winter with their paternal grandmother. (Louise's oldest sister, Joséphine, had married a first cousin from Lyons, Pierre Révoil; her sister Marie, the only sibling who occasionally tolerated Louise, lived with her husband in Nîmes.)

Grandmother Révoil resided in the Croix-Rousse section of Lyons, a pleasant neighborhood where Louise was to spend one of the happiest winters of her youth. Her lively, affectionate grandmother was as ardent a book-lover as Louise was. She read a novel a day and encouraged her granddaughter to read the prophets of French Romanticism considered most subversive by government censors—Madame de Staël, Victor Hugo, Benjamin Constant. She even permitted her to read those excessively Romantic British works, forbidden to French youth, that were the underground rage of the mid-1820s and that Louise's mother had frowned on: The fictions of Richardson, Sir Walter Scott, Mrs. Radcliffe—Gothic thrillers set in eerie abbeys or castles, replete with sexual aberration, murder, and adultery—would have great influence on Louise's own later fiction.

"I remember the caresses and gentle flatteries she showered on my nascent imagination," Louise recalled of her paternal grandmother in a memoir.

Seated in the large armchair under her grape bower, leaning her elbow on the edge of a clematis-covered well, she read without spectacles, and her vivacious eyes sparkled with the full glow of youth. She often

loaned me the book she had just read, and seated on a stool at her feet,
I'd devour those moving pages, which we went on to discuss. "Let
those beautiful fictions enter her spirit," she would say to my mother.
"They'll turn her away from the harm and pain of reality."

And so like Flaubert's fictional heroine Emma Bovary, many of whose
traits were modeled on Louise (Emma Bovary's romantic fantasies were
nurtured by the books given her by an aging laundress at her convent),
Louise was converted to romantic fiction, and to delusionary views of
love, by an older accomplice.

Louise's passion for literature, and her early conversion to Romanticism, must be seen in their historical context. To the generation of French
youth who came to adulthood in the mid-1820s, the reading of Romantic
literature was far more than a search for heightened emotion and subjectivity; it was a resurrection of the "new person" to a higher way of life. It
was also a dedication to political and social reform—a commitment particularly intensified among French liberals by the inept reign of King
Charles X, the youngest brother of Louis XVI and Louis XVIII. This
pompous archreactionary despot had fully restored the ceremonies of
ancien régime etiquette, dismantled most of the freedoms achieved by the
Revolution, and put curbs on the press that were even more stringent
than those of his Bourbon predecessors.

The Romanticism of mid-1820s France, on the social level, brought a
renewed commitment to the political, philosophical, and moral liberation
proclaimed by the revolution of 1789 and betrayed by Charles X. It re-
awakened a passion for exotic cultures, and support for the poor and the
oppressed; among many it also provoked a rebellion against the renewed
stranglehold of the Church, which consistently attacked Romanticism for
its subversion of the nation's most sacred values.

On the literary level, Romanticism was a defiance of the reign of "reason" preached by Neoclassicism. It preached a passionate new level of
subjectivity and exalted the view of the artist as sacred prophet, a theme
that would become central to Louise's view of life. Equally important to
Louise, it stressed social fluidity and the possibility of self-invention, the
individual's capacity to create a new persona through the sheer power of
imagination and will.

No such spiritual agitation had taken place in literature since the Renaissance. Romantic texts became scripts through which individuals emulated fictional heroes and enacted their lives; a shared taste for certain
kinds of literature became the principal foundation of many friendships.

The Romantic virus, which had already swept Germany and England in the late eighteenth century, only began to affect French society in the 1820s, at a time when national divisions were particularly exacerbated. The collapse of Napoleon's empire, the immense loss of men incurred by his wars, the occupation of France by "redcoat" British troops, which continued until 1818, were blows to national pride and kindled many forms of chauvinism and cultural isolationism. The age-old gulf between rich and poor, which the Revolution had not begun to bridge, was being aggravated by the industrial revolution and by the ineptness of Charles X. Mutual suspicion still divided those citizens who had supported the Revolution and the "ultraroyalist" émigrés repatriated after Napoleon's defeat. And even among those who had fought on the revolutionary side, there was still bitter division between the two main factions of revolutionary ideology: the moderate Girondins (so called because many of their deputies came from the Gironde province of France), who initially believed in a constitutional monarchy and wished Louis XVI's life spared; and the more radical Jacobins, who believed that no blood should be spared in dismantling every feature of the *ancien régime.*

Because of these divisions, the Romantic movement that ultimately conquered France in the late 1820s, several decades later than it had prevailed in Germany and England, met with far more hostility than in other cultures; and it caused schisms of unprecedented violence in French families. Disputes over the relative merits of Goethe, Musset, Byron (whose death in 1824 plunged all European liberals into mourning), caused blood kin to quarrel quite as bitterly as they would a half-century later over the Dreyfus affair. The estrangements formed by such disputes sometimes lasted for decades. Such was the case in the Révoil clan as Louise came of age in the third decade of the nineteenth century.

Upon returning from Lyons in 1827, the Révoil family settled year round to a penurious life at the Château de Servanes. Furniture was brought in from the Aix apartment; the paintings of Vesuvius were incongruously hung on the thick chalk-white walls of the rustic house. The Révoils were now forced to live the life of farmers. Louise and her mother fed the chickens and the sheep, worked in the kitchen when they were short of domestic help. At a time when few women of the gentry even knew how to boil water, Louise greatly enjoyed such tasks. Later, when she became a star of the Paris intelligentsia, the popularity of her salon was in part based on the excellence of her Provençal cooking.

But life at such close quarters with her hostile siblings proved increasingly difficult. Louise's eldest sister, Joséphine, was serving as the mistress of Servanes alongside her mother; Joséphine's husband, Pierre

Révoil, and Louise's two dour, reactionary bachelor brothers, Adolphe and Jean-Jérome, shared the management of the modest olive oil business that was the estate's principal source of income. One can gauge the character of Louise's kin by the behavior of her third brother, Auguste, who upon the family's return from Lyons, during one of his mother's grave illnesses, demanded an outlandish share of his father's inheritance. "To keep [Auguste] quiet and avoid all further troubles we gave him 40,000 francs," the forthright Henriette wrote in a letter to a relative. "You can imagine what hardships these sacrifices caused us, but at least we bought peace." A few years later, Auguste would serve a jail term on a charge of fraud and would be totally disowned by his family.

It was during the harsh Mouriès winters, when the entire family was forced to spend most of its days around the fireplace of a communal chamber that served as kitchen, parlor, and dining room, that tensions among the Révoil siblings reached their apogee. Louise's chief torturer in this period was her brother-in-law Pierre, an archconservative painter of "official" historical canvases. Pierre Révoil was a typical "ultra" of the restoration period that followed Napoleon's defeat, and he prided himself much on once having been received by his idol King Charles X. Révoil spent considerable time at the dinner table denouncing the major heroes of the French Revolution, and those same liberators and poets beginning to be published in France—Hugo, Byron, Lamartine—who were captivating Louise.

In the view of Louise's brother-in-law, General Lafayette was a subversive fool; the most revered young writer of the Romantic movement, Victor Hugo, deserved to be locked up at the Salpêtrière, France's dreaded mental asylum; even the very Christian Chateaubriand, who believed in a constitutional monarchy on the British model, was a renegade, another liberal undermining the authority of crown and church with his progressive talk.

What further deepened Louise's rift with her brother-in-law were his pretensions as a poet. In one poem condemning the idols of the French Romantic movement—Byron and his Greek friends—Pierre Révoil took on the voice of a Turkish sultan sworn to pursue unto death the "rascals of Missolonghi." His verses also celebrated the prison guards who tortured another idol of Louise's generation of Romantics, the Italian revolutionary poet Silvio Pellico. At all hours—over meals, sitting long evenings by the fire—the new master of Servanes smugly expounded on his royalist beliefs to admiring family members. They all fawned on him, with the notable exception of his mother-in-law, with whom he dared not argue, and Louise, whose scornful smile had irritated him since her earliest adolescence.

For added ammunition, Révoil would call on the village priest, an equally smug provincial bigot, who came to dinner every Sunday and relentlessly sermonized the subversive young Louise. This "assiduous parasite," as Louise referred to him, proclaimed as heretical every Enlightenment thinker—Montesquieu, Voltaire, Rousseau—who had inspired Louise's grandfather Jean-Baptiste Le Blanc to support the Revolution. These were the years when Louise, like many converts to Romanticism, became an ardent pantheist and ceased going to Mass, a decision certainly provoked by her revulsion against her brother-in-law and his reactionary clerical friends.

Family life in Servanes became even more oppressive after 1830, when the "Three Glorious Days" of that year's revolution dealt a blow to French conservatives by overthrowing Charles X in favor of the relatively liberal Louis Philippe. The phrase *"Les Trois Glorieuses"* had been coined by liberal insurrectionists in homage to the "Glorious Revolution" of 1688 Britain, which established a constitutional monarchy and gave the English people numerous new political freedoms.

Like "ultras" throughout France, Louise's brother-in-law and all her siblings were embittered by the overthrow of Charles X's autocratic regime. And from the beginning of Louis Philippe's "July Monarchy," as his reign was called, they grew more hostile than ever toward Louise's liberal views.

At the age of nineteen, Louise took solace in her long walks through the bleak olive groves that surround Servanes, where she composed new verses, mused on the eminent men and women to whom she had dedicated them, and read, read unceasingly.

Walking out into the barren landscape, Louise thought enviously of Madame de Staël's salons in Paris and Coppet, where the writer's intelligence and wit had captivated Talleyrand and Benjamin Constant, the most brilliant men of her time.

Along the dusty path to the dreary village of Mouriès, Louise recalled one of her most beloved role models, Germaine de Staël's fictional heroine Corinne, an acclaimed young bard who offered a new image of woman as literary genius.

Strolling the pebble-strewn moors surrounding Mouriès, Louise dreamed of meeting the statesman-author Chateaubriand, to whom she dedicated many poems. Trapped in her monotonous province, tortured by her family dissensions, she was gradually consumed with one obsession: getting the hell out of Servanes, any way she could, and creating her own literary fame in Paris.

During her last years in Provence, Louise's poetry frequently expressed her increasing longing for the French capital:

Paris! Bazaar of the world, immense capital!
Where power spreads in all its grandeur;
Your image kept invading my nights,
Waking my desires, soothing my sorrows . . .

Louise's early poems were filled with the word *gloire,* "glory," which must be read in the full scope of its meaning to young Romantics. It is a stock-in-trade notion of France's postrevolutionary era. (*"Allons enfants de la patrie, Le jour de* gloire *est arrivé."* I have only two passions, love and glory," Balzac wrote in the 1820s.) It has more communal associations than mere "fame" and is achieved only by individuals who benefit humanity and posterity. It is an extension of the cult of Great Men brought about by the upheaval of 1789, which replaced aristocratic hierarchy by an elite of talent and supplanted privilege by ideals of secular achievement. Far more than fame, "glory," to Louise's generation, denoted life's highest goal—a secular form of immortality that superseded the concept of eternal life once offered by the Church.

Oh do not speak to me of happiness and glory,
To me, poor ignored one on whom no one has smiled!

The world admired her; she was young and beautiful,
A brilliant future was beckoning to her,
Glory and friendship lulled her in turn.

Vainly had I followed, with ardent eye,
A thousand dreams of love, of glory and of friendship . . .

Only the prospect of Paris could reanimate Louise's faith in that "happiness and glory" denied her in her native Provence.

There was no way to get to Paris yet, so to escape her siblings' ever growing hostility, Louise began to spend part of the year in the neighboring city of Nîmes with her married sister Marie, the only sibling with whom she got along. And at least Nîmes was a city, not a desert of dusty olive groves.

By all accounts, the adolescent Louise was as beautiful as she was learned. She described herself as being "full-blown and tall as a Creole" at the age of twelve, implying that she had already reached physical puberty. Long before adulthood, she had created a "style" for herself, wearing only sky-blue dresses to match the color of her eyes. By the time she was thirteen, her beauty had begun to attract many admirers. The first of her conquests was a twenty-year-old law student at the University of Aix, who waited for her every week as she took her ritual Sunday stroll with her mother on the "people's" side of the Cours Mirabeau. Another suitor appeared when Louise was fifteen: a frail young man who used to wait for her by the main bridge of Nîmes—for the whole of seven years, she claims—each time she visited that city to stay with her sister Marie. She drew on these incidents for some early poems: "For seven years, ever paler, / Increasingly hopeless and wasted, / On the bridge, even in storms, / He came to wait for me, smiling." Shortly before dying of that most characteristic illness of the nineteenth century, consumption, the aspirant sent Louise two splendid orange trees to remember him by— "Two Genoan orange trees, /Worthy of a king's garden, / Which during his long days of sorrow / He had cultivated for me."

During her time in Nîmes, Louise was able to expand her education at that city's municipal library. There she experienced a passion as hopeless as that of her rejected suitors: She fell in love with a revolutionary hero she had never met or even glimpsed in a crowd.

In 1832, the Italian playwright and poet Silvio Pellico published *My Prisons,* in account of the eight years he spent in jail for participating in the "Carbonari" nationalist movement that sought to liberate Italy from Austrian rule. Placed on the Index by the Vatican, the book became an instant best-seller throughout Europe and was particularly popular in France during Louis Philippe's July Monarchy. Louise read it several times in a row, weeping throughout, and became enamored of Pellico's jail companion, his *Carbonaro* colleague Piero Maroncelli.

"What's the matter, dear child?" her mother asked when she saw her daughter's tears. "What romantic dream are you pursuing now?"

"I'm in love," Louise answered, "I'm in love for life with a martyr, and I shall have no husband but him. . . . He is poor, miserable, and I wish to console him with my love!"

She read aloud to her mother that passage of Pellico's in which he describes Maroncelli undergoing without a murmur the amputation of his gangrenous leg, as he inhaled the scent of a rose to ease his pain. "For two years I dreamed of this rose filled with a perfume of suffering," Louise wrote later, "and rediscovered it in all the roses that flowered about our house."

Louise's infatuation with a partly literary personage—par for the course for any young Romantic—seemed completely serious. Henriette Le Blanc Révoil advised her besotted daughter to inquire about her hero's whereabouts. Louise discovered that Maroncelli had married a German singer and settled into a bourgeois life in Turin. She wept just once more, out of disgust, and returned to her poetry for consolation.

Perhaps these imaginary loves obsessed her because despite her beauty and her many suitors, at the age of twenty-two Louise had not yet received any offers of marriage. Her aloof pride and independence? Her lack of dowry?

There was great anxiety among Louise's siblings concerning her unmarried state and the possibility that she might become a financial burden if she remained single. Louise's sister Marie and her stolid husband, Amédée Baragnon, the only siblings who lived in a city, took on the task of "settling" Louise. Louise's mother, however, had her own ideas regarding this delicate moment of her daughter's life: In direct contrast to most nineteenth-century parents, Henriette Révoil pleaded with her daughter not to rush into marriage.

"You're so comfortable at Servanes, I love you so," mother wrote daughter, "I would be so bereaved to part with you, that if these are not already reasons enough to refuse a suitable match, they are at least reasons to run no risks, and to avoid the peril of living a life to which you are not accustomed. Your mother and loving friend, Henriette."

For a brief while, it seems, Louise did have a serious suitor found by her relatives in Nîmes, a professional army man of noble family considered an excellent match by her brother-in-law; but she turned him down. Perhaps Louise's ambitions for a life in Paris overrode all other concerns; perhaps her mother could not stand her favorite child being assigned to some distant garrison. Henriette's only concern was for Louise's health and morale, which she felt was undermined by her increasingly passionate social concerns. "Your blood is fatiguing you," her mother counseled. "Your period is not regular enough and you're suffering violent headaches; take care of yourself darling child, use the little remedy I've advised you . . . don't worry too much about what poor women have to suffer throughout life, become a bit more selfish."

By the age of twenty-three, even Louise was expressing concern about her single state. "The love I sought has never been granted. Already my forehead pales and my spring comes to an end."

It was at this uneasy stage of her life that Louise was rescued by the first of many literary stars who would help establish her career.

2.
To Paris!

※

On a spring afternoon in 1832, a most interesting woman named Julie Candeille came to Servanes for tea. Once a close friend of Louise's maternal grandfather, Julie Candeille reigned over the most fashionable left-leaning library salon of the sleepy Provençal town of Nîmes. Walking about the estate during a visit to Louise's mother, she came upon Louise sitting under a grape bower scribbling poetry in her notebook. Madame Candeille asked to see some of the verses and proclaimed them to be exquisite. Entreating Louise to persevere, she invited the young woman to visit her in Nîmes.

Now in her late fifties, the vivacious Julie Candeille had enjoyed a decade of great celebrity during the Revolution, and remained famous well into the nineteenth century for having impersonated the Goddess of Reason, quite naked, at one of the secularized "altars" installed at the great Republican Festivals of 1793. But Julie Candeille was also an immensely popular artist. Daughter of the choirmaster of the Paris Opéra, she was educated as a musician and went on to become a dancer, an actress, a singer, a piano and harp virtuoso, a composer, poet, and playwright. In 1793, thousands of Parisians put their guns away to catch one of her versatile acts, her play *Catherine or The Beautiful Farm Girl,* for which she had also composed the songs and in which she starred and sang, accompanying herself on the harp. It had a goodly one year's run and was one of the few plays allowed to be performed in Paris during that year of the Terror.

Nearly forty years later, Julie Candeille was living in her native Nîmes with her third husband, Hilaire-Henri Périé, curator of the city's most distinguished historical monument, the Maison Carrée; and she had established a reputation as Provence's most influential hostess. Ardent converts to Romanticism, Julie and her husband enjoyed keeping up with "the youth" and launching new talents. Their salon was the principal meeting place for Nîmes's art- and music-lovers and was particularly popular as a center for poetry readings.

Imagine the exhilaration Louise felt—coming out of her isolated, tormenting family—upon first visiting the salon of a Parisian who so closely shared her own literary and political sensibilities; upon signing a guestbook that had been autographed by the most eminent poets and personalities of the day—Hugo, Lamartine, de Vigny, Madame de Staël, Madame Récamier!

As for Julie Candeille, who immediately demonstrated great affection for Louise, she may well have recognized in the young woman aspects of herself three decades earlier: exuberance, theatricality, a dose of exhibitionism, a desire to seek some form of public "glory." If these traits were only emerging in Louise, they were vastly encouraged by her short but intense friendship with Julie Candeille, who was writing her memoirs and regaled Louise by the hour with tales of her glamorous Paris life.

Until Louise's arrival, there had been two stars in Julie's salon, both of whom Louise immediately charmed: the poet Jules Canonge, who indulged in such excessive Romantic metaphors as "bitter chalices drained to the dregs"; and Jean Reboul, a more populist baker-turned-bard, who was championed by Alexandre Dumas and Alphonse de Lamartine and whose verses had recently brought him nationwide fame.

Louise, who was already known in her native Aix as "the pearl of the Bouches-du-Rhône"* for her beauty, was the only young woman poet of the Candeilie milieu. Her role had been waiting for her, and she had rehearsed it well: she became the "official" muse of the salon—a plaintive, beauteous damsel-poet dreaming of finding eternal glory through her verses.

At sixteen, Louise had already published a few of her poems anony-

---

* Bouches-du-Rhône, so called because of its proximity to the river Rhône, is the official name of the "department"—a legislative division somewhat akin to one of our fifty states—in which Aix, Avignon, Marseilles, and much of what is known as Provence is situated.

mously in the newspapers of provincial cities—Marseilles, Lyons—signing them "Une Femme." She had no literary friends, save for the correspondences she struck up with Reboul and Canonge, which became particularly precious. Reboul dedicated a simpering poem to Louise (it must have sent her into ecstasies), in which he both exalted her poetic gifts and deplored the misery of the poet's vocation: "You who should above all love / Festivals, pleasures, butterflies, roses, / You dream of an immortal name! / . . . I see that a superhuman lover / Has already slept on your breast / . . . Applaud, Muses! . . . Weep, O you Loves, weep /For this victim of genius!"

Unlike Reboul, who wished to continue his modest provincial life, Jules Canonge had aspirations of finding fame in Paris. In the spring of 1833, he sent Louise a poem in which he announced his departure for the capital: "I'm leaving to navigate / the capricious waves of a world unknown." (It was a Romantic fad, particularly in the provinces, to communicate exclusively in verse.) Louise replied: "Follow your divine pilgrimage / and your songs, rescued from the shipwreck, / will crown your memory."

But she also wrote Canonge a long and melancholy letter—one of the few pieces of Louise's early correspondence that have been preserved—about her own wish to flee her hostile home in Servanes and move to the capital (the emphases are hers).

You are leaving for Paris and you wish to be pitied! Oh! On my part, I must admit to you, sir, that I would be tempted to envy you. I can imagine the fact that the noisy pleasures of the city of mud do not seduce you; but how many delights for the poet and artist in that great town, how many admirable monuments to contemplate, how many magical paintings, how many artistic prodigies. . . .

You will probably see in Paris a few of the most celebrated men of our epoch. That is a delight I envy you all the more. How joyful it is to meet those one admires, those whose writings charm and entrance souls. . . .

You will realize one of my dreams. I don't know when I shall be able to visit Paris, but its image constantly pursues me. I fear that this beautiful Lutaetia will make you forget the sky of the Midi and those who can not leave it!

You would be most kind, Sir, to share your impressions of the city's pleasures by telling me all about them. I'm merely begging for a few crumbs of the feast. . . .

Adieu, Sir, please accept the assurance of the distinguished senti-
ments and the high consideration of

> Louise R.
> Servanes, May 19, 1833.

"To Paris, to Paris!" The attention-starved maiden is calling out for
the metropolis as ardently as the women of Chekhov's *Three Sisters* cried
"To Moscow, to Moscow!" Louise had already become the acknowledged muse of the Bouches-du-Rhône. She now aspired to be the Muse of
Paris.

There was yet another member of Julie Candeille's salon who reinforced that yearning, convincing Louise that Provence was intolerable for
a budding writer. His name was Arsène Thévenot; he was her age, a published poet. He had just returned to Nîmes after a long sojourn in Paris,
a confirmed Romantic with Byronic passions. Thévenot's motto was nothing less than "Religion! Humanity! Social Progress!"

For the first time in her life Louise had a peer and colleague to confide
in. For a few months, the friendship with Thévenot seems even to have
turned to romance. The two spent much time that summer at Servanes.
Louise listened avidly to her friend's reports on Parisian life. They visited
the Roman monuments of nearby Saint-Rémy, the craggy tragic landscape of Les Baux, the many sites of Provence where Louise, a misunderstood adolescent girl, had felt her poetic talents awakening.

They must have exchanged many Romantic clichés. Louise Révoil,
aged twenty-two: "Birth! Death! Life to come! Nothingness! Profound
eternity!" "Chatterton . . . like you I have felt that sharp pain / Which
leads us to desire the hemlock . . ." "Oh suffer and weep! That is regen-
eration. . . ."

Louise and Thévenot also shared long hours climbing the mountains
behind Servanes. From those peaks there is a distant view of the Mediterranean, evoking Byron's and Chateaubriand's exotic travels, reinforcing the most ardent aspiration of any young Romantic—a visit to the
Orient, i.e., the Near East.

Orient! Orient! At that very word
Their souls were lulled by an ideal love: Orient!

We do not know for sure what turned Louise away from Thévenot. A
lovers' quarrel, a dispute over suddenly diverging literary tastes, Maman
Révoil's concern that Louise marry a more stable fellow? The romance
lasted little more than six months, and by the summer of her twenty-third

year, Louise's references to this admirer, at least in her poetry, are jaded
and bitter.

At around the same time, the few safe havens Louise had created over
the past year—the cheer of Julie's salon in Nîmes, the occasional shelter
she still found in Servanes with her cherished mother—suddenly vanished. In February of 1834, Julie Candeille died in Paris, where she had
gone to seek medical help for a malignancy. Louise's mother, who had
also been suffering from cancer, died at Servanes a few weeks later, in
April of 1834, at the age of sixty-four. She was buried in the traditional
Provençal dress, wearing the white lace cap of the "Arlésienne" style.

Imagine Louise's despair as she attended the funeral ceremony with
her hostile brothers and sisters. Henriette's kindness and strength had
been the only buffer between Louise and her siblings. Thenceforth the
orphaned Louise was considered the "lowest" member of the Révoil clan:
even the opinions of her nephews, Benedict and Henri, twelve and eighteen years old, who were always served before her at the dining room
table, overrode Louise's in all family decisions.

Shortly after Henriette's death, Louise went to her room to fetch the
trousseau that her mother had painstakingly assembled for her over the
years and had hung in Louise's cupboards during her last illness. It was
gone. Joséphine and Pierre Révoil had spirited the trousseau away, claiming that Louise had no right to it and that it "belonged to the house."

Louise found herself totally isolated in the political and literary disputes
that had divided Servanes since her adolescence. They had grown all the
more heated since 1832, when Louise began to read, in a state of ecstatic
admiration, the immensely popular and controversial novels of a young
Paris author called George Sand. Sand, in real life the Baronne Aurore
Dudevant, was the first female author since Germaine de Staël to achieve
fame through her accomplishments as a woman of letters. And she was becoming a central role model for the women of Louise's generation. Six
years Louise's senior, Sand reinforced Louise's progressive ideas, her
views of the oppression of women, and her ideal of self-determination.

The George Sand issue created particularly bitter disputes at Servanes.
Her siblings called Louise impudent when she expressed her admiration
for the author: a woman who went about Paris in male dress, who had a
public affair in Venice with Alfred de Musset, who dared to write about
women's sexual passion! The arguments at Servanes grew more acrid on
the subject of Sand's close friend and mentor, the progressive Paris priest
Abbé de Lamennais. Lamennais, who was on the verge of being excom-
municated, preached a socialist style of Christianity that advocated radical social reforms. His book *The Words of a Believer* was immensely

popular in antiroyalist circles and an unprecedented best-seller in the history of French publishing.

A few months later after Louise's mother died, the subversive views of Abbé de Lamennais caused the harshest confrontation to date between Louise and her siblings at the dinner table, where most family conflicts seem to erupt in France.

One Sunday, as Louise was ardently praising Lamennais, the village priest of Mouriès, still a constant fixture at the Révoils' dinner table, shouted that she was a heretic and doomed to hell. Encouraged by the cleric, an aging uncle of Pierre Révoil's threw a glassful of water in Louise's face.

That was the throw of the dice—the *"alea jacta,"* as Louise would put it—the final blow to any family life at Servanes. She ran upstairs to her room, packed her modest bundle of clothes and her poetry, and ran down the long oak-lined alley of Servanes toward the village. There she sought refuge with her former nurse, Reine Picard. She went on to Nîmes the next day and moved in with her sister Marie Baragnon. It was the next-to-last time she would ever see the house that had been in her mother's family for two centuries.

Sometime during the previous year, in Nîmes, Louise had met a musician named Hippolyte Colet. The son of a veterinarian, he had grown up in the beautiful Provençal town of Uzès. At the age of twenty he had gone to Paris to study harmony and counterpoint at the Conservatory of Music with Anton Reicha, a popular Czech-born theorist who had taught Franz Liszt. Hippolyte Colet was a slight, prematurely stooped young man, three years Louise's elder. He had a certain effete handsomeness but a minimum of animal energy.

Colet aspired to be a composer and earned his living playing violin and flute in chamber music ensembles. He was a poor match for the dynamic Louise, but they shared several inclinations: vanity, a taste for Romanticism, progressive political views, overriding ambition, "desires of glory and of a brilliant future" (Hippolyte's stated yearning). Beyond these affinities, Hippolyte held a far more important trump card—he had just been offered a teaching position at the Paris Conservatory.

On condition that she marry him, Hippolyte invited Louise to join him in Paris! Louise might have married far worse to fulfill her highest ambition—a life in the longed-for "immense capital," "Bazaar of the world." Given her obsession with Paris, the bland Hippolyte seems to have been a fairly decent catch for the penniless beauty, who in spite of her independent character worried about becoming an unmarriageable spinster.

The two conducted the first phases of their courtship in secret (their first meeting probably took place in Julie Candeille's salon) for the sake of Hippolyte's career. In the spring of 1834, he had applied for a Prix de Rome in music, an honor which stipulated that its recipient be a bachelor. It may have rankled Louise to hear her suitor ponder his alternatives—his love for her or the perhaps greater happiness of a prestigious prize and a five-year stay in Rome. "My bliss is admixed with bitterness," Hippolyte Colet wrote to Louise in the early months of 1834, when the prize had not yet been announced. *"King's Fellow at the French Academy in Rome,* is that not an inebriating title for a young artist?"

But fate tipped the scales in favor of Louise. Hippolyte was awarded only second prize in the annual competition for the Prix de Rome. This consolation was accompanied by that modest teaching position in Paris which had so baited Louise; it assured their move to the capital. And so in late June, returning to Nîmes after learning that he had not received a Rome first, Hippolyte finally felt free to make an official proposal of marriage. By October of 1834 his love for Louise seems to have been heartfelt.

Oh yes, Louise, how I love you! You can't conceive of the happiness you offer me . . . you are promising to be that companion of whom I dreamed such a long time: From earliest adolescence, I felt that I needed an angel descended from the heavens to fulfill the needs of my heart. . . . You are so good, so loving. . . . I so fear losing you, you my sister, my friend. . . . I belong to you before God; I swore to be yours before God. . . . Divine soul, shall I ever be able to offer you all the happiness you deserve?

Using neoclassical metaphors, the letter repeatedly expressed the careerist ambition for "glory" that the two Romantics shared: "Watch this double crown blaze on our happy foreheads: Love and Glory. We shall unite these palms as we unite our Loves."

Swept up in the enthusiasm of his love for Louise, Hippolyte made an almost fatal mistake: Discarding his former secrecy, he cheerfully announced his forthcoming marriage to Louise, in writing, to two of his future brothers-in-law: Amédée Baragnon, the husband of Louise's sister Marie, and Adolphe Révoil, Louise's dour bachelor brother, who since his mother's death had gained great power in Servanes. Upon receiving Hippolyte's news, the entire Révoil clan burst out in indignation: a penniless veterinarian's son, an impoverished artist, having the presumption to marry into the "noble" Le Blanc-Révoil clan! The family intrigues that ensued prove once and for all that Louise's complaints concerning her siblings' maliciousness were not a whit exaggerated.

*　　*　　*

To begin with, brother-in-law Amédée Baragnon, furious that Louise had turned down his own attempts at matchmaking in favor of an upstart artist, wrote Hippolyte a letter defaming Louise's character and warning him that this union would turn him into "the most unhappy of men." Baragnon, very pleased with himself, then told Louise of his letter.

Louise, betrayed by her once friendly in-law, was overcome by anxiety over the prospect that Hippolyte, to defend her honor, might challenge Monsieur Baragnon to a fatal duel. "If Hippolyte feels outraged," she wrote her former suitor Thévenot, who had since become a close platonic friend, "can I keep him away from demanding a duel, should I . . .?" (Louise greatly overestimated her fiancé's valor—throughout their fifteen years of tormented married life, the passive Hippolyte would nearly always overlook such challenges to her honor.)

Louise was so terrified by the threat of not making it to Paris that she apologized repeatedly to her prospective father-in-law for her family's despicable behavior, reassuring him that her affection for Hippolyte remained undiminished.

My soul is ready to offer you and your kin the affection which my own family refuses. I shall prove to you, Sir, that in marrying your son I shall look on his family as my own, and that my brothers' idiotic vainglory is utterly foreign to my heart. My soul is elevated enough, thank God, to recognize that there are no merits and distinctions beyond honor and glory.

Louise's brothers residing at Servanes—Jean-Jérome and Adolphe—sprang to action next. A few weeks before the wedding was scheduled, Adolphe announced that Louise would receive no part of the inheritance still due from her mother's estate.

That autumn Louise had been living at the only shelter she had left since her altercation with the Baragnons—in Mouriès, with her beloved former nurse. Although Servanes was but a kilometer from the village, a ten-minute stroll, in the several months she has been at Mouriès, she had not once ventured in the direction of her family home. Upon receiving her brother's letter, she made an appointment with a good friend of her mother's, the mayor of Mouriès, to meet him a few days thence, with Hippolyte and her future father-in-law, and seek his counsel on "these revolting matters" of inheritance.

The night before the proposed meeting, upon hearing that Colet *père* and Colet *fils* had arrived in Mouriès, Adolphe Révoil went to see his sister Louise, threatening to challenge Hippolyte to a duel if she sought professional advice to settle the family finances.

Louise was again terrified that the frail Hippolyte might be killed in a duel. She headed off toward the mayor's house for help. A pack of her relatives—Joséphine Révoil and her husband, Pierre, brother Jean-Jérome, all led by the irate Adolphe—pursued her down the lane that led to the village cemetery. "I'll challenge him to a duel if you don't pledge to stay out of our money matters!" Adolphe shouted as he ran after his sister. "I'll challenge your so-called fiancé to a duel if you see him again before you settle this issue directly with us!"

It is possible that Louise loved Hippolyte at only two moments in her life: in these frantic weeks that preceded their marriage, when he was offering longed-for liberation from her siblings and from a solitary spinster's fate; and again a decade and a half later, in the months preceding his death, when after four years of separation she nursed him as devotedly as the most loving of spouses.

Louise's sole concern was to spare Hippolyte a duel. She stood for two hours at the roadside, arguing with Adolphe, and in the end she conceded to every one of her brother's demands if only to assure the safety of her beloved Hippolyte.

She even allowed Adolphe to take her back to Servanes, where he locked her into her childhood room and forced her to write a letter to the Colet family, breaking off all marriage plans. Feigning sincerity, Louise also promised to remain thenceforth at Servanes and allow Adolphe to censor all correspondence addressed to her.

But that very night, Louise tried to escape. Dressed only in her nightclothes, she ran out into the chill November night, back toward her nurse's house in the village. Led by Adolphe, her relatives caught up to her once more and dragged her back to her room, "in delirium, half dying," as she would describe it later.

This tragicomedy finally ended the next day. Upon the firm intervention of the mayor of Mouriès, who cited numerous legal injunctions against Louise's siblings, a deal was struck that seemed equitable enough to all sides: Louise agreed to limit her portion of the family inheritance to 24,500 francs (each of her mother's offspring was entitled to 30,000 francs; her siblings seemed placated by cheating Louise of 5,500 francs). Under the terms of this peace treaty, Louise also inherited a few pieces of furniture; and the trousseau that her mother had assembled for her a few months before her death was returned.

"I would have hoped to have a more considerable fortune," she wrote with humility to her prospective father-in-law. "I much regret not being richer. Oh, how happy I would have been to offer more to Hippolyte. . . ."

The wedding was set for Wednesday, December 3, 1834. Louise had to arrange all the details of the ceremony herself, showing characteristic decisiveness in her practical communications with Hippolyte, who was in Uzès with his family. "We need only two witnesses for the church blessing," she wrote him a few days before the ceremony. "Your brother Monsieur Charles and Monsieur Thévenot will suffice. As for the procedure at the *mairie,* we'll find two random witnesses in the village."

But come the day of the wedding, there was no sign of Hippolyte in Mouriès; he had not even responded to his fiancée's letter. Unfortunately, we lack the documents that might describe Louise's panic concerning her fiancé's curiously lackadaisical behavior. She had to reschedule the civil wedding for December 5, a Friday—the worst possible day, according to French rural superstitions, to get married. It was Hippolyte's twenty-seventh birthday.

The following morning, Saturday, the nuptial blessing was finally bestowed on the couple at the church of Saint-Jacques in Mouriès. Not one member of the Révoil family was in attendance.

But what did it matter? The couple spent their wedding night in a hotel in Nîmes; three days later, they were off to Paris.

"Servane la Rimembreza"—"Put Your Memory to Use"—had been the Le Blancs' family motto for two centuries. In light of their behavior, it is understandable that Louise's attitude toward her kin remained very bitter. She would never again be allowed to cross the threshold of the family house that inspired her first poetry, in which "my nascent Muse," as she wrote, "first lulled me with resplendent dreams." Even in her middle years, when she traveled to Mouriès for faithful visits with her former nurse, Louise never again walked through the doors of her childhood home.

As for the Révoil clan, they would expunge Louise Révoil Colet from their memory as totally as they had expunged her from their life. Even when she had become one of France's most famous authors, the women writer most frequently honored by the Académie Française, her name was never mentioned in family annals.

In fact, Louise Révoil Colet's name remained unknown to the descendants of this provincial clan until the 1970s, when journalists and literary historians began visiting Servanes in quest of the Romantic poet who was one of her generation's most prolific women authors and the muse, lover, and close friend of nineteenth-century France's greatest novelist, Gustave Flaubert.

P.S. SERVANES, 1993

The Révoils' domain at Servanes, little changed in aspect since Louise's time and still in the possession of the Révoil family, is now a flourishing hotel and golf resort.

I was greeted there on a recent spring day by the estate's present owner, Paul Révoil. He is Louise's great-great-grandnephew, a direct descendant of her sister Joséphine and her brother-in-law Pierre Révoil.

Paul Révoil is a sturdy man in his late sixties, with a silvery beard and a vigorous gait. As he came out to greet me, I recognized, unchanged, many details depicted in Louise's poems and memoirs—the spacious, ocher-hued two-story mas-type house; behind it, the craggy, chalky peaks of the Alpilles, or "little Alps," which stretch from Servanes to the neighboring town of Les Baux.

There are, admittedly, some startling contemporary details at present-day Servanes: The terrace in front of the main house is now dotted with merry candy-striped parasols and white metal tables, at which clients of the Hostellerie de Servanes sit over their aperitifs; adjacent to the residence is a sporty eighteen-hole golf course, whose bunkers and water holes are placed amid dense groves of oak and cypress trees; Servanes's former sheepfolds and granges have been transformed into a chic clubhouse, which mills with nattily attired golfers and streamlined golf carts.

Upon greeting me, Monsieur Révoil, a man with a manner both courteous and blunt, immediately stressed that he knew next to nothing about Louise Colet, that no one in his family had ever mentioned her until writers started coming to Servanes in the past decade. "We were all vaguely aware that there was some scandalous woman ancestor who lived it up in Paris in the nineteenth century," he said, "but my grandparents and parents refused to ever mention her by name. All we knew is that there was this black sheep in the family who horrified them. But now . . . .

"Now we're forced to talk about Louise Colet; there's an epidemic of interest in her!" he exclaimed, looking mystified. "You're the third person who's come around this year. Never read a word of hers—was she that good?"

Well, I said, she was awfully interesting. Was Monsieur Révoil acquainted with the works of Gustave Flaubert?

Flaubert? My host looked vague. Perhaps he'd read him way back at the lycée. "Nevertheless," he added with a friendly pat on my back, "I'll show you around the place where Louise Colet grew up, and you'll get the best dinner in town."

He took me through the spacious, chalk-white rooms of the main house. At the left of the entrance hall, the former library, where Louise steeped herself in the collection of her enlightened grandfather, had been turned into an office buzzing with fax machines and ringing phones. By the desk stood a case of golf accoutrements—spiked shoes, sunshades, bags of tees.

As we toured Servanes, Paul Révoil struck me as a man with exceptional reverence for family traditions. He immediately wished me to know that he was only the fourth person to have owned Servanes since Louise Colet's time, and he told me how he had come to turn Louise's ancestral home into a thriving resort.

Paul Révoil and his wife had returned to Aix-en-Provence in the late 1950s after spending a few decades as farmers in Algeria. ("We were chased out when independence came," my host said with resentment.) He inherited Servanes in the 1960s from his grandmother, the wife of Pierre and Josephine Révoil's grandson, who lived until the age of ninety-nine and appreciated Paul's great love for the estate. After struggling for a few years to live off Servanes's olive oil, the Révoils started renting a few of their rooms to paying guests, with such success that they soon doubled their accommodations. Their sons, who held degrees in finance, hotel management, and culinary arts, were fitting helpers for the new venture. "We started with six rooms, a big sports syndicate came to build a golf course at no expense to us, and voilà!" my beaming host said. "Two decades later, we're at twenty-two rooms and solidly booked for two thirds of the year."

Before my first visit to Servanes, I had engaged a room for a May weekend while I was still in the United States (it was weird to receive a faxed message confirming a reservation to stay in Louise's ancestral home). I drove down from Avignon. Servanes is reached in forty minutes, a superb trip on back roads through the heart of the Durance Valley. Five miles from my destination, after I had crossed Saint-Rémy and driven past the turnoff to Les Baux, the landscape grew increasingly barren and chalky. Arriving at the drowsy village of Mouriès, I found it barely changed since the day Louise wrote the following description of it:

Mouriès does not have any Roman ruins nor any debris of medieval monuments; around the village immense olive groves spread out as far as the eye can see, their pale dusty verdure covering the ground with a gray shroud. . . . Nothing picturesque in this village, nothing rustic in its environs; everywhere a tragic uniformity that speaks little to the soul, and yet mine is grasped here by the most powerful feelings. . . . That is because my mother's château hides behind the little chain of mountains that rises to the north; because at the west of the village, by a white wall, my mother is buried in a humble tomb surmounted by a simple cross, surrounded by those poor folk whom she so often assisted and who loved her so much throughout her life.

A few hundred yards from the drab church where Louise was married to Hippolyte Colet stood the sign for Servanes. And then, a half mile down that village road—the same road down which Louise's siblings had forcibly dragged her back home after her attempted escape—I reached a dirt driveway under a canopy of huge oaks and drove toward the gold-and-ocher buildings of Servanes.

My room was on the second floor, in the back of the house, looking out toward the golf course, the Alpilles hills, and a vast expanse of olive groves. On the table by my bed lay a scrapbook displaying the nineteenth-century labels and advertisements that promoted, in several languages, Servanes's renowned olive oil as the "champagne" of its species. The buzzing of cicadas and crickets mingled with the sharp whir of swinging golf clubs.

I took my evening meal in Servanes's little dining room amid quietly chatting fellow guests, feasting on a first-rate loup grillé au fenouil prepared by the hotel's chef—Louise Colet's great-great-great-grand-nephew, my host Paul Révoil's son. Servanes's dining room is the estate's former kitchen, a thickly vaulted eighteenth-century chamber with an immense smoke-blackened hearth that retains its original iron spits. This was the kitchen where Louise and her siblings sat, bickering about the olive harvest, hating each other all through those arduous Provençal winters. This was the hearth at which Pierre, Joséphine, Adolphe, and Jean-Jérome Révoil, dismissing Hugo and Lamartine as subversive brigands, mocked Louise for being an educated woman, for loving the Romantics, for being a poet. . . .

After dinner, trying to catch the sunset, I walked down the road to take an evening stroll in the landscape of Louise Révoil Colet's youth.

I started up the public road that continues past Servanes away from Mouriès, up a hill through extensive fields of olive trees. Periodically I found myself leaving the road to trudge westward through the pebbly gray stubble of the olive groves, trying to reach some crest of hill, some patch of unwooded terrain, where trees would not obscure my sight of the setting sun.

But there was no such place within walking distance. I'd walk a half mile west and uphill toward the rosy cast of sky where the sun must be setting, and still more olive trees obscured the view. There was no crest to any of the hills, no way of seeing the horizon. Each westward excursion off the road was like wading into a tide of olives, and at each step the gray pebbly soil grew more rugged, the olive trees were planted with increasingly threatening density.

So when Louise walked up this road as a young woman in her twenties to get away from her odious siblings, fiercely rhyming her verses, fiercely dreaming of her escape to Paris, this is all she saw—olive trees and more olive trees.

At the time of year I was seeing it—late May—the monotony of the fields that surround Louise's childhood home was relieved by a superb variety of wildflowers. Crimson globe thistle, patches of scarlet poppies and of tall fragrant lavender, allayed the sadness of the stony gray earth. But what must it have been like in the arduous winter months, with nothing eastward to look at but the same desolate mountains that form the rocky spectacle of Les Baux, nothing westward but this monotony of olives swaying in the brutal mistral wind?

No wonder Louise was ready to marry anyone, anyone who could assure her of escape to "Paris! Bazaar of the world, immense capital!"

Before I checked out of the Hostellerie de Servanes that weekend, Paul Révoil gave me a tour of the golf course in his four-wheel-drive Citroën. "We're in full Roman country here," he said. "Here's the second hole, where they found some beautiful Roman vases. There's hole four, where they found that second-century Roman oppidum. . . . They had to stop all construction on the golf course for over a year, orders from the Ministry of Culture."

Paul Révoil surveyed his estate with satisfaction. "I tell you, I love this ancient land, I love my work, I love having all of my children at arm's reach, in my control. . . . We Révoils have always put great emphasis on close family life—respectful, obedient, closely bonded."

I asked my host about Louise's renegade brother Auguste, who was said to have stolen all that money from his mother's estate, then ended up in jail.

Paul Révoil shot me an angry look. He'd never heard of great-great-granduncle Auguste's getting into any kind of trouble, and he didn't seem to like having the family name sullied by such tales. "I think you get this kind of antifamily propaganda from reading too many articles on Louise Colet," he said. "They're probably all slanted in her favor these days. After all, she's the one who married some bohemian musician and left for Paris and cut off all ties with her family. She was never allowed to set foot in the house after she married Colet.

"And probably for good reason!" he added.

Ardently conservative, enthusiasts of family tradition, wedded to their ancestral land: Plus ça change, plus c'est la même chose. Although far kinder and more gracious, the contemporary Révoils are not that different from those of Louise's generation.

3.
Her Conquest of
the Capital

❦

Finally, the ambitious beauty arrives in the promised land. She walks down Paris's teeming boulevards, visits its libraries and museums, stands on the heights of Montmartre, where she may have thought of the challenge flung out to the city by Rastignac, the hero of Balzac's *Le Père Goriot:* "It's between the two of us now!"

In the mid-1830s, the capital was animated by many entertainments that had been forbidden under the reign of Charles X. There was a craze for new dances—the *valse éperdue,* the *galop infernal,* and also the *cancan,* brought back by French soldiers after the conquest of Algeria. It was a decade of conspicuous consumption, of quests for instant fame and fortune.

Women's fashions had veered away from the straight-lined, flat-chested styles that had been in vogue since the Revolution; tightly laced corsets again emphasized the amplitude of hips and the treasures of décolletage, bodices sported extravagant mutton sleeves, pom-poms, rosettes. A giraffe sent to France as a gift from a Near Eastern potentate made a sensation at the zoo and launched a new vogue in headgear; "giraffe coiffures" inspired such intricate edifices that ladies had to sit on the floor of their carriages in order to keep their hairdos in place. "A monstrous, ridiculously anachronistic luxury pervades all classes of society," wrote the popular social chronicler Delphine de Girardin. "Its only goal is to display the shabbiness of our fortunes, the power of our bourgeoisie, the uncouthness of our manners, the flimsiness of our institutions." Smugness, prosperity, the triumph of the July Monarchy's bourgeoisie: Louis Philippe, the domestic "citizen king," made a point of walking in the boulevards with his family like any other Parisian and, when giving tours of the Tuileries Palace, ushered visitors into the bedroom he shared with his queen.

France had finally bowed to the Romantic movement. In 1830, the victorious fracas caused by Hugo's *Hernani,* at which claques of thousands of long-haired acolytes nightly shouted down the "classicist" opposition, established Romanticism as the nation's official aesthetic credo. And by 1835 Alfred de Vigny's stage drama *Chatterton,* which celebrated the heroism of poets destroyed by a philistine society, was playing to ecstatic crowds. Paris had also discovered opera, which drew hosts of devotees from most every stratum of society, like the rock festivals of our own time. There was keen competition for tickets to attend performances of Bellini, Donizetti, Meyerbeer; it was considered chic to attend opera twice a week, once with one's wife and once with one's mistress.

High-society marriages were far less sedate than that of the citizen king. "Among Parisian aristocracy, to busy oneself with one's wife is looked on as ridiculous," wrote Marie d'Agoult, another astute social chronicler of the July Monarchy. "To be seen at her side, be it at home or in the world, would brand one as foolish or unfortunate. . . . Hostesses do not enjoy entertaining husbands and wives together. Each should shine in different salons to relieve conjugal tedium."

The most important places to be seen in Paris in the 1830s were Marie d'Agoult's own salon, which starred Bulwer-Lytton, Chateaubriand, the critic Sainte-Beuve, the novelist Eugène Sue, and her lover Franz Lizst; the salon of Delphine de Girardin, wife of France's most powerful press lord, who wrote her poetry under her maiden name, Delphine Gay, and signed her popular newspaper column with the alias "Vicomte de Launay"; the salon of the radical Italian aristocrat Cristina Belgiojoso, who read fluent Hebrew, displayed a human skull on her desk, and entertained the leaders of Europe's nationalist and revolutionary movements in her dusky medieval decor.

At first Louise had little access to these spectacles and fashions. Upon her arrival in the capital, she discovered that Hippolyte's modest appointment at the Paris Conservatory, a lowly "rehearser" position which he supplemented by teaching the flute, earned a mere two thousand francs a year (the earning power of seven thousand contemporary dollars), barely enough to buy three of the multi-tiered Oriental turbans of gold lamé, lace, or tulle that were currently the fashion rage of Paris. So the young couple settled in a shabby flat at 6 *bis* Rue des Petites Écuries, in the poor working-class section of Montmartre, around the corner from Hippolyte's school. It was scarcely heated, a fourth-floor walk-up past greasy, refuse-littered stairs. Louise detested housekeeping, and she had few personal resources beyond a few pieces of her mother's jewelry. The Colets barely had enough money to buy groceries, not to mention the books and the theater and opera tickets Louise had dreamed of since adolescence, and the trinkets she needed to make a proper showing in the capital. Was this the grim reality of the City of Light? Shortly after her arrival, Louise hinted at her disappointment in a letter to her father-in-law:

"Hippolyte is the absolute master of our household, I can't spend a cent on anything without his giving it to me. But I do wish to stress that his love compensates for our many little troubles."

By no means did Louise regret her move, however. Having stayed in touch with a few friends in Provence, she learned of the strife that had plagued the Révoil clan since her departure. Joséphine and Pierre Révoil had moved out of Servanes and returned to Lyons, dividing the family into two enemy camps. Louise's sister Marie Baragnon and her eldest brother, Adolphe, were each claiming possession of the family estate (Adolphe would eventually win out). Meanwhile Louise's brother Auguste, just out of jail, had attempted to extort yet more money from those two siblings. Refused the funds, he had threatened to set fire to the house. The police had been called to safeguard the estate. How comforting even a modest life in the capital must have seemed to Louise.

Her most immediate quandary was how to earn a living. How would she break into the competitive melee of Parisian literati, who treated every newcomer as an enemy? The Paris literary world, which had been changing at dizzying speed throughout the 1830s, bore no relation to the cozy Provençal salons in which Louise had so easily scored her first triumphs.

Owing also to the increasingly rapid technology of publishing, to the relative liberalism of the new regime, and to the glamour that Romanticism accorded to men of letters, over one hundred new periodicals had been founded in the five years preceding the Colets' arrival in Paris. These publications maintained their cachet by serializing the fiction of popular novelists—Eugène Sue, Dumas, Balzac—but depended on advertising, fashion columns, and sensationalistic social gossip to break even financially.

Hordes of scribblers blitzed their way into this lucrative new calling and then jealously defended their turf against all future intruders. Louise's description of the "New Journalism" of mid-nineteenth century France has a very contemporary ring:

The literary "trade," as one now refers to that glorious profession of author and poet which, in antiquity, was almost priestly in its nature, is today the most miserable and lethal of vocations. How many victims for each of its conquerors! The evil and the struggle began in 1830 and since then have only increased; the excessive development of journalism is its principal cause. It is now in periodicals rather than in books that all literary works must be published in order to gain a readership. Hence the necessity, for an author, to be protected and patronized by newspaper editors. The violent bread and circuses that Romans once demanded from their leaders are now demanded by Parisian readers in the form of pulp fiction.

Her next paragraph is particularly prophetic:

Contemporary literature did not know how to elevate the people to its tastes, it lowered itself to them instead. Hence its vulgar aspects, its absence of style, its gratuitous effects, the improbable passions—devoid of truth or nuances—of its narratives. To shock, to surprise, to terrify with exaggerated portraits—this is now the ceaseless preoccupation of our breathless battalions of daily writers. . . .

In 1835, upon my arrival in Paris, this sad literary situation was just beginning, and it has only worsened since then. . . . At first I rushed into the melee with all the ardor and faith of early youth. . . .

So here is Louise, pages of her poetry in hand, making the rounds to dailies, weeklies, and other periodicals, each time subjected to interminable waits among male scribblers who poison the air with their reeking cigars. They whisper crude remarks as they stare at her décolletage; no one rises to offer her a seat. And after standing for hours in a smoke-polluted waiting room, chilled by icy blasts from the constantly opening door, Louise is finally allowed to see some ranking editor and is told that readers are far more interested in public scandals and titillating prose fictions than in her poetry.

Thus Louise spent much of her first season in Paris, traveling in muddy public coaches, her sparse clothes and footwear drenched by winter rain. Lesser characters might have been discouraged, but the awesomely stubborn Louise made a dent in the breach within six months—in part, one

suspects, because of her unusual beauty, but also because of a perseverance unusual in a woman of that time. She finally had a poem accepted in
a fairly prominent new periodical called *L'Artiste,* whose contributors
included George Sand and the painter Eugène Delacroix. A contemporary described Louise's first visit to *L'Artiste,* where she was greeted by its
gallant editor in chief, a Monsieur Ricourt.

> *Ricourt was chatting with a colleague on the day when Mlle Révoil, a*
> *little tremulous, entered the offices of "L'Artiste."*
>
> *Both the gentlemen stood up, marveling at this radiant vision, and*
> *Ricourt offered her an armchair.*
>
> *Louise handed him a little sheaf of paper, tied with a blue ribbon.*
>
> *"These are some of my verses," she said. "Would you have the*
> *kindness to glance at them?"*
>
> *"With pleasure, Madame, this very minute," Ricourt said.*
>
> *He takes the manuscript, unrolls it, and reads two or three stanzas to*
> *himself; then, increasingly enthused as he reads on, he speaks the last*
> *stanzas aloud.*
>
> *"But these are ravishing verses, Madame! You have the breath of a*
> *Victor Hugo, with a purer and more severe form."*
>
> *Louise bowed before this unexpected praise. . . .*
>
> *Upon these words, he rang for a copyboy.*
>
> *"Carry this text to the printer's, and tell them to put it on the front*
> *page!"*
>
> *Louise saluted him with her prettiest curtsy and left.*
>
> *"Heavens," the editor's friend exclaimed after Louise made her*
> *exit, "when I saw that delicious woman appear I thought I was in the*
> *presence of one of the Three Graces!"*
>
> *"Oh, better than that!" said Ricourt. "You have seen the creature*
> *whom the master sculptors have called Poetry!"*

Throughout the following year, *L'Artiste* served as the principal show-
case for Louise's verses. But the pennies she earned from that magazine,
equivalent to fees contemporary poets receive from the *Partisan Review,*
brought little relief to the Colets. Like other women writers who come to
mind—George Sand, Colette, Isak Dinesen—Louise was a spendthrift
and needed to create an identity through her costumes and public image
as well as through her talent. In order to make her mark on Paris society,
the budding woman writer needed to attend the theater, buy piles of
magazines and books, take an occasional cab during those incessant winter visits to the press, and purchase a few clothes to enchant prospective
editors at evening gatherings.

Thanks to Louise's tenacity, and a few letters of introduction from friends in Provence, the Colets had found some important entrées into the Paris literary world. They frequented Charles Nodier's salon at the Bibliothèque de l'Arsenal, a legendary hotbed of early Romanticism, where Louise's beauty much impressed one of her future lovers, Alfred de Musset. They were invited to the homes of the Duke de Marliani, the Spanish ambassador; of the celebrated portraitist Madame Vigée-Lebrun, to whom Louise dedicated eulogious verses in the way of a thank-you note: "Oh, it is you who are the poet, / you whose soul, from its very birth, / received from God, as his interpreter, / a paintbrush instead of a lyre." They visited the writer Delphine de Girardin and her husband, Émile, the S. I. Newhouse of the July Monarchy, whose phenomenally successful newspaper Le Siècle would eventually serialize many of Louise's prose works.

At all such gatherings, Louise's style was hampered by Hippolyte's jealousy. He forbade his wife to wear the fashionable low-cut dresses, insisting that she appear in public with high necklines and sleeves fastened down to the wrists. Upon their first meeting, Musset complained that the beauty was as wretchedly attired as "a Quakeress."

Driven by a fierce need to gain financial independence from Hippolyte, Louise decided to edit the poems she had written during her years in Provence and publish them as a little anthology: That, surely, would be more remunerative than the pittance she earned at L'Artiste. For the last months of 1835 Louise worked on this collection, which she entitled Fleurs du Midi, "Flowers of the South."

Once the book was finished, but before she could even start to knock at book publishers' doors, Louise had to plan the most important strategy for any writer's first published volume: Some distinguished literary figure must extend his support through what we now call a "blurb," a custom as de rigueur in 1835 as it is today. As newcomers to the literary scene, women particularly needed to find a champion among the four major literary cult figures of the period: the idolized poets Victor Hugo and Alfred de Vigny; the elder statesman of Romanticism, François René de Chateaubriand; or Charles-Augustin Sainte-Beuve, France's most eminent literary critic.

Among these stars, Sainte-Beuve might have provided the most prestigious blurb. The founder of modern critical method, he was the first French essayist to look on criticism as a form of moral inquiry, to analyze literary works in their full sociohistorical dimensions rather than merely use them as springboards for personal reflections.

Sainte-Beuve was a stocky, pocked-faced man with a complex private life. He was terrified of his bouts of impotence, and only the thrill of first conquest ensured his virility. In order to avoid repeated sexual fiascos, he had evolved the theory that the happiest liaisons are those founded on a single sexual encounter; he called it *le clou d'or,* the "golden nail," which could "implant" the seeds of a long and serene platonic friendship. In 1835, Sainte-Beuve had begun a liaison of this sort with Adèle Hugo, the wife of Victor Hugo, which would last many years. Yet he was ever ready to implant more "golden nails." Louise's blond-locked splendor might well have moved Sainte-Beuve to kindness if she had not ruined her approach with those traits of behavior that would persistently harm her career—impatience and tactlessness.

Having received an introduction to Sainte-Beuve through a mutual friend in Provence, Louise submitted a poem to him several months after her arrival in Paris, with a plea for a candid evaluation. Sainte-Beuve replied with an incisive letter in which a few encouragements were interspersed with several harsh criticisms—too many prosaic words and harsh rhyming patterns, he complained, a lack of the originality that might distinguish her from "those hordes of other young poets overly influenced by Lamartine."

Notwithstanding this put-down, Louise stubbornly sent Sainte-Beuve the entire *Fleurs du Midi* before it had found a publisher, asking him for an advance blurb. The request went unanswered.

Her attempt to corral the one member of the literary pantheon to whom she had an introduction having failed, Louise had to turn to another member of France's Big Four. The aristocratic Vigny was notoriously indifferent to younger colleagues. Hugo had grown into such a national idol that he was unapproachable to all but his closest friends. Louise decided to try her chances with the nation's greatest prose writer, Chateaubriand, who, noted for his generosity, had offered support to several young writers.

A quixotic blend of progressive, Christian, and royalist ideals, Chateaubriand had spent most of the revolutionary years in the United States and Great Britain. Since 1830 he had devoted himself to the writing of his greatest book, *Mémoires d'outre-tombe,* "Memories from Beyond the Tomb," and to living an idyll in Paris with the love of his late life, the legendary, aging Juliette Récamier.

Louise had a great gift for self-promotion, for detecting the advantages that any literary lion could bring her. Approaching the "Homer of Melancholy," as Chateaubriand was called, she had some trump cards up her sleeve: Two poems in the collection she was trying to publish—"Chateaubriand and Lamartine" and "Torments of a Poet"—were tributes to the writer's genius. "It is you, Chateaubriand, you, magic Ariel, / God of an ideal world; it is you, living lyre, / Who directs with one sound a seething crowd."

Louise had the nerve to pay the great man an unsolicited visit. She simply appeared at Chateaubriand's home in Montparnasse one afternoon, manuscript in hand. She recounted the visit in a memoir: "It is hard to describe the emotions I felt while approaching that calm and isolated site. . . . I was overwhelmed as I was about to face the majesty of his genius."

Notwithstanding the flattery she showered upon him, and the additional requests she forwarded to him through his concierge, Chateaubriand remained reserved toward Louise's verses. "In my opinion," he finally responded in a carefully noncommittal note, "the woman who wrote a poem such as 'Consolation to an American Poet' has the right to every kind of suffrage. But, Madame, only poets can announce a poet: Choose among those who have glory, they will be honor-bound to predict yours."

Louise was too smart not to sense Chateaubriand's ambivalence about her work. But she decided to include his letter anyhow as a frontispiece of *Fleurs du Midi*. However guarded his praise, the very name of the august writer guaranteed a modest success for the volume, which was published by the Paris editor Dumont in the spring of 1836. The gift copies sent out by Louise may well have been double the number of copies sold. Among the recipients were the Duchesse d'Orléans, daughter of King Louis Philippe, and the king himself, who later bought several copies of the book.

Next, of course, Louise had to face the problem of getting the book reviewed. Undaunted by Sainte-Beuve's rebuffs the preceding fall, she sent him the volume once more, repeating the request—in several successive letters—that he publish a critique of it in France's most noted periodical, *La Revue des deux mondes*.

She wanted a review in that prestigious magazine? She got it. Sainte-Beuve responded to Louise's repeated assaults with a fairly scathing critique:

> *All possible aspirations to enthusiasm and to the Infinite—applied in turn to vast landscape depictions, to the famous and most desirable cities of one's dreams, to the illustrious poets whom one would wish to meet in person and whose glory devours and pursues us—are the commonplace themes of this muse who lacks neither force nor audacity. . . . The volume's greatest flaw is that she has not focused her inspira-*

tion on one central theme and does not offer a truly distinctive style. It is to this double aim that the author should henceforth aspire, having revealed, in this first attempt, a true and uncommon facility.

These icy comments marked the beginning of three decades of strained relations between Louise and the most eminent critic of her time.

Louise then redirected her charms upon earlier fans. Monsieur Ricourt, who had been publishing her poems in *L'Artiste,* praised it in his own magazine and pressed another important periodical, *La Quotidienne,* for a favorable review. *Fleurs du Midi* also received much praise in *Gazette de France,* whose critic, unwittingly, wrote eerily prophetic words about Louise's most tragic flaws of character:

The verse of this intelligent and sensitive poet . . . offers a model of perfection which she demands from the created universe, which she conceives of but cannot find. . . . One sympathizes with this suffering soul, one weeps with her, for the love which she demands does not exist on earth. The happiness of which she has dreamed is but an illusion, the existence filled with truth and glory which she demands is that of a future life.

Book advances to a newcomer such as Louise were still tiny in the 1830s. The country's most famous authors—Hugo, Eugène Sue—might receive three or four thousand francs, the equivalent of ten to fourteen thousand contemporary dollars. But even novelists of "average" esteem, such as Balzac, were advanced a maximum of only one thousand francs for a book; the more obscure writers—Théophile Gautier, Louise Colet—were lucky to get between two hundred and five hundred francs.

With the prestige of a published book behind her, Louise found a humble new source of income in selling short prose fictions, book reviews, and social chronicles to various periodicals. Another modest source of support came from the royal court: Marie d'Orléans, Louis Philippe's daughter, enjoyed greatly the Romantic effusions of *Fleurs du Midi* and arranged a very modest pension for Louise. Granted by the Ministry of Instruction, which funded the only stipends then available to artists and writers, it amounted to some four hundred francs a year, or fourteen hundred contemporary dollars.

But these new pittances, added to her husband's meager wages, still could not pay for the cabs Louise needed for her visits to editors and publishers, the dozens of copies of her own book she had to purchase for gifts to the eminent. Throughout the following year, her dreams of glory were further diminished by the numerous faux pas of her unfortunate husband. Louise had married Hippolyte with the notion that he would be her passport to Paris and instant success; he was proving to be more of a burden.

The very month her book was published, for instance, when Louise most needed him to escort her to literary gatherings, the quick-tempered Hippolyte clumsily got himself arrested by the Paris police on charges of assaulting a policeman and was sentenced to several days in jail. On other occasions, when Louise was getting dressed for a ball, her husband pleaded a sudden illness, cloistering her at home. Hippolyte's gaucheness also lost him a potential advancement at the music conservatory where he was teaching: Upon the death of his former professor of harmony, Anton Reicha, Hippolyte immediately put in a bid for his job. Irked by Colet's pushiness, the conservatory's director, composer Luigi Cherubini, citing the gross error of counterpoint theory that had lost Hippolyte the Prix de Rome two years before, denied him the position.

Moreover, Hippolyte's character and demeanor, after two unfruitful years in Paris, were turning out to be very different from those of the amiable young man who had courted Louise in Provence. Financial difficulties strained the Colets' marriage, and Hippolyte became increasingly vindictive as he grew jealous of his wife's modest successes. He opened her mail and frequently forged letters to her correspondents behind her back.

Hippolyte was not only proving to be a miser, counting each penny he doled out for the makings of the weekly *pot-au-feu;* he was also a petty despot, throwing tantrums when he came home from his music school if he saw a cold stove and books on the kitchen table. The Colets' marriage was further soured by the dismal failure of their one joint effort. A year after their arrival in Paris, they collaborated on a comically inept mini-opera entitled *Le Marabout de Sidi-Brahim,* which never got near the boards. Dedicated to the French Army, which had captured Algiers in 1830, *Le Marabout* attempted to capitalize on the nation's enthusiasm for the colonization of North Africa and on the vogue for Orientalia that attended the new imperialism. A sampling of its facile verses reveal why it failed to see the light of day: *"Rata-plan-rata-plan plan-plan"*—so goes its refrain, emulating the beating of martial drums. "All these little struggles / Heat up our tempers; / So let's strike with mighty blows / As all of France watches us." The manuscript of this "opera" made the rounds of every theater in Pairs, with no success.

So as time passed, Louise and Hippolyte began to see each other's faults in an increasingly harsh light. Their funds remained minimal, and there were bitter recriminations, violent domestic scenes between the two hotheaded Provençals. Some of their acquaintances reported that Hippolyte had a sadistic streak and enjoyed "breaking his best violins" on his wife's head. And yet they needed each other. Louise needed Hippolyte to give her status as a "respectable" married woman. Hippolyte, in turn, had little to show the world beyond his wife's charm and exhilarating beauty. For the time being, they were stuck with each other.

Three years after her arrival in Paris, when she felt at an impasse in her marriage and her career, Louise was rescued by a distinguished fellow Aixois whom she knew from her days in Provence, François Mignet. He suggested that Louise enter the poetry competition held every two years by the Académie Française, that august body of forty male citizens singled out for their contributions to the arts or sciences and referred to, as they are still, as "The Immortals." Mignet, the leading historian of the French Revolution, was himself a member of the Académie. Louise took his advice to heart.

Since its founding in 1671, under Louis XIV, the Académie Française had awarded its poetry prize to a woman only four times.

It was the Académie's custom to set a specific theme for each of its biennial competitions. In 1839, the assigned topic was "The Museum of Versailles." Sacked to near destruction by the Revolution and closed for nearly half a century, the museum had been restored and inaugurated again with great fanfare the previous year.

According to Louise, she learned about the theme of that year's competition only a few days before the entry deadline. It was with the extraordinarily rapid composition of this poem that legends of Louise Colet's awesome facility began to spread. After having rushed to Versailles to visit its new museum, she is said to have worked around the clock for three days, pounding out fifty-eight stanzas without once changing out of her housecoat.

Louise Colet's contribution so pleased "The Immortals" that they chose her work above fifty-nine other entries for the first prize.

Louise found the central inspiration for her poem in Versaille's "Pantheon of Great Men," a gallery of the castle's museum in which dozens of sculptures of French history's most distinguished citizens had recently been installed. One work had particularly moved Louise: a statue of Joan of Arc executed by King Louis Philippe's daughter Marie d'Orléans, who had died tragically a few months before the competition was announced, at the age of twenty-six.

The poem opens with a vision of Louis XIV as he orders the construction of Versailles, a faerie structure and sumptuous gardens in which "human art returns us to the Garden of Eden." Once created, the castle is metaphorically transformed into the ecstatic bride of the Sun King, awaiting "the splendors of the nuptial night." But within a century, so the poem's imagery evolves, the kingdom falls into corrupt and feeble hands; the people rebel and overthrow the monarchy. In turn, the people themselves become corrupt, turning liberty into terror. The desolate Queen Versailles, diadem torn off her head, is raped by a bloody-armed rabble. The regal palace is left deserted for decades, until the "three glorious angry days" of the 1830 revolution, when a "popular prince" (who but Louis Philippe?) resurrects Versailles to her former glory.

The poet's vision ends in Versailles's gallery of famous men, lingering on the busts of Corneille, Molière, Mirabeau, and finally resting on the virgin heroine Joan of Arc, who "with her child's arm liberated the French people from the British yoke." The sculptor of this sacred image—the virginal Marie d'Orléans—has herself fled to the heavens above, becoming, like Versailles, like Joan of Arc, a female mediator between the will of the people and the power of the monarchy. The poem ends with an exalted apotheosis of all these populist symbols—representatives of the people kneeling reverently before the statue of Joan of Arc, ecstatic ghost of the king's artist daughter wrapping her shroud over her sculpted white marble heroine, immortal souls of the great men rising in unison to share nocturnal feasts with virginal heroine and royal artist. . . .

Rereading "Le Musée de Versailles" today, one might be amused by the kitschy inflation of Colet's images. And one would perhaps find them more palatable than much of the equally "official" salon painting of that decade, such as the depictions of France's victorious battles in Algeria cranked out by the most popular painter of the 1830s, the understandably forgotten Horace Vernet. Louise was the first to admit that she dashed off her bombastic poem with the principal goal of earning money: "Impelled by financial need," she wrote a few years later in a memoir, "I was incited by the hope of winning a two-thousand-franc prize to finish my work on time. I sent the poem to the Academy all sealed, as was the custom. I did not know any of my judges."

That last statement was not totally true. In addition to her friend François Mignet, Louise was already acquainted with one of the Académie's most influential senior members, the seventy-three-year-old Népomucène Lemercier. It is probable that this aging playwright, still very sensitive to feminine charm, overlooked the Académie's rule of anonymity and allowed Louise to read her poem aloud to him. Much taken with her and moved by her financial plight, he may well have tried to help the lady in distress by recommending her talents to his colleagues on the jury, particularly to the most eminent philosopher of nineteenth-century France, Victor Cousin. Such literary friendships have often earned writers their first palms.

The Académie was spruced up festively on May 30 of 1839, for the awarding of its coveted poetry prize to Madame Colet's "Le Musée de Versailles." If the description of the event in the Paris press sounds inflated, one must recall the spell Louise's face cast on her contemporaries. (One of many enamored portraits: "The flaxen radiance of her blond hair, which fell unto each temple in cascades of curls, had golden gleams which recalled the dazzling halos of saints.")

A contemporary chronicler's description of Louise's first official triumph reads:

> The basket of roses was utterly filled, that eternal basket formed by the reunion, at the center of the room, of the daughters, nieces, wives, or widows of academicians. . . . Why this unusual exhibit of fresh white linen and decorations? Why this holiday mood and these reciprocal felicitations and these smiles as mysterious as those of newlyweds?
>
> Ah! The reason is that today the poetry laureate is a woman! And the old men will rise before Helen, and the advent of a woman to the academic prize stirs our forty immortals from their torpor!
>
> . . . There was a most beautiful moment: when the young woman rose to receive . . . the glorious medal, symbol of her triumph. The amphitheater and the loges trembled, everyone stared at her amid a chaos of whispers; then, when the inspired young woman appeared on the highest step of the green stage, the crowd broke into admiring applause. . . .
>
> Madame Colet's triumph continued into the great open courtyard of the Institute. The crowd pressed about her as she entered her cab; and it gave the impression that it was about to unharness its coaches, an honor of which a pretty woman is as worthy as a member of our parliament.

Népomucène Lemercier was so taken with this impoverished new celebrity that he ordered the habitual Académie stipend of two thousand francs doubled.

Louise waited impatiently for the reviews of her prize-winning poem. But the prevailing view of woman-as-ornament, so evident in the euphoric report on the Académie festivities, hardly assured the critical success of women's literary efforts. Louise was shattered, in fact, to read these phrases concerning her work in the nation's most prestigious literary gazette, *La Revue de Paris:* ". . . parasitic epithets, words bordering on barbarism, emphatic, inflated commonplaces, outrageous metaphors which deliver Versailles like a prostitute to the heated embraces of royalty and popular lies."

Louise's pique at the critics was in part allayed when she received the most desirable invitation in Paris: King Louis Philippe's two sons, the dukes of Aumale and of Montpensier, had been present at the Académie's prize-giving celebration and had been very taken with Louise. She was summoned to the Tuileries Palace. In 1839, that was an invitation which even the most progressive citizen would not have declined.

At Louise's side during the palace visit, of course, was her tight-lipped passport husband, Hippolyte, effetely handsome in his new suit. Hippolyte was enough of a snob to enjoy his wife's triumph, even as their marriage was deteriorating. He had become something of a philanderer, plumping up his income by giving private music lessons, and more, to Parisian society ladies. One of his favorite students—Byron's former mistress, the strawberry-haired Teresa Guiccioli—had been Hippolyte's lover for several recent months. Many Parisians wondered what this sought-after beauty saw in the somber little musician.

Louise, who so far had been a model of fidelity, would soon begin to fulfill her own yearnings for romance.

It was a point of etiquette for all writers honored by the Académie Française to make a round of thank-you visits to those members who had cast a vote for them. Once she learned from Népomucène Lemercier the names of her supporters, Louise decided to pay her first call on the most famous of them, Victor Cousin. The meeting would change the course of her life.

The forty-six-year-old Cousin, a wizened, dapper bachelor who had been the first scholar to translate Plato into the French vernacular, had risen meteorically from very humble origins. His mother was a laundress, his father a clockmaker; the family lived in a tawdry garret reached by a stepladder. Until the age of ten, he was another rough Paris street kid, vagabonding the time away until he could find an apprenticeship in some menial trade.

Young Cousin lived a few blocks away from the Lycée Charlemagne, France's most prestigious school. One day he saw a gang of students savagely pursuing and beating one of their classmates, a shy, sickly boy who was weeping pitifully, unable to fight back. Young Victor Cousin took on the persecutors with his fists and quickly dispersed them. The victim's grateful mother took an interest in her son's rescuer. Upon discovering that he had already taught himself to read and write, she assumed the cost of his schooling.

At age eleven, Cousin was enrolled at the Lycée Charlemagne, where he showed such prodigious gifts that he skipped a class every two years and won every prize available. He advanced so quickly in the university world that at the unprecedented age of twenty he had become professor of classics at his alma mater, the École Normale. At thirty-five he was generally considered to be the most important "thinker" of his generation.

Cousin's fame and popularity were heightened by the persecution he suffered during the reign of Charles X, when he was censured for teaching the writings of such "subversive" foreign thinkers as John Locke. After serving a six-month jail term, he sought exile in Germany. There he formed a lifetime friendship with Hegel and began his studies of Fichte and Kant, whose work was then totally unknown in France.

A centrist, eclectic scholar who did not develop any original philosophical theories, Cousin nevertheless had a vast impact on French culture. He introduced the major Greek philosophers, the German idealists, and medieval scholastics such as Abelard into France's philosophical curriculum. Later, as minister of education, he decreed, rather immodestly, that his famous book *On the True, the Beautiful, and the Good* be required reading for all French *lycéens;* it remained mandatory well into the twentieth century, and the Rue Victor Cousin is still a main thoroughfare of the Sorbonne area in Paris.

A frail-bodied man with a gaunt face, Cousin was also noted for his oratory. Stendhal wrote of his "boundless influence on my generation," describing Cousin's Sorbonne discourses as "electrifying all our youth." Young Balzac returned from those lectures with his "head on fire." Sainte-Beuve claimed that they left "an almost legendary memory" and created "a revolution in French philosophy."

By the time he met Louise, this celebrity who had been born in a garret had become a peer of France, was president of the Sorbonne, and held a lifetime chair at several other universities. Cousin was a curious combination of worldliness and monastic frugality and was known for his stinginess. His breakfast consisted of a bowl of cabbage soup brought up by his concierge, and this hermit's meal would last him until suppertime, when he invariably went to dinner at some great person's house. Known as "Plato" to his friends, Cousin had a considerable ego and loved the high society that celebrated his intellectual gifts: *"Il faut paraître"* and *"La philosophie, c'est moi!"* were among his favorite phrases.

There was another interesting sideline to Cousin's career which helps to explain his instant infatuation with Louise: He had long been enamored of those Amazon bluestockings of seventeenth-century French society—Mademoiselle de Scudéry, Madame de Sablé, Madame de Chevreuse—who were known as *précieuses ridicules* for the uninhibited manner in which they displayed their erudition, and who reigned over the most brilliant salons of Paris. Cousin's fascination with these commanding females, to whose accomplishments he had devoted eight large volumes, could not but prepare him to fall in love—at very first sight—with the gorgeous bluestocking Louise Révoil Colet.

And how could she not have been flattered by that love? Cousin's popularity was such among the Paris intelligentsia that his eloquence was compared to that of Thomas Aquinas. Moreover, the life story of "Plato" was made to order for Louise's liberal, populist ideals: The son of a humble craftsman, a self-made intellectual grandee who had suffered long, painful exiles for his progressive views.

After years with a plaintive washout husband whose only achievement was the publication of a musical treatise called *La Panharmonie Musicale; ou, Cours Complet de Composition Théorique et Pratique,* Louise must have been very taken with the honey-tongued Victor Cousin.

Numerous male critics have tried to prove that Louise was already having an affair with Cousin before she was awarded her Academy prize for "Le Musée de Versailles" and that "Plato" single-handedly engineered her award. But all kinds of evidence—Cousin's own letters, the Académie's official documents—disprove these allegations. In point of fact, Cousin was so ignorant of Louise's identity that when he read her entry he "attributed her poetic talent to a man, and upon opening the seal was most surprised to find that it was the work of a young woman."

The prize was awarded to Louise on May 30, 1839. She only met Cousin the following week, at the Sorbonne. And it was not until July 1, after a few such formal meetings at his office, that "Plato" was invited to dinner at the Colets' flat on the Rue Saint-Lazare, where he patiently listened to Hippolyte complain about his arguments with Cherubini about counterpoint and his recurring migraines. Cousin's first letter to

Louise consists of a brief note on July 2 thanking her for dinner and for "our nice little talk of yesterday, which I hope did not fatigue you too much or increase M. Colet's headache."

In deciphering the correspondences (often coded to avoid a husband's suspicions) that attend such nascent romances, the most telling phrases of all can be the tersest: A note written by Cousin to Louise on July 16, a few weeks after that first family dinner, read: "Yesterday at two P.M. Memory!" That word "Memory!" is like the tenderest of sighs. On the afternoon of July 15, Professor Cousin had evidently returned to the Colets' flat while Hippolyte was giving flute lessons at the conservatory and had not found the beautiful Louise reluctant.

Cousin left Paris toward the end of that month to take the waters at a fashionable provincial spa, a discreet cover-up for his budding passion. Yet however guarded the language of his letters in the next weeks (he continues to address Louise as "Chère Madame"), one easily senses the depth of his infatuation. In the beginning of autumn, the "Madame" was replaced by "Chère Amie." By November all subterfuges had been abandoned, and the lovers were an official "couple" of the Paris scene. The importance of this relationship in the crafting of Louise's public image cannot be overestimated.

For in those days no Parisian woman could aspire to be an official "muse" without also playing the part of the sexually emancipated woman, the passionate Romantic mistress. Just as she had needed a husband as a passport to Paris, Louise, if she had not been courted by the famous Cousin, would have had to take some other respectable lover to help her assume the next role in the constant rescripting of her life—becoming a Literary Celebrity.

Our contemporary mores seem provincial in comparison to those decades of the nineteenth century when publicly displayed extramarital affairs were not only de rigueur among the intelligentsia but also a mark of liberty and class. The Romantic ethos glorified the passions that drive women to commit outrageous follies, to leave their families and the most privileged lives. Such abandonment, in the Byronic or Stendhalian sense, confirmed the superiority of a woman's soul and her assertion of individual freedom. Although it was more widely known than others because of her eccentric dress and her unique celebrity in French letters, George Sand's romance with Frédéric Chopin was only one of numerous liaisons that characterized the freedom of the Romantic era.

Every major writer and artist of the century would have his "official" mistress-muse, every celebrated beauty her official lover. Benjamin Constant and Germaine de Staël, Chateaubriand and Madame Récamier,

Hector Berlioz and the actress Harriet Smithson, Alfred de Vigny and Marie Dorval, Baudelaire and Jeanne Duval—the list is endless. Two Romantic mistresses of Louise's generation were particularly notable:

Countess Marie d'Agoult, born into the highest French aristocracy, had left her husband, her two daughters, and her grand country estate to live with Franz Lizst, to whom she bore three more children (one of those offspring would become Cosima Wagner). Assuming the pen name Daniel Stern, Marie d'Agoult became a prominent writer, publishing a score of novels and sociopolitical treatises, and one of the most respected chronicles of the revolution of 1848.

After a long liaison with France's most popular sculptor, James Pradier (at whose salon Louise would meet Gustave Flaubert), the actress Juliette Drouet began a decades-long idyll with Victor Hugo. The most reclusive of mistress-muses, Juliette dedicated herself far more tenderly to Hugo than the writer's wife, Adèle, ever had. Acting as his confidante and secretary, she would remain at his side during his nineteen years of political exile on the Channel Islands. And shortly before their deaths in 1883, Juliette Drouet and Victor Hugo celebrated their fiftieth anniversary as lovers.

With such idylls to aspire to, no wonder that by the fall season of 1839, after Victor Cousin had returned from his spa, Louise took great pleasure in being seen with her lover at the opera and theater; at the most stylish restaurants, such as Troîs Frères Provençeaux (which still stands in the vicinity of the Palais-Royal); at the merry studio gatherings of James Pradier, who much admired Louise and made several sculptures of her.

Within a few months of their initial meeting, Victor Cousin had become much more than a lover to Louise; the peer of France acted as her protector and principal literary adviser. Attempting to improve the Colets' disastrous finances, he even lobbied for Hippolyte at the music conservatory, securing for him twice the income and a promotion in its teaching ranks. Maneuvering for Louise at the Ministry of Education, Cousin managed to have her government pension tripled, from four hundred to twelve hundred francs. Promoting her in the theater world, he pressured the Théâtre de la Renaissance to give another chance to a disastrous little verse drama of Louise's entitled *La Jeunesse de Goethe,* a literary trifle based on an imaginary episode in the poet's life. Elaborating on an injustice done to Goethe by one of his antagonists, the critic Johann Elias Schlegel, the play offered Louise an opportunity to avenge herself against those Paris critics who had attacked her prize-winning poem on Versailles:

The Critic, you see, is an impotent being....
He envies the genius, the talent he has not,
Vengeance is his only justice....

"Madame Colet interests us in the highest degree," Cousin wrote to the director of the Théâtre de la Renaissance, "and I speak for my colleagues [at the Académie] in expressing the wish that her play be presented more frequently."

Under Cousin's pressure, *La Jeunesse de Goethe* went back to the boards for a few weeks, but his intervention did not ensure its critical success; the reviews were scathing. "This supposed comedy crawls with verses disagreeable to any critic," Théophile Gautier wrote. "The poet laureate's verses are feeble, colorless, and of mediocre taste; her phrases are clammy and totally lack style. For a crowned muse, this is not powerful." Concentrating on the issue of gender, another prominent reviewer attacked Louise in that tone of disdainful condescension which informed most critiques of women's writing in mid-nineteenth-century France:

Nothing is more touching, in our view, than the sight of a young and beautiful woman who forswears the divine weaknesses of her sex, abdicates her sweetest privileges—the chaste obscurity, the modest silence of domestic life—to bravely mount the boards, arm her white hand with a metal gauntlet, and publicly slap around the most snarling critics of our time. I know some vile detractors who must have spent a rough night....

And yet the reprimand ended with a cynical denial of any prejudices toward the author's sex:

Isn't Madame Colet exaggerating the enmities incited by her budding fame?... Is it true that her brow is bleeding from the thorns of glory? Does Madame Colet (née Révoil) have any enemies?... Eh, no, Madame, you do not have enemies!... Eh, no, your brow is not bleeding!... Eh, no, the poet is not accursed on this planet! M. de Lamartine is not accursed, M. Hugo is not accursed.... No, we are not outraging you! No, you are not dealing with cowardly pamphleteers! You have dreamed up all this, Madame!

The agitated tone of this male critic might have opened Louise's eyes to the obstacles that confronted her and most any independent-minded woman of her time.

P.S. THE TRIALS OF MID-NINETEENTH-CENTURY FRENCH WOMEN

Woman was created to love and to be loved, and for no other reason.

Since woman is claiming her rights, we permit her only one: the right to please.

Guy de Maupassant

Enlighten the spirit of a young woman, form her character, give her a good education, and she will become a pedant, which is the world's most disagreeable and degraded being. All of us would prefer to spend our lives with a woman servant than with a woman savant.

Stendhal

Woman, a vulgar animal . . .

Woman is a production of man; she is a mere result of civilization, a factitious creation.

Gustave Flaubert

Woman . . . is the intermediary link between man and the animal world.

Pierre-Joseph Proudhon

Such pronouncements, voiced by hundreds of influential French men of Louise's time and evidently reflecting the opinions of millions, expose one of the most curious paradoxes of French culture:

Since the Middle Ages, French women lived in an environment of far more benevolent attitudes, and enjoyed much greater esteem, than their peers in Anglo-Saxon or Mediterranean societies. France produced a greater quantity of successful women authors, and a greater abundance of outspokenly feminist texts, than any other Western culture that comes to mind. At times, particularly in the seventeenth and eighteenth centuries, women literally ran the nation through the backstairs influence of their political and literary salons.

Why, then, was a tradition of publicly expressed misogyny more widespread in nineteenth-century France than anywhere else in the West?

In tracing the violent sexist prejudices that began to pervade French culture in the last decade of the eighteenth century, one central historical factor must be emphasized: the impact of the 1789 revolution on that society's views of women. In the communal psyche, this uprising endowed women with an immense potential for violence. Female citizens had been extraordinarily militant throughout the century of revolts that preceded the Revolution. The bread riots of 1709, the uprisings protesting the price of cotton in 1752, the next great wave of bread riots that spread in the 1780s, were, in the words of historian Jules Michelet, "predominantly led by women." And on July 14, 1789, the Bastille was seized by a huge crowd composed of both sexes.

Throughout the first three years of the civil war that broke out in 1789, women were encouraged by the revolutionary leadership to carry arms, dress like men, and fight at men's sides. They were also incited to form their own political clubs, in which they swore to "live by the Revolution and die by her." Many members of these women's groups allied themselves with the Revolution's most radical fringes, such as the "Enragés," a faction more extreme than the Jacobins; and they published some of the century's most fiery revolutionary pamphlets.

But the Amazonic images stamped upon the communal psyche by these female militants provoked growing fear among male citizens. In 1792, in one of the more capricious turnabouts in political history, both the radical and the centrist factions of the revolutionary leadership began to engage in a systematic repression of women. All women's political clubs were ordered closed. The Convention of 1795 stated that such groups had gone against "natural order" because "they emancipated [females] from their exclusively private, familial roles." It ruled that "All citizenesses must retire to their respective domiciles" and decreed that women publicly gathered in groups of more than five would be dispersed by armed force and arrested. And a convention deputy who had belonged to the Revolution's single most radical fringe, the sans-culottes, actually proposed that a statute be passed entitled "A Prohibition Against Teaching Girls to Read." In sum, the nation's male leadership invited women to assume militantly masculine roles when it needed them; as soon as the Revolution's goals were achieved, it segregated them more rigidly than ever in their "private, familial roles."

In those years, the Revolution's most prominent leaders—Babeuf, Marat, Robespierre—delivered harangues in the new French parliament on the innate inferiority of women and denigrated the female sex in brutal terms. Epithets hurled on the floor of the convention at those citizenesses who attempted to remain active in politics included: "licentious monsters," "public leeches," "hideous tricksters," "bacchantes splurging on men and wine." (Before the Revolution, to slander women in such a public manner would have been considered a moral offense.)

Ironically, the fraternal equality newly declared among men seemed to increase their despotism. The Revolution granted only two of the rights demanded by women in 1789: a law that offered them equality with men in the inheritance of property; and divorce legislation, which was to be very short-lived. The Napoleonic Code of 1804 revoked the divorce laws passed in the early phases of the Revolution and further institutionalized women's inferior status. The code's double standard toward adultery was striking: An adulterous wife, when observed by a third party, could receive between three months and two years in jail; and if the husband himself found her in flagrante delicto, he could legally justify murdering her. Whereas a man caught in the act, even by his wife, would pay a maximum penalty of two thousand francs.

The anti-woman polemics engaged in by male writers of the period reflected these double standards. Alexandre Dumas fils maintained that cuckolded husbands should take justice into their own hands. The founder of the French socialist movement. Pierre-Joseph Proudhon, agreed: In cases of a woman's drunkenness, thieving, or other forms of dissipation, a husband had the right to kill his wife "according to the rigor of paternal justice."

When surveying the misogynous tradition that flourished in nineteenth-century France, one must differentiate between several different attitudes that prevailed in that epoch: the virulent gynephobic rhetoric of the journalistic and essayist genres; an exaltation of women's purity and nobility of heart, expressed by a few poets and novelists—Stendhal, Hugo, Musset—which often verged on protective condescension; and the uniquely French blend of idealization and denigration expressed in the following statements, penned by some of the most influential writers of the mid-nineteenth century:

Woman . . . that idol, perhaps stupid, but dazzling and enchanting, who holds our destinies and wills suspended on her gaze . . .
Charles Baudelaire

As instructed as a woman might be, you'll soon see that she knows nothing and that her banter is more insupportable than the prattle of ignorance. . . .

Please remain what we have always demanded you to be: gentle, reserved, cloistered, devoted, modest; only in this state can we set you on a pedestal and dedicate ourselves to you in body and soul.

Pierre-Joseph Proudhon

The emancipation of woman! It resembles the sight of a deity who has abandoned her altar and now drags her feet through mud, hobnobbing with her crowd of adulators for the mere pleasure of sending up incense toward her now empty niche—it seems that even in heaven, she was bored.

Alphonse Karr

The anti-woman polemic provoked by the events of 1789 had long-lasting effects. When Louise Colet and her peers were chastised by male literary critics for abandoning "the modest silence of the domestic life" and becoming self-supporting women, they were still suffering from the backlash of the French Revolution. In his many vicious attacks on Colet, for instance, the influential writer Barbey d'Aurevilly, an exemplar of nineteenth-century male attitudes, harped on Louise's "revolutionary" bluestocking ideologies. In d'Aurevilly's view, the "violent" and "outrageous" Colet was a "fastidiously impious, Jacobin, insulting, Vesuvian, reddish bluestocking . . . radical to the point of being bloodthirsty. . . . This devil of a [Louise Colet] . . . had nothing in common with the humanitarian bluestocking who slobbers about peace, fraternity, and universal well-being. Madame Colet's pedantry is disheveled, sibylline, enraged. . . . It's the Revolution that this horrible gargoyle keeps spouting out of her mouth! Only revolutionary hatred could have been coupled with the frantic vanity that filled Madame Colet's soul, if one could even use the word 'soul' in speaking of her. . . ."

At the same time, one cannot ignore the considerable role played by French women themselves in the growth of this male virulence. Beginning in the 1830s, for the first time since the Revolution, thousands of female citizens were founding or joining their own political and literary clubs. Encouraged by the phenomenal growth of the press under Louis Philippe, a large new class of self-educated bluestockings were entering the literary profession, publicly demanding the right to vote and to divorce. "Literature and politics," Balzac wrote, "are now what devoutness used to be in women's lives—the last refuge of their pretensions."

Throughout the 1830s and '40s, the male psyche was further threatened by small but highly publicized fringe groups such as the Fourierists and Saint-Simonists, who preached mystical views of women's liberation: Demanding that women be given full political rights, they declared that social progress grew in measure with the increase of women's liberty, and described the marriage contract as "worse than prostitution."

One should note that ideology had little to do with what we would now call "politically correct" attitudes on the woman issue. The royalist and republican press expressed equally forceful misogynous opinions. In his lithograph series Les Divorceuses, the notably progressive Honoré Daumier, who served a jail term for his socialist sympathies, offered some of the most gynophobic images ever conceived by a great artist. Under the leadership of Proudhon, the socialist literature that began to proliferate in midcentury was as violently prejudiced against women as any in the land.

Against Emancipated Women:
> You displease us in this form: we find you ugly, stupid, and venomous. . . . Whom do you wish to please? Your colleague witches, your King Charles spaniels? Go ahead, and when men have regained their reason they will drown you and your lovers in a pond.
> Do you reply that we displease you equally? Let it be. War is declared.
>
> Pierre-Joseph Proudhon

Woman's very aspect reveals that she is destined neither to serious works of the intelligence nor to serious physical work.
> Guy de Maupassant

So they are today, the bluestockings of our republic . . . women's blue stockings have stretched far above the garters and become whole-body sheaths; women now are blue from head to foot, equal to men, ferociously equal, ready to devour men. . . . These gargoyles vomiting stupid or atrocious declamations, they're blue up the lips, like ancient Negresses.

We now have majestic professors who would admit to literary and scientific institutions, with the aim of turning them into doctors

or lawyers, little girls who should immediately be sent back to playing with their dolls. . . .
It's bluestockingism that makes most men wish to kill.

Barbey d'Aurevilly

There are seven capital sins for the seven days of the week. Woman is the eighth capital sin.

Arsène Houssaye

Woman . . . is the only unfinished work which God left for man to complete.
According to the Bible, woman is the last thing created by God. He made her on Saturday night. One feels the fatigue.

Alexandre Dumas fils

4.

Penserosa

❧

Like Emma Bovary, like innumerable women living in the French provinces, Louise Colet had dreamed since adolescence of having a literary salon.

A salon like that of Mademoiselle de Scudéry, the seventeenth-century bluestocking so admired by Victor Cousin, who maneuvered the hiring and firing of state ministers through the intrigues of her drawing room; like that of the much-missed Madame de Staël, den mother of the Romantics; like that of the aging beauty Juliette Récamier, Benjamin Constant's and Chateaubriand's muse, whom Louise yearned to meet. A salon like those of countless other French women who for centuries had helped to shape their nation's culture through the backstairs influence of their intelligence and wit.

Now that she had an official lover—an indispensable ornament for any woman's salon—Louise began to succeed in that aspiration. In the winter of 1841, her literary successes enabled her to move to more respectable quarters, on the Rue de Bréra, near Place Pigalle, an area much in vogue among the High Bohemia of Parisian writers and artists. Although not much larger than her shabby previous flats, it was the first one that had a little drawing room in which she could receive properly.

Louise's salon was held on Thursday evenings to accommodate the schedule of Victor Cousin's colleagues, the Immortals of the Académie Française, who held their weekly session that day. The gatherings began on a small scale—a dozen people sharing lively talk and Louise's delectable *poulet à la provençale*; over the years they would remain more informal, more politically activist, than their fashionable rivals, the soirees held by Countess d'Agoult, Princess Belgiojoso, or Delphine de Girardin. Eventually Louise's home became the principal gathering place for the capital's progressive intelligentsia.

In the first year of her salon, Louise's guest list focused on those members of the Académie Française who had helped her obtain her literary prize. It included Victor Cousin, of course; the literary historian Abel-François Villemain, who had obtained a chair at the Sorbonne at the unprecedented age of twenty-six and had a secret infatuation for Louise; the distinguished Latinist Aimé de Pongerville, whose wife would become godmother to Louise's daughter; and Eugène Scribe, radical deputy to the French parliament and author of librettos for some of the decade's most popular operas, such as Meyerbeer's *Robert le Diable*.

Another habitué, and one of Louise's most flamboyant fans, was the great bibliophile Paul Lacroix, known as "Jacob." Dressed from morning to night in a black satin waistcoat, his pockets perpetually crammed with books, Jacob was a man of astounding culture and extravagant imagination. He enjoyed shocking his friends with the most sensational revisionist theories of the day. He affirmed that Marat was the abandoned son of Jean-Jacques Rousseau and that Joan of Arc's combative virginity was due to the fact that she had never menstruated.

Amid Louise's meager furnishings—shawls hastily thrown over wooden crates, seedy secondhand chairs awaiting the sale of a new volume of verse to be reupholstered—the company might discuss the latest nationalist uprising in Poland; the ovation received by the extraordinary new star of the Comédie Française, Rachel, in Racine's *Andromaque;* the success at a recent salon of Louise's friend James Pradier, whose erotically charged statuettes were so popular that his fans stood in line for six, eight hours to crowd within sight of them; or the virtuoso gifts of the Italian violinist Paganini, who was rumored to have extracted the G string of his magic instrument from the intestine of a mistress he had murdered.

And at the center of the group stood the ravishing hostess, now known to her friends as the "Muse," appreciated for her literary erudition, her warm Provençal hospitality, her talent for listening, her gift for friendship. A description of her in those years by her contemporary the poet Théodore de Banville: "Sovereignly beautiful, with a charming and imposing face, reflecting the sky in her soft and proud eyes, enchanting all onlookers by the vivid crimson of her flower lips, her superb queenly head, and her white rose-nailed hands, a nose fit to overthrow empires, she was both poet and fitting subject for poetry."

In the challenge she'd thrown out to Paris upon arriving from Provence, Louise was beginning to triumph. She had attained two essentials of the successful Parisian woman's life: a prominent lover and a distinguished salon.

Louise commemorated those happy first months of her romance with Cousin in a poem entitled "Song of Héloïse," a reference to Cousin's extensive studies of the medieval scholar and lover Abelard:

> *. . . My trembling mouth,*
> *My lowered glances,*
> *Tell you enough*
> *When we're together.*
>
> *I love your shadowed forehead,*
> *Your soft deep eyes,*
> *Your dark head*
> *Next to my blond hair!*

This is pillow talk all right. It was published in 1841 in a new collection called *Penserosa* (Cousin had told Louise that her languorous pose reminded him of the Penseroso of Milton's poem). His benevolent influence on her career had begun to bear fruit: The enthusiastic review of this book in *Revue des deux mondes* was written by none other than the previously ornery Sainte-Beuve:

> *The latest poet laureate of the Académie, Madame Colet, has published under the name of* Penserosa *(an appellation perhaps more pensive than the contents suggest) an elegant and brilliant volume which henceforth promises her a high rank among our muses. It is impossible to deny the harmony of her verses . . . their firmness, their wide and sonorous touch.*

Sainte-Beuve gently chastised Madame Colet for a sporadic overdose of "vehemence," an occasional lack of deep emotion, and for those "armed attacks" against critics that the "beautiful Amazon" had launched the previous year. He concluded with a put-down repeatedly issued to women poets by nineteenth-century male literati: "We most admire Madame Colet in her expressions of love." Still, it was a welcome change after the critic's previous censure.

Sainte-Beuve's about-face typified the power plays that characterized Paris's competitive literary world: He had turned mellow toward Louise because he coveted election to the Académie Française. Cousin was one of its two or three most powerful members, and Sainte-Beuve was actively wooing the philosopher's support.

Plato paid almost daily visits to Louise. When her concierge went out to fetch the philosopher a cab—they could be hard to find—Cousin even took over the concierge's duties. Passersby were amazed to see the peer of France playing doorman at Louise's building, gravely opening the door for its inhabitants.

"Be assured that your life is filled with habits I would like to alter," he wrote her in his New Year's greeting of 1840, only faintly veiling his passion from the brooding Hippolyte Colet, "with bonds I would like to shatter, with barriers I would like to see vanish. . . ."

That year Cousin acquired another power base in French society, as minister of public instruction. He maneuvered to have the Muse's government pension increased to three thousand francs a year. Minister Cousin, by then, was acting as bookkeeper for both members of the impecunious Colet ménage; he even seemed ready to check the maid's grocery accounts. "There you have it for the essentials," he wrote Louise:

1,000 francs for your lodgings, 1,200 francs for food, the rest for Celina [the maid], incidental expenses, clothing, etc. But when M. Colet becomes a full professor at the conservatory, his clientele will be augmented. And I promise again to do all I can to see that one of his operas will be staged—all that would add some 1,000 francs to his income: there you have it, 4,000 francs assured. . . .

You will be able to work more calmly . . . I kiss you with all my heart. May I continue to do so for many long years.

Cousin's expressions of tenderness were anything but rhetorical. A few months after their affair became public, Louise found that she was pregnant. Since the Colets had remained childless throughout their five years of marriage, there was little doubt in anyone's mind concerning the child's paternity. Such were the circumstances that led to one of the most celebrated scandals of the Parisian mid-century, the *"Affaire Colet-Karr."*

*   *   *

Alphonse Karr was a very popular, lively journalist who has gone down in history for coining the epigram *"Plus ça change, plus c'est la même chose,"* his phrase for the disillusionment that followed the revolution of 1848. He edited France's most scandalmongering periodical, a satirical monthly called *Les Guêpes,* "The Wasps," and excelled at antifeminist polemics. By the time Karr began to sting Louise in his "Wasps," his reputation was already tainted by allegations of depraved sexual behavior. He had been the lover of the beautiful young actress Juliette Drouet, Hugo's future life companion, when she was barely nineteen and had tried to persuade her to refine her erotic gifts in a brothel. ("My spirit's desires are no less powerful than my body's, and a thousand times more ardent," the pure-of-heart young woman had replied in outrage.)

Ever since its first edition, Karr's periodical had relentlessly stung Victor Cousin, singling him out for his miserliness and favoritism. In April of 1840, Karr intensified his campaign against Cousin with two insinuating articles on the philosopher's relationship with Louise:

> *The philosopher Cousin often makes sacrifices to the Graces. . . . Before joining the Ministry of Education, he asked the then minister of education, M. Villemain, for an increased pension for Mme Colet, née Révoil, who recently won the poetry prize at the Académie. . . . Upon M. Villemain's objecting, the philosopher Cousin cried out, "But she is so beautiful!" And having joined the ministry, he augmented her pension. . . .*
>
> *Literature is falling into the gutter under the tutelage of that dear M. Cousin. . . . Everyone now agrees that under his rule, it is essential to be a pretty woman in order to receive a pension as man of letters.*

But Karr's most outright invective against the lovers concerned Louise's pregnancy. Here is an excerpt from the article that ultimately provoked Louise to take vengeance against Karr:

> *Mme Révoil, after a union of many years with M. Collet [sic], has finally seen her marriage blessed. She is about to give birth to something other than an alexandrine. Since the venerable minister of public instruction heard this news . . . he has surrounded her with all manner of attention and care; he does not permit her to go out of her house in any vehicle other than his own coach. He went himself to Nanterre to find a wet nurse for the child of letters who is about to arrive, and one hopes that he will not refuse to be its godfather. Well!*

Karr added to these insults with a scurrilous pun, which he circulated in Parisian salons: The Muse, he said, had been impregnated by *"une piqûre de Cousin,"* which could be translated as "Cousin's sting" or "Cousin's prick." With this ultimate caddishness Karr risked his life. For within a week, Louise acted decisively, and with extravagant drama.

She first tried to retaliate in a traditional manner: She asked her husband to avenge her honor through a duel. But Hippolyte, fearful of combat as he had been during Louise's family battles in Provence, was terrified of taking on Karr, who was known to be an expert fencer and one of the best marksmen in Paris. Hippolyte backed off.

Louise, determined to teach her husband a lesson in virility, decided to take revenge into her own hands. Here is Louise's own account of her attempted murder of Karr, which begins with a rhetorical device she often used—allusions to her noble and ancient Provençal lineage and to her grandfather Le Blanc's valor as a hero of the French Revolution:

I spent the night in a state of insomnia, of stupor and rage: The blood of my grandfather, member of the Revolutionary Convention, the blood of his daughter—my proud and holy mother—trembled within me. I also heard the child trembling in my womb and shouting out: "This man must die!"

(Many murderess heroines had filled Louise's imagination since her adolescence—Lady Macbeth, Lucrezia Borgia, Charlotte Corday. It was central to the Romantic ethos to act out one's favorite literary roles.)

I waited for the proper day, I counted the hours. When I was alone . . . I put on my clothes; I took a kitchen knife as my weapon. . . .

(The next passage is enchanting:)

. . . To arm myself with a more elegant weapon would have been theatrical. I only wished to act with simplicity, as is suitable to any great sorrow.

(Louise is nearly nine months pregnant, enormous—she would always put on a great deal of weight during her difficult pregnancies. She has been in bed for weeks with terrible leg pains. She drags herself to the villain's house, the knife hidden in her umbrella. . . .)

I lived in the vicinity of that man's lodgings; I walked toward it, reso-lute. I found him at his threshold, in his shirtsleeves. "I must speak to you—" Those were my only words. He asked me to come in, and as he leaned toward his porter's lodge I struck him in the lower back. A few drops of blood spurted out. The kitchen knife had slipped. Anxious about his calumnies, he is said to have put on an iron vest. He swiftly turned around and disarmed me. . . .

(The outraged Muse is surprised; her indignation surpasses any fear she might have concerning her victim's reprisal. . . .)

After having failed, I did not speak a word. He pretended that he had called a cab for me and offered me his hand to help me into it. A ridiculous gesture! How could I have touched that man's hand! He would write about me: "She was quite beautiful, but of too massive a beauty." Atrocious phrase! I was as massive as any mother about to bring a child into the world.

In the aftermath, the Colet-Cousin ménage à trois went into pandemonium. Cousin took pride in his mistress's boldness. He even devised a flattering Latin epigram for her: *"Maxime sum mulier; sed vicut vir ago."* ("I am a quintessential woman, but I know how to act like a man.") Minister Cousin, however, was determined to keep the scandal from becoming a lawsuit. He dispatched Sainte-Beuve, who still coveted membership in the Académie Française, to intercede with Karr. Probably exhorting some favor of his own from Sainte-Beuve, Karr promised not to bring suit against Louise.

The Cousin-Colet trio anxiously awaited the next issue of Karr's periodical. Plato's intercession through Sainte-Beuve was rewarded, for to their relief, Karr's postscript began with an admiring apology: "I don't believe that [Madame Colet] was absolutely wrong. In her resolve to avenge an injury by herself, alone, in full daylight, there is indeed an energy and courage that borders on nobility. . . . I acted in bad taste, and I beg all women's forgiveness."

Alphonse Karr's own account of the incident, which he also published in *Guêpes,* did not vary much from Louise's version. " 'Forgive me for not prolonging this little conversation,' " he quoted himself as saying to the Muse upon being stabbed. " 'Accompany this lady to the door,' " he then told his concierge.

Karr ended on this biting reflection, which alluded mockingly to Louise's appetite for publicity:

I certainly would have been gravely harmed if my attacker had struck me with a direct horizontal blow instead of lifting her arm high over her head in a tragedian's gesture, surely in anticipation of some forthcoming lithograph of the incident.

"If only it had not been a *kitchen* knife," Karr added. "These women of letters are terrible housekeepers."

Karr would commemorate the incident by keeping Louise's knife in a vitrine of his drawing room, with the following inscription:

Offered by Madame Colet
In the back

Karr aimed one last sting at Cousin. Shortly after the uproar over the stabbing incident had calmed down, he wrote in "Wasps" that Sainte-Beuve had been given the curatorship of the distinguished Bibliothèque Mazarine—Minister Cousin's reward for interceding in his mistress's favor.

Meanwhile the feckless Hippolyte had tried to reclaim his honor. He wrote the following account of the *"Affaire Colet-Karr"* to his brother, a career army officer who had attended the Colets' wedding in Provence:

I cried out that I would kill the slanderer. My resolve was all there. Louise heard me. Yet while I was giving a lesson at the conservatory, she decided to take revenge by herself. . . .

(Hippolyte, leaning over his desk, desperately tries to regild his manly image in his sibling's eyes.)

And this poor suffering woman, a few hours away from childbirth, massive as a Roman matron, all the more powerful because she was an outraged mother about to avenge the honor of an unborn child, this poor woman had the courage to confront the defamer all by herself. . . .

(Even Hippolyte seems to admire Louise at this moment.)

But Alas, the power of her arm could not match the energy of her
spirit, and the weapon, which must have been guided by God, barely
even bruised the villain's skin. If you could have seen the pallor, the
tremor of that man, you would have said: "Hell is already in his soul!"

The child who might well have caused Karr's death and Louise's life
imprisonment was a girl, born in August of 1840. Louise called her daughter Henriette, after her mother. It was Cousin, as Karr had alleged, who
went to the suburban town of Nanterre to find the best possible wet nurse
for the infant to live with. This does not signal any lack of maternal emotion on the part of Louise. City air being considered noxious to infants, it
was the custom of the time among the middle and upper classes of French
society to send babies to board with a wet nurse in the country for their
first two years.

Cousin continued to lavish every solicitude on Louise for the next
several seasons. He praised her writings anonymously in various periodicals. "Dear friend, could you see to it . . . that this critique gets published
in either *La Revue de Paris* or *La Revue des deux mondes*?" he scribbled
in a note to Sainte-Beuve concerning one of his unsigned praises to the
Muse. "In my view, the overall handling of the work is felicitous. . . . I ask
you to arrange this as soon as possible."

At times Cousin was too protective. Louise received a small yearly sum
from him for her daughter's upkeep, but although she was constantly in
debt, she never accepted a penny for her own use. So far, all government
support she received came from the Ministry of Education, the habitual
conduit for writers' pensions, and she was vain enough to believe that it
was given her for the high value of her work. Cousin's offers to lobby for
an additional pension from the Ministry of the Interior, which would
have had little to do with her literary achievements, made her furious. The
lovers quarreled violently over such issues; but according to the philosopher, some of their reconciliations were so sweet that they more than
compensated.

"I'm in love with a lioness rather than a dove," he wrote Louise, "and
I'm doing my best to tame her. . . . I'm limited, O roaring lioness, to
kissing the tips of your claws."

Louise's temper was so fierce, however, that Cousin, heretofore an
ardent champion of female intellectuals, began to lose his admiration for
literary women. A few years into their affair, Cousin's writings started to
show strong misgivings concerning professional women writers. This
burgeoning prejudice in Cousin exemplified a prevailing attitude in

nineteenth-century France: Too precious to be corrupted by the public world, women should remain both physically and psychologically secluded and must not display their inner emotions in writing. "What is there to say about women authors?" Cousin wrote.

About a woman with no public cause to defend who rushes to the public forum . . . and uncovers herself to all eyes, puts herself to bid as if at auction, exposes to the commercial scrutiny of booksellers, readers, and journalists her most secret beauties, her most touching and mysterious charms, her soul, her feelings, her sufferings, her interior struggles! That is what we now witness every day . . . that is what will be eternally impossible for us to comprehend.

Notwithstanding many such reservations concerning the confessionalism of her verses, Louise Colet was well established by the early 1840s as one of France's leading women poets. In an essay in the eminent periodical *Le Moniteur,* she was ranked alongside several older colleagues: her friends Marceline Desbordes-Valmore and Anaïs Ségalas, and the prolific Delphine Gay, who at the age of nineteen had preceded Louise as one of the four women ever awarded the poetry prize of the Académie Française. While the article faulted Louise for her occasional "affectation and precious obscurity" (flaws that one could equally attribute to the sister poets mentioned above), it praised the maturity of her thought and the confidence of her voice.

Another sign of her growing fame: In the spring of 1842, Louise received an extravagant gift from an anonymous admirer: A multivolume set of *The Poetry of Madame Colet,* gilt-edged and bound in red morocco leather and presented in inlaid ebony boxes, it was published in a special edition of twenty-five copies. The gift was accompanied by an unsigned letter:

If I were a great philosopher or physicist, I would address to you dialogues on the nature of light and other mysteries of nature. If I were a celebrated man of letters, I would congratulate you as M. Chateaubriand has. And if I were a poet, I would apply myself to imitating you. Since I am but a simple man, devoid of genius or grandeur and endowed solely with the faculty of admiration, suffer, Madame, to accept the book of a great poet. This is an edition similar to those published in the Louvre for the works of Corneille. . . .

At first Louise thought this sumptuous gift might be from Victor Cousin; but he was too stingy to have made such a present, not modest enough to have written such a note. Investigating the mystery, she discovered that the volumes had come from a prosperous provincial pharmacist, a Monsieur Quéneville, who had been writing her admiring letters for several years. He had also sent her flowers, opera tickets, invitations to supper, none of them acknowledged.

The same age as Louise, Quéneville had made his fortune by manufacturing curative powders extracted from the sulfurous waters of the spa of Barèges.

After writing her admirer to thank him for this superb present, Louise's one-woman public relations factory immediately put the books to use. She sent copies of the luxury edition to monarchs and prominent men throughout Europe: to King Frederick William of Prussia; to the Czar of All Russias, Nicholas I, whose minister, Prince Ouvaroff, replied with a flattering note accompanied by a large gold medal of the czar; to a hero of her early years, the radical Abbé de Lamennais, who was currently serving a jail term for his socialist views.

Louise also sent a copy of the volume to another idol of her youth, the Italian revolutionary activist Silvio Pellico. Pellico replied: "Your poetry is so beautiful, I'm so proud of having such a glorious place in it, the edition is magnificent, your gift is so kind that I have no words with which to express my gratitude. . . ." The cycle of admiration had come full circle: It was Pellico, a fan of Louise's verse and a pen pal of her admirer Quéneville, who had suggested to the pharmacist that he might score a hit with the Parisian beauty by producing a lavish edition of her work.

Louise sent copies to a score of French literary celebrities whom she had not yet tackled for their attention—Victor Hugo, Lamartine, and the most famous poet of the French midcentury, Pierre-Jean de Béranger, with whom she would form a lifelong friendship.

These signs of growing recognition emboldened Louise to aspire to grander themes, to historical and political topics. She wrote a long eulogy on the most momentous French event of the early 1840s, the return of Napoleon's ashes to Paris. She also published a book on the youth of the revolutionary leader Mirabeau, the hero of her childhood who had been a close friend of her grandfather's. She dedicated the book to her mother, whose beauty had led Mirabeau to choose her as his partner for the last great ball held in Aix before the revolution of 1789.

La Jeunesse de Mirabeau is one of Colet's most enjoyable works, filled with a vivid, painterly historical prose that might ultimately have won her far more "glory" than she gained for her pretty, ordinary verses. A captivating hybrid of biography, novella, and moral fable, it documents the first thirty years in the life of Comte Honoré-Gabriel de Mirabeau, the greatest orator and political thinker of the French Revolution's early phase.

Mirabeau's tormented youth was an inspired theme for Louise, ideally suited to her passion for republican topics and to her leanings toward Gothic melodrama and moral extremes. Mirabeau's father, France's most prominent economist, was a pitiless tyrant who repressed his son because he feared his precocious genius and superiority. Soon after young Mirabeau's loveless marriage to a wealthy girl of the Aix-en-Provence aristocracy, Mirabeau senior had his son incarcerated in a series of increasingly harsh prisons.

The confinement lasted an entire decade and had the approval of Mirabeau's malicious wife, who sought happiness in the arms of fortune-seekers. Having failed to break his son's spirit, Mirabeau *père* set him free a few years before the Revolution. Young Mirabeau displayed his oratorical gifts in a famous trial against his faithless spouse, which made him the hero of Aix-en-Provence. Renouncing the decadent aristocracy into which he'd been born, he began his career as radical reformer and with the outbreak of the Revolution was elected deputy to the Revolutionary Convention as a member of the *Tiers État,* the plebeian sector of the French nation, to whose liberation he dedicated his life.

La Jeunesse de Mirabeau gains its moral authority from its political subtext: The perverse egotism and self-indulgence of the hero's father and wife are pitted against Mirabeau's probity. The narrative symbolizes the conflict between the cruel excesses of France's *ancien régime* and the virtue of the nation's oppressed people, or, in the author's words, "that clash between the ancient and the new which produced the Revolution."

Colet's *Mirabeau* was widely read when it was serialized in Émile de Girardin's popular newspaper, *La Presse.* Louise sent a copy of the book to the most famous woman writer of her time, George Sand, whose celebrity Louise may have envied even more than her talent.

At the time she started corresponding with Louise, George Sand was at the height of her fame. Baudelaire referred to her as "a latrine"; Chateaubriand saw her as "the Byron of France"; other progressive compatriots hailed her as the equal of Hugo, Balzac, and Dumas; the notably misogynous novelist Barbey d'Aurevilly boasted that he "dressed in red, like an executioner," to write his violent attacks on her books.

George Sand, too, had been born into country gentry, though into a family more prosperous than Louise's. She, too, was amply sexed, prodigally generous and spendthrift, and a devoted mother. Also like Louise, Sand had made a disastrous first marriage to a weak-willed and jealous husband ("Marriage is one of the most barbaric institutions society has engendered," she wrote) and soon had consoled herself with a dazzling sequence of lovers.

The most scandalous of Sand's early affairs (in 1832, when Louise was defending her in bitter arguments with her Provençal siblings) was with the fetching and dissolute poet Alfred de Musset. The lovers had set off together for Italy, where Sand reversed traditional gender stereotypes by playing to the hilt the role of aggressive seducer: She ravished a handsome Italian doctor, whom she brought back to Paris, creating mayhem in the life of the heartbroken Musset. The Italian was eventually dispatched back to Italy, and the liaison with Musset came to a stormy close. Sand was dismayed that society condemned as scandalous a behavior it had so admired in Byron.

The life of this eccentric woman, who went on to have an equally turbulent affair with Frédéric Chopin, was a balancing act of erotic adventurism and devoted family life. Juggling the care of frequently ailing children, their moody and often enamored tutors, many other jealous and sickly lovers, and an alcoholic, gun-toting husband, Sand moved from house to house to lessen debts, or escape various men, or improve her lovers' and offspring's health. She frequently traveled the three hundred kilometers to her beloved family home at Nohant, in central France, and could gallop five hours on horseback for an amorous rendezvous. Throughout this chaos she cranked out more than two books a year to keep the debtors at bay, writing all night, sustained by coffee and cigars.

A few weeks after Louise sent Sand her novella, she received her first letter from her. This lengthy missive had a mother-superior tone. It praised a few aspects of Louise's technique but expressed strong political reservations concerning Louise's glorification of Mirabeau and her views of the 1789 revolution, which were more conservative than Sand's own.

Ironically, although Louise would evolve a more concrete and committed feminist stance than Sand, their political discord on the issue of the Revolution would remain an obstacle to any friendship the two women might ever have shared. In their correspondence, Sand kept emphasizing that she and Louise belonged to opposite factions of republican ideology.

Louise, Sand maintained, was in the camp of the moderate Girondins, who initially believed in a constitutional monarchy and would have preferred to spare Louis XVI's life. She, Sand, was committed to the Jacobins, who wanted to abolish the monarchy and believed that all violence was justified in the process of dismantling the *ancien régime*. "I am most grateful to you, Madame, for having sent me your books," George Sand began her first letter.

They appear to be very beautiful and contain very noble sentiments. However, I do not share your view of Mirabeau's work. . . . I do not believe that it covers the range of revolutionary achievement. In my view, it merely served to create a transition between monarchy and the republic. It is only after the death of that great man that his great revolution became significant, efficacious, providential, and sublime.

Sand then asserted that Colet was simply too young to understand that the more extreme militants whom she had censured in her book on Mirabeau—Marat, Robespierre—were the Revolution's truest apostles. The letter moved on to more personal topics, voicing dismay at Louise's social conduct of the past years (as if Sand were in a position to judge!) and berating Louise's quest for fame. For Sand seemed to have observed Louise from afar with great interest. She was well informed about Louise's melodramatic conduct in the Karr-Cousin-Colet scandal. Details had probably been supplied by her close friend Sainte-Beuve.

I look upon you as a child filled with genius who does not yet know where it will go but who will open its wings and fly toward the light if it finds the proper path to seek. This path is one of absolute independence toward the petty prides and prejudices of our century. You have almost shattered yourself on those, madame . . . you have an ardent soul, an impetuous and courageous character. But your future should be aimed in a direction totally opposed to the one you have taken. . . .

I prefer that you leave this letter unanswered. I understand you better than you understand yourself. I have never sought to meet you. You love glory and literature too much for us to be able to converse with each other, although I do not blame you for loving things which bore me.

There appears to be a whiff of hypocrisy here. Sand is suggesting that Louise is a publicity hound; but could any woman who chose to parade about Paris in men's clothes, chain-smoking cigars and flaunting her melodramatic love affairs, be exempt from the charge of exhibitionism?

Throughout the following year, Louise explored another facet of French revolutionary history. "The Revolution and the Empire are our Homeric ages," she had written in her preface to *La Jeunesse de Mirabeau*. "Epics and dramas will burst forth forever from these two fecund epochs." Her next literary venture focused on two of the Revolution's most prominent women activists. One of them was Madame Roland, a Girondin leader, who was put to death during the Terror on the orders of Jean-Paul Marat and is best remembered for the last words she spoke before being guillotined: "O Liberty, what crimes are committed in thy name!" The other heroine was also a Girondin: Charlotte Corday, a twenty-five-year-old woman of the Normandy gentry who was put to death after she stabbed Marat as he sat in his bath.

Colet saw both Corday and Roland as emblems of the martyred women throughout history who have sacrificed themselves to noble causes. But her identification with Corday might also have been based, however subconsciously, on her own attack on Karr, in which she had wielded the same weapon. Parisian wits had wagged that Louise had played out the role of *"une Corday contemporaine."*

Louise studied for many months before she started writing, interviewing the few remaining witnesses who had known Corday and Roland, boning up on Madame Roland's memoirs, the court records of the women's trials, Montesquieu's reflections on regicide. But the crucial moment in her research—that spark many writers need to ignite their creative process—was her visit to the "Museum of the Terror" installed by the revolutionary activist Comte Alexandre de Saint-Albain. At his home on the Île Saint-Louis, Saint-Albain had assembled an extensive collection of posters, pamphlets, and paintings related to the 1789 uprising.

Louise was transfixed by one particular item of this collection: a portrait of Charlotte Corday which depicted her as she climbed the steps toward the guillotine, wearing the red shirt assigned to those condemned to death. As Louise studied the painting, her eyes welled up with tears. As in the instance of her visit to the Versailles "Pantheon of Great Men," Louise's legend factory immediately went to work; she would later report that she had written the sixty-page play in one sitting, overwhelmed by the vision of her heroine rising to the scaffold.

Charlotte Corday was a direct descendant of the great playwright Corneille, and Louise capitalized on this kinship. In her scenario, Corday impersonates Corneille's Judith, righteous murderess of the villain Holofernes. Louise emulated the terseness and control of Corneille's verse—a tone not characteristic of her habitually florid style—and it beautifully offsets the histrionic violence of its theme.

As the play begins, Charlotte Corday, attending a meeting of Girondins in her native Normandy during the Terror of 1793, hears her male colleagues denounce the carnage being caused by the radical Jacobin leader Marat. "And you will allow him to live?" Charlotte asks her male peers. "Good-bye, gentlemen, I shall outdo you." She returns to her father's house, picks up her Bible, and rereads the Book of Judith. She meditates on the legitimacy of regicide and affirms her decision to kill, calling on her forebear Corneille: "Your shadow, O my ancestor, arms my trembling hand."

Pretending that she is carrying evidence of a Girondin plot against his life, Corday is given permission to visit Marat. His guards usher her into his bathroom, where the tyrant spends much of his time immersed in warm water, a writing desk installed over his tub, seeking relief from a painful skin disease.

"I will send them all, all to the guillotine!" Marat cries out as he reads the document Charlotte has brought him. Charlotte strengthens her resolve with another invocation from Corneille's *Judith:* "Lord God of Israel, fortify my soul!" She then strikes the tyrant in the chest (far more accurately than Louise struck at Alphonse Karr). "His death will deliver France!" she exclaims. Seized by a squad of Marat's bodyguards, Charlotte says she is ready for the scaffold.

Colet's depiction of Charlotte Corday's trial draws on the original court record. It contains some lines that have become famous among French schoolchildren, such as "I have killed one man to rescue a hundred thousand." The last scene takes place in the Conciergerie Prison, where Charlotte waits for the executioner while thinking of all those she loved. "I leave you regretfully. . . . But do not mourn me: My task is fulfilled."

This fine "docudrama," as we would call it today, gains its power from the controlled austerity of its verse style. It is flawed mostly by excessive moral symmetry—its simplistic Manichaean juxtaposition of the evil Marat and the virtuous regicide Corday. *Charlotte Corday,* though published as a book, was never performed on the stage. Because it expressed centrist-progressive opinions, it was considered suspect by both leftists like George Sand, who maintained strong pro-Jacobin sentiments, and those numerous French citizens who had remained royalists. Above all, the play thoroughly confused male critics, who did not think women were fit to deal with such grand historical themes and chafed at its implicit feminism. One commentary on *Charlotte Corday* criticized Louise particularly for focusing on the Revolution's two most celebrated women. "She seems to be saying that the Gironde produced only one important action, and a woman was the actor, that the Gironde had only one great politician, and that woman was the wife of Roland," *La Revue Indépendante* complained.

So much for the attitudes of conservative males. The play was not any better received by George Sand, who, so Louise hoped, might have helped to get it onto the stage—Sand was too much on Marat's side. "You will someday reflect more clearly on revolutionary achievements which you don't yet want to accept," Sand scolded her upon receiving the manuscripts of *Charlotte Corday* and *Madame Roland.*

> *After all, you're not a cowardly little woman. You love Charlotte Corday, bloodshed does not seem to disturb you. That is not what bothers you; you would have struck down Marat without an afterthought. You are led by false notions which the Girondins passed on to you. . . .*

"For since your heart is fundamentally with the people," Sand's letter continued, in a let-me-give-you-a-history-lesson tone,

> *you seem to be in constant contradiction with yourself. . . . What passion so animates you against those terrorists whom Goethe, Schiller, could not help admiring? It is said that women do not think in a fully logical manner. Why don't you work to refute that opinion? Either admit your hate for Equality, or else respect those who proclaimed it! As long as I will have the opportunity to communicate with you, I'll continue to repeat that you refuse to understand the Revolution! . . . I always maintain a certain respect for fanatics. They are always logical, because they act according to their beliefs.*

Colet and Sand clearly had a complex relationship. In one of their few face-to-face encounters, the Muse had recited some of her poetry at a private home in front of a distinguished audience that included Sand. Louise fully expected some compliments from her, but all Sand said to her was: "Madame, you have the shoulders and arms of a Greek statue." This comment, adequate enough if it had come from a male admirer, was interpreted by Louise as a denigration of her talent. George Sand's attitude toward her junior colleague was equally ambivalent. She was obviously fascinated by her destiny as well as by her talents; and she was impressed enough with Louise to send her many thoughtful, pedagogic letters. Yet she preferred to keep her at a distance. "I dared already to tell you that you do not understand the Revolution," she wrote Louise again a fortnight later.

> I dare repeat it again, and repeat that you will eventually come to understand it, for your heart is made for the truth. Up to now, you have been too preoccupied with facts. Facts to not prove as much as you would wish them to. If you decided to be more preoccupied with ideas, you would very soon realize that the furor and delirium of a political party do not disprove the Idea which produced and launched them.

The necessity of the Jacobins' bloodthirsty acts versus the Girondins' semiroyalist compromises—this contrast continued to inform Sand's critiques of Colet's play.

> If inebriation has its part in it, the fault lies in the infirmity of human nature, and the virtues of your Girondins will not make their notions any wider or warmer. I would have loved them, I would have mourned them: but I would not have been on their side.

Louise persevered. That same month, she had sent Sand some poems concerning "The Downtrodden People," which she had dedicated to her friend Pierre-Jean de Béranger, France's "national bard." Sand dismantled them as meticulously as she has dismantled Louise's works on Mirabeau, Roland, and Corday.

> Béranger, you, and the men presently in power consecrate their energy and their genius to the education of that oppressed class which you show us to be so mean, so ugly, and so stupid. Your muse was indignant rather than compassionate when she made you sing in this manner. . . . I fear that in abusing her divine right, you might have a bit too much disgust for those who are poor in spirit.

Louise was infuriated. Sand must have totally misunderstood her verses. How could she have detected a "hatred of The People" in these poems, Louise raged, when Louise was attempting to defend The People against its exploiters? And so she wrote back to Sand: What she had meant to say was that the lower classes, besotted by misery, illness, exploitation of all sorts, had not yet become conscious of their need to rebel.

The radical schoolmarm wrote back the very same evening: "I see, Madame, that I made you very angry, and I am happy that I have. If I was mistaken in your intent, I thank God that I changed my mind, for a talent such as yours is not a sympathy which one could lose without regret. . . ."

Sand reiterated that notwithstanding her keen interest in Louise and her work, she led "too reclusive" a life for them to ever meet. That, too, was a bit hypocritical. Sand moved in a very elitist circle of friends who saw each other with nearly incestuous frequency. Beyond Chopin, her intimates included Franz Lizst, his mistress Marie d'Agoult, the painter Delacroix, and the prominent actress Marie Dorval, with whom Sand was rumored to have had lesbian interludes. And despite her evident fascination with the flamboyant Colet, Sand may well have been wary of allowing such a seductive and opportunistic beauty to invade her cozy circle, possibly to snare one of its precious males.

But Sand's aloof attitude to Louise was not at all typical; she was one of the few celebrities who deliberately refused her offer of friendship. The passionate and lifelong platonic friendships Louise enjoyed with France's most popular poet, Béranger, with its preeminent sculptor, James Pradier, and with the legendary Madame Récamier, are more characteristic of the devotion Louise Colet received from the intelligentsia of mid-nineteenth-century Paris.

5.

Three Great
Friendships:
1842–1846

⚜

Pierre-Jean de Béranger, an author of light ditties still studied today as outstanding examples of "popular" verse in nineteenth-century France, was the country's official "national bard," his fame far more widespread than Hugo's or Lamartine's. In him Louise found a protector whose influence was greater than theirs and whose populist tastes responded warmly to her work.

Born in 1780 into a lower-middle-class family, Pierre-Jean de Béranger was carried on his grandfather's shoulders to witness the storming of the Bastille. His first collection of verse, which came out right after the downfall of Napoleon, was marked by extreme anticlericalism and a violent hatred for the restored Bourbon monarchy. The prison term he subsequently served under Charles X for committing "outrage to public and religious morality" turned him into a martyr and a hero of France's progressive citizenry. Béranger was bailed out of jail on funds raised by several hundred thousand citizens, and he remained a national hero until his death in 1857, when he was given the grandest state funeral since Mirabeau's.

The verses of "Papa Béranger," as he was known throughout France, were designed to be sung to well-known melodies at the *guinguettes*, or workmen's singing clubs, that had sprung up since the fall of the empire. Sincere and often naive in their directness, Béranger's simplistic words and titles ("The Children of France," "The Old Flag," "The Old Corporal") made his art accessible to the working-class. But the wide social spectrum of his devotees—unique in the history of French literature— went beyond the peasantry, the new urban proletariat, or the disgruntled veterans of Napoleon's armies. The incisiveness of his satires, which ridiculed conservative clergy, greedy deputies, and the excesses of state power, also earned him the respect of Europe's most distinguished men of letters. Hugo and Lamartine memorized his verses, Sainte-Beuve rated him "only a little below Horace," Stendhal hailed him as "the finest French poet alive" and "the one whose works have the greatest chance of seeing the twentieth century." And Béranger's legendary generosity and modesty turned him into the Saint Francis of French literature. (He refused a seat in the Académie Française, a rejection perhaps unique in that century.)

Louise's friendship with Béranger began when she sent him the pharmacist's luxury edition of her work. Béranger wrote to the Muse to thank her. His first letter was full of warnings about the dangerous glibness of her verse, but in fact it revealed a "feminist," uncondescending admiration of women writers rare among his generation.

Chère Madame, I love the warmth, the power, the abundance of your generous spirit. You possess that courage of thought often lacking to the poetic superiority that honors your gender. The forthrightness of your expression seems to be reflected in your character, and it would be a pleasure to see you direct your energy at the reprimanding of the male community, avenging women for men's idiotic pretensions. . . .

"You poor women of letters!" Béranger commiserated in another letter to Louise. "Only too often are you denigrated by your own sex and crushed by ours."

Béranger and Louise met, and within a few months they exchanged dozens more letters. The "Madame" soon became "Chère Muse" and "Chère Enfant," and the two writers struck up such a close friendship that for the next fifteen years they visited with each other nearly every day. They saw eye to eye on political and social issues. Until the end of his days, Béranger would serve Louise as literary counselor, guru, and father confessor, and their friendship would remain one of the treasures of Louise's life.

At the time he met Louise, Béranger was in his early sixties, a genial, portly bachelor who lived in a modest cottage in Passy; later he moved to a few servants' rooms in the middle of Paris. He took time off from his work to agitate for numerous social reforms, to visit workmen's cafés along the Seine, to lobby for favors on behalf of one of his younger colleagues. Louise would drop in on Béranger in Passy when she went to Nanterre to visit her little daughter, Henriette; and Béranger would scold her for some instance of tactlessness or devise some favor he might do for her.

"Here is a volume which Mme Colet asked me to send you . . . in hopes that you might support it at the committee on translations," Béranger wrote to the Secretary of the Académie Française as he tried to secure for Louise a reward for her translations of the poems of the seventeenth-century Italian heretic Tommaso Campanella. "It has the particular merit of being the first translation ever of that writer's poems. . . . Be good enough to write me a word on this issue, and do continue all your goodwill for Mme Colet."

There was a great deal more for Béranger to counsel his young friend about. Within the first five years of her arrival in Paris, Louise Colet had become not only a famous writer, and a paradigm of that bluestocking French men so feared and derided, but also a somewhat legendary figure who tended to overdo her pose as Romantic Muse. The 1830s marked the beginning of media cults, the fashioning of artists' public personae as indispensable assets to success. And the Romantic movement itself had much to do with self-invention, with the individual's capacity to surmount every possible social obstacle through passion, gumption, and commitment.

Louise excelled at those techniques. Paris was rife with accounts of her phenomenal facility and speed of execution, her singular faculty for scribbling verses while surrounded by the domestic mayhem of her boudoir-study, amid a hodgepodge of manuscripts, cologne bottles, and grocers' accounts. It was considered awesome, for instance, that Madame Colet had written her prize-winning poem "Le Musée de Versailles" in three consecutive sleepless days without once getting out of her housecoat; that she had finished her verse play on Charlotte Corday in twenty-four hours, after having wept before a portrait of the scaffold-bound Charlotte; that she had risen from her sickbed, after an inspirational talk with Béranger, to write a fifty-stanza poem on Molière in one sitting (those verses would earn her another prize from the Académie Française).

Louise's generosity—for gift-giving, for helping younger writers and artists—was as legendary as her often slipshod writing practices. One of her first biographers recounted the following incident: Upon learning that a penniless young artist had failed to come to her Sunday salon because of illness, Louise walked over to his garret with a hot meal, took home a dozen of his canvases, and organized a lottery at her salon for the paintings, bringing him the proceeds the same evening.

There were less flattering rumors as well, of Louise's hotheadedness and fits of temper, aimed not only at the monster Alphonse Karr, her henpecked lover, Cousin, or her increasingly bitter husband, Hippolyte. One of the Colets' frequently dismissed domestic servants spread this tale: Quarreling with her maid one day, right after emerging from her bath, Louise had pursued the girl to the door of the apartment, kitchen tongs in hand. During a tussle at the door, the maid locked the door from the inside, leaving Louise stranded on the upstairs landing (so the maid claimed), quite naked.

Béranger went about Paris trying to downplay his protégée's faux pas, polish her image, curb her impetuosity. His most frequent criticisms concerned her hurried working methods:

> If I may so dare [the national bard warned her], I wish to remind you that you might take to heart a dictum attributed to Buffon: "Genius is nothing but an aptitude for patience." Do you not lack a bit of that patience . . .? French verse requires a long reflective labor, of which few women have been capable; and it seems to me that in a few passages you have lacked a bit of that patience which, even if it does not assure genius, is one of its principal instruments. . . . You're writing too fast; let it decant, and then give it another careful reading. . . .

During a face-to-face meeting, the tempestuous beauty might have greeted Béranger as she greeted all her friends, in the modest parlor that served as her salon, dressing room, and study, sitting at a dilapidated table that was heaped with unfinished manuscripts, letters from creditors, and cosmetic jars. "But I need to published three books a year to make ends meet!" she would say. "You know how our critics tear most women's works to shreds! When will society do something to help women get along?"

Her mentor would explain that if Louise put more *patience* into her work, she would better avenge her own gender.

"But I need money!" one can hear Louise cry out to Béranger. "I need to support a child and an ailing husband! I have no family to lean on, not a cent of my own! What do you bachelors know of all that?"

The other issue Béranger nagged Louise about, often in unison with Cousin, was her spendthrift ways. Her extensive correspondence with

European personages had inspired her to assemble an autograph album in which she wished to include the greatest celebrities of her time. The thank-you notes from Russian and German heads of state having gone to her head, Louise went on to purchase—often for exorbitant sums—the signatures of Rossini, Manzoni, Meyerbeer, and the scientist Humboldt. The fatherly Béranger fruitlessly advised her against the project:

> In such ephemeral times as ours, you should be saving those one-thousand-franc notes for your daughter, rather than wasting them on the signatures of dubiously "great" men, mere twigs thrown upon the river to measure its course . . . but I'm talking to a deaf woman.

Louise replied that the autograph album was as fine an investment as she could make, that she could resell it for a minimum of ten thousand francs. On this particular issue her arguments with Béranger grew heated. She sulked for days. He corresponded with Cousin concerning Louise's moodiness. "Oh, Plato, you neglect Aristotle!" he wrote Cousin. "I've known for some time that I'm trying to address a madwoman."

Cousin tried to reconcile the two new friends. "Perhaps Béranger feels his advice to you is not getting the attention merited by his age, his renown, and his protection," he wrote his stormy mistress. "I've heard him complain that he is called only to repair your mistakes and not to prevent them. He has a reverent flock, like all good pastors, and you are not his most docile lamb."

Louise continued to spend as recklessly, to scribble as speedily and prolifically, as ever, and to give vent to her hot temper. One of her frequent rages betrayed her continued resentment of her siblings in Provence: Walking down the Rue Montmartre one day in 1841, she happened upon her nephew Benedict Révoil, son of her sister Joséphine. The eccentric Benedict, only six years Louise's junior, had become a colleague of sorts: His several trips to the United States, where he had struck up a close friendship with Davy Crockett, had inspired a series of books on animal husbandry and hunting, such as *Chasse et pêche dans l'autre monde, L'Exposition universelle des chiens, Histoire physiologique et anecdotique de tout les chiens de toutes les races.*

Louise noted that after gazing at her in a very disdainful manner, Benedict had brushed by her without saying a word. She approached her nephew and slapped him in the face. Benedict thought of nothing better to do than to race to the Paris Opera, where Hippolyte Colet was rehearsing, and slap him in turn. Hippolyte, this time, did not shy away from a duel; he immediately demanded one in a note sent to Benedict via his two

proposed witnesses. Benedict's reply typifies the impertinence of the
Révoil clan.

*Sir, you seem to have forgotten the facts, and I find it necessary to
remind you of them:*

*At the moment when your hand lifted toward me, I broke my cane
on your face.*

*As to your epithet of "cowardly," it has been long bestowed on
you in Paris circles.*

*I fully understand that you seek to flaunt your courage at a time
when you know that an unfortunate family kinship makes a duel between us impossible.*

*And so if you henceforth ever challenge me again, I shall respond
with a stick.*

Consider yourself forewarned,
Benedict Révoil

Louise had not returned to Provence since 1834, when she left in
search of fame and glory. In the summer of 1842, she set off on a two-
month trip to the Midi with her husband and child. The expedition was
planned in part to improve the health of Hippolyte, who was suffering
from an increasingly serious lung ailment, and in part out of nostalgia for
the landscape of her childhood: "Those lands where the sun is only occasionally veiled by swiftly passing clouds, where our blood boils, where
our soul is warmed in the sun's heat."

The prodigal daughter was feted in Nîmes, Arles, Avignon, and her
native Aix. Citizens of Provence fought for the honor of holding parties in
her honor, offered her banquets, and held grand ceremonies in their municipal libraries. After their triumphant tour of Provençal cities, Louise
and the two-year-old Henriette traveled on to spend a week at Mouriès.
They visited Louise's beloved childhood nurse, Reine Picard, and stayed
with the widow of the town's former mayor; like her husband, she had
generously aided Louise during the family feuding at the time of her marriage, and Louise had remained devoted to her.

Louise's brother-in-law Pierre Révoil had died that spring, her sister
Joséphine had moved to Lyons, and the family estate was now run by
Louise's bachelor brother, Adolphe. This trip proved that the family enmities that had plagued Louise's youth were as powerful as ever. Not
once during that week in Mouriès was Louise able to visit Servanes, even
though it is a ten-minute walk from the village. She wrote about her frustration concerning Servanes and her kin in the memoir of Provence she

published shortly after her trip, *Deux mois d'émotions,* "Two Months of Emotion." Although it was a book of nonfiction, a classic travel essay, Louise included a fictional encounter with Adolphe.

The way Louise narrated the episode, by 1842 Servanes had been sold to a Belgian industrialist, notorious in the region for his meanness. Louise, who wished to say a prayer in the room in which her mother had died, stood at the gate of the estate, asking the new owner's permission to enter the house for a few minutes. The Belgian forbade her access: "What right do you have to enter my property without my consent? . . . You will not enter, Madame." If only Servanes were inhabited by one of her brothers or sisters, Louise thought as she stared desolately at the windows of her mother's former bedroom, "their hearts would have opened, their arms would have received me."

Servanes, in fact, never left the possession of the Révoil family, and Adolphe remained the lord of the manor from the mid-1840s until the 1860s. So one can only conclude that this fictional episode was a disguised version of a very painful real-life encounter Louise had with her brother, in which *he* barred her from their family home.

Back in Paris, the Colets moved to a new Montmartre flat, their fifth apartment in six years, at 21 Rue Fontaine Saint-George. It would be the last domicile they would share.

Louise was pregnant again. She looked forward so eagerly to the birth that she did not seem to care whether it was the child of Hippolyte or of Victor Cousin, with whom she continued an increasingly stormy liaison. Often ailing from her pregnancy, refusing as proudly as ever Cousin's offers of any financial aid beyond a small pension for her daughter, Louise made ends meet by dashing off three books in ten months: The travel book on Provence was followed by Louise's preface to the collected writings of the prominent eighteenth-century bluestocking Madame de Lambert, which she turned into an essay on the unacknowledged influence of women on historical events. Then she produced a collection of romantic novelettes about oppressed or exploited women, *Les Coeurs brisés,* "Broken Hearts," a fashionably gothic work offering case histories of women tormented by debauched lovers or sadistic husbands.

"Broken Hearts" is a fitting description of the grief Louise began to face in the last months of 1843. Hippolyte's lung ailment was growing more acute, and he spent a great amount of time at spas in the Pyrenees. The critical establishment was continuing to give her trouble: That winter she was hatcheted by a critic in *Revue des deux mondes.* It was an exemplary bit of nineteenth-century male venom, which skewered her along with France's most prominent women poets—Marceline Desbordes-Valmore, Anaïs Ségalas, even the very protected Delphine Gay, who was the wife of the press lord Émile de Girardin.

The "little upstart," as Louise called him, took the women poets to task for being "a bizarre race of Amazons and Hermaphrodites," who had forgotten that women had only two proper roles—as mothers or as courtesans. He singled out Louise as "The Muse of abysms and tempests, of desperate doubts and flaming passions," as "a woman who went astray on the tracks of Byron."

Louise was having a difficult pregnancy. It was a very hot summer. Her relations with Cousin were deteriorating, for he sensed that the child might not be his. Up to then he had been cordial toward Hippolyte, even protective, but after a recent insult he refused to talk to him. "Hippolyte acted so rudely with Mr. Cousin," Louise wrote a relative in Provence, "that we do not see him anymore."

In July, Louise gave birth to a boy, who died within a few weeks of a lung infirmity. Her sorrow was so great that the doctor feared for her life. The loss further embittered her marriage with Hippolyte, and she was unable to work for some months. Throughout this most difficult time, Louise's sanity may have been rescued by a devoted new woman friend— the celebrated Juliette Récamier.

Jeanne-Françoise-Julie de Récamier, daughter of a prosperous Paris lawyer, was married at the age of fifteen, at the height of the Revolution's Reign of Terror, to a wealthy banker twenty-seven years her senior. Few women have acquired such fame for doing so little: Reclining on a daybed of simple geometric grace (a style to which she would lend her name), she smiled, occasionally talked, and for forty years charmed distinguished men and women into spiritual slavery with her mysterious magnetism.

In 1799, under the Directoire, twenty-one-year-old Juliette Récamier had revived an ancient French tradition by opening the first salon to be held in Paris after the Revolution. She attracted to it those politicians who had survived the Revolution and the most eminent literary figures of her time, and she infused these gatherings with the new cosmopolitanism of France's postrevolutionary years. She became a Parisian cult figure. Mobbed by hundreds of fans at every public occasion she appeared at, she seduced through the charisma of the Eternal Teaser, the Never Attainable.

Récamier was a small, delicate woman with a timid, whispering voice and an appearance that was comely rather than beautiful—pert oval face, pearly teeth, incomparably radiant skin. Her manner was at once chaste and coquettish. Each of Récamier's homes was referred to as a "Temple of Taste" because of the elegance of its furnishings. Her famous mahogany bed, canopied in violet damask and set on a two-stepped dais, surmounted by swans of shining bronze shrouded in clouds of spangled white muslin, set the fashion in decor for generations to come.

However, Juliette's way of dress imposed a deliberate austerity upon the styles of the Directoire and the early imperial years. She wore only severe white Grecian tunics—made famous by David's portrait of her—which she might enhance, at night, with a thread of blue or gold. Her hair was gathered upward in the antique style, fastened with a girlish ribbon. One pearl bracelet, or a cameo, was the only ornament she ever wore. Few dictators of style have better exemplified the motto "Less is more."

Juliette Récamier's seduction lay indeed in strategies of refusal and resistance. There is ample proof that her alliance with Récamier was a "white" marriage, never physically consummated because of her dread of sex and her husband's decision to "respect her sensibilities." Although Juliette's maidenly gracefulness exerted an irresistible attraction on men, she would remain a virgin until her forties, when she began a liaison with Chateaubriand that lasted until her death.

Madame Récamier's many suitors discovered that falling in love with the goddess of chaste seduction could be an infernal experience. Flirting with virtually every man she knew, playing with passion but terrified of surrendering to it, Juliette tormented even those men whom she truly wanted to love. The deepest bond of Récamier's life was with the writer Germaine de Staël, who was exiled by Napoleon to her family home in Coppet, Switzerland—where she remained throughout most of the emperor's reign—for "not thinking French" in writings that he considered subversive.

Récamier, too, was exiled on occasion, ostensibly for her association with the dangerous Madame de Staël. But several of her forced exiles were probably caused by her resistance to the advances of Napoleon himself. She would later resist the passion of one of the great French Romantics, the novelist Benjamin Constant, and many enamored European nobles, including Prince Bernadotte (future king of Sweden) and Prince Augustus of Saxony.

Even after her husband went bankrupt in 1810, Madame Récamier continued to charm and refuse admirers, in a series of increasingly modest homes. She spent much of her time with her young orphaned niece, whom she legally adopted when the child was nine.

In 1819, a few years after Napoleon's final defeat at Waterloo, Récamier, now widowed, settled in a little suite of rooms at L'Abbaye-aux-Bois. This ancient Paris convent for women of the aristocracy rented out a few remodeled flats to lay persons. (Part of the building survives today in a small street called Impasse Récamier, off the junction of Boulevard Raspail and Rue de Sèvres, a block from the present Hotel Lutétia.) Even in these modest circumstances, this kind, shrewd woman remained so powerful that, as Sainte-Beuve put it, "she could find a good ministerial post for every one of her pharmacist's bastards." Her last Paris salon, L'Abbaye-aux-Bois, maintained a prerevolutionary ceremoniousness and would be dominated for three decades by the extraordinary author and statesman René de Chateaubriand, French Romanticism's first prophet. Chateaubriand and Juliette Récamier had first met at the deathbed of their mutual friend Germaine de Staël. Chateaubriand was "timidly addressed" by the reclusive fortyish Récamier, and the passion kindled between the two lasted the rest of their days and offered Juliette her first and last knowledge of carnal love.

By 1843, when Louise first met Juliette Récamier, Chateaubriand was living in a small flat in Montparnasse, dividing his time between daily visits with Juliette and writing his autobiography, *Mémoires d'outre tombe*. Chateaubriand and Juliette met every afternoon at three o'clock, an hour before her official salon hours. The dulcet monotony of the sweethearts' domestic routine was famous throughout Paris: "To see them, one would think they were having tea together for the first time in their lives," one witness of this ritual wrote. " 'Would you like some tea, Monsieur de Chateaubriand?' (He had been saying yes for the past ten years.) 'After you, Madame.' 'And shall I add some milk?' 'Just a few drops.' 'May I offer you a second cup?' And so on for half an hour."

Louise Colet had already had a glimpse of Chateaubriand seven years earlier, when she solicited his support for her first book of verse, *Fleurs du Midi*. By the time Louise met the aging lovebirds together, Chateaubriand was seventy-four and Juliette was sixty-five, very deaf and nearly blind. Juliette used every possible ruse to keep her lover from discovering her afflictions. One of her favorite tactics for retaining the loyalty of her male entourage was to invite bright young female literati to her salon and praise their charms. It was for this purpose, and also to satisfy her endless curiosity, that Récamier sought out the rising new star Louise Colet. Having admired the verses Louise had sent to Chateaubriand in previous years, Récamier dispatched a message, via the philosopher Pierre Ballanche, a mutual acquaintance who had been a friend of Louise's father in Lyons days, that she very much wished to receive the Muse's visit.

Even brashly ambitious Louise had never dared to hope for such a summons into the *crème de la crème* of Parisian literary society.

And so Louise passed the metal gate of the august convent where generations of noble ladies—widowed or abandoned or dishonored—had sought solace from the world's pains. Madame Récamier's tiny flat was on the third floor, reached by a shabby staircase. Louise walked into the little drawing room, appointed with what remained of the hostess's famous furniture—bergères and chaises of rare Brazilian rosewood decorated with the winged sphinxes and palm-leaf footings of that Directoire style which was in good part Récamier's own creation.

Chateaubriand, his gray hair as tousled as it had been during his rebellious youth, was sitting in front of a white marble fireplace surmounted by a Regency clock of gilt bronze, his hands on the pommel of his cane, his chin on his hands. Opposite him, still dressed in chaste white chiffon, Madame Récamier reclined languidly on her famous sofa, talking almost inaudibly about the past to the historian Jean-Jacques Ampère, son of the famous physicist who invented the telegraph.

In the face of the plump, nearly blind Juliette, Louise saw little of that beauty which had broken a thousand hearts. But she recognized the perpetually startled gaze, the angelic sweetness of manner, and the compulsion to seduce that had been the fount of Récamier's charm. Juliette complimented Louise on her poetry as soon as she walked in, addressing her as "Dear Penserosa," the nickname heretofore known only to her most intimate friends.

Louise, many decades her hosts' junior, did not feel shy that afternoon. In spite of Récamier's and Chateaubriand's conservative views (far to the right of most of Louise's generation of writers, they believed in a constitutional monarchy), Louise proclaimed her republican sympathies and announced her support of the most daring art being shown in the capital. One must call for the return of Delacroix's *Death of Sardanapalus* to the official salons, pay tribute to his genius! Théophile Gautier's *Mademoiselle de Maupin* is a masterpiece; his handling of lesbianism shows consummate talent!

Louise was judged astonishingly cultivated and refreshingly bold. A few days after the visit, Louise sent Juliette the poems she had dedicated to Benjamin Constant; they were declared "very beautiful" at the Temple of Taste.

Thenceforth Louise became Madame Récamier's most frequent guest. Juliette, genuinely captivated by the young poet, reported to mutual friends that she had been charmed by the energy imprinted on Louise's "haughty and imperious" face and by her forthrightness, which reminded her of her beloved lost friend Germaine de Staël. After a few visits, a place was always set for Louise at Récamier's dinner table. Juliette wished the young poet to take a flat near hers so that they could be together even more often. A few years later, Louise complied by moving to the Rue de Sèvres, a stone's throw from Récamier's door.

So thoroughly did the two charmers seduce each other that Récamier eventually offered Louise the ultimate proof of her affection and esteem: She entrusted her with copies of her correspondence with Benjamin Constant, whom Louise considered a vastly underestimated genius of French Romanticism and the writer most mistreated by the "ultras" of the Bourbon Restoration. Récamier attached the following note to the bundle: "I give Madame Colet a copy of Benjamin Constant's letters, trusting her to use them in whatever manner she deems most fitting to his memory, on the condition that these letters can be published only after my death."

This legacy would have grave consequences for Louise in subsequent years.

Despite the unwavering support of her new friend, Louise had found it difficult to work during her son's brief, fatal illness. She visited the baby every day at the wet nurse's home; she became increasingly emotional about her daughter, now three years old and growing up healthy in the neighboring countryside. She would bring the beautiful Henriette home with her for days at a time, not letting her out of her sight. Meanwhile, the ailing Hippolyte required more and more care. Louise's worries were draining the little energy she had left. She cast about desperately for a new theme, a new direction for her work.

This time it was the devoted Béranger who came to the rescue. The Académie Française was holding another of its biennial poetry competitions. The theme assigned in 1843 was "The Fountain of Molière," a reference to the monument to the playwright inaugurated earlier that year on the Rue de Richelieu. (It still stands on its original site in the Palais-Royal area, a few hundred yards from the Comédie Française.) You need the money, you need to boost your morale, Béranger advised his friend; why not enter the Académie's competition again?

Béranger, always protective of Louise, wanted to make sure that her poem would be politically correct. "In your analogy between Molière and Shakespeare," he wrote her, "couldn't you mention, as I'd already suggested, his tempestuous, often impoverished life, which makes men of us before making poets."

Victor Cousin also offered Louise advice about her entry. "Don't attack the clergy directly," he counseled. "Anyone who attacks the clergy directly these days is seen as uncouth. Just attack the Jesuits; that's a popular stance, which aims at the very heart of the Church."

Louise's tribute to Molière was dedicated to Béranger. "In the last hours of a cold, paling day, / Two nuns bend over a bed," it began, "And the infinite gentleness of their care, / Consoled the agony of a dying poet." The poem ended: "He achieved greatness, souls bent before his glory! / But what numerous enmities! What hateful plots / Were sallied against this proud genius!"

In 1843, gossip concerning the Académie's poetry competition, and the intrigues and lobbying of the various contestants, was even more widespread than in previous years. Louise's name was seldom mentioned, on the assumption that she would not dare to enter so soon after her last triumph. But when the prize was announced, the winner was again Madame Louise Colet!

Louise was happy to pocket the two thousand francs, but she found the establishment no kinder than it had been after her first victory. The devious Sainte-Beuve may have felt that he had no favors to gain from Victor Cousin anymore because of the deteriorating relationship between him and the Muse; and his remarks exemplify the hostility with which France's nineteenth-century male writers viewed their women colleagues and the particular bias they had against the blunt Louise Colet.

The poetry of Madame Colet has a je ne sais quoi *that is a simulation of the good, a false effect of the beautiful. Her poetry has a rather beautiful* busk, *or bust if you wish, like the lady herself. —Do you find her beautiful? I was recently asked. —Yes, I replied,* she has the air of being beautiful.

Such an identification of a woman's body with the quality of her writing is more than boorish. It appeared in the same period as the death of Louise's infant son.

Louise was on the edge of a nervous breakdown, and her close friends were worried. "Allow me to express my doubts concerning your constant visits to the cemetery," Béranger wrote her. "I realize that they offer a painful solace, but you must renounce them as a sacrifice to your daughter. Your health is indispensable to her; so maintain it well and cease to undermine it by these exposures to rain, to the cold, and to a sorrow that is irremediable."

In these months, Louise was more hard-pressed financially than ever, for she had become a self-supporting single mother. Hippolyte, depressed by his deteriorating health, which vastly reduced his teaching salary, moved out to his own tiny flat. The Colets filed for a legal separation, which at that time took several years to obtain.

To relieve Louise's financial distress, Béranger and Cousin devised a contract whereby a publisher would offer Louise short-term payments for three years in exchange for exclusive rights to her works. But Louise discovered the ruse, was insulted, and called off the contract. Cousin asked Béranger to reconcile her to the project; but Louise insisted that she refused gifts or favors, that she wished only to "earn what she merited," that she was more determined than ever to make her living by her pen alone.

"I ran over to try and repair the damage, but there was nothing to do," Béranger complained to Cousin. "She exhausted my eloquence.... I must admit, dear philosopher, that the reasons she gave me for her refusal were so principled that I could not pursue our little lies to their limit."

It may have been the fervor of nationalist revolutions beginning to spread throughout Europe in the 1840s, or perhaps it was Louise's need to change her life in order to heal her sorrow over her dead child: She now began to engage herself even more passionately in political causes. She lent her name to and helped subsidize France's first socialist-feminist journal, *L'Union ouvrière,* published by the controversial Flora Tristan. It was during these years that distinctly feminist concerns began to inform Louise's writings. The short stories in her 1845 collection, *Saintes et folles,* "Saints and Madwomen," deal with women who are marginalized by powerlessness, exploited by a mercenary patriarchal system. In these gothic stories, fair maidens are sold by corrupt relatives to be deflowered by lecherous noblemen or cardinals and are forced to flee to convents. A woman who is coerced into a monastery after being raped by a wealthy lord is reunited in the hospital of her abbey with the penniless poet whom she had loved decades before. She dies joyfully in his arms.

In these tales, the nascent feminist Colet tries to pinpoint the principal villains responsible for the victimization of women. She searches for them in various threads of the social structure. As a good republican, she often blames the cupidity and corruption of the French nobility and clergy, but she also condemns male lust and parental indifference.

In early 1846, Louise's verse took on another kind of political commitment. Her poetry anthology of that year, *Chants des vaincus,* "Songs of the Vanquished," celebrates the nationalist uprisings that were sweeping Europe: "The old world is no more; tyranny everywhere / Is being vanquished by Liberty!" Louise was re-creating herself as a political activist. She joined the French intelligentsia's most popular cause—that of the Polish revolutionaries.

The ancient kingdom of Poland had been divided for booty by the Prussian and Russian empires in 1815 at the Congress of Vienna. From the 1830s on, nationalist groups led by the Polish Democratic Society had issued manifestos demanding their nation's independence and a return to its eighteenth-century borders. Secret revolutionary cells had been established throughout the country and their leaders had been jailed or exiled by the repressive regimes of the Russian czar and the Prussian emperor.

This had led thousands of Polish patriots to seek exile in Paris in the early decades of the nineteenth century. Thousands more arrived in the first months of 1846, when armed rebellions arose in Galicia. In February of that year, Louise attended a soiree at the Hotel Lambert on the Île Saint-Louis given by Princess Czartoriska, Paris's most prominent Polish exile, who was raising money for her insurgent compatriots. The emotional gathering, addressed by many fiery Polish nationalists, drew an audience of four thousand. Among many others in the crowd Louise recognized George Sand, Frédéric Chopin, and the former lover of Byron and of Hippolyte Colet, Teresa Guiccioli, with whom she would strike up a warm friendship.

Louise, who had attended many such gatherings for the Polish cause, did not come to hobnob with her peers. She took notes on the speeches and over the next weeks buried herself in libraries, researching Polish history. The result was a stirring poem, not without merit, which she published under the title *Le Réveil de la Pologne,* "The Awakening of Poland."

The nation whom all wish to destroy
Is rising and calling out to life.
The martyred people sleeps in its tomb,
And the czar's white eagle flies over Warsaw.

Proud Poland, immortal and vanquished,
Your noble struggle, alas, has little hope,
But you fight on,
Enslaved yet unconquerable.

It was probably at one of these many gatherings held in support of the Polish uprising that Louise met the young Polish exile Boris Christien, who was to be her lover for several months. She was extraordinarily discreet about the affair, perhaps because of the risks faced by all Polish activists in Paris: Several of them had been kidnapped or assassinated by Russian secret agents dispatched by the czar to the French capital. So we know little about Boris beyond the fact that he was Louise's age and that she found him handsome, tender, and vigorous. He was only her second lover, and he was clearly the first man with whom she enjoyed ecstatic sex.

The affair with the young Polish revolutionary ended bitterly, if we decode the following line from "The Awakening of Poland": "If [your nation] fell, if its glory is tarnished, / It is because it had more than one unworthy son."

Many women writers have turned to introverted, soul-searching new literary genres at the end of distressing love affairs. Toward the end of her liaison with the Polish exile, Louise began keeping a journal. She referred to these jottings as "Mementos." They have become a precious source of information on the literary circles of mid-nineteenth-century Paris and provide an invaluable documentation on eight years of Gustave Flaubert's career. Louise maintained this journal, on and off, through the most tumultuous period of her life, recording her sorrows, her enthusiasms, her meetings with great men, her ultimate disillusionment with that "glory" she had come to seek in Paris.

Louise's Mementos are written in a curiously haphazard form, which helps to account for the fragility and paucity of entries left us. She often scribbled them on pieces of torn paper and corners of envelopes, as if she were ambivalent about sharing her intimate thoughts with posterity. Her first journal entry, dated Saturday, June 14, 1845, is in the form of a self-portrait.

Why start this journal today rather than a decade ago when I arrived in Paris, when, filled with enthusiasm, curious to see and know everything, I still had illusions about great men, emotion, glory?

I am now thirty-four years old, neither less nor more. I have put on weight; my waist is no longer willowy but is still elegant and well defined. My throat, my shoulders, my arms, are exceptionally lovely. My neck is still admired for the manner in which it is joined to my head, but that is actually a defect because it causes my face to appear too round. I remedy this flaw with my hairstyle, which consists of very long curls falling over my temples, hiding my cheeks and tumbling to ı.`y shoulders.

Louise confesses that her hair, which is abundant and ash blond in color, is worked on almost daily by a coiffeur. She admits that her hair has been "one of the curses of my vanity," for she began to note some prematurely gray strands in it when she was in her mid-twenties. Every Saturday of the past three years, she reveals, her coiffeur had pulled out the graying culprits with no damaging effect, and she puts her time at the beauty parlor to good use by reading or writing throughout the ordeal.

She continues downward: Her eyes are "dark blue and large, beautiful when they flare up in reaction to a thought or emotion, but often tired by work and tears." There is "nothing remarkable" about her mouth. Her smile is said to be "agreeable, kind, and even naive" but then she has never observed herself smiling. She has lost only one tooth to date (an extraordinary record in that century), and she is content with her well-shaped legs and slender ankles.

"My hand is equally thin, white and fine," she concludes tersely. "That's a rather long portrait. I don't think I'm worthy of it. Someday I'll make it shorter."

Vanity here, but no exaggeration—if anything, Louise tends to understate her great beauty, which was raved about by Paris's more exacting womanizers and conceded by her bitterest enemies. Alfred de Musset referred to her as a "Venus of hot marble," and even her most enraged critic, the notoriously reactionary author Barbey d'Aurevilly, acknowledged that "In these days of revolutionary orgy—which, for her, would have been happy days—she was a truly republican beauty, hewed as if for a huge-breasted statue of the Goddess of Liberty to set on the altars of Notre Dame."

Few men in Paris more admired the statuesque splendor of the "Tenth Muse," as Louise had also come to be known, than the sculptor James Pradier, who befriended her soon after her arrival from Provence. The colorful Pradier deserves our full attention, for it was he who introduced Louise to the love of her life, an obscure young provincial named Gustave Flaubert.

James Pradier, the most popular sculptor of mid-nineteenth-century Paris, was considered by some of his contemporaries to be the Michelangelo of France. A Provençal by birth, Pradier had come to Paris at the age of twenty to study at the Beaux Arts, where he prided himself on having met Napoleon. A year before Waterloo, the emperor had asked to meet the art school's most gifted pupil. Young Pradier had been thrust forward by his teacher. The emperor took the young artist's face between his hands, orphically touched his forehead, and said, "Work with courage, my boy. You have a special gift."

The monarch's prophecy came true. Within a year, Pradier had won the Prix de Rome, and after returning to Paris he was awarded a lifelong professorship at the Beaux Arts. He made his debut at the Salon of 1819 with a controversial bronze *Bacchante,* whose unabashed sensuality broke radically with the puritanism of the then prevailing classical tradition and became a trademark of his work. In the following decade, as Romanticism became France's official aesthetic credo, Pradier, called "Phidias" by his friends, was commissioned to execute dozens of civic works throughout the country.

Of the many Pradier works still on-site in Paris, the most eminent are the two heroic statues at the southeast corner of the Place de la Concorde, majestic seated women personifying the cities of Lille and Strasbourg. They are said to be likenesses of Louise Colet. There are also the twelve life-size *Victories* at the crypt of Napoleon I's tomb in the Invalides; the Molière Fountain adjoining the Comédie Francaise, whose eulogy won Louise her second prize from the Académie; the heroic-scale sculptures of *Liberty, Public Order* and *Public Instruction* at the Chamber of Deputies; and the clock face at the Palais du Luxembourg, with which Pradier characteristically defied custom by personifying Time with a female figure.

The mystique of Woman dominated Pradier's work more powerfully than that of any other nineteenth-century sculptor before Rodin. The female protagonist of his *Satyr and Bacchante,* exhibited at the Salon of 1833, again created a scandal because of its erotic character and earned Pradier the epithet "last of the pagans." His foot-high portrait statuettes of Parisian women, which expressed the emancipated "new woman" of the 1830s, her increasingly assertive emotional and physical freedom, were equally controversial. One of the first models for these genre pieces was Louise Colet, whom Pradier nicknamed "Sappho." His portrait of Louise, which shows her seated on a rock in a contemplative pose, is still in the collection of the Louvre.

The private life of the dapper, sexually obsessed Pradier, who sported very long hair, a Mephistophelian Van Dyke beard, red velvet tunics, and yards of lace jabots, was no less flashy and controversial than his art. Seldom seen without a demimondaine beauty on his arm, he had a love of luxury, gossip, and erotic intrigue. He satisfied these tastes with the extraordinary young woman he married in 1832, Louise "Ludovica" d'Arcet, a volcanic beauty who would play an important role in Louise's affair with Flaubert.

Ludovica d'Arcet was born into a family of gentry and high academic circles. Her scientist father, a friend of Gustave Flaubert's family, was a government minister under Louis Philippe and one of the most respected chemists of his time (he was awarded his ministry post for having invented gelatinous soups). Young Ludovica was noted from adolescence for her fabulous beauty. (Louise Colet's occasional friend Maxime Du Camp described her "abundance of admirable, curly red hair, blue eyes, dazzling teeth, her laughter vibrating like a harmonica.") Ludovica married Pradier at the age of nineteen, and the couple started a social life more prodigal in its excesses than any described in Fellini's *La Dolce Vita* or Andy Warhol's *Diaries.*

Flamboyant fetes and costume balls succeeded one another at the Pradiers' home on Quai Voltaire or their weekend house in Auteuil. A single party might cost as much as ten thousand francs, the contemporary equivalent of forty thousand dollars. The Pradiers entertained a blend of the capital's demimonde and three-quarter *monde*—its leading musicians, poets, courtesans, academicians, artists, with a dash of the free-thinking aristocracy. Champagne flowed, and an average evening featured an orchestra of eight instrumentalists and an equal number of vocalists dressed in period costumes.

"Beauty is compulsory," Ludovica Pradier used to write on her invitation cards. At her costume balls Madame Pradier enjoyed appearing in the guise of Venus Genetrix, dressed in a transparent tunic embroidered with gold filigree. "Under the influence of this adorable paganism," so one guest recorded it, "Olympus was resuscitated with its entire retinue of deities." "I never felt as sad as on the morrow of these evenings," wrote the critic Arsène Houssaye, a frequent guest at the Pradiers' household, "when one had to return to reality after such flights and inebriations."

Ludovica admitted that she had never been able to resist anyone. Of her three children, only the first was fathered by her husband. She seldom carried on fewer than four affairs at one time and maintained several superbly furnished trysting flats in different parts of Paris, so as to entertain each of her lovers in style. One of her favorite pastimes was to assemble as many of her current lovers as possible at the lunch table with her husband (whose own philandering was notorious) and lead a gallantly spirited conversation. Her paramours included Louis Jadin, the leading dog painter of the mid-nineteenth century and the father of Ludovica's second child; a minister of the navy, father of her third offspring; and young Alexandre Dumas *fils,* who left us this description of his first assignation with Ludovica, in the spring of 1843:

The beautiful Mme Pradier paid her first visit to me, dressed in a flower-embroidered white silk dress with shawl to match and a straw hat. I was eighteen, I was just finishing school. It was the first time that a so-called femme du monde was crossing the threshold of my bachelor flat. She was remarkably beautiful—that mass of red-golden hair, those sapphire eyes, those pearly teeth, and the little bouquet of golden hair between the breasts. . . . She didn't lose any time, I must say, and immediately stood before me totally naked, being equally devoid of physical flaws and modesty.

We shall keep in close touch with Ludovica and James Pradier, for they will play crucial roles in the central obsession of Louise's life—her tempestuous eight-year liaison with the aspiring young writer Gustave Flaubert. It was at James Pradier's studio that Louise and Flaubert met and fell in love, and it was Ludovica Pradier who would occasion their first falling-out.

6.
Lui

❧⚜❧

HIS CHILDHOOD

When Gustave Flaubert was born, on December 2, 1821, his father had just been appointed head surgeon of Normandy's most prestigious hospital, the Hôtel-Dieu in Rouen. Dr. Achille-Cléophas Flaubert had risen from modest origins through his own talent as a man of science: his grandfather, father, and brothers had worked as veterinarians in the Norman countryside.

Dr. Flaubert was complex and work-obsessed. Although he was a hardheaded pragmatist, he often displayed a hysterical streak and was easily moved to tears. He was a Puritan but he liked to give his medical students twenty francs to go to whorehouses and sometimes flaunted his own sexuality. During a family trip to Brittany, Flaubert *père* stopped for an hour at the home of one of his former mistresses, as his wife and teenage children waited for him outside in the coach.

Gustave's mother had lost both her parents as a child. Raised by stern relatives, a shy girl with no real home of her own, she grew up anxious and aloof. She met Dr. Flaubert, nine years her senior, at the home of an aunt when she was sixteen. He requested that she be sent to boarding school until the eve of their marriage. In the words of Jean-Paul Sartre, whose quixotic biography of Gustave Flaubert, *The Family Idiot,* I shall frequently cite to decode the neuroses of the Flaubert clan: "She waited in her monastic cell for the hour when she could sleep with her father."

The first of the Flauberts' children, Gustave's older brother Achille, was a strong, healthy boy; their next three offspring, also sons, died in infancy. The bereaved mother ardently wished for a girl. But the next child was Gustave, and only three years later, his sister Caroline was born. One might be drawn to Sartre's view that Gustave felt like a usurper, replacing a much-desired daughter.

When Dr. Flaubert was appointed head surgeon of Rouen's Hôtel-Dieu, the family moved to a flat on the hospital's second floor. It would be Gustave's home for his first twenty-one years. Its windows opened onto the courtyard, where bandaged patients wearing long white robes were often seen. Directly across the courtyard was the dissecting room, from which dogs were often ran out, pieces of human flesh dangling from their jaws.

Playing in the family's tiny private garden, Gustave and Caroline would climb a wall that overlooked the dissecting room and watch their father giving anatomy courses to students who set their lit cigars on the corpses' limbs. The doctor would occasionally look up from his work and shoo his offspring away. "The same flies that alighted upon us alighted there, retuned buzzing to us," Flaubert wrote in a letter to Louise Colet. "I still see my father raising his head over his dissection and ordering us to go away. He was yet another cadaver."

One can assume that these macabre surroundings made Madame Flaubert all the more nervous and remote. Flaubert's friends describe her as a tall, dour woman with sunken cheeks and a glacial manner. Gustave's youth was burdened by his mother's neurotic ailments, which are amply documented in the many letters his beloved sister wrote him when he was studying law in Paris. Caroline was usually assigned to relay messages to Gustave on her mother's behalf, because even writing a note could aggravate Maman's recurring headaches. "Mother is in too much pain to write you herself tonight" is the standard opening of Caroline's letters, or "We've just finished dinner, dear friend, and I am writing in mother's stead because she neither can nor wishes to write you while she is digesting."

Madame Flaubert constantly extended her hypochondria to Gustave. At twenty-five, Gustave, who was a powerful swimmer and enjoyed sailing, gave up these pastimes because they made his mother nervous. He missed his sports dreadfully, he wrote to a friend years later, but he had to make sacrifices "to avoid certain allusions and glances" from his overbearing mother, who was exceptionally gifted in the art of maternal blackmail.

These domestic oppressions were not mitigated by Gustave's father, who was quite aloof from his two younger children. He preferred the company of Gustave's brother Achille, who had followed him in the medical profession and would eventually step into his shoes as chief surgeon of the Rouen hospital.

At the age of eleven, Flaubert found respite from these somber home surroundings when he was enrolled at Rouen's most prestigious boys' school, the Collège Royal, still thriving today under the name Lycée Corneille. Here, for the next several years, Flaubert excelled in literature and history. Here he was converted, like many of his schoolmates, to the Romantic movement that was sweeping France: He exchanged forbidden copies of Victor Hugo with his chums, kept copies of Chateaubriand under his bedspread, and carried a dagger under his shirt in case he suddenly decided to follow Chatterton's visionary way into early death. Here, too, he first sensed a literary vocation and produced his earliest writings. By the time he was twenty-two, when, pressured by his father, he was studying law in Paris, he had already finished three book-length works, *Smarrh, Novembre,* and *Mémoires d'un fou.* These uneven but gifted novels, which only Louise Colet and two or three other friends would read during his lifetime, were all published posthumously.

Having bowed to his father's will to go to Paris and to study law, Flaubert found life in the capital detestable. The lectures at the law school were boring. He hated his ugly furnished room and the cheap students' restaurants, and found the bohemianism of the Latin Quarter tawdry. Beyond the company of a few friends, his only solace was his visits to the exhilaratingly nonconformist Pradier family, friends of his parents, at whose lavish parties he was thrilled to make the acquaintance of Victor Hugo.

Having completed his novel *Novembre* with unexpected ease, Flaubert began a longer and more complex narrative, entitled *L'Éducation sentimentale* (it was the first draft of the masterpiece he published a quarter of a century later). But it was slow going, constantly interrupted by his studies, and he grew anxious at the sight of the unfinished manuscript that lay on his desk.

Flaubert looked on his two years of studying law in Paris as a form of "moral castration" committed by his father, aimed at aborting his promising literary career. The first of his many "nervous seizures," which would recur throughout his life and were most probably caused by a form of epilepsy, was doubtless triggered by his abhorrence of the vocation his father tried to impose on him.

Flaubert suffered his first seizure when he was twenty-two, during a Christmas vacation from law school. While driving back from Deauville to Rouen in a horse-drawn coach with his brother Achille, he found himself, as he would later describe it, "being suddenly carried off by a torrent of flames," his vision clouded "by shapes resembling strands of hair or firework explosions."

This first attack, after which his father and brother nursed him devotedly, had a momentous impact on his life: The black-sheep rebel whose artistic inclinations so terrified his philistine family was allowed to give up the law and dedicate himself to literature. "I have been feeling very well," he wrote at the age of twenty-three to a close friend, "ever since I decided to be *un*well."

To say that Flaubert's parents were intrusive would be an understatement. A year after Gustave's first illness, when his sister married the ordinary and weak-willed Émile Hamard, the entire family accompanied them on their nightmarish honeymoon to Italy. Father Flaubert's eyes ached so that he kept to his hotel room in every city in which they stopped; Caroline had kidney stones; Maman "nearly died of worry" over her daughter's health; and Gustave, exasperated by his insipid brother-in-law and furious at "seeing the Mediterranean through the eyes of a grocer," suffered two more seizures.

That same year, the Flauberts moved from their apartment in the hospital to a riverside home four miles from the center of Rouen. Flaubert was to spend the rest of his life in that house. It was a graceful two-story structure on the banks of the Seine, in a rural settlement called Croisset. Dr. Flaubert did not enjoy his new home for long. Two years after he had moved his family to Croisset, he died during an operation (on an abscess of the hip) performed by his own son. Five weeks later, Gustave's sister Caroline also died, shortly after giving birth to a daughter, named after her, who would be brought up by her grandmother and her uncle Gustave.

After these tragedies, life at Croisset became more stifling than ever. Madame Flaubert's anxiety about her younger son increased. Gustave had to tiptoe about the house at night to get his firewood, candles, or tobacco, ever fearful of alarming his mother, who "spent her days imagining the illnesses and accidents that could befall me." Gustave's epileptic attacks, however, occurred much less frequently after his father's death. "I am perhaps healed," he wrote a friend. "It's as if a process of burning removed the wound."

In this hothouse of neuroses, Flaubert gradually fell into a rigid daily ritual centered about his literary needs, which would remain unchanged for most of his life. A late-night worker, he woke at about ten A.M. and rang for his servant, who would run upstairs with the mail, newspapers, a glass of water, and a filled pipe. As he read his mail, Gustave knocked loudly on the wall to beckon Maman, who came and sat with him until he got up to dress. At eleven, Gustave's little harem joined him for brunch— Maman, his young niece Caroline, and her nurse. The trio then followed him as he strolled down the lovely little alley of linden trees, still standing today, that flanks the Croisset residence.

At one o'clock, when the steamboat that shuttled between Rouen and Croisset gave its midday whistle, the family walked back to the house. Flaubert might then give a few lessons to Caroline or else settle right down to work in his study, which was the house's grandest room, a corner chamber with five large windows. There was dinner at seven P.M., a chat with Maman until nine P.M. Then he went back to work until the early-morning hours, only interrupting his writing to kiss his mother good night when she was installed in her bed.

In his upstairs room overlooking the Seine, amid hushed, tiptoeing domestic servants who were forbidden to perform any noisy tasks or talk above a whisper, this master of lapidary prose worked into the dawn hours, going through many dozens of drafts, chiseling his clauses so meticulously that he seldom finished more than a paragraph or two a day. "Only one page this week!" he would complain to Louise Colet. "Only 111 pages in ten months!"

Notwithstanding the bizarre *folie à deux* of Flaubert's family life—two damaged recluses, mother and son, both under the illusion that they remained together to save each other—the writer would continue this routine until his mother's death, which preceded his own by eight years. Diseases bodily and psychic, genuine or hysterical, plagued the Oedipal couple from the very beginning, and the mother's lifelong mourning affected every aspect of her son's life.

Yet the "hermit of Croisset," as Flaubert came to be called, was anything but a gloomy monk. He was a strapping, six-foot-tall bon vivant with a thundering voice, Rabelaisian humor, and a booming laugh. His fair-haired good looks led some of his friends to compare him to "a young Viking god." Take the description of twenty-four-year-old Gustave by one of his closest friends, Maxime Du Camp: "He was of heroic beauty . . . white skin, rose-tinged cheeks, long, fine, flowing hair, tall and wide-shouldered body, abundant blond beard, enormous sea-green eyes shielded by dark brows, his voice as resounding as a trumpet."

Flaubert was also said to be a gifted lover. "Life! Life! To have erections!" he wrote in one of his more than one hundred twenty letters to Louise Colet. The object of Gustave's first infatuation, which occurred when he was fifteen and decades later would inspire the writing of *Sentimental Education,* was a married woman in her twenties. He had first glimpsed her on a beach in Normandy as she sat on a dune, breast bared, nursing her baby. This was Elisa Schlesinger, who was born in the same week and year as Louise Colet. Gustave became acquainted with Madame Schlesinger's husband and suffered agonies of love and jealousy. Upon returning to Rouen that fall, he had his sexual initiation with his mother's chambermaid. The experience filled him with disgust.

In his late teens Flaubert began to frequent whorehouses, a pastime he indulged in throughout much of his life. At nineteen, he had a serious sexual encounter with a handsome, aggressive divorcée in Marseilles. Élalie Foucauld, a hotelkeeper in her mid-thirties, seems to have overwhelmed the handsome adolescent. The writers Jules and Edmond de Goncourt, to whom Flaubert talked at length about his sex life decades later, wrote in their memoirs: "This woman came in the evening to [Flaubert's] hotel room and immediately proceeded to suck his cock. . . . This was followed by an orgy of fucking, and then an exchange of letters."

Madame Foucauld, Louise Colet, Gustave's childhood friend and occasional lover Ludovica Pradier—Gustave seems to have always turned to energetic, amazonic older women for the little sex he enjoyed outside of whorehouses.

BUDDIES AND BORDELLOS

Gustave's father had thought his son was quite devoid of talent. His mother agreed, even after the publication of *Madame Bovary* and his other celebrated novels. From childhood on he found his chief solace and emotional support in the company of male peers. Few artists' lives have been structured so intensely around friendship. Flaubert's dedication to his friends, a lifelong need for male bondings, was already in evidence in the letters he wrote as a child. At eight, he wrote to his favorite classmate, Ernest Chevalier: "I am devoured by impatience to see the best of my friends, him with whom I shall always remain friends we shall love each other, o friend who will always be in my heart. Yes your friend since birth unto death."

Again, to Chevalier, that same year (I am following young Gustave's original punctuation): "If you were not to visit me I would go on all fours like King Louis Philippe's dogs . . . to carry you back and I think you would do the same for me. For a fraternal love unites us. Yes, I who have feeling would walk a thousand leagues if need be to rejoin the best of my friends, for nothing is as sweet as friendship oh sweet friendship . . . without this bonding how would we live One sees this sentiment down to the smallest animals without friendship how would the weak live how would women and children survive."

By the time he was ten, Flaubert was already linking his friendships with men to literary inspiration and to a rebellion against bourgeois platitudes. He wrote to the same classmate, Chevalier: "I shall send you my comic plays. If you wish we can create a literary team, I shall write comedy and you will write your dreams, and since there's a lady who often comes to see papa and always speaks inanities I shall write them down." Gustave aged thirteen, to the same pal, assuming the fashionable *mal du siècle* pose of young Frenchmen being converted to Romanticism: "Without you . . . I would be totally disgusted, and a bullet would have long ago delivered me from this buffooning joke we call life."

For decades to come, both in his life and in his fiction, Flaubert would continue to see friendship with his male comrades as the cornerstone of a good life, a way of perfection that ideally involves living and studying together. The male protagonists of his first novel, *Novembre,* and, later, of *Sentimental Education,* swear to live under the same roof, perpetuating until death the rites of joint literary projects and of long evening conversations over pipes and wine. The protagonists of his last novel, *Bouvard et Pécuchet,* are bachelor roommates who even share a double desk. One of the novel's crucial lines reads: " 'No more women, right? Let's live without them!' They tenderly embraced each other."

The most passionate infatuation of Flaubert's youth was for his fellow Rouennais Alfred de Poittevin. Poittevin and Flaubert had been a few classes apart at school in Rouen and had close family ties. The boys' mothers had been schoolmates; their fathers were best friends and godfathers of each other's sons.

Alfred de Poittevin, five years Flaubert's senior, was the scion of a family wealthier and even more conventional than the Flauberts. Poittevin *père* was one of Normandy's leading textile manufacturers. Young Poittevin offers an exemplary case study of the alienated French bourgeois youth of the 1840s. Playing to the hilt the decadent *mal du siècle* pose—long disheveled hair, languidly stooping shoulders, cynical aphorisms about the loathsomeness of life—Poittevin described himself as "a Greek of the late empire." His cosmopolitanism, his frailty, his pale, doomed, melancholic air, intoxicated the large-boned, rustic Gustave.

Poittevin and Flaubert became inseparable during their time together in Paris, where they were both forced into law school by their fathers. Their hatred of the law was equally fierce. Both wanted to be writers. And both experienced the deep sense of political disenchantment that afflicted much of France's intelligentsia in midcentury. By the 1840s, as Flaubert and Poittevin saw it, the liberal promises of the Three Glorious Days that had brought Louis Philippe had all but disappeared: The Bourgeois King's reign had only effected the triumph of a materialistic bourgeoisie. Seeing the hopelessness of the world, Poittevin determined that the only sublime way of life was to "put oneself at the service of the useless." From his adolescence, Poittevin seems to have chosen a sublimely "useless" life and an early death, induced by numerous forms of excess: alcohol, prostitutes, and above all boredom, which he believed was the inevitable consequence of a bourgeois upbringing and could be conquered only by debauch. "Man feels his weakening body resurrected / In the fires of brutal orgy," he wrote in one of his poems.

Not wanting to be outdone by his contemporaries' chic decadence, Flaubert, for many years, elaborated on his own *mal du siècle* pose by expressing admiration for the most debauched epochs of history: "I was born to be emperor of Cochin China," he wrote in his early twenties, "to own . . . 6,000 women and 1,400 eunuchs, to build cemeteries for those people I shoot for not liking their face, and all I have is immense and insatiable desires, atrocious boredom, and continual yawns. . . ."

In the same vein: "It was imperial Rome I loved, that beautiful queen rolling itself in orgy, fouling its vestments in the wine of debauch." "I have a profound veneration for the tyrannical regimes of ancient times, which I look on as the most beautiful achievement of mankind."

An equally important friend of Flaubert's early and middle years was the dandyish Maxime Du Camp. Like Poittevin, Du Camp, a rising star of the young Paris intelligentsia, befriended Flaubert during their school years in Paris. Du Camp, too, was the son of a fashionable surgeon and an impassioned early convert to Romanticism. At thirteen, attending the first night of Alfred de Vigny's epochal play *Chatterton* with his widowed mother, Du Camp had fainted from the ecstasy that Vigny's words provoked within him, and upon recovering burst into uncontrollable sobs. His mother had to hold his hand all the rest of the night to help him survive his emotions.

Du Camp's family fortune allowed him to devote a major part of his youth to writing erudite essays; to studying Oriental themes and traveling to the Near East; to sitting about in Paris cafés in the company of other well-heeled young Romantics, castigating the bourgeoisie into which they had been born and languishing for the Middle Ages, the lost glory of chivalry, and the Crusades.

After Gustave had begun his convalescent seclusion in Croisset, it was to Du Camp that he read his novel *Novembre,* written when he was nineteen. "A great writer has been born to us," Maxime solemnly said, "and I am among the first to receive the news." Du Camp would become very possessive about Flaubert's work. Notwithstanding their extreme unreliability, Du Camp's gossipy *Souvenirs littéraires,* published a half century later, became a rich (though often deceptive) source of Flaubert lore for generations of literary scholars.

The intensity of Flaubert's friendships with men had homoerotic overtones. "Let me reassure you concerning the fate of that phallus of mine which you love well and has equal emotions toward you," Maxime Du Camp wrote Gustave in 1844, shortly after they had both expressed their fears of having caught the clap in a Paris bordello. Homosexual allusions were even more blatant in Poittevin's letters to Flaubert. "I kiss your Priapus," Poittevin wrote frequently to Flaubert. "Adieu, dear Pederast," "Adieu, old buddy, I kiss you and socratize you," were standard greetings in Poittevin's missives to his friend in Croisset. Were such phrases written in earnest, or were they composed in jest, as part of that decadent rhetorical pose so frequently assumed by literati of Flaubert's generation *pour épater les copains,* to impress the pals? Flaubert scholars remain divided on this issue.

Another striking trait of Flaubert's circle of friends is their obsessive need to brag about their sexual feats. The prevalent expression for coming to orgasm among Flaubert's buddies was *"tirer un coup,"* "fire a shot" (or "shoot your wad," as American parlance has it). "You know that Arles's women have a good reputation," Maxime wrote Gustave from Provence in 1846, "so your Max fired a shot four times like a man."

Poittevin shared Du Camp's and Flaubert's fascination for brothels—it was Poittevin who had introduced Flaubert, at nineteen, to the bordello culture. And he swapped stories with his friends about their adventures with prostitutes in painstaking detail. Responding to Flaubert's description of a whore, Poittevin wrote him: "What a vision to see Léonie kneeling between your legs, intoxicated by the scent of your cheesy cock! . . . As for Anna, I twice-fucked her *without catching the clap* . . . but your Léonie's ass is better turned, and if I hadn't just come home [to Rouen] I'd return tonight to Paris to check on your eulogies."

Two weeks later, concerning two other whores of their acquaintance: "La Boisgontier made me return. . . . I passed great hours there and fired four shots in her. Do go and present yourself to this woman." "Have you seen Elodie again . . . and sniffed at the fog of her clitoris? . . . You too, as if to tempt fate, parade your happy phallus among the cunts of Parisian whores, as if you wanted to catch the clap. But the filthiest cunts seem to return your cock intact." (Alas, Poittevin was being optimistic. Flaubert would be syphilitic at twenty-nine. By the time he was fifty, mercury treatments had so polluted his body that his saliva was black and he had one tooth left in his mouth.)

Throughout these exchanges, female sexuality seems mainly to serve as a disposable conduit for bonds between men, and prostitutes are ritual fetishes that serve to deepen male solidarity. Might the psychological gang banging indulged in by Flaubert's circle—either through consecutive possession of the same female or through scatological exchanges of information—be a way of sublimating homosexual desire? Whatever implications one assigns to their conduct, the libidinous lifestyle of Flaubert and his friends would greatly affect the course of their love affairs with "respectable" women.

"I have never loved anyone, man or woman, as much as him," Flaubert wrote about Alfred de Poittevin in his later years. When Poittevin married, Flaubert felt betrayed. It occurred in the summer of 1846, just a few weeks before Flaubert's first encounter with Louise Colet. As if in cynical capitulation to his parents' wishes, Poittevin was marrying a girl of the highest Normandy gentry, Louise de Maupassant, whose brother was the future father of the writer Guy. This was at the height of Gustave's friendship with Poittevin, two years after he had begun his monastic literary routine at Croisset, a few months after his sister's and father's deaths.

In Flaubert's view, to marry was to renounce the life of imagination and study, to risk being "infected" by bourgeois values. At the age of eighteen, he had scoffed at his older brother's marriage: "Achille . . . will become a settled man, like those polyps fixed on rocks. Every day he will be enlightened by his beloved's cunt, and happiness will shine as brightly on him as sun on a pile of shit." At thirty, when his mother asked him when he planned to marry, Flaubert replied: "Marriage *would be an apostasy which terrifies me.*"

When it involved his closest friend, marriage was far worse than apostasy. It was an act of treachery that threatened the core of his emotional life. Gustave felt "the profound pain of jealousy," he confessed upon hearing of Poittevin's betrothal. In fact, he regarded Poittevin's marriage as his friend's first death, and he experienced this loss far more painfully than the second, physical death that came to the dissipated Alfred two years later. "For me, Alfred died twice," Gustave often wrote.

Revolted and infuriated by the news of Poittevin's forthcoming marriage, Flaubert deepened his friendship with Maxime Du Camp. And he began to spend more time with another friend, Louis Bouilhet. Like Du Camp, Bouilhet would play an important role in the unraveling of Flaubert's liaison with Louise Colet and would become a central catalyst in Flaubert's literary career. Bouilhet, also an aspiring writer, was a shy young man who had been a scholarship student at Gustave's school in Rouen. After a few years at university, he supported himself by tutoring lycée students in Greek and Latin. By the summer of 1846, Flaubert and Bouilhet, who bore a striking resemblance to each other, were often spending weekends together in Croisset, translating Aristophanes and Plautus or collaborating on salacious burlesque plays that satirized the bourgeoisie. (Eventually Bouilhet, a mediocre writer but an editor of genius, would become, along with Louise Colet, Flaubert's closest literary confidant in the composition of *Madame Bovary*.)

The forging of this intimate cluster of new friends was Flaubert's initial response to Poittevin's disloyalty. But in the crucial month of July 1846 he took a far more subtle revenge—he followed some advice of Poittevin's and found himself a mistress in Paris.

Reenter the ever present Pradier ménage—the famous sculptor and his extravagant wife, Ludovica, highborn beauty turned courtesan. ("Never have I seen a more shameless degree of libertinism," Maxime Du Camp wrote in his memoirs about Ludovica. "She wallowed and floundered in vice as if it were her natural element.")

Although they moved in extremely different milieus, both James Pradier and Jean-Pierre d'Arcet, Ludovica's father, were good friends of the well-connected Flaubert family. (Pradier was commissioned to do a statue of the doctor, after his death, for the municipality of Rouen.) "I advise you to cultivate this house," Alfred de Poittevin had written Flaubert in reference to the Pradiers while Gustave was still studying law in Paris. "There is much for you to gain there, perhaps a mistress, etc."

Although Flaubert was not yet ready at twenty-two to take a mistress, he had visited the Pradiers frequently. Their total lack of bourgeois scruples captivated him. But by May of 1845, Ludovica's debauchery and extravagance had led her husband to start divorce proceedings. A few months after the couple's separation, Flaubert called on Pradier while staying in Paris with his parents and enjoyed his first man-to-man talks with the sculptor. His admiration for Pradier was immense. "Phidias . . . is an excellent person and a great artist," he wrote in a letter. "Yes, a great artist, a true Greek, and the most ancient of all our moderns."

During his visits with Pradier in 1845, Flaubert seems to have discussed the recurrence of his epileptic fits; and he told him that since his first seizure, he had monastically refrained from sex. ("It's been nearly two years since I've engaged in coitus," Flaubert had written Poittevin that year. "I must have fallen pretty low, since even the bordello does not entice me.") During this stay in Paris, Flaubert jotted a cryptic phrase into the diary he had begun to keep the previous year: "Pradier's medical advice." Pradier, hearing that his young friend still lived in his stifling parental home, had evidently traced the cause of Flaubert's illness to solitude and celibacy. Like Poittevin two years earlier, he counseled Flaubert, in characteristically raunchy language, to get out from under his mother's skirts, take a mistress, and enjoy a normal sex life.

The meaning of the cryptic jotting "Pradier's medical advice" is made evident in a letter Flaubert wrote to Poittevin a few days after that visit to the sculptor. The note also reveals Flaubert's terror of any permanent heterosexual liaison:

I have reflected on Pradier's advice; it is sound. But how shall I follow it? And then where would I be able to stop? . . . It is what I should do, and it is what I shall not do. A normal, solid, punctual schedule of fucking would take me too much out of myself, would disturb me. It would lead me into a life of action, into physical reality, in sum into platitudes, and all of that has been repugnant to me each time I've tried it.

However, by the summer of the following year—the pivotal year 1846—Flaubert had been struck by the tragedies of his youth: the deaths five weeks apart, of his father and of his adored twenty-two-year-old sister and the treasonous "death marriage," four months later, of his beloved Alfred de Poittevin. Despite all his earlier protests, the time was ripe for his meeting Louise Colet.

It is worth nothing that Flaubert met and fell in love with Louise a mere three weeks after Poittevin's perfidious marriage; that he met her, moreover, in James Pradier's salon—in precisely the place where Poittevin had counseled him to find a mistress.

So it came to pass that Louise, sitting on a high stool in Pradier's studio as she posed for yet another portrait, surrounded by antique casts, mounds of damp clay, groups of rowdy literati exchanging gossip over their pipes and champagne glasses, met the love of her life, an obscure young provincial who aspired to be a writer.

P.S. MALE BONDING AND THE CARNAL ACT

*The primacy of Flaubert's friendships with men and his fascination
for prostitutes were in part caused by the constrained sexual mores
affecting all young bourgeois in the nineteenth century. The severity of
that era's sexual taboos created immense chasms between the realm of
"pure and untouchable" women—sister, mother, bride—and the less
honored "available" females. Young men had only two ways to channel their sexual energies: brothels or liaisons with considerably older
married women. And friendships with male peers were the only outlets
through which men could analyze and confess—if not absolve—their
sexual experiences, inside and outside the bordello.*

*Brothels had proliferated greatly under the reign of Louis Philippe.
Their growth can be attributed to the expansive economic climate of
the decade that followed the July Revolution of 1830; the suspension of
many forms of censorship imposed under the previous Bourbon rulers; and the social upheavals caused by the industrial revolution: vast
numbers of rural women migrated to cities to earn pitiful wages in
factories and were easily drawn into the sexual market by a network of
ruthless recruiters.*

*The structure of mid-nineteenth-century brothels had many similar-
ities to that of convents or prisons. Unlike their wealthier colleagues of
past centuries, whores in the 1840s lived in a state of pathetic indebt-
edness, owning nothing in the world, not even their clothing. Successful
escapes were very rare, for the patronnes of brothels averted defections
by bribing the police handsomely to hunt down any deserter.*

*Bordello fanciers who did not have a communal information net-
work such as Flaubert's and Poittevin's could consult guidebooks that
ranked these establishments with precise descriptions of services, the
way Michelins rank contemporary restaurants. Clients could choose
from a wide spectrum of sexual pleasures. According to police records
and the very rare prostitutes' diaries that have survived, fellatio was
requested by eight clients out of ten, and the custom of anal coitus was
extremely frequent; no prostitute stopped working during her men-
strual period, and pregnant women were greatly prized.*

*There was also a considerable demand for child prostitutes in the
nineteenth century. They were sold to bordellos by their parents and
lodged in thick-walled, heavily upholstered rooms to make sure their
shouts of pain were not heard. (Child prostitution was not abolished in*

France until 1908.) Successful bordellos prided themselves on satisfying the most finicky customers—some gentlemen desired uncombed, unwashed twelve-year-old factory workers in their filthy work clothes; other deviants found joy in pain through the use of whips or sliver-thin silver needles inserted by their partners under their foreskins. Tableaux vivants, particularly those depicting lesbian sex or the rape of nuns, were extremely popular.

The fascination for prostitutes manifested by Flaubert and his friends was characteristic of their generation of intelligentsia. "I love prostitution for itself, independently of what it offers," Flaubert wrote Louise a few years into their affair. "In the very notion of prostitution there is such a complex convergence of lust and bitterness, such a frenzy of muscle and sound of gold . . . that the very sight of it makes one dizzy! And how much is learned there! And one dreams so well of love! . . . Yes, he who has never woken up in a nameless bed, who has never seen sleeping on his pillow a face he will never see again, is missing a great deal."

Patronage of the bordello culture was a rebellion against middle-class propriety and was well suited to the mal du siècle disaffection cultivated in Flaubert's circle. Their attitude toward the debased mid-nineteenth-century prostitute was highly convoluted, involving a dual relationship of identification and revulsion. Experiencing their alienation from society far more poignantly than their generational peers in other cultures, the intelligentsia of the French Romantic movement could even find in the prostitute a spiritual mirror image of their own marginal state, an emblem of their defiance of both classical and bourgeois norms. After 1830 the prostitute began to appear in innumerable fictions—in that decade alone, one can cite Victor Hugo's Marion Delorme, Eugène Sue's Mysteries of Paris, Balzac's Girl with the Golden Eyes, Théophile Gautier's Mademoiselle de Maupin, and Flaubert's own youthful novel Novembre.

This attraction to whores was also a way of acting out the misogyny that had swept through France in the decades after the Revolution. At a time when women of the intelligentsia were becoming increasingly independent, associating with purchased women might well have been a way for men to regain an illusion of control over the female sex. A need to humiliate women impelled many habitués of bordellos: Flaubert often boasted that upon entering such an establishment he chose the ugliest whore he could find and took her in front of his pals, puffing on a cigar, his hat still on his head.

*   *   *

The sexual braggadocio indulged in by Flaubert's set was another ear-
mark of their generation. The literati who came of age in the 1820s and
1830s tended to assert their cultural and sexual identities by chronicling their genital adventures in journals and letters. Victor Hugo (who
boasted in his diary of having eleven orgasms on his wedding night),
Alfred de Vigny, Stendhal, and numerous other writers were prolific at
this coital arithmetic, whining about their "fiascos" in their diaries and
correspondence, or documenting the three, five, or seven times they
"fired a shot" with a mistress or whore.

In such bachelor circles as Flaubert's, every detail of sexual prow-
ess, not only with prostitutes but also with the most distinguished
women of Paris society, was discussed with a candor that would appall
our most libertine contemporaries. A characteristic example of this
brazenness can be found in Maxime Du Camp's letters to Flaubert
describing his trysts with Valentine Delessert, his mistress during some
of the years in which Flaubert and Louise Colet were lovers.

Madame Delessert, thirteen years Du Camp's senior, was an eminent Paris socialite, the wife of a wealthy banker who served for some
years as the capital's prefect of police. Du Camp portrayed their first
visit this way:

> I asked her to give herself to me forthrightly, without an after-
> thought. She took my arm and we went up to her room. There, still
> standing, we enjoyed a few second of mutual bilingualism. She has
> lips of singular flexibility, which promise great blow jobs. She sat
> down, I knelt before her, exhibiting Thomas, she took it and in-
> serted it. She had terrific orgasms, she was very moved. . . . I came,
> she received my ejaculation into her handkerchief, which she after-
> wards kissed. . . .

This particular visit was ended (safely) by sounds of the husband's
imminent arrival. A subsequent visit to Du Camp's mistress, again
chronicled for Flaubert's delectation:

> My cock is faring fine and is fucking the woman of advanced age
> with much pleasure. She's going out of her mind with pleasure. . . .
> She opens her thighs, she French-kisses me, she screams! She emits
> her moistures, she has her orgasms! She swoons, she brings me to
> orgasm . . . she puts her handkerchief soaking with my sperm on her

chest . . . she squirms with agility, inserts with skill, emits charming little swinish snorting sounds, and spits in my mouth to prove her affection. . . .

One more report to Gustave on Du Camp's affair with his distinguished mistress:

Valentine has so exhausted me that I can barely write. It is all superb. . . . If I sense it right, some delectably farcical complications may be in the offing: her daughter is currently staying with her— wouldn't it be dandy to fuck the father after having gone through the wife and the daughter?

I dare my readers to cite a writer who has portrayed, with equal crudeness, his relations with a "respectable" woman who was his mistress for seven years.

This was the world that confronted Louise Colet as she began her affair with Gustave Flaubert.

7.
Love Letters

❧❧

It was a sad moment in James Pradier's own life when Flaubert came to call on him to commission a sculpture of his dead sister, Caroline. In July of 1846, Pradier was mourning the death a month earlier of his oldest child, the twenty-one-year-old daughter of his former mistress Juliette Drouet. At the same time, Pradier, a man as loyal as he was sybaritic, was single-handedly educating the three children of his ex-wife, Ludovica, only one of whom was his.

Nonetheless, "Phidias" looked two decades younger than his sixty years, ever the gregarious, generous, eccentric High Bohemian attired in extravagant lace jabots and gold-embroidered leotards. He continued to receive guests nearly every day—even during his working hours—at his studio on the Quai Voltaire, still a popular meeting place for Paris's artists and writers.

Imagine the setting of Louise's and Flaubert's first meeting at Pradier's, on July 28, 1846: It is a Tuesday afternoon. Groups of men drinking, talking, gambling at little tables set up in the large, statue-filled studio. Among the blocks of marble, the Greek and Roman casts, in corners of the clay-dusty, sunlit space, clusters of pretty young women gossip over tea. As Flaubert enters the studio, he sees a strikingly beautiful woman sitting on a high stool at the center of the room, dressed in her trademark azure-blue dress, posing for her host.

This detailed account of their first moments is comically rapturous:

> *The Muse was posing. Her Olympian hair was resplendent in the summer light; in the middle of the dusty statues and rough models wrapped in their humid cloths, her golden hair resembled a ray of Provençal sun; its curls rolled about her shoulders and upon the least movement caressed her perfect throat and her white arms. She had a charming nose, whose nostrils fluttered when her blue gaze, deep as the sea off Italy, rested on the handsome young Norman. Her mouth was round and vermilion. Her body was majestic.*
>
> *"What a beautiful creature!" Flaubert said to himself, dazzled. Coquettish, she smiled. . . .*
>
> *The Viking shuddered, burned to his inner depths by the desire to possess this woman of living marble, to know the embrace of such perfect arms. His emotion was evident, and Pradier, a prince of a man, whispered to his young friend:*
>
> *"Go on, my boy! She's a famous woman, and since you want to be a writer, she will help you."*

She, the thirty-six-year-old poetess, already twice honored by the prestigious Académie Française, admired by a vast circle of luminaries for her wit and talent, hostess of one of Paris's most popular literary salons. And he, a prodigiously cultivated twenty-four-year-old Adonis who has not yet published a word.

The encounters that followed their first meeting at Pradier's studio have to be reconstructed from Flaubert's correspondence. No journal entries in Louise's Mementos have survived for that year, and we know what might have happened to the letters she wrote Gustave.

The very following evening, Wednesday, Flaubert arrives at Louise's flat unannounced. She opens the door herself. Her daughter, Henriette, is out with the maid.

If Louise is surprised, she does not let on. A well-mannered boy (let's remember that according to the French legal system of the time, he will remain a minor until he reaches the age of twenty-six), Flaubert pretends to be very interested in his hostess's modest flat, its thrift-shop furnishings. The living room, fragrant with her favorite scent of musk, is draped with a blue silk that matches her dress. The alabaster lamp hanging by a chain from the ceiling gives a soft, intimate glow. The visitor probably tells Louise that he lived in a fairly similar apartment in his law school days, that upon entering her flat he is returning to a painful past. . . .

The light is fading; Louise lights her lamp. They talk. "Tell me all about yourself."

Her obsession has begun. She is re-creating herself into yet another role, that of the Romantic mistress ready to throw all caution to the wind, commit herself to every folly to satisfy her infatuation. . . . She has thought about Flaubert ceaselessly since their meeting at Pradier's studio. He is even more seductive than she remembers him: that monumental body, the guarded yet gentle sea-green eyes.

The visitor doesn't seem to like talking about his private life. He launches into his literary aspirations, his favorite books. He stares at her searchingly, yet evades her glance. He finished his first novel, *Smarrh,* at the age of thirteen, he tells her. When he was sixteen, a chapter of his second novel was published in Rouen's daily paper, he adds. But this led to terrible humiliation, and he decided that he was ready to work for decades—for all his life if need be—in obscurity, without publishing a word, with no thought of fame or renown. . . .

That is remarkable, Louise tells him. Do you not occasionally need money?

Gustave's eyes avoid hers. He is living at home, he says, he *must* live at home for a while because . . . three months ago a terrible double tragedy occurred. In fact, he has come to Paris this week to commission a portrait of his dead sister. There is his mother and his infant niece to take care of, he is the head of the family, they have no one else.

They sip on orange-flower water, which Louise has brought from the sideboard and poured into delicate unmatched glasses. The young bourgeois in his overly formal black suit is examining the room. It is not the furnishings he seems to be examining—the tattered antimacassars, the tufted blue divan with the worn velvet cover. He is trying to figure out who lives here, whether there is a husband, a lover, a child.

Louise knows men don't like unpleasant surprises. She skips her husband—the subject has become a source of humiliation—and decides to save Victor Cousin for another day. She launches into praise of her daughter, who is at boarding school several days of the week. It is a very good school, she scrimps and saves all year long, publishes continually in order to afford her child the best education possible. . . . The subject of schooling allows Louise to approach the most important topic of conversation for any member of Gustave's and Louise's milieu: What do you most love to *read?*

Louise knows she has struck the right note—to an aspiring writer of the time, the act of reading is akin to a liturgical experience; shared literary tastes are the seeds of all genuine friendships. . . . The young man stands up and starts pacing the room, gesticulating fiercely about Shakespeare, that colossus across the Channel, shame on the French for being so slow to understand his greatness! Has Madame Colet recently read *The Tempest, King Lear, A Midsummer Night's Dream?* Does she know anything to compare with their genius? No, she doesn't; Shakespeare is indeed the greatest prodigy of world history . . . She rises, walks to her bookshelf, and takes out several volumes. She translated some passages from those plays when she was younger, she adds modestly; if Monsieur Flaubert is interested he can take a look.

"Read to me!" the blond giant commands. "Please read."

Louise sits down on the couch next to her guest. She is aware of the flattering glow cast by her alabaster lamp as she reads him a passage from her translation of *The Tempest.*

Habitants des ruisseaux, des rochers, de l'espace,
Vous, dont le pied léger ne laisse point de trace,
Lorsque vous poursuivez sur le sable mouvant
Neptune, dont le flot recule en s'élevant;
Vous, qui vous enfuyez lorsque ardent et sauvage
Il revient à son tour vous poursuivre au rivage. . . .*

He listens intently, his eyes never swerving from her face.

There is an uneasy silence when she ends. Is Madame Colet quite sure that classical French alexandrines are the proper medium of translation for those great lines? he asks. Mightn't free verse better capture the genius of Shakespeare's metaphors? Does she write all her own verse in alexandrine couplets?

Oh, no, no! she swiftly replies. I write and translate in a great variety of meters—here, listen:

N'aie pas peur; l'île est pleine de sons et d'airs
ravissants qui charment et ne nuisent pas; parfois des

**The Tempest,* Act V, Scene 1: "Ye elves of hills, brooks, standing lakes, and groves . . ."

*milliers d'instruments retentissent confusément à mes
oreilles; d'autre fois ce sont des voix si douces, que,
lorsque je m'éveille après un long sommeil, elles me portent
à dormir encore . . .* *

"Ah, that's better." Gustave sighs with relief.

Louise walks back to the bookshelf, returns with a few other volumes. Here are her two long poems, "Le Musée de Versailles" and "Le Tombeau de Molière," for which she received prizes (this is said casually) from the Académie Française. And here is her first collection, *Fleurs du Midi,* with a quotation from Byron on the title page; here also is *Penserosa,* so called because "a great philosopher"—Louise catches herself here; perhaps she disclosed this detail too readily, but after all, the visitor will eventually know—because an old friend had given her that Miltonian name. . . .

The young man doesn't seem to have noticed the allusion to another man in Madame Colet's life; he is holding her books respectfully, reading swiftly through the pages. God! she thinks, the directness and beauty of his eyes—how undaunted, how self-possessed he is for his age!

Can I be utterly frank? he asks. Of course, of course! Tell me exactly what you think!

Some of these lines are very beautiful, he says; others seem . . . well, a little bit rushed and facile; and others are just plain *commonplace,* he adds quietly. For instance, has Madame Colet thought of how trivial her use of the word "glory" might be? Here: "Do not speak to me of happiness or *glory,*" and only three pages later, "*glory* and fame," and there again, "by youth or by *glory.*" Should she not pause more often, craft her work more carefully, avoid what he's come to call "accepted ideas"?

Louise is taken aback. She's seldom received such levelheaded criticism. Why, Monsieur Flaubert, Pradier told me to take you under my wing; perhaps it's *you* who should be *my* mentor. . . .

The room is getting dim; the evening sun is casting long shadows into Louise's little flat. Now that they can speak as colleagues, their talk becomes more direct. The two writers sit side by side on the couch, looking through dozens of volumes—Chateaubriand, Byron, Hugo, Vigny, more Shakespeare—commenting, arguing. And when Monsieur Flaubert's powerful arm brushes Louise's in one of his expansive gestures, she turns

---

*Act III, Scene 2: "Be not afeard, the isle is full of noises,/Sounds, and sweet airs, that give delight and hurt not."

and smiles up at him. The next thing she knows, he is not touching her arm by accident. What is she going to do? She desires this man as she's never desired anyone in her life. Is it possible that he might liberate her from the invalid Hippolyte, the unctuous Victor Cousin?

But here it is seven-thirty, and Henriette, who is on vacation from school, could be coming home with the maid at any moment. Louise is a dutiful mother, who tries to maintain decorum in her daughter's eyes. . . .

"There's so little time," she whispers as he embraces her, "so little time. You must leave very soon. . . ."

They kiss, but after a while she has to push him gently away. Her daughter, Henriette, she repeats, is about to return. . . . They make a date for the following day.

In the early, infatuated phase of their relationship, Flaubert's letters to Louise will often return to the long hansom cab rides they take together in the days that follow in the Bois de Boulogne. On the first occasion, little Henriette is in the cab with them but reclines on the cushions of the coach seat, her eyes sleepily closed. As the horse-drawn coach ascends the Champs Élysées on a quiet moonlit night, the enamored pair hear only the sound of the horses' clacking hooves. They exchange few words, but their hands, their glances, tell all. When the child falls asleep, Louise abandons herself to his caresses.

As they return to the door of her flat, Louise gently lifts her daughter down from the cab. Henriette clutches at her mother's skirt, whining, confused. Gustave leaves them at the door.

The following afternoon, Louise rushes to Pradier's studio and waits for Gustave's arrival. She waits into the evening. He never appears. At first Pradier teases her, then he consoles her, trying to warn her of the complexities of this enigmatic young man. Flaubert's passions have all been chaste, he tells her, art has been his only love, he prefers the solitude of his Normandy retreat to all the glamour of Paris. And yet Pradier has never seen him so infatuated with anyone as he seems to be with Louise. Louise returns home, goes to bed perplexed, filled with sorrow and desire.

Late the next afternoon, again unannounced, Gustave returns to Louise's flat. They take their second coach ride. This time they are alone. Fireworks light the city, for it is the sixteenth anniversary of the "Glorious" 1830 revolution, which toppled the oppressive regime of Charles X and ushered in the reign of Louis Philippe. Their cab drives past the flower-bedecked obelisks of the Champs Élysées and the Arc de Triomphe. It proceeds toward the Bois de Boulogne, whose alleys are draped with luminous garlands. The coach moves slowly amid a raging lightning storm, amid bursts of flashing rockets and patriotic shouting; the thunder is deafening throughout Paris; flashes of lightning seem to celebrate their lust. As Gustave would write Louise a few days later, "They blazed for us . . . like a flaming beginning of love."

Sartre is certain that Louise's and Gustave's first lovemaking took place then and there, inside that black hansom cab, and that Flaubert was impotent on his first try. This "fiasco" is revealed in a letter he wrote to Louise a few days later: "What happened to me with you had never happened to me before (I was so worn out from the previous three days, and my nerves were taut like cello strings)."

Whatever occurred in the hansom cab, there are many successful moments later that night, when Louise accompanies Gustave to his hotel room. During a respite, he contemplates her at length as she lies in his bed, in a pose he will recall ecstatically in his letters: " . . . your hair spread about your pale face, your palms joined, speaking mad words." (An archetypal pose of postorgasmic ecstasy in mid-nineteenth-century France: To retain decorum after having made love like the most skilled courtesan, a "New Woman" like Louise, who retains many bourgeois scruples, must play the role of the innocent seduced girl.) And Gustave is also playing his role, acting like a young man who has had his first true night of love.

The following evening, little Henriette is away visiting friends, but Louise cannot call off her weekly salon at such short notice. Gustave brings her a large bouquet of flowers and is forced to mingle with her guests—dear "Phidias" Pradier, the poet Anaïs Ségalas, the bibliophile Jacob. The hostess has spread her table with the habitual dish of *poulet à la provençale,* prepared with her own hands. I doubt if Gustave or Louise pays much attention to Phidias's good-natured jokes, Ségalas's giggles, the book collector's learned chatter. Gustave will recall only Louise's anxious azure eyes, the blazing whiteness of those shoulders traversed by fine blue veins. The evening drags on; will there ever be an end to it? The worldly Phidias soon discerns the lovers' torment and leaves soon after the meal, taking the guests with him.

Gustave goes down the stairs with Louise's friends, accompanies them for a few blocks. Pretending that he is taking a shortcut to his hotel, he then returns to Louise's flat.

The next morning at dawn, Gustave steals away with his booty—Louise's bedroom slippers, a handkerchief spotted with blood, and two volumes of her writings, including *Saintes et folles,* "Saints and Madwomen" (a title appropriate to the author's past few nights).

That day, Monday, August 3, Louise is too overwhelmed to work or even to leave her house. She dines with Gustave, they spend one last night together at his hotel. In the morning Gustave flees Louise, this time for many weeks, to return to his treasured retreat at Croisset, to that study, adjoining his mother's room, where he can "remain a bear in my den, in my lair, in my skin, in my old bear's skin."

Letters: Month One

"Twelve hours ago we were still together. Yesterday at this very hour I still held you in my arms. . . . Do you remember? How distant it all is already! The night is now warm and gentle, I hear the great tulip tree by my window tremble in the wind and, raising my head, see the moon's reflection on the water."

So it began, one of the great love correspondences of all time.

"Your little slippers are here even as I write, facing me, I stare at them. . . . I would like to offer you only joy, to surround you with a continuous and warm felicity in exchange for all that you've given me in the prodigality of your love. I am afraid of being cold, selfish, and yet God only knows what is churning in me at this hour. What memories! And what desire . . .

"Ah, our two promenades by coach, how beautiful they were! Especially the second one, with all its lightning! I recall the color of the trees lit up by lanterns, and the swaying of the coach's springs. . . .

"When looking at those little brown slippers I dream of the movement of your feet when they filled them and were still warm. The handkerchief is also with them, I see your blood—I wish it were drenched with it."

A note of foreboding in the next lines:

"My mother was waiting for me at the railroad station. She wept to see me return. You wept upon seeing me leave. Is our misery so great that we cannot move a mile without causing tears on both sides?"

He signs off in grand romantic fashion:

"I only wished to send you one more kiss before I went to sleep, to tell you that I loved you. . . . So, a kiss, a quick one, you know what kind, and one more, and oh again still more, and still more under your chin, in that spot I love on your very soft skin, and on your chest, where I place my heart."

* * *

This first letter of Gustave's, written on the night of Tuesday-to-Wednesday and mailed on Wednesday morning, arrived in Paris *that very afternoon.* When reading through this correspondence, it is essential to note the remarkable efficiency of the nineteenth-century postal system, whose speed had a considerable influence on the denouement of Louise and Gustave's affair. If Louise wrote her lover on the same Wednesday evening that she received his letter and posted it the next morning, as she was wont to do, Gustave would have her reply Thursday night, thus securing a response to every one of his letters a mere thirty-six hours after sending them. Given these lovers' impulsive, tempestuous natures, might this swiftness of exchange—made possible by the recent opening of the Rouen–Paris train line and speedier than our contemporary express mail systems—have contributed to the frequent storminess of their correspondence?

By week's end, with Gustave's second letter, many notes of discord are already evident: One immediately feels the devouring exigency of Louise's passion, her imperious demands that her lover instantly return to Paris; one detects also Gustave's strategy of resistance, the jaded pessimism with which he expresses his postcoital *tristesse:*

"I am broken, dizzied, as after a long orgy, I am bored to death. I have an incredible void in my heart. I once so proud of my serenity, I who worked from morning to night with a sustained rigor, can neither read nor think nor write. Your love has made me sad. I can see that you're suffering, I foresee that I shall make you suffer. For your sake first, then for mine, *I wish I had never known you....* " (It is Louise who underlined those last seven words of Flaubert's letter, adding several exclamation marks.)

Gustave's subsequent lines reflect Louise's reproaches of the previous day, her recurring fear that she might have lost her "reputation" in his eyes.

"Let lightning strike me, let all possible maledictions befall me if I ever forget you. I, disdain you, you write me, because you gave yourself to me too soon! What can you be thinking of? *Never, never,* whatever you make of it, whatever happens. I am devoted to you for life, to your daughter, to all those for whom you would wish my devotion. That is an oath, keep it in mind, use it. I make it because I know I can keep it.

"Yes, I desire you and I think of you. Yes, I love you more than I loved you in Paris. I keep seeing you again in [Pradier's] studio, standing by your portrait bust, your blond curls moving about your white shoulders, your blue dress, your arm, your face...."

But Louise wasn't satisfied by such assurances. She seems to have fussed (one of her fatal bourgeois faux pas) about the lack of the word "forever" in Gustave's missives.

"Ever since we said we loved each other you've wondered why I never added the word 'forever,'" he responds. "Why? Because I can always forecast the future. I've never looked at a child without thinking that it would grow old, never glimpsed a cradle without thinking of a tomb. The sight of a naked woman makes me think of a skeleton. . . . After our frenzied moments together have passed, my heart swoons with sadness. . . . I have a foreboding of immense unhappiness for you. . . . And you, child, do you think that you will love me 'forever'? Forever! What presumption on human lips . . ."

He pacifies her with recollections of their unleashed sex.

"Oh, what forgetfulness of all, what exclusion of the world . . . How soft the skin of your naked body . . . I'll always remember the expression on your face when you were squatting on the floor by my knees, your inebriated smile when we left each other. . . ."

Then, the plea that the devouring Louise might well have heeded more attentively:

"You tell me . . . to write you every day, and if I do not I know you will reproach me. But the very idea that you want a letter every morning will prevent me from writing it! Let me love you in my manner. . . . Don't force me to do anything, and I shall do everything. Understand me, and don't reproach me. If I thought you were frivolous and stupid, like other women, I would inundate you with promises, oaths . . . but I prefer to express less, not more, than the true feelings of my heart. A thousand kisses, everywhere, *everywhere*."

("I kiss you everywhere" was such a regular phrase in Gustave's letters to Louise that it provided the title, in France, for several plays based on their correspondence.)

Letter three was written late on a Saturday night, a few hours after Gustave received the note Louise mailed him that morning. Maman Flaubert's lugubrious presence was beginning to seep into the correspondence:

"My mother has been in a terrible state for the past two days, suffering from sinister hallucinations. . . . You don't know what a burden it is to carry such despair alone. If you ever think yourself to be the world's most miserable woman, remember what I've just said: There is one who is unhappier than anyone can bear to be, one degree below death or total madness."

This letter goes on for a dozen pages. In it, one begins to sense that

Gustave preferred his lover absent, unseen; that notwithstanding his lust
for Louise, he continued to suffer from the mayhem she had thrown into
his reclusive writing schedule.

"Before knowing you I had become calm. . . . I had understood, clas-
sified, put myself in order so well. . . . It is as if you came along and stirred
it all up with your finger. The old dregs boiled up again, the lake of my
heart began to tremble. Only oceans can survive storms! When you stir
up a swamp such as mine, only foul odors rise up. . . . I have to love you
to tell you all this. Forget me if you can, tear out your soul with your two
hands and stamp on it to erase the imprint I left on it."

(Remember: They had became lovers only a week earlier!)

"I'm not made to enjoy life," he states pointedly on the same page (this
time the emphasis is his). "Happiness is a monstrosity! It punishes all
who seek it."

"Go on, don't get angry!" Then he changes his tone. "No, I kiss you,
I embrace you, I am crazed. If you were there, I would bite you. . . . "

Clearly, he is obsessed with the memory of their last cab ride: "A week
ago we were taking our beautiful drive in the Bois de Boulogne. What an
abyss since that day! . . . It was a radiant moment whose glow will always
brighten our hearts. It was beautiful in its joy and tenderness. . . . If I were
rich I would buy that carriage and put it in my stable and never use it
again. . . . "

(Watch Flaubert's mention of purchasing that black hansom cab in
which he first seduced his mistress. Louise will later remind him of that
hyperbole, rub it in. And Flaubert will transpose his hansom cab seduction of Louise into a crucial passage of *Madame Bovary.*)

"What a good idea it was to steal away with your bedroom slippers! If
you knew how often I look at them!"

(Watch also for the recurrence of Louise's slippers in Gustave's letters.
Psychoanalytically inclined critics, like Jean-Paul Sartre, have had a field
day with those slippers: This man who tried to repress his considerable
sexual appetite was a pervert and a fetishist, Sartre says, preferring the
"denoted object of absence" to his mistress's real body. Gustave had not
wanted to sleep with Louise *for real,* Sartre adds; he would have preferred
to maintain "an erection in the void," to *control* her symbolically through
those possessions of hers he kept in his desk drawer—her slippers, her
handkerchief, her portrait, her lock of hair.)

Gustave did indeed love to dwell on Louise fetishes, such as her blood-
spotted handkerchief, often linking them to the brevity of human love.
("The spots of blood are yellowing, paling, is it their fault? We'll do the

same: a year, two years, what does it matter? All that one can measure passes, has a term.")

On that first week of their correspondence, he does try to pacify her with promises of a forthcoming reunion, but the date depends on when Pradier finishes the portrait of his sister. For Gustave cannot go to Paris without giving Maman a reasonable excuse for leaving home.

"So we'll inaugurate your blue dress together," he writes. "I'll try to arrive some evening around 6 P.M. We'll have all that night and the next day."

(*One night!* Louise must have exclaimed, enraged.)

"We'll set fire to that night! . . . We shall feast on each other to see if we can ever get sated. Never, no, never! Your heart is an endless source, you make me drink huge drafts of it. It floods me. It penetrates me. I drown in it. . . . So there, I'm going to visit your slippers again. Ah! those won't ever leave me! I think I love them as much as I love you. . . . Good-bye, my love, good-bye, my life, a thousand kisses everywhere. I shall come to you as soon as I hear from Pradier. . . . Adieu. I kiss you there where I shall kiss you, there where I have wished to in the past. I put my mouth on it, I roll on you, a thousand kisses."

The next morning, Gustave responds to Louise's ire.

"My child, your folly is carrying you too far. Calm yourself. Be more sparing with your shouts; they torture me. What do you want me to do? Can I leave everything here and go live in Paris? Impossible. If I were free I should do it, for with you in Paris I should not have the force to keep myself away."

Perfectly content to wait another three weeks before making the three-hour train trip to Paris, he tries to buy a few days of peace: "I await a letter [from Phidias] which will give me a pretext to go to Paris for a day. Then, toward September, I will find another pretext for going to some town between Paris and Rouen—Mantes or Vernon—where you can meet me. After that, we'll see. . . . Adieu, dear soul. I have just gone down into the garden and have gathered this little rose, which I am sending you. I have kissed it; put it quickly to your mouth, and then—guess where. Adieu! A thousand kisses. I am yours from night to day, from day to night."

By the second week, Gustave is fending off a tide of protests.

"Forget everything I said in my letter of Sunday. . . . I'll torment you no longer. I will draw in my quills. With a little goodwill, even a porcupine is tamed! . . . You don't thank me for my frankness. (Women wish to be deceived; they force you to deceive them, and if you resist they reproach you!) . . . Why do you reproach me for my phrase, 'I wish we had never met'? I know of none more tender. What more can anyone say when his heart is faltering because it is so full?

"I must ask you not to write me such commonplaces as the following: that I'm unhappy because I have never had to earn my living, that I should be better off if I had to work. As though all one had to do to escape from the boredom of this world was to become a druggist's clerk, or a baker, or a wine merchant! Too many bourgeois have told me those things over and over again to make me want to hear them from you.

"Adieu. A thousand kisses, unending. Till soon, my beautiful one, till soon!"

But by "soon" Flaubert hardly meant what his sweetheart wished him to mean. This was already the third week, and he was expressing growing scruples regarding his dour, demanding mother. He asked Louise to address all her letters to "Monsieur Du Camp, care of Monsieur Gustave Flaubert." Flaubert had arranged for his friend and his mistress to meet in Paris. Maxime then arrived at Croisset with a letter and a little engraved portrait of Louise, which she had asked him to deliver to Gustave.

". . . My mother has seen [the portrait]. She likes your face, thinks you are pretty. You have 'an animated, open, pleasant expression,' she says. (I have pretended to her that proofs of the engraving happened to be delivered on an afternoon when I had been taken to see you and that you presented some of them to your visitors.)"

Although he remained adamant in his refusal to return to Paris, Gustave's desire for Louise seems to have been very powerful and real.

"What beautiful verses you sent me! Their rhythm is as soft as the caresses of your voice when you mix my name in your tender chirping. Allow me to find them the most beautiful of your verses. . . .

"Oh, if I seem cold to you, if my satires are harsh and wound you, I wish to cover you with love, indulgence, ecstasy when I see you next. I wish to gorge you with fleshly raptures, sate you with them, make you die. I wish you to be amazed by me, to admit that you had never even dreamed that such transports were possible. . . . I wish you to recall them so well in your old age that your dry bones will tremble at the memory."

Finally—finally—a few days later, Pradier lets him know that he has finished the sculpture of Caroline.

"I'll be with you tomorrow between 4:30 and 5 P.M. . . . Shall we take Phidias along for dinner? What do you think? Flow speedily, day! Flow on, long night!"

* * *

Although limited to twenty-four hours, Gustave and Louise's second rendezvous seems to have been splendid. As they strolled the boulevards just before his departure, Gustave purchased a Jacques Callot engraving of Saint Anthony as inspiration for a book he was researching on the third-century anchorite. Might Gustave have been reminding Louise of his often monastic behavior, his ability to master temptation?

Back in Croisset, where he hung the image of Saint Anthony directly across from his desk, he wrote Louise, repeatedly returning to their most recent moments of bliss, apparently thrilled by his performance: "I recall our last *reunion* at the hotel, with your silk dress way open, and the lace winding down your breast." "Remember how violent my caresses were, how powerful my hands, you were trembling! I made you shout out a few times."

"When the evening has returned, when I am securely alone, when everyone else has gone to bed and I'm certain of not being disturbed, I open the drawer of the chest I have mentioned and I take out the relics, which I spread on my table: first your little slippers, then your handkerchief, your locks of hair, the envelope with your letters. I read them again, touch them again. . . ."

Ah yes, those slippers.

Month Two

In the last days of August, Louise must have fretted about the fact that her lover had accorded her only one meeting since they first met. A confrontational tone set in.

"Dear God, your anger, and sourness, and tartness, and rawness!" Gustave wrote. "What does it all mean? Do you truly like these disputes, recriminations, and bitter daily attacks, which end up making life a living hell? . . . If I cannot come to Paris as you desire me to, it is because my mother needs me."

He tried to placate her by offering a meeting in Mantes, a romantic little city halfway between Rouen and Paris. Often painted by Corot, the place has been known for centuries as "Mantes-la-Jolie" and had been chosen by many French monarchs as a site for their castles. But Gustave was proposing a meeting of five hours! This was his Byzantine game plan, conceived, as ever, to keep Maman's suspicions at bay:

"Du Camp is returning to Paris, and I'm supposedly accompanying him as far as Gaillon to see a château a few miles away. But instead of that I will go on to Mantes, where I shall stay until the six o'clock train, arriv-

ing back here at eight. Such is the plan I have been hatching. Let's hope that my brother-in-law, or my mother herself, doesn't have the unfortunate idea of accompanying me. . . . We'd have five wonderful hours together . . . it's at least something, and I foresee no possibility of being able to come to Paris for some time. . . . Till then adieu, I am yours, on top of you [*à toi, sur toi*]."

The brevity of this projected visit, and the complexity of its Oedipal scruples, seems only to have triggered Louise's rage. She launched an accusation that particularly irritated Gustave:

"I thought you would kiss me for the idea of our going to Mantes, and instead you are reproaching me in advance for not staying there longer. You thought you would find my vulnerable point in my vanity, saying 'So you are watched over like a young girl.' If this phrase had been addressed to me five or six years ago it would have made me do something desperate—I would have killed myself, if necessary, to cancel the effect it had on me. But now it rolls off me like water from the neck of a swan; it has not humiliated me at all."

All right, then, Gustave conceded, they could add two hours to their stay at Mantes's Hôtel du Grand Cerf, as long as he was home by ten P.M.

The rendezvous in Mantes turned out to be a delirium of pleasure. Save for a delectable lunch of shellfish served right in their room, and a brief outdoor stroll at sunset by the Seine, Louise and Gustave seem barely to have left their bed. If we read through Gustave's lines, they shared thrilling frenzies.

"That was our most beautiful time together," he recalled in a letter a few hours after returning home to Croisset. "We loved each other better than ever before, we shared exquisite joys. . . . You told me that you'd never known such rapture, that your ecstasy set you on fire. I'm so proud; did I truly please you? . . . What a beautiful memory! It deserves a commemorative Mass! . . . Do you remember, yesterday at this very hour you were shouting, 'Bite me, Bite me!' "

And what a victory Louise had won that evening in Mantes! Their lovemaking was so euphoric that Gustave defied his mother and spent the entire night with Louise in their love nest at the Hôtel du Cerf. Madame Flaubert met his train at eleven P.M., went home, and lay awake the entire night, fretting. The next morning Gustave found her on the station platform in a state of terrible anxiety. "She didn't utter the slightest reproach," he wrote Louise in the same latter, "but her expression was the greatest reproach possible."

"I keep recalling your face under your night bonnet," he continued two days later, "the curls emerging from it when you were on top of me, suspended above me; your eyes shone, your mouth trembled, your teeth chattered. . . . Adieu, receive all my kisses, those that you told me I'd taught you, those with which I would like to continually cover all your limbs. I imagine that you're still there, swooning under their moist pressure."

Their sex must indeed have been steamy, if not kinky. There is frequent mention of bloodstained handkerchiefs (not necessarily caused by Louise's period), which the lovers exchanged as keepsakes. There are references to Louise letting her nails grow very long because Gustave preferred them that way. The missionary position seems to have been infrequent, and there are numerous instances when Gustave recalls the rapture of seeing "your head at my knees."

The very infrequency of the lovers' meetings, the state of sexual starvation Louise must have experienced between their rare reunions, points to another aspect of Flaubert's sensuality. Beyond his latent homoeroticism and his fascination with brothels, his tastes appear to have tended toward fetishism, sadomasochism, and masturbation (those slippers!). He enjoyed playing the part of the seduced girl; the long periods of celibacy he imposed on the multiorgasmic Louise must have led her to attack him voraciously at each of their meetings, which is precisely what he desired. Whenever he was not paying for sex, only the most aggressive partners seemed to satisfy his occasional lust.

In fact, the Goncourts, drawing on their extensive conversations with Flaubert, state that in her angrier moments Louise physically beat and molested Gustave, provoking in him fantasies of killing her. "There was a natural truculence in Flaubert which led him to seek out women terrifying in their sensuality and frenetic emotions," they comment, "women who destroyed love through brutal transports, demented passions." Sartre also sees Flaubert as an archetypal fetishist who preferred "complex erotic games directed at masturbation" to actual sex, and diminished his impulse to commit violence by masturbating over the Louise-objects stored in his drawer.

But even if we do not agree with these interpretations, it is clear that Flaubert preferred assuaging his bouts of passion in brief dizzy moments. Many of Louise's mannerisms, and details of her life story, would infuse Emma Bovary. One recalls instantly Gustave and Louise's fervid meetings in Mantes when reading Flaubert's description of Emma's famished reunions with her lover in Rouen hotel rooms. "She un-

dressed brutally, tearing the slim lacings of her corset about her hips
like a snake . . . and then with one gesture she let all her vestments fall;
and pale, without speaking, aerial, she fell against his chest with a great
shudder."

Throughout Gustave's descriptions of marvelous sex, one is also struck
by the narcissism of his attraction for Louise. The two were evidently
trying to dazzle each other in bed. But one senses that Gustave was above
all trying to dazzle himself (Sartre refers to Flaubert's erotic tactics as
"opération miroir"). He frequently described the violence and skill of his
caresses, striking the pose of a sexual superman offering superecstasy. (In
typical nineteenth-century macho style, Flaubert told his male friends
that he offered Louise such stupendous orgasms during their encounters
in Mantes that "her shouts of pleasure awakened the occupants of the
entire hotel.")

In the second month of the affair, a new concern surfaced in the lovers'
letters. Louise, who recorded her periods assiduously, noted at one point
that she was running a week late and was suffering from nausea. Gustave
brooded terribly about that "cursed blood which doesn't return," about
the absence of "the British." (Throughout their years of correspondence
"the British," or "Lord Palmerston," would be the lovers' code name for
menstruation, derived from the French custom of referring to British
soldiers as "redcoats.")

Louise mentioned the possibility of going to Switzerland for an abor-
tion. Gustave urged her to see a doctor before undertaking such a trip
and in the same breath pleaded with her to burn this particular letter of
his "out of prudence." Gustave had already responded heatedly, the previous month, to Louise's statement that she would be joyful to bear his
child. "The very idea sends chills down my spine," he wrote; he would
rather "jump into the Seine this very moment with a 36-pound cannon-
ball attached to my feet" than learn that he has propagated life. He apologized for the "imprudences" he had committed and promised that "In
our future raptures I shall take greater care." (Louise's journals intimate
that the lovers occasionally practiced coitus interruptus as a way of birth
control; that Gustave sometimes ejaculated in a handkerchief, kept at
Louise's bedside, which she preserved as a keepsake.)

When the "British redcoats" finally arrived, they were greeted by
Gustave with consummate cynicism. "Thank God, one less wretch on
earth. One victim less to boredom, vice, or crime. . . . Thank God I shall
not have any posterity!"

Months Three and Four

Winter was nearing; the days were growing shorter, colder. In his letters, Gustave chatted to Louise about his research on Saint Anthony. He was steeped in the Greek classics, the Bahgavad Gita, the Church Fathers. He seemed to emulate the asceticism of his protagonist, never leaving his house, seeing absolutely no one beyond his immediate family and Louis Bouilhet, who continued to visit him on weekends to work by his side. He grew increasingly impatient with Louise's insistent cries of "Come to Paris, come to Paris!" "In the name of God, talk to me about something other than coming to Paris" became his usual response.

Gustave's tactic to counter Louise's constant needling, her pleas to allow her to visit Croisset, was to emphasize his outstanding capacity for self-control and his family duties.

"A long time ago I used to go to whores at New Year's to celebrate the New Year. . . . Now when I have desires, a bowl of cold water gets rid of them."

"My life is tied to another life, and will be as long as that other life lasts."

"Why have you wanted to encroach upon a life which does not belong to me, and change my whole existence to satisfy your desires?"

That fall, perhaps in retribution for an angry letter, Louise sent him a cigar case with an agate seal stamped with the motto *Amor nel cor,* "Love in the heart." Gustave responded in a cool, perplexed manner: "What does this mean? Is this a challenge? A reproach? A taunt? I'm lost. *Amor nel cor!* You're right; this heart of mine, which, as you put it, is not as full of devotion as 'those of other men,' is indeed unlike the hearts of others." (The *Amor nel cor* seal is yet another detail of his life with Louise that Flaubert would utilize in *Madame Bovary*.)

"People in love can go for years without seeing each other," he nonchalantly answered one of Louise's "Come to Paris!" demands. ("What to make of *that*?" she scribbled on the margin of the page.)

He told Louise to drink plenty of chamomile tea to "calm" herself and to take many hot baths.

Meanwhile Gustave continued to keep Maxime Du Camp informed of the progress of his liaison. "Praise God, old pal, that you're out of a dreadful pickle," Du Camp commented when he heard that Louise's "Brits" had returned. "I send my sincere compliments to you and also to her, whatever she might have to say about it; you would have been burdened for a good part of your life, and without any great reward."

*　　*　　*

How would one feel in Louise's place? Throughout the autumn, as she wrote Gustave about her whirls in Paris society—the solace of her daily visits with Béranger, the increasingly sinister presence of the still-ardent Victor Cousin—she suffered from Flaubert's heartlessness, such as: "I'm not forgetting you yet, that time hasn't yet come. We'll cross that bridge when we come to it." He was crueler yet in the following exchange: Hearing that a mutual friend was about to leave Paris for Marseilles, he asked Louise to pass on a letter addressed to his paramour of six years before— Madame Foucauld, the "gorgeously titted broad," as he had described her to friends, with whom he spent such delirious hours in his adolescence. Gustave left the letter unsealed, provoking Louise, whose jealousy erupted as readily as her temper.

Understandably puzzled by this man of prodigious amorous skills who kept emphasizing his preference for nearly total abstinence, Louise reacted with increasing ire. By December the love duet became a duel. Flaubert had begun to feel that his initially negative reaction to Pradier's "medical advice" was prophetic. His first attempt at "normal love" was proving to be a catastrophic interruption of all that he most cherished— the calm and fruitful triad of Mother/Work/Male Friends. His correspondence with Louise had grown "apoplectic"—his own word. One wonders what kept these two together beyond their mutual interest in literature and their rare, ecstatic moments in bed.

It would be hard to envision more different personalities: Louise Colet was an exuberant Mediterranean extrovert, terrified of solitude. She was an archetype of what the French called *les grandes amoureuses*—the gifted nineteenth-century women (George Sand, Marie d'Agoult, Juliette Drouet) who, however talented, were brainwashed by the Romantic view of consuming love and were ever ready to sacrifice their work to it; whereas the introverted Gustave was fundamentally reclusive. In spite of his moments of expansive wit and conversation, he prized his solitude, enjoying little human company beyond that of his family and two or three carefully chosen friends.

Louise's sensuality was forthright and abundant, and she referred to her appetites in a manner that was considered "masculine" in her time. Flaubert's sexuality, on the other hand, was cryptic and convoluted; love was hardly the "main course" of his life, as it was of Louise's, but an occasional and highly disposable "seasoning." However much he enjoyed "firing his shots," his innumerable amorous metaphors for the act of writing suggest that language and literature were the true objects of his long-ings. When his writing went well, Flaubert said, "Something deep and extra-voluptuous flows out of me in concentrated jets, like an ejaculation of the soul." He advised Bouilhet: "Save your Priapism for style, fuck your inkwell. . . . One ounce of sperm spent equals three liters of blood lost."

There were further points of misunderstanding: Flaubert, who lived without a financial concern as his mother's companion, saw literature as a priesthood, the most austere of callings; Louise looked on it as a means to "glory" and above all as a way of earning a living for herself and her child. Whereas she was able to compose her couplets in bed during their trysts, a night of lovemaking could cost Flaubert a fortnight of work. Louise dashed off her prize-winning poems in a legendary few days. Flaubert's mature style was an arduous, years-long process of erasing and rewriting through many dozens of drafts.

Flaubert's aesthetic credos were as close to a religious belief as he had. The couple's violent disagreements over literary practice were often the source of their frequent estrangements, and Gustave had profound con-tempt for Louise's facile, volatile manner of working.

For in her more self-indulgent moments, Louise's writing—floridly sentimental, lacking irony, infused with earnest liberalism—was a con-tradiction of all Flaubert believed in. Indeed, it is incongruous that the Muse of the writer who pioneered a revolutionary new doctrine of im-personality was a nineteenth-century Erica Jong who recklessly splashed her life and loves across her poetry and prose, barely distinguishing the line between fact and fiction. After his first few months of infatuation, Flaubert began to criticize Louise's work harshly. He may have been particularly embarrassed by a verse in which, evoking their most recent raptures, Louise commemorated his speed of sexual recuperation— "Like a wild buffalo of the American desert / Never wearying, you keep infusing me with life." ("It made me roar with laughter," he commented.) And how could this master of restrained style have felt about such lines as: "Your pure embalmed mouth / Hung on my tongue / Two tongues in the same mouth / Exchanged unctuous lickings / Our joined bodies pounded the bed / Under our ardent transports."

On the other hand, the pioneer feminist Colet, one of the first nineteenth-century women writers to protest the subservience of women, had to endure the many misogynous statements with which her lover enjoyed offending her: "Women mistake their cunt for their heart and think the moon is made to illuminate their boudoir." "Why do you always take the defense [of the female sex]? One must always be on the side of the strong." "When has a woman ever died of rape?"

Throughout the eight years of their on-again, off-again liaison, the dedicated liberal Louise Colet—an embattled supporter of women, the working class, Polish and Turkish rebels, victims of any oppression—must have been equally appalled by Flaubert's repeatedly stated belief in an enlightened oligarchy. He constantly affronted her with such statements as: "I would like to be rich enough to offer the superfluous to those who are not in any need." Or, directly attacking Louise's most fervent ideals: "Your notions of morality, patriotism, duty, your tastes in literature—all that is repugnant to my taste . . . How could I be enthused by the domestic and democratic virtues you wish me to admire?"

But the most interesting aspect of the Colet-Flaubert liaison was the fact that Louise so violently threw Flaubert off balance, so totally confused him. At those times in history when women were redefining their status in society, men have had a powerful need to categorize them in order to maintain their control, and have been panicked by those whom they could not classify. Flaubert was thoroughly intimidated by the versatility of this "New Woman" who loudly proclaimed her sexual appetites in life and in art. He was too mired in archaic bourgeois distinctions between sacred "untouchable" mother versus unclassifiable "New Woman" mistress to know whether he should disdain or respect Louise. And the greatest single dispute between the lovers, over the years, was linked to Flaubert's need to typify and categorize all human relations. He was infuriated by Louise's repeated requests to visit Croisset and meet Maman.

Flaubert found it "strange," as he put it, that Louise persisted in this demand. She maintained that his tenacious refusal to allow an encounter of "two sentiments of totally different sources" was equally curious. Flaubert continued to look on his home as a convent, whose walls Louise must never transgress.

Yet one of the many paradoxes of this odd affair is that it may have thriven on the very "separation" that Louise protested. In light of Flaubert's Oedipal loyalty, his Byzantine strategies of sexual postponement, could this tempestuous idyll have lasted for more than a fortnight if the lovers had lived in the same city?

Moreover, it must be emphasized that beneath these huge differences of temperament there were subtle factors that drew the lovers together. Not only was the ego of this insecure, provincial young man flattered by a famous poet's passion and by her prophetic trust in his genius; Louise's spell on Gustave also had to do with her extraordinary gift for listening and with the delicate confessional relationship they evolved: Although Gustave mostly preferred to keep Louise unseen (symbolically behind him, as in the patient-doctor positioning of traditional psychoanalysis), for some years she was the only one to whom he seemed able freely to express his melancholy problems.

They shared another important affinity that it would have been impossible for Louise and Gustave, or any of their contemporaries, to diagnose: Both were out of sync with their time. They were each alienated from most members of their generation—he through his rebellion against the bourgeoisie into which he was born, she by her repudiation of the nineteenth-century credo of male dominance.

8.

Tempests

❧

In late October, Pradier sent word that he had finished the cast of a statue of Flaubert's father, commissioned by the city of Rouen. At last Gustave had an excuse to give Maman for going to Paris. He told Louise to check with Du Camp about where to meet him on the appointed day.

"A thousand kisses," he signed off, and "I keep remembering the shudder of joy I experienced, in bed, when I felt your thigh on my belly and your waist in my arms."

It appears that this particular reunion did not go well. Louise refused Gustave's good-bye kiss. She even refused to take her hand out of her muff to shake his hand. In the letters that followed this Paris meeting, she used the formal *vous* for the first time. Gustave sought a reconciliation. He tried to rekindle her passion by telling her he wanted to possess her right in her living room ("from the back"), when she was wearing her most elegant dress. Two weeks later, he again expressed relief that "the British have landed."

During those last months of 1846, Louise made a series of serious mistakes on the issue most sacred to Flaubert—literature. In his letters, he often harks back to an impetuous phrase she had uttered when they met in Mantes. As she lay in bed by his side, she had declared that she would "not exchange her present happiness for all the fame of Corneille." To prefer any terrestrial bliss to the sublime Corneille! Flaubert stormed. Worse, to mention Corneille's *fame* as the reason to envy that supreme writer! Why, Louise, to *feel oneself* Corneille, that would be a bliss far higher than any sensual perfection. Her misjudgment, he feared, pointed to a grave flaw in his lover. "I sense that you do not much adore Genius, that you do not tremble to your innards in the contemplation of the Beautiful."

A while later, Louise's possessiveness incited her to berate Gustave for speaking admiringly about a new armchair he had brought into his study at Croisset. "Is it possible that you even reproach the innocent affection I feel for this armchair?" he answered peevishly. "If I so much as mentioned my boots you would be jealous."

Louise must have reproached Gustave once too often for not allowing her to come and see him at Croisset. For five months he had been telling her that she must not violate his life's frontiers. "What would I risk? . . . It is for *your* sake that I told you not to come, for the sake of your good name, your honor. Let's not talk anymore about it."

By the end of December, Flaubert also was using the formal *vous*. "It is impossible for me to continue a correspondence that is becoming epileptic. . . . You pretend that I am treating you like a *woman of low rank*. I don't know the difference between first rank or last rank or second rank women."

As his feelings for Louise cooled, Gustave, characteristically, turned to his male buddies to get his hatchetwork done.

Maxime Du Camp was playing an increasingly important role in the running of Gustave's liaison. Initially, "Bel Ami," as Louise called Du Camp, had served as courier and goodwill ambassador, bringing her letters she did not wish her husband to see and soothing her worries concerning Flaubert's aloofness. The devious Du Camp found it useful at first to proffer a tender friendship. He called her *"chère soeur,"* "dear sister," and never ended his letters without a greeting to Louise's daughter: "A kiss to Henriette."

As tensions between Gustave and Louise grew (many of them created by Du Camp's jealousy of Louise and the malignant Paris gossip about her he doled out to Flaubert), Gustave appointed Maxime his henchman. Shortly before Christmas, Maxime wrote Louise the following advice: "He loves you, but he loves you in his way, like a good comrade. . . .

Don't despair, don't let him see your tears, never be exigent." "As you sadly put it yourself, you love him too much."

By year's end, however, Maxime began to express a coolness toward Louise. He was particularly appalled by her suggestion that the two of them set off together for a visit to Croisset. "Go to Rouen together? He would never forgive us! He'd never forgive you for going, and me for accompanying you!"

In January of 1847, Maxime tried to curb Louise's needling by suggesting that Gustave's emotions for her had become platonic. "Have the courage to hear me out: He has strong affection for you, a warm friendship, but I think that's all. . . . The *only* way to retain him a bit is to contain yourself to a friendship, to that camaraderie which you've already agreed on."

Louise was not reconciled to such a resolution. Sure that Gustave had taken up with another woman, she spied on him during a few of his unannounced trips to Paris. One night, having followed his every movement in the city, she burst into the private dining room of the Trois Frères Provençeaux restaurant, ready to kill her rival. She was met by an explosion of male laughter. Flaubert was enjoying a stag dinner with his pals Maxime Du Camp and Louis Bouilhet.

By the end of January, Louise, who was getting nowhere with her efforts to see Gustave, turned her guns directly on Du Camp. She had just heard that the two men were planning a four-month backpacking trip to Brittany the following May (four whole months with his friend, whereas in five months Gustave had granted *her* only four brief visits). Louise accused Maxime of treachery, of scheming to ruin her relationship with the man she loved.

"I didn't merit your anger or your reproaches," Maxime responded. "Since you've written me '*I shall never see or write to him again,*' why do you storm so about our trip to Brittany?"

In mid-February, Maxime wrote Louise that he was expecting Gustave in Paris, and added a cautionary note that enraged her further. "I would advise you not to try to see him on this trip: that would be the best way of healing your wounded heart. . . . If you do wish to be with Gustave a bit, it would be best not to indulge in any reproaches and to avoid all tears; on these issues he is like all men . . . he wishes above all to be amused."

It was during that particular visit to the capital—February 17, 1847—that Gustave and Louise engaged in their stormiest confrontation yet. It was so violent, in fact, that a few hours after leaving Louise, Gustave suffered one of his dreaded epileptic fits—the first in over a year.

To clarify this incident, one must return again to Flaubert's friend Ludovica Pradier.

It is evident that Flaubert had a long-lasting fascination for Ludovica, whom he knew from his earliest youth. Ludovica's tomboy sensuality, both masculine and whorelike in its total lack of commitment, beguiled Gustave as much as her bawdily humorous view of all matters sexual. Amused by Poittevin's suggestion a few years back that Ludovica might take from him "five francs out of sheer wantonness" if he bedded her, Flaubert had certainly fantasized about an affair with her. Ludovica's spell on the twenty-four-year-old was evident in letters he wrote to Poittevin during his stay in Paris in May 1845, after James Pradier had filed for divorce and Ludovica had been forced to take separate lodgings.

> I rushed to 42 Rue Laffitte [to see] this lost woman. . . . Ah, the beautiful study I made there! And how well I looked doing it! Didn't I come on like a goodhearted rake! I approved her conduct, I declared myself the champion of adultery, and I even may have startled her with my indulgence. What is certain is that she was extremely flattered by my visit, and she even asked me to lunch on my next visit. All this demands to be written up with great detail, imaged, chiseled. . . . [Note the wheels of the novelist's mind churning.]
>
> I even pity the degradation of all those folk who're up in arms against this poor woman because she opened her thighs to a penis other than the one assigned her by His Eminence the Mayor. They've taken away her children, they've taken away everything. She lives on six thousand francs in a furnished room, without a maid, in a state of misery. And upon my previous visit to her she had sparkled in salons with gilt ceilings and furniture upholstered in violet silk. . . .

To Poittevin later that month:

> I'll go and lunch again with that kind Mme Pradier, as you recommended and as I promised to do . . . but it is doubtful that I shall do any more than lunch, unless she invites me to it very openly. Fucking doesn't teach me anything new these days.

So, six months after he had begun his affair with Louise, Gustave went to Paris because his friend Félix d'Arcet, Ludovica's brother, had just died. Gustave wished to pay a visit of condolence.

An hour before Gustave planned to set off from his hotel to see the grieving family, Louise seems to have burst into his room. After a particularly vicious argument with his mistress, Gustave walked out on her and went to call on Madame d'Arcet. Here is Du Camp's account—written to Louise three days later—of the seizure that felled Flaubert that evening:

You saw him at six o'clock. He was off to the d'Arcets, he came to me at about eleven, and ten minutes after his arrival he had an attack on my bed. I don't reproach you for it, poor sister, but it was uniquely due, I'm sadly convinced, to what had taken place between you; at 3 A.M. I drove him back to his hotel. The following day, I guarded him and watched over him the whole day long, and I must admit that he did not want to go see you. At 11:30 P.M., after he had spent the evening with me, I took him back to his hotel, and he must have left either at midnight or at 6 A.M. . . . . He was evidently most troubled; his dreadful sickness worries him terribly, and he dreaded yet another crisis today.

The frenzied confrontation between Gustave and Louise was caused by Louise's instant resentment concerning the "other Louise," Ludovica Pradier. Ludovica's central role in Gustave and Louise's quarrel is clearly stated in Flaubert's next letter to Louise, written two weeks later from Croisset:

"When I reread your suspicions concerning Phidias's wife I said to myself, 'This is the living end!' How to react to such notions? If Phidias spoke of it to you himself, I'm sure he was joking. . . . I address the artist in you: This woman interests me only as the archetypal female, as a veritable orchestra of female instincts. . . . " Flaubert went on to emphasize that he had enjoyed no more than "a rather amusing familiarity" with his old friend Ludovica.

One can imagine the jealousy Louise must have felt, confronted by a rival of that mettle—the rakish, gorgeous Ludovica Pradier. It seems, however, that on this score Louise was telepathic. Flaubert's protestation, as of February 1847, that he was not "holding [Ludovica] in my arms" may have been quite true. But it would not remain true for long, as one of his several affairs with Ludovica was about to begin. How else to interpret the following comments, made a few months later in a letter from Du Camp to Flaubert?

In the visit I recently made to Pradier, he asked me very brusquely, in the middle of our conversation, "And Gustave, whom does he fuck in

Paris?" . . . I answered . . . "Eh, dear God! He's fucking a big, horsey kept woman called Madame Valory . . ." I played my part well, and the old man swallowed it hook, line, and sinker.

Flaubert's affair with Ludovica, which began in the spring of 1847, was discussed in detail in letters exchanged by Flaubert and Du Camp throughout the next year.

"I've just received a letter from Ludovica," Du Camp wrote, "it says that she can come to see you next week. . . . I'm off to see her tomorrow at noon, we'll talk about her trip to Rouen." And "Bel Ami" goes on to give some details about where Ludovica was to stay in Rouen, where she had sublet some rooms.

Another letter written by Du Camp to Flaubert, in December 1847, makes it clear that Gustave's affair with Ludovica lasted at least six months. (The two men continue to share all details of their sexual life with great candor.)

I stayed until midnight at Ludovica's yesterday . . . I asked this venerable lady if I could fuck her: She took my hands and said she was most fond of me but that she couldn't go all the way, because she was persuaded that it would hurt your feelings. . . .—I pressed her a bit, we kissed, we even did a few tongues. I saw that her body was getting the upper hand, that she was about to say "yes," and I feared that she might regret it later. . . . So I was stupid (or too loyal to you) and stopped. . . . She wept a great deal on my shoulder. . . . she . . . kept repeating all the while: "I beg you, let's not do anything; I must see Gustave before such things and discuss it with him seriously."

Maxime concluded: "I came home in despair, furious not to have 200 thousand pounds of annual income to share among the three of us."

Five months later still, Flaubert wrote Du Camp: "Guess what's presently on Ludovica's mind? She wants to eventually live right next to my 'estate,' in a little farm I would rent for her. . . . Can you imagine her on a farm and me on my nearby estate? . . . She's presently in England and not happy about her stay. Her current Englishman refuses to indulge in cunnilingus, which he finds 'shocking.' Poor Ludovica!"

Gustave's violent confrontation with Louise over Ludovica during his trip to Paris in February 1847 terrified him. He had structured his life so as to avoid his dreaded epileptic fits. The scene in that Paris hotel room put a definitive end to the first phase of their relationship: Although Flaubert and Colet would continue to write each other until the summer of 1848, they would not see each other again before Flaubert's departure for the Near East, in the fall of 1849. In fact, they would not see each other again for some four and a half years.

The limping correspondence that continued between the estranged lovers throughout the following year reveals the depth and confusion of Flaubert's feelings for Louise. How easy it would have been for him to make a clean break! By the summer of 1847, after all, Louise was finally heeding Du Camp's advice and was resigned to having all relations and correspondence cease. It was Gustave who insisted on resuming their exchange of letters, on filling them with his half-baked explanations and vague promises, only to receive her savage missives in return.

"Have you tried to forget me through silence?" Flaubert wrote to Louise from his walking tour of Brittany with Du Camp, on which Madame Flaubert followed them by coach, meeting them for the night at any town that had a decent hotel. "Give me at least a word! A word which would say, 'I do not wish to think of you, adieu.' "

What, indeed, was the nature of Flaubert's reluctance to make a final break with Louise after he settled into an affair with the undemanding Ludovica? Was it a sadistic streak that incited him to reopen Louise's wounds every three weeks, continually fretting that she had not answered his letters? Or did he miss the candor, the unfettered stream of consciousness, with which he could write to his first close woman friend?

Or might the seeds of some Bovary-type novel already be germinating in Flaubert's mind? Might he have wished to preserve a bit of Louise's passion in his desk drawer (along with her slippers, etc.), as a reservoir of inspiration for a future heroine? (A few years later, Flaubert would resume his liaison with Louise the very fortnight he started writing *Madame Bovary*.)

In the summer of 1847, Gustave having taunted her with shreds of renewed tenderness, Louise wrote to him with a barrage of sentimental grievances: The first anniversary of their meeting, July 28, had passed by, and he had neither gone to see her nor sent her flowers to mark that momentous event! (He blamed these omissions on his great current sorrow—he had just learned that his friend Poittevin was fatally ill.) Toward summer's end, responding to another letter from Gustave, Louise coaxed him to come to Paris to observe her name day, the feast of Saint Louis. (He got out of that by saying he could find no "pretext" to give his mother for absenting himself from Croisset for two days. And for the umpteenth time he reiterated that there was no question of Louise's coming to Croisset. "Patience, dear heart," he wrote her in August of 1847. "This winter I hope to go to Paris for a fortnight, then I'll invent the pretext of having to study a bit at the Bibliothèque Nationale.")

Louise's state of mind throughout these months is clearer than Gustave's. A few months after the tempest in Gustave's Paris hotel room and his ensuing seizure, she confided her frustration and sorrow to her journals. "Fatally driven to visit Phidias," she noted in the habitually terse, telegraphic style of her Mementos. ". . . The advice he offers me. Terrific common sense about the world. My heart heavy with tears of indignation and love. To forget! . . . Oh dear God, what a fate. Yet he [Flaubert] can be kind and delicate; with others!! . . . Always that bizarre flaw of his intelligence . . ."

In November (by now they hadn't seen each other for eight months), Louise seems to have rebelled at Flaubert's addressing her as "old friend"; she also renewed her campaign against Du Camp. "Du Camp!" Gustave raged in turn. "Eternally Du Camp! It's becoming chronic!" He had derided Louise's jealousy of Du Camp for several months. "That's the rule, there's no wife or mistress who likes her husband's best friend. They're afraid, they're jealous. I've known some women who were jealous of a dog, others of pipes."

He talked about a long trip to the Near East with Du Camp, which he was planning for the following year. And he reminded Louise of the error she had committed the previous year in Mantes concerning Corneille, again attacking her bourgeois conceptions of art, which she mixed "with love, patriotism, God knows what."

The chronicler of this strange romance is now rewarded by a rare treasure: one of the only three letters from Louise to Gustave that have been preserved from the Great Fire. Dated later that month, it is written in the formal *vous* and harks back to her faux pas concerning Corneille and to Flaubert's wish, stated in a frenzied moment of love, to purchase the hansom cab in which he had first seduced Louise.

"Don't you yourself have a little hyperbole on your conscience?" [Louise asked Gustave in this letter]. "Didn't you one day write me that you would like to purchase the coach in which we took our ride together? Notwithstanding the tenderness of that sentiment, wasn't it rather arcane and ridiculous? Whereas at this present moment, you wouldn't spend four cents to come see me. If anyone offered you that coach

today, what would you do with it? Nothing much more, I would guess, than logs for the fire.

Thus it is with my own hyperbole. I deny it, I renounce it, and now that I know the quality of your love I find it pretty stupid. If you were to offer me this very moment one hundred nights in Mantes in exchange for the satisfaction of having written my last play, I would answer, I prefer the play, my dear, I prefer the play. And yet, having written that very mediocre piece, I am far from thinking myself as a Corneille. . . .

You tell me very gallantly, dear courteous knight, that I occupied too much of Du Camp's time and that I ended up by tiring him. In the world in which I live, a man who has deliberately made himself the confidant of a woman feels conscience-bound to maintain a certain respect for her. . . . But it seems that in the world of students, high livers, and humbugs, things are different, and that when a woman begins to bore you—be it in matters of friendship or love—one writes her insolences and sends her packing. That has more chic.

Anyhow, the weather is gentle, tepid, and sad, and made to order for long philosophical strolls. I take advantage of it for walking a great deal and clarifying my wits. . . .

Upon this, dear friend, I cordially kiss your beautiful eyes, dazzled by all their visions of the Orient, compared to which (whenever they deign to look down upon me) I must seem like a most bourgeois and drab image.

I remain your old, faithful, and very platonic friend . . .

That moderate, only occasionally sassy letter did little to assuage Gustave. He detested being put in the company of "students, high livers, and humbugs." In his fortnightly letters of the following months he repeatedly made sarcastic attacks against Louise's dear friend Béranger ("the staple of the lower middle class, the boiled beef of contemporary poetry"). He wrote her of the enthusiasm with which he had taken up fencing again. And he went to Paris numerous times without telling Louise.

Celibacy did not suit Louise. At some point in the spring or summer of 1847, while Gustave was either diverting himself with Ludovica or walking the moors of Brittany with Du Camp, Louise took another Polish lover.

This one's first name was Franc. We do not know his last name. We know only that he was part of that large colony of Polish émigrés—exiled in Paris since the bloody antiroyalist uprisings of the previous few years in his country—who had a considerable romantic cachet among the emancipated women of Sand and Colet's generation.

We also know that Franc was younger than Louise, blond and vigorous; and that like her previous Polish lover, he lived a semiclandestine existence, always in dread of the undercover Polish royalist agents who roamed Paris in that decade. By the fall of 1847 (she would not let Flaubert know until two months before the baby's birth), Louise was pregnant by *"le Polonais Franc."*

The political mood of 1848 France was very different from the smug contentment of the first years of Louis Philippe's reign. Urban workers had been radicalized by a swiftly growing socialist movement. Liberals were increasingly angered by Louis Philippe's concessions to the conservative factions of the French parliament, which were threatening to revoke many of the liberties brought by the revolution of July 1830. The nation's most popular writers—Hugo, Michelet, Lamartine—publicly denounced the loss of progress achieved by the great revolution of 1789. In the last months of December 1847, during a particularly volatile political season, the public's loathing for the king's prime minister, Henri Guizot, created a new wave of unrest. The first phase of the 1848 revolution broke out on February 27.

On that day Louise was in the Paris suburbs, visiting France's leading actress, Rachel. Louise had had as difficult a year as any in her life. The judicial process needed to ensure her legal separation from Hippolyte was dragging on. Her friend Chateaubriand, now paralyzed, was in his last months, brought every day on a stretcher to the house of Madame Récamier, who had closed her salon for the season.

Rachel, like Louise, was pregnant. The day she went to visit her, Louise read Rachel her new play, *Madeleine*—which concerned yet another heroic woman of the 1789 revolution—in hopes that the actress might agree to star in it. Hearing of an uprising, the friends decided to take a cab into the center of Paris. The Champs Élysées was filled with insurgent troops. All traffic had been stopped and crowds throughout the city were singing the "Marseillaise." The two pregnant women walked down the street, joining in the elated chanting, hugging each other with joy.

Louise came home to find Béranger waiting for her, worried that there would be bloodshed that evening. He was right. Throughout the night, the insurgents paraded corpses through the streets of Paris to arouse the citizens, and royalist forces shot randomly into the crowds. In the following twenty-four hours, several thousand people were killed and tens of thousands wounded. Within a few days, Louis Philippe had abdicated and fled to exile in England; the Tuileries palace was sacked; the newly empowered Republican party—a centrist coalition—appointed the poet and deputy Lamartine head of a provisional government; and the national idol Victor Hugo was made mayor of a Paris district.

Flaubert had written Louise that he was coming to Paris the week of the uprising to observe the impending revolution "from the point of view of art," but she had not answered his letter. He and Bouilhet took rooms at a hotel on the Left Bank. As blood flowed in the streets, they dined in an excellent restaurant, and afterward they sat around Maxime Du Camp's fireplace listening to Bouilhet read them the first canto of his poem about ancient Rome. The next day the friends observed (from a safe distance) the sacking of the Tuileries. Then, after hearing the Second Republic proclaimed from the steps of the Hôtel-de-Ville, they returned contentedly to Rouen.

"I don't know whether the new form of government and the resultant social conditions will be favorable to art," Gustave wrote Louise from Croisset. "Certainly they can't be more bourgeois or ineffectual than the old, and I wonder whether they can be more stupid."

A few weeks after the February 1848 uprising, Louise decided, in the context of a rather circuitous letter, to notify Flaubert of her pregnancy. She did not need to tell him that the child was not his.

"Why all those roundabouts to announce *the news* to me?" he wrote back in a curiously bitter tone. "You could have broken it more directly. I shall spare you the reflections and the sentiments it caused. There would be far too much to say. I pity you. I pity you much. I have suffered for you—to put it better, I have seen through all of it. You understand, don't you? I'm addressing myself to the artist in you. Whatever happens, always count on me. Even at the time when we shall not write each other, when we shall never see each other, there will always remain a link between us that can never be dissolved. Adieu, I send you a kiss."

It was the second-to-last time Gustave would write to Louise before cutting off all communication for three years.

There is an interesting timing about this last exchange of letters and about Flaubert's decision finally to break with Louise. It reveals the continuing primacy of men's friendships in Flaubert's life, and the particular power Alfred de Poittevin wielded over him.

Poittevin had been gravely ill throughout the winter. Now that he was dying, Flaubert did not need to avenge the treachery of his friend's marriage through his liaison with Louise. Just as he had found Louise a fortnight after Poittevin's wedding, precisely where his friend had suggested he should find his first mistress, he effected his first rupture with Louise within a week or so of Poittevin's "second" death, in April of 1848.

Poittevin's actual death seems to have been less painful to Flaubert than his "first death," his marriage. Flaubert wrote to Du Camp describing the devoted manner in which he buried his friend:

> It was I who wrapped him in his shroud, I who gave him the last kiss, I who saw the coffin nailed down. I spent two long days and nights beside him, reading Kreuzer's Religions of Antiquity as I watched over him. . . .
>
> Now and then I went over to him and lifted the veil covering his face. . . . At daybreak the attendant and I began our task. I lifted him, turned him, covered him. . . . We wrapped him in a double shroud. When it was done he looked like an Egyptian mummy in its bandages, and I was filled with an indescribable sense of joy and relief on his account.

Joy and relief. The dead Alfred was far more powerful a presence to Gustave than he had been in the last two years of his married, bourgeois life. No longer separated from Gustave by his wife and child, Alfred was resurrected in Gustave's affections. And Gustave finally felt free to leave his mistress.

The spring and summer of 1848 were increasingly tormented for Louise. By May she had premonitions that some tragedy would affect her pregnancy. She began to put her papers in order as if she were preparing for death, classifying her manuscripts and all her correspondence. Leafing through the packet of letters from Benjamin Constant that Madame Récamier had given her, she decided to place them in safekeeping with her colleague and friend the poet Marceline Desbordes-Valmore.

"My nerves are at their end, I constantly weep and grow sadder," Louise wrote in a note that accompanied the carton of letters. "Courage fails me precisely when I most need it." Marceline assured her that should Louise die in childbirth, she would take the letters to Madame Récamier by hand.

In mid-June, Louise gave birth to a boy, whom she named Marcel. From the very start, the child was as frail and sickly as his doomed half-brother five years earlier. She put him to wet-nurse in the country. She felt guilty: perhaps, at the age of thirty-seven, she was too old to be a mother. She decided to move to the suburbs of the city, where the air would be healthier when the infant returned from the wet nurse. Her new apartment was close to the summer homes of Madame Récamier and Béranger, whom she saw more often than ever.

The second phase of the 1848 revolution occurred in late June and was instigated by radical factions dissatisfied with the centrist provisional government headed by Lamartine. The "Bloody June Days"—the twenty-third through the twenty-sixth of that month—were led by unemployed workers, students, and artisans. This conflict was even more violent than the February uprising and the insurgents were swiftly crushed by the new republic's national guard.

On one of the June Days, Maxime Du Camp was shot in the leg while storming the insurgents' barricades; he would be decorated for "bravery under fire." Flaubert and Bouilhet briefly joined Du Camp at the battlefront. For a few minutes Flaubert even mounted the barricades himself, hunting gun in hand. He did not shoot, and avoided all injuries. But two decades later, the incident inspired him to write, in his novel *Sentimental Education,* a brilliant and cynical depiction of the uprising.

> *The first floor of the Palais-Royal was filled with national guardsmen. There was shooting from every window; bullets whistled through the air; the fountain's water mingled with blood; one slipped in the mud on men's clothing, hats, weapons; Frederic felt something soft underfoot; it was the hand of a sergeant in a gray cape, lying facedown in the street. . . . A dog howled. It made people laugh.*

When he returned to Croisset, Flaubert went back to work on his *Temptation of Saint Anthony,* the book that had been suggested to him by Poittevin three years earlier.

Louise, usually impassioned by political events, had given birth ten days before the June Revolution; she was too ill, and too upset by her baby's poor condition, to go out of her house. A week after the insurrection, her sorrow was deepened by the death of Chateaubriand. Louise managed to rise from her bed to pay her respects to the writer at his home on the Rue du Bac. He was lying in his little white metal cot, his tawny face lit by four candles, a priest praying at his side.

Louise leaned down to cut off a lock of the great man's hair. It was a custom of the time, and in keeping with her sentimental nature. Soon afterward she sent part of this keepsake to Flaubert. She must have accompanied it with a few of her recent poems, for a month and half later, Flaubert sent her the following laconic note:

> *Thank you for the gift.*
> *Thank you for your very beautiful verses.*
> *Thank you for the memory.*
> *Yours, G.*

And that was that for a long while. Flaubert and Du Camp were preparing for their long voyage to the Near East, a journey Louise and any true Romantic would have dreamed of all their lives.

9.
The Years
Without Him:
1848–1851

❧

The winter of 1848 was difficult for Louise. She had become deeply attached to the sickly child born the previous June. "Yesterday went to see my son," she noted in a memento. "Profound joy that his smile fills me with. The face of an angel." A few weeks later, the baby died, the second child she had lost in four years. She buried him at the Cimetière Montparnasse, next to his brother, and resumed her obsessive visits to the grave site.

She was also confronting the possibility that Flaubert, preparing for his long trip to the Near East, might be lost to her.

Moreover, her relationship with her longtime protector was becoming a source of humiliation. Victor Cousin, who realized he had lost Louise's affection, had begun to doubt that he was Henriette's father. He tried to recapture Louise's affection by financial blackmail, threatening, whenever she took up with someone, to diminish the stipend he had pledged for the child's schooling.

And who *was* Henriette's father? Most probably (but not necessarily) it was Cousin. The issue has never been resolved, because Louise, herself unsure, was too honest to claim him as the father just to ensure his financial support. In her Mementos, she only once hinted at the possibility that Henriette might have been the daughter of Hippolyte Colet, writing, when Henriette was twelve years old, "My daughter's character fills me with pain; she has the envious and trifling spirit of her father" (traits more descriptive of Colet than of Cousin).

In spite of the uncertainty, Cousin's tenderness toward Louise's child never waned. "Even though she isn't my daughter, I love Henriette because she is yours," he wrote Louise, "because I saw her being born, because I felt her move in that womb which I often covered with my hands."

So Henriette enjoyed the love of two fathers and was doted on by Cousin until his death, when she was twenty-seven. She would grow into the precise opposite of Louise, a conformist, rigidly devout Catholic housewife. These traits, ironically, were fostered by her mother, who had not yet espoused anticlericalism when Henriette was young. Louise objected to any sign of normal girlish frivolity and encouraged her to be decorous and serious. In a letter to the headmistress of her daughter's boarding school, Louise expressed her wish that Henriette be brought up with the most traditional bourgeois etiquette and Catholic piety:

Madame, here is my dear little girl, whom I place in your care with the greatest trust.

My little Henriette will arrive on Wednesday with the black uniform you required and a gown of violet velvet. As soon as the weather turns warmer I will send her dresses and uniforms made of lighter muslin.

I am entrusting you, Madame, with all that is dearest in the world to me. . . . I would be most grateful if you could see to it that Henriette says her prayers both in the morning and in the evening on every one of her school days.

Since Sundays are the students' day off, I shall be sure to reserve that day to bring her home. . . .

In the late 1840s, Cousin renewed his efforts to regain Louise's affection by offers of marriage. Marceline Desbordes-Valmore kept pleading with her, in letters, to "reshape your private life, your future and your daughter's," by agreeing to marry the philosopher. If Louise could not find much happiness in a marriage with Cousin, Valmore suggested, she would at least enjoy "the proud contentment of a duty fulfilled . . . in a world so terrible for women."

But Louise remained adamantly opposed to any living arrangement that might limit her independence (the only exception was Flaubert, whom she would have followed to the ends of the earth). Continuing to send a pension for Henriette, Cousin, who retired from public life in 1849, expressed his sorrow in this melancholy letter:

> *I am no more the head of a great opposition party destined to form a new ministry; I am no more an ambassador nor a minister; I am nothing. That is the reason why I have the right to more delicate consideration. . . . I am nothing but a shadow who might be satisfied with the shadow of a friendship in the Elysian Fields of our Republic. . . .*
>
> *Let us spend a half hour or an hour together from time to time. . . . An affectionate cordiality, such will be our bond.*

In the meantime, Hippolyte Colet, who had spent the previous year living in bachelor quarters, was now very ill. The lung ailment that had plagued him for a decade—he was wasted to the bone, tormented by coughing fits—eventually came to such a critical stage that he asked his estranged wife to offer him shelter. Louise welcomed him tenderly, and she cared for him with immense devotion until the day when he died in her arms.

Louise buried Hippolyte at the Montparnasse cemetery, next to the tombs of her two infant sons. She commissioned a bas-relief medallion portrait of him for his grave. And she wrote a surprisingly tender elegy to her spouse of fifteen troubled years: "Oh! If you'd only desired it, / How fate could have smiled down upon us! / . . . You were my life's most secret love, / My heart's most sacred regrets."

In January of 1849, in part to relieve her grief over the loss of her third child, Louise had moved to yet another apartment, right across the street from Madame Récamier, who had repeatedly pleaded with her friend to move closer. This new flat was at 21 Rue de Sèvres, right off the Boulevard Raspail. Its three rooms were more spacious than any Louise had enjoyed before, and from her living room window she could see into the courtyard of Madame Récamier's dwelling in L'Abbaye-aux-Bois.

Louise painted the walls of all her rooms sky blue, her trademark color. She resettled all her family memorabilia—books and bibelots from her childhood home at Servanes, portraits of her mother and her maternal grandfather. And she delighted in her visits with Récamier, who, almost totally blind now, was in deep mourning for Chateaubriand and relied more than ever on the loyalty of a few close friends. "She wished to have me constantly at her side," Louise wrote later in a memoir. "She often told me: 'If you were only free, I would ask you to never leave me.' "

Sitting at Madame Récamier's side, Louise enjoyed studying the folder of letters from Benjamin Constant that Récamier had entrusted to her three years earlier. Louise and Juliette agreed that Constant was the most underestimated political and literary genius of his generation. Believing him to have been defamed by the Bourbon rulers, they were convinced that his reputation must be rehabilitated at all costs. Louise would suffer a great deal for acting on this conviction.

The author and statesman Benjamin Constant had been one of the most prominent figures of the Napoleonic and restoration eras. An impetuous adventurer with a particular appetite for prostitutes, he was exiled during many years of Napoleon's reign for his republican ideals. His fiction *Adolphe,* a forerunner of the twentieth-century psychological novel, was a roman à clef of his twelve-year affair with Juliette Récamier's close friend Madame de Staël.

During Récamier's romance with Constant, she kept him perpetually suspended between hope and despair, as she did with every admirer she had. Rendezvous were promised and canceled, or were kept in the presence of rivals. She alternated among moods of frivolous coquetry, sisterly compassion, and glacial coldness—and Constant responded like a puppet to all of Juliette's seduction games, frequently driven to the verge of suicide. Toward the end of his infatuation, Constant confided to friends in utter seriousness that he was attempting to conjure the devil in order to sell his soul in exchange for Juliette's body. Ever a volatile man, he announced two weeks later, with equal fervor, that he had "emerged from his delirium" and ceased to love Juliette.

During the year of his obsession, Constant wrote some sixty passionate letters to Récamier, which she considered great works of art but did not wish to have published until after her death. These were the letters she had entrusted to Louise in 1846.

Récamier had to make a difficult decision: How should she handle these expressions of lust by one of France's most distinguished and controversial men? She had given the correspondence from her other eminent friends—Madame de Staël, Chateaubriand, the entire Bonaparte family—to her niece and legal heir, Madame Lenormant. But it would have been risky to leave her Constant's letters, for Lenormant, an ultra-conservative royalist, would never acknowledge their value. If anything, she might destroy them, offended by Constant's philandering, his debt-ridden life, and his anticlericalism. Far shrewder than she ever let on,

Récamier entrusted the letters to Louise, to use in whatever manner she deemed "most fitting to Constant's memory."

In the spring of 1849, an epidemic of cholera swept through Paris, killing tens of thousands in a few weeks. Several areas of the city were totally evacuated, theaters and stores were closed, and many families fled the capital for the country. Madame Récamier left her flat, in the center of town, to seek refuge with her niece, who lived in a safer district. But this precaution came to naught. Juliette Récamier died of cholera in May.

Thus ended one of Louise's most cherished friendships, one of her only comforts during that painful year. Louise immediately wrote an introduction to the Constant correspondence and set about the task of getting it published. Acting, as usual, too impulsively (in part because she was so pressed for money), a month after Récamier's death Louise brought the correspondence to *La Presse,* one of the country's two most popular dailies. Its editor, Émile de Girardin, jumped at the offer.

On June 30, *La Presse* ran a large advertisement announcing the imminent publication of Constant's love letters to Juliette Récamier. The letters began to appear the following week, on July 3 and 4. On the third day, spellbound readers of *La Presse* were grieved to see that the correspondence was abruptly discontinued. Juliette Récamier's legal heir, Madame Lenormant, got an injunction against Girardin, putting a stop to any further publication of the Constant-Récamier correspondence, and accused Louise of fraud and forgery.

This trial concerning the love affair between two of the most legendary figures of nineteenth-century France enthralled the nation during the last week of July 1849. It became the most publicized legal happening of the year, a media extravaganza that prompted thousands of Parisians to delay their summer vacations and line up at dawn for entrance to the courthouse.

The prosecution alleged that Louise had insinuated herself into Madame Récamier's good graces for materialistic reasons and taken advantage of her near blindness to get her to sign a forged deed of donation. It suggested that it would have been against the grain of her reclusive personality for Récamier to seek such publicity, even after her death.

Louise's defense lawyer provided numerous proofs of the high esteem and affection Madame Récamier had for Louise. One of his most convincing pieces of evidence was a letter to Louise from Béranger confirming that Madame Récamier had entrusted Louise with the Constant letters:

The confidence with which [Madame Récamier] told me that she had made you this gift was equal to the trust she had in you, whose proud and independent character, whose devoted, disinterested, and recklessly generous heart, she so admired. So what a surprise to see you accused of fraud and ruse, you whose overly Mediterranean energies have led you to be exposed to precisely opposite kinds of reproaches! . . . If there is a scandalous aspect to these proceedings, it is the trial set in motion against you.

Furthermore, Louise's lawyer pleaded, if Madame Récamier was as reclusive, as averse to publicity, as the prosecution claimed her to be, would she have sat for the many portraits of her—by Canova, Gérard, David—and allowed the numerous written depictions by Chateaubriand, who had dedicated an entire chapter to her life story in his *Mémoires d'outre tombe?*

Despite their strained relations, Victor Cousin also upheld Louise during the trial. He wrote to an influential Parisian editor, urging him not to testify for the prosecution:

Poor Madame Colet . . . is as capable of fraud as I am of stealing your handkerchief. She has neither the qualities nor the faults for such skills. . . . She has an excellent heart but a poor head. . . . She is quite innocent of the baseness of which these excellent Christians accuse her.

Finally, Louise's lawyer argued, considering Madame Lenormant's indifference to literature and Madame Colet's prominence as a woman of letters, wasn't Madame Colet an eminently suited editor for these letters? "I'm not the one who claims she's a poet," the defense attorney exclaimed in one of his final arguments. "That is the opinion of Chateaubriand, Béranger, Victor Hugo, Lamartine, Alfred de Vigny, Manzoni, Silvio Pellico. . . ."

The verdict handed down after the ten-day trial was a Pyrrhic victory for both sides. Louise and Émile de Girardin were prohibited from publishing any more of Constant's correspondence and were asked to pay restitution for any damages. But Louise was acquitted of all charges of fraud and dupery. Her honor was in good part saved, though at a great cost of energy and peace of mind.

*   *   *

Prior to Récamier's death and the harrowing experience of the trial, Louise had begun enjoying the company of a new lover, Franz Noller, twelve years her junior. For a while the relationship was intense. Noller lived in a hotel on the Rue du Bac, a ten-minute walk from her flat, where Louise joined him every evening unless Henriette was home from school (she remained scrupulous about the image she presented to her daughter).

She also began a warm platonic friendship with another suitor twelve years her junior, the sculptor Hippolyte Ferrat, a fellow native of Aix, whom she met at Pradier's studio. Ferrat, a gentle fellow with a delicately chiseled face and long curly hair, remained abjectly in love with Louise for several years. But she refused him resolutely, for like most great Romantic mistresses, Louise needed to be possessed, to be dominated by a powerful man, and Ferrat's character bore a resemblance to that of his insipid namesake, Louise's unfortunate late husband; the young man was seldom mentioned in Louise's journals without his name being prefaced with the word "poor." "Poor soul, I see that he is consumed with love. Yet I can never love him, never. He does not even have the semblance of the qualities that attract me in others—force of character, independence. . . ."

So Louise maintained Ferrat as a faithful errand boy and confidant—perhaps because he was acquainted with Flaubert, who would continue to dominate her thoughts throughout their three-year separation. Ferrat faithfully told Louise everything he knew about Gustave's peregrinations.

Louise's journal entries, her Mementos, are very sparse for 1848, the year she made her first break with Flaubert. They become more frequent in 1849, when she was dreading his impending departure for the Near East. Telegraphic in rhythm, filled with unorthodox punctuation, they reflect like bits of shattered glass her turbulent emotions.

In an entry for July 1849, she deplores Gustave's silence on the third anniversary of their first meeting.

Dreadful torture of the past few days. This evening, tears and sad emotions. Dined with Ferrat, talked about Gustave. His inexplicable conduct! He came to Paris six weeks ago. Not even the memory of a friendship. Is this the fatal illness? . . . Oh sad, sad heart.

The "fatal illness" refers to Gustave's epileptic fits; he had come to Paris that summer (so Louise heard from Hippolyte Ferrat) to seek medical advice, fearing that any seizure he might suffer during his trip to Egypt would be fatal.

Another Memento, written two months later, shows Louise's continuing state of bereavement concerning her rupture with Gustave, and also with her lover of that spring, Franz Noller.

Friday, September 28, 1849. 8 A.M. I spent the night in a state of fever. I would like to die, and if it weren't for my daughter I would fulfill that desire. Nothing in the present, nothing in the past, to sustain me. Will I receive a letter from Franz? I should have gotten one six days ago! Will he be like the others? No better!

[Gustave] may leave for the Orient . . . without seeing me, without writing me! Inexplicable heart! Mine would prefer to cease beating and feeling! There's too much pain! . . . I'm suffering physically my condition is aggravated! What will become of me without friends, without counsel, without money? And yet I must go on living, for my daughter's sake! For this hope, for this despair!

She ends that journal entry by comparing women's capacity for tenderness to men's crudeness.

Men punish and carve up the most passionate, the truest, the noblest sentiments experienced by women, and among themselves they only boast of smut. What lies in store for us women in the society of the future? Who can say? The present state of things is a long martyrdom.

Later that month:

Today Ferrat told me that Gustave is about to come to Paris on his way to his long voyage to the Orient. He will leave without writing me, without seeing me again, without telling me what he has done with my letters and my souvenirs. No traces in the heart of man, while in my heart wounds never heal, and remain eternally open!

A few weeks later still:

Saturday morning, the first of the month, I read in a paper that Maxime and Gustave had embarked for Egypt. Heartbreak, reopening of the wound! What, not one word to say adieu? And now the oceans separate us.

My God, how I suffer! I wept openly in front of Ferrat, against my will, in the midst of my tears I spoke of Gustave. I am very unhappy. I would like to die. I shudder increasingly. Always alone.

Well, our dear Muse was not constantly alone. She may well have been plagued by a sense of isolation and estrangement—what self-supporting single woman was not in her time?—but she was not solitary. Her Mementos record numerous theater outings, frequent heart-to-heart talks with Béranger and with her affectionate colleague Marceline Desbordes-Valmore, meals and promenades with the attentive Ferrat and many others.

Moreover, by the fall of 1850 she was busy reopening her salon, which had been closed since the last months of her affair with Flaubert. However she complained in her journals about her solitude, Louise's salon was more crowded and popular than ever. The "Venus of the Rue de Sèvres," as she had come to be called, now received twice a week: Her Thursday salon was still dedicated to members of the Académie Française, who held their weekly reunions that day in their building on the Quai Malaquais, a ten minute walk from Louise's flat. As for her Sunday salon, it attracted a more informal and bohemian crowd—artists, poets, politicians, and journalists of progressive anti-Bonapartist bent.

A sampling of Louise's guest list:

Émile de Girardin, renowned throughout Europe as the founder of modern popular journalism.

François Mignet, from Aix, the most eminent historian of the French Revolution, who had encouraged Louise to enter her first poetry competition at the Académie Française.

Abel-François Villemain, a professor of literature and former minister of education, nicknamed Aesop because of his deformed back, who had helped Louise obtain her first Académie Française prize and had been enamored with her for over a decade. Villemain always wore the same malodorous, mud-spattered black suit and was treasured for the verve and impudence of his table talk.

Equally unkempt was the eminent physicist and astronomer Jacques Babinet, a fat, amiable drunk who stumbled up the stairs to Louise's flat to offer his latest theories on comets and planetary cooling.

Two former lovers of George Sand's were among the habitués: Eugène Pelletan, a journalist and radical activist who began his literary career as tutor to Sand's children; and the Aix-born jurist and politician Michel de Bourges, radical member of the Chamber of Deputies.

These guests were all embattled progressives fighting to save "the republic" at a particularly perilous moment in French history. Six months after the Bloody June Days of the 1848 revolution, Louis Napoleon Bonaparte, nephew of the emperor, exiled for years in Great Britain, had been elected president of the Second Republic by a landslide. His first year in office was peaceful enough, but by the end of 1850 he had begun to lose the support of both radical and monarchist deputies. His alternatives were to step down or revoke the Constitution of 1848 and stage a coup d'état (in December 1851, he would choose the latter course). Louise's salon, in those stormy years, was looked on as a hotbed of "opposition" politics struggling to safeguard the constitution won with so much bloodshed.

But there were numerous writers at Louise's salons, who cared more for art than for ideology. Among its stars:

The poet Leconte de Lisle, whose talent was discovered by Louise when he arrived in Paris in the late 1840s, poor and unknown, and who would later pioneer the Parnassian school of poetry. Louise admired de Lisle's mystical socialism and became his principal supporter, finding him publishers and stipends, helping to feed and lodge his family when they were in need.

Also seen at Louise's salon were Théophile Gautier and the prolific Alexandre Dumas. Baudelaire passed through the salon a few times, but he preferred gatherings centered on the visual arts, and perhaps Louise was too much of a bluestocking for Baudelaire's taste—"To love intelligent women," he is reported to have said, "is a homosexual's preference."

The popular painter Leon Gérôme occasionally strayed into Louise's weekly gatherings, but her old friend James Pradier was notably absent. Louise and Pradier had had several quarrels. The sculptor had sold a ring that Louise and Gustave had given him the year of their meeting; he had also used a piece of marble originally destined for a new bust of Louise to make a portrait of someone else. Louise never forgave such breaches of sentiment.

There were other interesting Parisians at Louise's Sunday gatherings who had not yet achieved notoriety, among them the two sons of Victor Hugo, Charles-Victor and François-Victor, charming playboys whom Louise invited because she idolized their father.

Antony Deschamps, often mentioned in her journals, was one of Louise's most frequent opera and theater escorts. A prominent translator of Dante, he was an archetypal Romantic devastated by *mal du siècle* melancholia, who managed to publish bits of brilliant verse between hospitalizations for bouts of depression.

Louise's favorite "walker" seemed to be Stanislas d'Arpentigny, an eccentric retired army officer in his early sixties, who dressed in gilt-braided navy uniforms and dyed his hair green to recapture his youth as a bohemian student. A popular social gadfly involved in many forms of occult lore, d'Arpentigny was the author of a widely read book entitled *Chiromancy; or, The Art of Recognizing Traits of Intelligence According to the Forms of the Hand.*

This was a sizable crowd, and since Louise was always broke, they were fed and entertained on a shoestring and sheer enthusiasm. (Victor Cousin, who may have understood Louise better than any of her other suitors, used to tease her about her "Slavic temperament.") When a large company was expected, she borrowed spoons and cups from the teachers at Henriette's school. In particularly destitute weeks, she brought her mother's silver tea sets to pawnshops on Monday and redeemed them on Saturday to set the table for Sunday's salon. Any uneaten biscuits were stored until the following weekend and reheated for the next shift of visitors. Occasionally Louise was forced to save tea leaves from one week to the next, setting them on the windowsill to dry and reusing them for the ensuing salon. At supper, she reserved the neck of the *poulet à la provençale* for herself, pretending it was her favorite part.

What about the women who attended these gatherings? They were relatively few, and Louise seldom mentions them in her journals. On both sides of the English Channel, the late-Romantic epoch was a sexually competitive era, which seemed to discourage female friendships as passionate as Germaine de Staël and Juliette Récamier's, or Mary Wollstonecraft and Fanny Blood's. Just as George Sand was reluctant to include Louise among her intimates, so Louise seemed hesitant to invite women of beauty and talent to her home.

In the 1840s and early 1850s, one can cite only three women, beyond the much-missed Madame Récamier, who became close friends of Louise's and habitués of her salon: the literary socialites Aglaë Didier and Edma Roger des Genettes (who would play an important role in the second phase of Louise's affair with Flaubert); and the poet Marceline Desbordes-Valmore, twenty-four years Louise's senior and a close friend of Juliette Récamier's.

Desbordes-Valmore, a woman of minimal education who had supported herself as an itinerant actress throughout her orphaned youth, was an uncommon phenomenon in French letters. She was the only nineteenth-century woman author whom contemporary male critics—the severe Sainte-Beuve and even extreme misogynists such as Baudelaire and Barbey d'Aurevilly—unanimously acclaimed as a great writer. Desbordes-Valmore achieved this distinction because unlike Colet, Sand, d'Agoult, and an entire generation of threatening bluestockings, she had no pretensions to intellectual gifts and restricted herself to what critics called "properly female emotions"—chaste lamentations of unrequited love, paeans to childhood, and religious exultations.

Throughout their correspondence, which began in the mid-1840s and was the most extensive Louise would share with a woman, Marceline defended and admired Louise's impetuosity. She called her "a pure terrifying tempest" and concluded that Louise's "expansive Mediterranean character is neither understood nor forgiven in this conventional [Paris] world, which strikes fear into my heart." "So good, so maternal, and such a good poet, how many reasons there are to love you," she told her friend. She dedicated to Louise these honeyed verses, which are among her most famous:

La Beauté, n'est-ce pas? c'est le bonheur, Madame;
Aussi vous en avez plein les yeux et plein l'âme;
Et sous vos cheveux blonds, si j'ai surpris des pleurs,
C'est qu'il faut, n'est-ce pas? quelque rosée aux fleurs.*

Marceline gave Louise emotional support at the time of the trial over the Constant-Récamier correspondence: "To see you pursued by such ignorant enemies at the moment when your life is being undone by your mourning the death of that beloved friend [Récamier] and other loved ones," she wrote Louise, "this has so pained me . . . that I have been running a fever for four days." The depth of Desbordes-Valmore's esteem and affection for Louise is beautifully summed up by the following phrase: "I wish I could share my heart with the entire world in order that you be better judged."

So that was another tender friendship which allayed Louise's solitude during her years without Flaubert. But *philia* and *caritas* never satisfied Louise if she was not enjoying equally large doses of *eros*. And one cannot

---

*Isn't Beauty the greatest happiness, Madame?
That is what fills your eyes and your soul.
And if I've discerned tears under your blond hair—
Don't flowers need occasional dew?

grasp Louise's character without knowing the extent of her dependence on romantic passion.

Like Germaine de Staël and George Sand, like the fictional Emma Bovary she inspired, Louise felt most fulfilled when she was in the thrall of exalted infatuation. That was the price she paid for taking Romanticism too seriously. Among the hackneyed clichés of the movement that Louise had ingested lock, stock, and barrel was that of the Passionate Mistress who looks on love as the most sublime source of suffering and redemption. But her Romanticism was more problematic than Sand's or de Staël's, because she remained far more bourgeois than they were, and was a docile consumer of Romantic stereotypes of rhetoric and behavior: the only true love is "forever"; no birthday or feast day should go by without the swain bringing flowers or candy; it is improper to leave the country without making a former lover an official good-bye visit.

Louise castigated not only Gustave but each of her lovers for months after an affair had ceased. "In the park, I thought only of Franz, of the letters he wrote me!" she noted in an 1850 entry in her Mementos. "I see again his little hotel room, the hotel courtyard where we used to dine! . . . And I met him again eight days ago . . . and he walked by me like a stranger! . . . What spirits, dear God!"

All this mourning for a lost lover in the very weeks when she was enjoying a liaison with a man she probably loved more than any other after Flaubert.

Désiré Bancel was another habitué of her salon, and again he was twelve years her junior. A radical member of the Chamber of Deputies, Bancel was a leader of the faction opposing President Bonaparte's increasingly conservative policies, which had already repealed the laws for universal male suffrage passed in 1848 and restricted freedom of the press. Bancel was one of the most fiery orators of the opposition party. And he had begun the affair with Louise with expressions of suitably high-flown romantic sentiments.

"It is impossible for me to leave this damned Assembly," Bancel wrote Louise on one of the numerous occasions when he had to cancel a rendezvous for reasons of state. "So . . . my Nereid as white as milk and as sprightly as a bird, think of me and save me your heart and your lips until tomorrow. I love you against all fate and I kiss your transparent teeth."

But Bancel was an ambitious young man consumed by political duties. He often postponed meetings with Louise or else forgot them altogether, or he paid her surprise visits and left just as abruptly. This volatile behav-

ior readily incited Louise to long angry letters; and her affair with Bancel
is particularly well documented because she often copied the first drafts
of these invectives into her Mementos. "Oh how well you understood
what my heart needs!" she writes Bancel after he has pledged her his
"fraternal devotion and faithful friendship."

> *How preferable such sentiments are to love! Love, among you men, is
> doled out to all kinds of women, while affection, which your heart
> reserves for me, is accorded only to those you esteem and admire. I'm
> so proud of inspiring you with it.*
>
> *Seeing the potentially fatal illness* which you have suffered and
> which might recur, it's honest of you to wish only for my friendship!*
>
> *I haven't wanted to wait for your visit, which your innumerable
> duties and pleasures might force you to postpone, to write you. I shall
> drop off this letter at the Chamber of Deputies, where I am heading
> later. Yes, I'm committing this folly, against the doctor's advice. . . . It
> is true that I have just had a serious accident which kept me in bed for
> three weeks. The lover remained indifferent to my suffering, but the
> brother would have been moved.*

Louise was evidently pregnant by Bancel and had suffered a dangerous
miscarriage. Wryly refusing Bancel's offers of fraternal friendship, the
letter ends on a note of feminist militancy.

> *If ever the struggle becomes grandiose and bloody I wish to partake of
> it, I wish to unite all women, all mothers, all these sisters in pain and
> misery, and make them understand what must be said, what must be
> done, what must be demanded! . . . To keep them from eternally re-
> maining machines for pleasure and for the reproduction of the species!
> Until then I shall steep myself in solitude and meditation.*

In a far brasher letter she sent Bancel some days later, Louise intimated
again that she had been pregnant with his child and miscarried (letters
from friends reveal that Louise was indeed critically ill in the first half of
1850):

> *. . . three months ago, in the very room in which I write you, you swore
> that you had no other liaison, that you found in me the ideal of your*

---

* The illness Louise refers to seems to be a venereal disease.

dreams, adesso e sempre, etc. . . . yet fifteen days later, when you left me dying, perhaps pregnant! . . . you told me that the true motive of your cowardly and brutal rupture with me was caused not by illness but by the return of a woman whom you had not seen for two years and who might not even love you!

Bancel may have wavered between two excuses for breaking with Louise—the clap and another woman—and gotten trapped in the web of his inventions.

But you lied to me [the infuriated Louise continues]. The real motive of your breaking was an illness that you doubtless incurred with prostitutes during those very weeks you were in my arms! Yes, now I'm convinced of it, you changed none of your habitual lusts during our short relationship. I served as no more than an interlude to your orgies and doubtless an object of derision and wagers between you and your friends!

(That is another recurring dread of such pioneers of sexual liberation, catching the feared disease—indeed, one wonders how the sexually liberated "New Women" of Louise's generation did not contract syphilis more often.)

Hear me out and let this remain engraved in your memory: You don't know what kind of soul you have mortally wounded. . . . Between us now, it is man to man. . . . So be it, I pledge my life to the furies!

Intimating (rather outlandishly) that Bancel's coarse behavior could come only from a man of conservative ideology, Louise accused Bancel of being a political fake.

She struck her lover's vulnerability there. In plaintive tones, Bancel denied Louise's accusations that he was a closet reactionary. He claimed to be dedicating himself day and night to fighting against pending legislation that would "violate the sovereignty of the people and mutilate the Republic."

Louise answered him the very same evening. On such occasions she could turn into a fury.

You are a wretch. . . . You came to sully my life, you treated me like a whore, you constantly lied to me while swearing false oaths on the

Republic. . . . I repeat, between us it's now man to man . . . what do any
sacred issues matter to a socialist hack? You exclusively value your
little lusts, orgasms, well-being, while smashing all else underfoot. . . .
Spare me your painful phrases; your bastard heart does not compre-
hend the simplest indignation.

Since only three of her missives to Flaubert have survived—relatively
tame ones—these letters to Bancel are the only documents left that show
Louise in the full wrath of jealousy and spurned love and give us an in-
kling of the rages that must have confronted Flaubert during the stormier
phases of their affair.

The imposed chastity that followed Bancel's defection lasted only a
few months. By the end of August 1850, Louise allowed one of the guests
at her Sunday salon to stay behind after the others left. Octave Lacroix
was a handsome and erudite young poet seventeen years—no surprise—
her junior. He earned his living as Sainte-Beuve's secretary and had been
a habitué of Louise's salon for several seasons.

This time Louise had to wallow in an overabundance of sentiment.
Lacroix was the direct opposite of Bancel, as fervent and attentive as
lovers come, bringing Louise statuettes of Charlotte Corday as birthday
presents, showering her with his love sonnets and letters: "My poor heart
is full of you, Madame; I carry you there with respect and adoration, like
the highest religion of my youth, like my life's most serene glory. . . . "

At first Louise tried to resist this torrent of love. Here's the record of
her change of mind.

[Memento, August 29, 1850] I answered him on Monday, I told him I
could not love him. I told him that the memory of another filled my
heart. Torture of my solitude. He comes the evening of Wednesday the
14th, his profound sadness . . . what does glory matter to him if I do
not love him, he asks me. I abandon myself to his kisses . . . to him.
Astonishing surprise of his power. Daily passion and assiduous-
ness. . . .

Louise wanted lyric effusions of love? Lacroix's exaltations approached delirium. "I would like to be a poet, a great poet, to have you
for my Laura or my Beatrice, to have become illustrious through you, to
climb on your wings while clasping you to my heart." His passion became

alarming: "Only I would tell you this: Come flee with me, let us go die together wherever you wish, we would die within our love."

Always terrified of solitude, Louise did not dare break with Lacroix until the end of the year, when she would offer him merely sisterly affection. Another lover had entered her life, a Lyons-born lawyer named Auguste Vetter, only eleven years her junior. She was receptive to his advances but, prizing her freedom, denied him a deeper commitment.

Do I love Auguste? It is friendship rather than love. He has a noble character. . . . But his suggestion that we live together: impossible! Living together! . . . In truth, I rather like isolation, work, the company of my daughter, and frequent gatherings with a few sympathetic friends.

As adamantly as she had always refused a penny of support from Cousin beyond his pittance for her daughter's schooling, Louise remained steadfast about maintaining her independence. Moreover, in the first months of 1851 she became haunted by the possibility that Flaubert might be returning from his long journey. In her last two Mementos before Gustave reentered her life, she mourned the loved ones she had lost in recent years.

Sad and somber day. . . . At one o'clock left with Ferrat to go to the cemetery, stopped off at my daughter's school on the way to give her a kiss. . . . Standing before the tomb of Madame Récamier. Profound sadness before Hippolyte's grave. Dejection. Here is the end of so many vain agitations, heartfelt passions. All of us one day shall be cadavers in these narrow boxes.

Coming out of this sad earth flowered by our putrefied remains . . . went to the Sorbonne. [Cousin] is in his bed, sick, touched by my visit (some eye ailment).

Poor philosopher! Although he had temporarily ceased his offers of marriage, the loyal Cousin still fought to be part of her life. "You returned from Madame Valmore on foot at ten P.M. in horrible weather last night," he wrote her in early 1851. "That is pure folly. Next time, I shall force you to go home with me in a carriage; we shall gently talk by your fire for an hour; then I shall serve as your chambermaid; I shall put you to bed, alas without me in it, and after having tenderly kissed you good night I shall let you sleep. . . ."

"Renascent passion of the Philosopher, his transports," Louise noted in her Mementos.

But nothing could have interested her less than the devotion of this faithful famous man. There was only one emotion devouring her: "Sometime in the near future," she noted in her Mementos, "I shall go to Rouen to reclaim my letters and take news of Gustave."

Some weeks later, she wrote in a Memento:

Saturday May 31 1851: There are spring nights when I would like to clasp with one single embrace all those I have loved, for my love for all of them was genuine, and it would never have ceased if they had wished.

Will Gustave come? Here is the letter I wrote him!

Louise interrupted that journal entry to copy the draft of a letter she wrote Flaubert in mid-May, as he was heading back to France, via Italy, from the Near East.

Eighteen months ago [it began], I learned that you had gone through Paris to make that long voyage to the Orient which you had planned for such a long time. My heart ached at the thought that you did not think to shake my hand at the moment when you were leaving France, perhaps never to return. . . .

What I ask of you [it ended], and I wait for it with trust, as if you had sworn it on your honor, is the following: when you come through Paris, I ask you to see me, whatever the month, the day, the hour, to see me for an instant. . . . I desire this last meeting, the last of our lives; you will not refuse it. You will see that it will be gentle and calm and that it will also do you good.

I have your promise, don't I? I shall wait with certainty. . . . Understand me.

Louise was taking an immense gamble by resuming her correspondence with Flaubert. But this time it would serve her well.

10.

Flaubert in Egypt, and Back

❧❧❧

As they sat in their boat on the upper reaches of the Nile on the morning of March 6, 1850, Flaubert and Maxime Du Camp were approached by a young woman veiled in blue, who started shouting to them in Arabic. Their interpreter explained that she was a messenger from one of the area's most famous dancers and courtesans, Kuchuk Hanem, who was inviting the foreign gentlemen to pay her a call.

The very mention of Kuchuk Hanem would later lead to many disputes between Flaubert and Louise Colet. The woman belonged to a class of prostitutes called in Arabic *almeh,* whose vocation was decided for them in earliest adolescence by their parents. In Egyptian etymology, the word *almeh* also denoted "pendantic, learned woman," a fact that Flaubert, ever ready with a misogynous joke, would repeat with gusto to his male friends for many years.

Flaubert and Du Camp accepted the almeh's invitation, and that very afternoon their guide took them to Kuchuk Hanem's home, a few blocks behind the town mosque.

As they opened the door into a courtyard, they saw a vision that would haunt Flaubert for much of his life. Outlined against the blinding blue of the sky, Kuchuk Hanem was standing at the top of the stairs, her tall, superb body glimmering under a sheath of rose and violet gauze, her naked feet shod in yellow babouches. Her curly black hair was braided with ropes of gleaming sequins; great golden bracelets hugged her neck, her slender ankles and wrists; dazzlingly white teeth sparkled under her delicate lips as she spoke her unintelligible welcome.

With many a salaam, Kuchuk Hanem ushered her visitors into a large white room and bade them sit on pillows on the floor. The travelers, their heads covered with Arabic tarboosh hats, sat cross-legged, according to local custom. The woman poured rose-petal water on their hands and, after some ritual ablutions, made a few languorous signs, which Flaubert and Du Camp correctly interpreted as an erotic invitation. Du Camp rose from his pillow. *"Buono!"* exclaimed the hostess (the only European word known by most Egyptians at the time). She took Maxime into her bedroom, where they spent a half hour. When they returned, Flaubert rose and stretched out his hand to Kuchuk Hanem, and she took him in turn to her bed. Flaubert lay down on her reed-woven mat, still warm from his friend's body, and focused his attention on the large, firm breasts, unctuous with rose oil, of the hospitable almeh.

Afterward, Flaubert's tarboosh set on her head teasingly, Kuchuk Hanem performed some marvelous dances, which recalled to Flaubert "the painting on ancient Greek vases." She continued to tease the travelers as she accompanied them back into town, jesting playfully about the foreigners' skulls, which they had shaved, in the manner of the country, to avoid lice. They promised to come back later.

They returned that night after a visit to a moonlit temple. Kuchuk Hanem was waiting for them in her living room, with glasses of raki. The room was lit by dozens of little golden-hued oil lamps. There was more dancing, with four of her young attendants, and lascivious simultaneous embraces with both men. At about ten P.M. Flaubert asked his hostess if he could spend the night with her. *Buono!* She was delighted. Flaubert described the night in one of his weekly letters to the friend he had left in France, Louis Bouilhet.

That night we returned to Kuchuk Hanem's: there were four women dancers and singers—almehs. (The word almeh *means "learned woman," "bluestocking," or "whore"—which proves, Monsieur, that in all countries women of letters . . . ! ! !) . . .*

When it was time to leave I didn't leave. . . .

I sucked her furiously—her body was covered with sweat—she was tired after dancing—she was cold—I covered her with my pelisse, and she fell asleep with her fingers in mine. As for me, I scarcely shut my eyes. Watching that beautiful creature asleep (she snored, her head against my arm: I had slipped my forefinger under her necklace), my night was one long, infinitely intense reverie. . . . At three o'clock I got up to piss in the street—the stars were shining. The sky was clear and immensely distant. The fucks were good—the third especially was ferocious, and the last tender—we told each other many sweet things— toward the end there was something sad and loving in the way we embraced.

. . . In my absorption in all those things, mon pauvre vieux, you never ceased to be present.

From the beginning of his stay in Egypt, Flaubert had been informing Bouilhet of his erotic experiences with members of both sexes. One of his early letters from Cairo enlightened Bouilhet on some local customs.

Speaking of bardashes, male whores, this is what I know about them. It is quite accepted here. One admits one's sodomy, and at the hotel one speaks of it openly at table. Sometimes you do a bit of denying, and then everybody teases you and you end up confessing. Traveling as we are for educational purposes, and charged with a mission by the government, we have considered it our duty to indulge in this form of ejaculation. So far the occasion has not presented itself. We continue to seek it, however. It's at the baths that such things take place. You reserve the bath for yourself (five francs including masseurs, pipe, coffee, sheet, and towel), and you skewer your lad in one of the rooms. Be informed, furthermore, that all the bath boys are bardashes, male whores. . . . The day before yesterday, my bath boy was rubbing me gently, and when he came to the noble parts he lifted up my balls to clean them, then continuing to rub my chest with his left hand he began to pull with his right on my cock, and as he drew it up and down he leaned over my shoulder and said "baksheesh, baksheesh." He was a man in his fifties, ignoble, disgusting—imagine the effect, and the word "baksheesh, baksheesh." I pushed him away a little, saying, "lah, lah" ("no, no")—he thought I was angry and took on a craven look— then I gave him a few pats on the shoulder, saying, "lah, lah" again but more gently—he smiled a smile that meant, "You're not fooling me— you like it as much as anybody, but today you've decided against it for

some reason." I laughed aloud like a dirty old man, and the shadowy
vault of the bath echoed with the sound.

Getting to the Near East—an obsession of all nineteenth-century literati—had not been easy for Flaubert. He had desired the trip especially
because of his chagrin over the disastrous failure of *The Temptation of*
Saint Anthony, which he had researched during the years of his liaison
with Louise and written after they separated. The friends to whom he had
read it aloud—Bouilhet and Du Camp—had been critical of the work's
overwrought romanticism. The reading at Croisset had lasted four days—
noon to four P.M., eight P.M. to midnight.

The night of the last reading, after he had finished, Flaubert had struck
his fist on the table and loudly said, "Up to the three of us now—tell me
frankly what you think." "We think," Bouilhet replied, "that it has to be
thrown into the fire and never mentioned again." Flaubert leaped out of
his chair with a cry of pain. His friends went on to say that the book was
drowned in bombastic metaphors, pompous rhetoric, incessant digressions into obscure religious heresies . . . The critique lasted until eight A.M.

After a few hours' sleep, Du Camp and Bouilhet were sitting in the
garden, trying to cheer Flaubert. Instead of continuing to exploit high-
flown medieval themes, Bouilhet suggested to his friend, why don't you
write about a very modest, prosaic event of contemporary life? He cited
a story recently published in the Rouen newspapers about a woman
named Delphine Delamare, the adulterous wife of a local country doctor,
a former student of Dr. Flaubert's, who was said to have committed suicide after running up scandalous debts. "Why not write her story?"
Bouilhet said.

"What a fine idea!" Flaubert responded, looking up joyfully.

The Delamare saga seems to have lain dormant in the young writer's
consciousness for the following year, and the trip to the Near East provided a perfect gestation for it. A few weeks after their arrival in Egypt,
Flaubert and Du Camp spent a night in a small hostelry run by a Frenchman named Bouvaret. Some months later, as they were standing at the
second cataract of the Nile, Flaubert exclaimed to Du Camp: "Eureka!
I've found it! I'll call her Emma Bovary!" And he repeated the word
"Bovary" many times with delight.

Du Camp, already a seasoned traveler to the Near East, had long been
planning this voyage for himself. In past years he had taken pity on Flaubert for his provincial seclusion, his illnesses, his longing to visit exotic

places. Moreover, doctors had recommended that the best cure for Flaubert's recurrent seizures would be a sojourn in hot dry climates. But formidable obstacles had been set by Madame Flaubert, who had surreptitiously come to visit Du Camp at eight o'clock one morning and told him that there were many countries "as hot as Egypt, Nubia, Palestine, Persia, and Asia Minor" that might prove less fatiguing to Gustave. She had asked him to confine their trip to a year's stay on the island of Madeira. "The climate is beautiful, and I shall not be tormented." Du Camp firmly held his own, saying their decision was irrevocable. Madame Flaubert left in great anger and never spoke to Du Camp again.

The maternal veto overcome, Flaubert spent many months making the extensive preparations this kind of trip then required. On November 15, 1849, the travelers landed in Alexandria, and a few weeks later they reached Cairo. In February 1850, in the company of Du Camp's faithful Corsican manservant, they boarded the large flat-bottom boat on which they were to remain for six months and from which they made their memorable visit to Kuchuk Hanem. It is from that boat that Flaubert wrote his salacious letters to Bouilhet.

When we returned to Beni Suef we found a whore in a wretched hut so low that you have to crawl on all fours to get in. You can only stay in it lying down, or crouching. You fuck there on a straw mat, between four little walls of Nile mud mounded under bunches of reeds, in the light of a lamp set into the filthy wall.

At Isna I came five times in one day and sucked three, and let me add that I enjoyed it.

Some weeks later, between Girga and Asyût:

At Qena I had a beautiful whore who liked me very much and told me in sign language that I had beautiful eyes. . . . And there was another fat pig on top of whom I enjoyed myself immensely and who stank of rancid butter.

In the same twenty-page letter to Bouilhet, more share-gals-with-pals banter about conquests back home:

When you go to Paris, go and see . . . [Ludovica Pradier], 2 Rue de la Paix. You'll give her my news and you'll have a tryst with the hostess. It will be pleasurable for you, and for me. She's a lovely lay. . . .

A few pages on, what seems to be evidence of Flaubert's homosexual experimentation:

You ask me whether I consummated that piece of work in the baths. Yes, I did. It was with a big young guy covered with smallpox marks who wore an enormous white turban. It made me laugh, that's about it. But I'll do it again. In order for an experience to be real, it has to be repeated.

Jean-Paul Sartre has wondered whether Flaubert truly "consummated" anything with this young man in the baths or with the several other males mentioned in Flaubert's Egyptian letters. He does not believe any of this homosexual banter is for real. He sees it as a continuation of the buddies' macho posing, a sophisticated traveler wanting to impress a provincial stay-at-home with his exotica (there was Bouilhet, marinating in dreary Rouen, panting over his friend's letters). But opinions on this passage vary wildly among Flaubertists.

There were many chaste letters to Flaubert's mother, of course, describing the decor of French consuls' homes in various Egyptian cities, the hue of flowers and the tints of skies in different countries—and his horror of the institution of marriage, always reiterating his intense love for Maman.

Marriage, for me, would be an apostasy which terrifies me. . . . When I think of your good sad loving face, of the pleasure I have in living with you, I know that I'll never love another woman as I've loved you, go on, have no fears, you'll never have a rival.

From Constantinople, in the fall of 1850, Flaubert wrote Bouilhet about the onset of his syphilis:

I must tell you, my dear sir, that I picked up in Beirut (I discovered them at Rhodes, land of the dragon) seven skin chancres, which eventually combined to form two, then one. I traveled in that condition from Marmaris to Smyrna on horseback. Each night and morning I dressed my poor prick. Finally it healed. In two more days the scar will have closed. I am madly taking care of myself. I suspect a Maronite—or was it a little Turk?—of having given me this present. Was it the Turkish lass? The Christian one? Which of the two? Problème! Food for thought!!!

In the environs of the gulf of Cos, Maxime shot his wad with a child (female) who barely knew what it was about. It was a little girl, approximately twelve, thirteen years old. He jacked off with the child's hands grasping his cock.

Six months after leaving France, Flaubert wound his way back to Paris via Italy. His niece Caroline was now six years old. His friend Louis Bouilhet had settled into a sedate ménage in Rouen with a working-class woman and her illegitimate child. The nation lived in dread of President Louis Napoleon's staging a coup d'état and reinstating a monarchy. And Louise Colet was waiting for Flaubert's arrival.

❦

On Monday, June 16, 1851, Louise received definitive news that Gustave had returned. Her journal entry for that day: "After dinner, Ferrat comes; he tells me that Gustave is back. He has known it for three days. Stupidity and meanness. I write this morning."

In this Memento, Louise mentions that she went to the hotel where Gustave usually stayed during his trips to Paris and asked if he was still there. She learned that he had just left with his mother for Rouen.

The news must have affected Louise deeply, for she was particularly restless that afternoon. She dropped in on her friend Ferrat and her former lover Bancel, and since neither of them was home, she continued on to the flat of yet another former lover, Franz Noller.

Then she went back to her flat, where she found some music that her current suitor, Auguste Vetter, had brought her. "I'm very depressed," she commented in a Memento that evening. "Not one person who attracts me or who loves me, on whom I can lean. The Philosopher sent me some strawberries. . . . Always the same uptight miser. What sad company he would be."

And then the journal entry abruptly stops; into the same page, Louise copied the first draft of another letter to Flaubert.

Wednesday morning.

Life is very short, its vanities and raptures too transient, to be that forgetful of what we all owe each other. Since things have reached this stage, since . . . you have resolved to never see me again, my letters and all that might remind you of me must be odious. Please assemble them, all my letters, and send them back to me.

I shall give the packet of your letters to whatever messenger you send. When I was so ill, 18 months ago, I prepared it in order for it to be sent to you if I died. Oh! What I'm doing today is very sad! I waited five years, I would have waited forever, if only you had come to shake my hand.

I bear you no harsh feelings.

This letter remains unsigned, and it is more than probable that Louise never sent it. Even if she had, she was about to take a far greater gamble: A fortnight later, she traveled to Croisset and finally attempted to cross its long-forbidden threshold.

Louise had spent a painful night sorting out her correspondence: her letters to Hippolyte as a young girl, those of their separation, Cousin's love letters, and finally Gustave's, over which she wept bitterly. "He loved me," she wrote in her Memento that night in one of those rare moments when she fully admitted her own mistakes. "It was my fault. Or rather that of my character. . . . I suffered too much, I was irritated, I exaggerated everything, I didn't have the adequate skills and shrewdness to charm him. . . ."

The next morning, the letters spread about her like faded blossoms, Louise made her decision. She was going to Croisset. She was going to decide her own destiny instead of waiting for men to do it for her. She would make Gustave welcome her, and she would recapture his love.

On Thursday, June 23, 1851, Louise boarded the train for Rouen, the same train she used to take to her rendezvous with Gustave in Mantes. Before reaching her hotel room in Rouen, she dashed off a note to him: "It is absolutely essential for me to see you. . . . You told me in your first letter of 1846: 'Remember this oath and recall it to me in ten years if I forget it, I don't know what will happen to our love but whatever happens, count on me.' So here I am, receive me as a friend with a good smile. L."

Afterward, she tried to dine, freshened up, and took a cab to the boat landing for the ten-minute trip along the Seine to Croisset. At her first glimpse of Gustave's house, her pain became nearly intolerable.

Croisset, parts of which remain unchanged to this day, is a charming English-style estate leaning against a steep hill, surrounded by a green lawn and flowered parterres, separated from the Seine by an iron grille and a narrow road. Louise lands a few hundred yards from the residence and walks toward its iron gate, which is partially open. What calm, freshness, and opulence! She enters the tiny farmhouse that adjoins the gate. Two women are sitting there, one of them holding a little girl, who must be Flaubert's niece Caroline. Louise hands them her note and asks to have it taken to Monsieur Flaubert. She waits in the courtyard, surrounded by cackling hens. It is six-thirty P.M.

The woman returns and tells her that Monsieur Flaubert cannot receive her, that he will write her. Louise thinks that Gustave may not even have read her note before giving that answer. A few minutes later, a chambermaid comes down from the house and repeats the message more precisely: "Monsieur is at table with foreign guests. He asks madame her address in Rouen; he will go to see her there."

Louise answers that she is leaving Rouen that very evening and that she merely wishes to speak to Monsieur Flaubert for a moment. The maid returns: "Monsieur will join madame at eight o'clock if madame will give her address; it's impossible for monsieur to receive madame here." Louise, devastated that she is again denied the right to enter Gustave's sanctuary, says all right, she will leave.

She looks with despair at this house, which her imagination has so often filled with people, furniture, flowers, from which Gustave has written her such beautiful, loving letters. She at least wishes to take one last look at this building that will remain forever locked to her. She paces up and down the riverbank in front of the iron gate, staring at the open windows of the white house, at the dining room, where several people appear to be having their supper.

As she starts walking to the boat landing, the gate of the farmyard opens. It is Gustave, much transformed. Fatter, balder, sporting a long, pendulous mustache, he is dressed like some Chinaman in flowing pants, a gauze shirt, a gold-filigreed silk cravat. "He looked more like a seal than like a Viking," Louise noted in the lengthy Memento that records this encounter. His eyes no longer have the nervous tic they used to, or the tenderness.

She goes toward him, stretches out her hand. "What do you wish from me, madame?" he asks.

"I have to speak to you."

"It is impossible to do so here."

"So you chase me away. Would my visit dishonor your gracious mother?"

"That's not it. It's impossible."

"Ah, monsieur, if you or any of your kin were to come to me, all my doors would be open."

"Madame, I shall rejoin you in Rouen by steamboat, at eight P.M. Is that all right with you?"

"What's the use?"

"Yes or no, do you wish to see me?"

"So be it," she says. She walks toward the riverbank. He disappears back into his house.

Overwhelmed, Louise sits in the boat, looking silently at the flowing river, at Croisset disappearing in the distance. The humiliation of women in love! The boat moves very slowly. She is nervous; the boatman tells her they might not get to Rouen ahead of the eight o'clock steamer. But as they approach the shore, Louise sees Gustave disembarking at the crowded landing. He looks for her, sees her, comes forward, offers her his arm. He seems moved. They cut through the dense crowd on the main boulevard and go into Louise's hotel.

Once in her room, he sits down. "What do you wish of me?"

"If your heart is as closed to me as your door is, why should I tell you what's in mine?"

Flaubert scolds Louise for going to his house and asking for him. If he did not receive her, it's because the house is not his, but his mother's. So strange a visit might have taken his mother off guard; Louise might not have been received in a manner worthy of her. That's what has always troubled him most, these impulsive gestures of hers. . . .

She answers, "But this is so essential, so serious, that I didn't hesitate to take this trip, if only to see you for a few minutes."

"A friend is listening to you," Gustave says pensively. "You can talk."

Louise tells Gustave about her worries concerning her daughter's future and Victor Cousin's renewed courtship. She admits her liaison with Auguste Vetter (she does not tell him about Franz Noller, or Bancel, or Lacroix).

"Marry Cousin," Gustave tells her.

"But there's only one fate I wish for," she says. "To live in some little village near you, to bring up my daughter there and be at your disposal whenever you wish to see me. That would be my only happiness, if you loved me."

"Marry the philosopher," he repeats.

She kisses his hands, weeping. It would be wrong for him to lie to her, he says. He can do nothing for her happiness; he isn't attracted to her or to any woman. He has total self-mastery, he adds; he can readily go for years without making love; during his trip to Egypt he met those almehs; it was beautiful, exciting, but since Louise, he hasn't loved anyone. . . .

Louise continues to weep. She confesses her own past mistakes, blames them on her fierce desire, a desire aroused by his letters. Gustave listens to her attentively, brings the candle nearer her face to see her better. Finally, he clutches her hands and kisses them. She tries to smile through her tears. Will he give in? No, he controls himself again.

"So I'll never be in your arms again," she whispers.

"Marry the philosopher," he repeats, with a laugh, "and we'll see each other again."

So that's it, Louise thinks. . . . Once she is married, there will be less risk of his bourgeois existence being disturbed, and when desire returns to him he can just go and fire his shots, as the men put it. . . . Gustave is thirty years old, she is forty-one, but as usual she feels far, far younger than he. He is always the one who acts like an old man.

It is ten-thirty. Gustave speaks of going home. Louise gives him her new play to read, *Madeleine.* He will bring it back when he comes to see her this summer, he says, but it's useless for her to write him. When he rises from his chair, she bursts into tears, kisses him with passion. He returns her kiss, but with coolness.

Outside, Louise accompanies Gustave for several blocks. She tries to be gay, to joke. He stops three times, with the words "This is where we must say good-bye." Each time she gains a few more yards, saying, "Wait until the next lamppost." The night is resplendent, the stars are shining, the air is summer-fragrant. She gives him one final kiss, the most passionate one; he hugs her briefly to him. And says, *Au revoir.*

Louise returns slowly to her hotel through Rouen's deserted streets.

For some months Louise had been planning a trip to London to visit the first Great International Exhibition, which had opened that spring. She was also hoping to sell the album of autographs on which she had lavished her savings, those same autographs Béranger and Cousin had so opposed her spending money on. The trip was a considerable expense for her, and she had to borrow funds from a sympathetic cousin in Aix. She left in the first week of July with Henriette, now eleven years old, and took a room in the most modest hotel she could find. It was Louise's first trip to Great Britain, but she had fluent English—she had taught it to herself as a young woman in Provence.

Louise took her daughter to see all the sights of London. "Queen Victoria is very ugly, her husband is very seductive, Windsor is admirable, Westminster mediocre," she wrote a friend in Paris. "Saint Paul caricatures the Pantheon the way British fashion caricatures ours. . . . The abundant glitter of British women's outrageous style drives me to paroxysms of laughter. . . . Henriette is faring splendidly and is much admired."

Louise had a few acquaintances in London: her friend Teresa Guiccioli, who had been Byron's lover and also Hippolyte Colet's, and was now married to a Marquis de Boissy; the Italian revolutionary leader Giuseppe Mazzini, living in exile there; and some Hungarian revolutionaries. She even managed a one-night stand with yet another exiled Polish patriot, a young sculptor referred to in her journals as "the Pole from London," who would come to visit her in Paris.

Louise had no luck selling the autograph album. She returned to Paris, her finances in desperate straits. At the end of August she barely had ten francs left—far less than a domestic servant or a factory worker lived on for a week—to buy food for herself and her child. And she could not expect the quarterly payment on her government pension until October. What could the future hold for a destitute widow; how to avert the malicious gossip to which single women were exposed? Marry the philosopher, Gustave had advised her. Indeed, Cousin had once more offered her "a perennial arrangement" whereby they would live under the same roof; but however it might assure her survival, the idea continued to repel her.

When she returned to Paris, Louise hoped to hear from Gustave, wondering whether he would keep his word.

And indeed, a few days after her return, four weeks after their meeting in Rouen, a letter from Gustave arrived.

July 26 [1851]

I write you because "my heart prompts me to speak to you kindly," pauvre amie. If I could make you happy, I would do so with joy: it would be only fair. The thought that I have made you suffer so much weighs on me heavily: you know that, don't you? . . .

You must have found me very cold the other day in Rouen. But I was as warm as I possibly could be. I made every effort to be kind. Tender, no: that would have been dishonorable, hypocritical, an insult to your sincerity. . . .

I wish you were in such a state that we could see each other calmly. I love your company when it is not tempestuous. The storms one so enjoys in youth are tiring in maturity. . . . I am growing very old; every jolt upsets me, and feeling is as repugnant to me as action.

I will see you soon in Paris, if you are there. . . .

Farewell. God bless you, poor child.

That last line was written in English. Unlike Louise, Flaubert had little command of the language, but he liked to show off the little he knew.

Exultant, Louise decided to wait patiently for Gustave's next move. Sure enough, within a week she received another note, announcing that he was coming to Paris for a week in the first days of September and wished to see her.

The morning of his arrival, as if drawn by one lodestone, several of her lovers of the past few years almost simultaneously converged upon her. Here is her Memento for that curious day.

Singular conjunction . . . I was planning to spend a delirious day with Gustave. Upon waking, I receive a letter from Octave [Lacroix]. As I was going out to take my daughter to her boarding school the Pole from London arrived. Returning from school, loaded with groceries for Gustave's dinner, I bumped into the Pole Christian; hardly had I come home than I received a note from the Philosopher, proposing an excursion. Finally, Gustave arrives, handsome, charming. We go for a stroll in the Bois, we dine together at my house, etc. . . . Sadness follows; I do not feel loved in the way I love him.

The "etc." is telling. It seems to mark the resumption of what we delicately call "relations." So does the letter Gustave sent Louise two weeks later, upon his beginning to write the most famous French novel of the nineteenth century, *Madame Bovary*.

[September 20, 1851]
Chère amie,
. . . Last night I began my novel. Now I foresee difficulties of style, and they terrify me. It is no small thing to be simple. I'm afraid of becoming a kind of Chateaubriand-ized Balzac. . . .
And you? How are you?
. . . Adieu, chère Louise; I kiss your white neck. A long kiss.

The cannibal writer has chosen Louise to be his mistress again, needing her as Muse.

For the next three years, Louise will again be Flaubert's "good, beautiful and dear Louise," his "dear dove" and "dear love," his "dear good Muse," "dear well-beloved Muse," "good Musette." "My darling poet," he will call her, and "my good Muse, dear colleague of every kind." In Louise's more irate moments she will again be Flaubert's "dear volcano," his "tempestuous one," "dear savage," "untamable savage," his "dear old ferocious one." In passages that must have particularly delighted Louise, she will occasionally be his "dear spouse" and even his "legitimate and fatal spouse."

Louise was about to have the happiest two years of her life.

11.
Amor Nel Cor

❧

Louise Colet was truly Flaubert's muse and a midwife for his Emma Bovary. It is to her that the hermit of Croisset chronicled, in over a hundred letters, the progress of his first published novel: It is exclusively to Louise that he wrote his famous reflections about the craft of literature—prophetic passages that would become the most familiar credos of twentieth-century modernism.

Gustave to Louise, three months after they had resumed their affair: "What I should like to write is a book about nothing, a book dependent on nothing external, which would be held together by the internal strength of its style. . . . From the standpoint of pure Art, one might even establish the axiom that there is no such thing as subject—style in itself being an absolute manner of seeing things."

In another letter, he wrote: "The author in his work must be like God in the universe, everywhere present and nowhere visible. Art being a second nature, the creator of that nature must behave similarly [to God]: In all its atoms, in all its aspects, let there be sensed an infinite and hidden impassibility."

Other reflections to Louise that are strikingly precursive of postmodernism in all the arts (Thomas Mann would emulate them closely in his novel *Doctor Faustus*):

"The time for beauty is over. Mankind may return to it, but it has no use for it at present. The more Art develops, the more scientific it will be, just as science will become more artistic. Separated in their early stages, the two will become one when both reach their culmination."

Equally prophetic were Flaubert's meditations to Louise on the modern artist's alienation from a philistine public: "Between the crowd and ourselves—literati, scribblers—no bond exists. . . . [We must] climb up our ivory tower and there, like an aloof princess with her perfumes, dwell alone with our dreams."

In other letters to Louise, Gustave revealed insights into the fundamentals of good writing that would become precious to aspiring writers: "A good prose sentence should be like a good line of verse, *unchangeable*, equally rhythmic and sonorous." "I conceive of a style . . . that someone will invent someday, ten years or ten centuries from now, that would be as rhythmic as verse, precise as the language of the sciences, undulant, deep-voiced as a cello, tipped with flame. . . . Always keep in mind that prose was born yesterday, verse is the form par excellence of ancient literature."

Flaubert's maxims on the impersonality of all good art, the need to purge it of sentiment, were often in response to his distaste for the confessionalism of Louise Colet's writings.

"Exhalations of the soul, lyricism, do not make for style. . . . A curse on all those who talk to you of their lost loves, their mothers' tombs, their blessed memories . . . who weep at the moon, wax tenderly effusive at the sight of children, assume a pensive air before the ocean. Jokers, jokers and triple mountebanks, jumping on the springboards of their heart to reach to gibberish!"

Artists have admonished each other with another precept Flaubert expounded to Louise: "This ought to be a practical dogma in the artist's life . . . live like a bourgeois and think like a demigod."

Only Flaubert's letters to Louise reveal the extraordinarily slow, laborious process in which this master wrote his fiction. ("Only half a page this week!" "Only three pages in one month!") Thanks to his trust in her, we can see the process of *Madame Bovary*'s gestation—the precise dates at which he wrote certain crucial scenes, which chapters caused him most anguish and which led to writer's block. One such crisis occurred as he was writing the episode in which Emma, just arrived at the Yonville inn, exchanges Romantic platitudes with her future lover, the clerk Léon:

"What trouble my *Bovary* is giving me! Never in my life have I written anything more difficult than what I am doing now—trivial dialogue. This one inn scene will perhaps take me three months, I can't tell. There are moments when I want to weep, I feel so powerless. . . . I have to portray, simultaneously and in the same conversation . . . five or six characters . . . and the entire town, giving physical descriptions of people and objects; and in the midst of all that I have to show a man and a woman who are beginning (through a similarity in tastes) to be a little taken with each other."

Throughout this phase of their correspondence, from 1851 to 1854, Flaubert so often sought Louise's advice on details that her daughter and literary executor, Henriette Colet Bissieu, would later demand (somewhat preposterously) that her mother's collaboration in *Madame Bovary* be officially acknowledged.

"For two days now I have been trying to enter into the dreams of young girls," Flaubert wrote Louise shortly before one of their reunions in Mantes, "and for this I have been navigating the milky oceans of books about castles and troubadours in white-plumed velvet hats. Remind me to speak to you about this. You can give me the exact details I need." (Louise had doubtless told him that she developed her Romantic fantasies while in her teens, from the novels passed on to her by her grandmother Révoil in Lyons. In *Madame Bovary,* the adolescent Emma's delusions about life and love are created by the same kinds of books, passed on to her by an aging laundress at her convent.)

But the current of literary inspiration flowed both ways. It was during this calmest phase of her liaison with Gustave that Louise wrote most prolifically. It was also during these years with her rather reactionary lover that her writings revealed a new level of political commitment.

Louise's first major achievement, in the period that followed her reunion with Flaubert, was the long poem "La Colonie de Mettray." The theme of Mettray—a pioneering new French penal colony, which aimed to reform young convicts instead of merely punishing them and where the writer Jean Genet would spend time a century later—had first been assigned by the Académie Française in 1851; the Académie having decided to postpone its awards, it was again the theme in 1852. Louise submitted her entry to both contests anonymously. Victor Hugo, a member of the Académie's literary jury the first time round, was certain that Louise's poem was written by a man. He praised "this youth's extraordinary talents" and pleaded with his colleagues that it receive the award.

By 1852 the theme had become more timely than ever. In December of the preceding year, Prince Louis Napoleon (officially President Bonaparte) had staged a coup d'état and revoked the constitution earned by much bloodshed in 1848. Protests erupted throughout the nation, with several hundred people killed and over twenty thousand arrested. Victor Hugo was banished from France a few days after the coup for taking part in the insurrection, and after several months in Belgium would spend the next eighteen years in exile on the British Channel islands of Jersey and Guernsey. Louise Colet herself was grazed by a bullet as she stood at a barricade in Montmartre, shouting her rage against Bonaparte. Despite considerable backing from the middle classes, Bonaparte was facing powerful opposition from the liberal citizenry. He was determined to regain their support, and the humanitarian theme of Mettray was well suited to this particular goal.

Louise's poem urged society to take pity rather than revenge upon its younger criminals. It upheld the model of the Working Christ as a way of salvation and compared the two Frenchmen who had pioneered the colony to Saint Vincent de Paul, who had put convicts' manacles on his own wrists. In a politically volatile season, this message was very bold. Many may have been surprised to learn that the winner of the 1852 Académie contest on the penal colony of Mettray was again Madame Louise Colet!

In recognition of her newest triumph, she was crowned with the laurel wreath at a festive ceremony attended by her daughter, the two of them in identical dresses made by Louise for the occasion. The audience included many of her lovers and admirers, past and present: Octave Lacroix; Victor Cousin, rejected but ever faithful, who had told Henriette "your Maman will win again." The audience even included Flaubert and his friend Louis Bouilhet, who had come to Paris for the occasion. After the festivities, the two lovers went out for dinner with Bouilhet.

The poetry prize offered the "Goddess of the Romantics," as Louise had also come to be called, another precious reward—the warm friendship of the exiled Victor Hugo, known throughout France as "Olympio." Upon learning that Hugo had supported her poem during the preceding year's competition, Louise had sent him a letter of gratitude and a poem, and received the following letter from the island of Jersey:

Do you realize, Madame, that your verses are perhaps the most beautiful to ever have been composed by a poet's soul and a woman's heart? Do you realize that you have sent this convict the most magnificent of consolations—glory? . . . I kneel in gratitude to have received this exile from the hands of Providence and this crown from your hands.

When shall we ever meet, Madame? . . . Soon, I hope. Probably in France, for Louis Bonaparte must be punished. Or perhaps in Jersey, for you merit being exiled. Upon that day, you will allow me to shake your hand like a man's and to kiss your feet as I would an angel's.

Although Hugo had never met Louise, he knew her by reputation as a gifted bard and a celebrated beauty, and she soon became one of his favorite correspondents. She relieved his solitude by sending him long accounts of Parisian political and literary events, and gave him news of his friends. At considerable risk to her own freedom, she eventually served as his principal "mail drop" in France and distributed some of his most inflammatory pamphlets, such as *Le Petit Napoléon.*

Louise Colet's next major work was a vast epic entitled *Le Poème de la femme* which expressed her growing feminism. It was dedicated to the precept, much contested, that women at every level of society were victimized by men's injustice; and each of its sections was to depict a different class of women—"The Peasant Girl," "The Servant," "The Nun," "The Bourgeoise," and "The Woman Artist."

Flaubert and Bouilhet, who rejected Romantic ideals and opposed all "sociopolitical" literature, were appalled by the notion of Louise's writing a poem cycle dedicated to women. But when Louise confided the plan of the epic to Béranger and to her new friend Victor Hugo, the only men in the French literary establishment to support the emancipation of women, both were enthusiastic. "Put men to shame," Hugo encouraged Louise. "Show them the strength, the grandeur, the energy, the resolve that accompany your grace and beauty. . . . While they vote, and prostitute themselves, and crawl in the mud, fly above them, singing in higher spheres."

The first poem in the cycle, "La Paysanne," set during the Napoleonic War, is hackneyed in its familiar Romantic themes of frustrated passion and belated epiphanies. But its bleak condemnation of aristocratic corruption makes it one of Colet's more powerful works. The marriage of its star-crossed lovers—the peasant girl Jeanneton and the rural nobleman Jean—is thwarted by Jean's parents, who arrange to have their son called into the army. Early in the conflict, Jean is presumed dead. Jeanneton gives birth to their child, who dies in infancy. Forced by the village priest to marry a brutal local drunk who has raped her, she dies after decades spent as an impoverished farmhand, sustained solely by the memory of her great love. Meanwhile Jean, who had been abandoned in Russia during Napoleon's invasion, returns to his native village. Now an aging beggar, he earns a few pennies digging graves. One day, while digging up the ground in the local cemetery, he comes upon a woman's skeleton that bears the locket he once gave Jeanneton. Jean dies happy, knowing that she was true to his memory.

Hugo praised "La Paysanne" as "virile without ever ceasing to be feminine," called its ending "the most painful and finest blend I know of idyll and of elegy," and committed entire passages of it to heart. Even the skeptical Flaubert declared "La Paysanne" to be "a work of genius" that was informed by "virile mettle" (the highest compliment doled out to women writers of Louise's generation); he read it to his mother, who reportedly was moved to tears.

The poem's feminist sympathies, however, made it hard to market: Louise had to hawk it for a year before it found a publisher. It was a commercial failure, severely panned by Louise's perennial antagonists in the critics' pantheon, Théophile Gautier and Sainte-Beuve, whom she had alienated a decade before with her brashness. She also had an enemy in her former supporter and salon habitué Abel-François Villemain, dean of France's literary historians. The influential Villemain, who had been fruitlessly in love with Louise for over a decade, had recently abandoned his protégée after she called him *"vile canaille,"* "vile cad," rebuking one of his bolder amorous advances with a blow that had sent him reeling to the floor.

As a result of this failure, Louise again found herself in financial straits. Her health was poor that season; she was suffering from severe stomach pains and vomiting. Louise was forced to borrow eight hundred francs from Flaubert, a considerable embarrassment to her that would eventually strain their relations. She had to resort to potboilers and to children's literature, for which she had a gift. Contemporary readers might find them among the most delightful of her works.

One such venture was *Enfances célèbres,* "Famous Childhoods." This excellent example of children's writing offers a dozen geniuses of art, literature, and politics as models for French youth, presenting early turning points in great men's lives that provided the "Eureka" of their vocations. Eight-year-old Filippo Lippi's gift for drawing is recognized by a band of wealthy brigands, who free the child's captive family in return for one of his drawings and persuade Filippo's grateful father to apprentice his son to the great Masaccio. Young Benjamin Franklin, sitting despondently on a beach after he has been disowned by his family for printing seditious pamphlets, receives his inspiration for the invention of the lightning rod by watching a storm over the ocean.

Pascal, Linnaeus, Mozart, Rameau, Pico della Mirandola, and a half dozen other great men are chronicled. *Enfances célèbres,* published by Hachette, went through twelve editions and stayed in print well into the twentieth century, gaining Louise more readers than any other work.

In addition to children's books and her long verse epics on historical and political themes, between 1851 and 1854 Louise published collections of short poems, such as *Ce qui est dans le coeur des femmes,* "What Women's Hearts Reveal." Drawing, as did most Romantic poetry, on personal experience, this volume celebrated her troubled youth among the classical antiquities of Provence, and the superiority of love to art, a sentiment clearly aimed at Flaubert's ivory-tower aestheticism: "You tell me that art is worthier than love, / that all sentiments must one day perish . . . I answer: The poet's song / distorts all sentiment . . . / Love is our only grandeur!"

These poems again drew the ire of Paris's literary critics. This "collection of sensualist verses under a title which engages not only herself but her entire sex," so one powerful critic pronounced, "this totally materialistic exaltation, this poem of the human body, all this is false poetry. . . ."

Throughout these years of material difficulty and of critical hostility, Louise's epistolary friendship with the exiled Victor Hugo proved to be a major solace.

Over the previous two decades, Hugo had become far more than France's most admired literary personality. "Olympio" was also looked on as the chief standard-bearer of the country's democratic ideals, the father figure to whom liberal citizens turned when the nation's civil liberties were threatened. Such a moment had come on December 2, 1851, when President Bonaparte, unable to reach an agreement with a factious parliament, staged his long-expected coup d'état and put an end to the Second Republic.

Hugo had instantly joined the street fighting that erupted in protest against the coup, and the very next day a warrant was issued for his arrest. With fiery speeches delivered in the most dangerous public places, he incited all Parisian citizens to take up arms. He only escaped arrest, or death under fire, through the devotion and shrewdness of his mistress of many years, Juliette Drouet, who deceived sentries, gave spies false clues, and found Hugo secret hiding places. But nine days after the conflict had erupted, Hugo, Drouet, and members of his family decided that for the sake of his survival he must flee the country.

After some months in Belgium (Adèle Hugo, Hugo's wife, spent most of this time in Paris to run family affairs), Hugo and Juliette Drouet decided to move to Jersey. Here, and later on Guernsey, bleak islands where they remained eighteen years, Hugo wrote some of his greatest masterpieces—*La Légende des siècles, Les Misérables, Les Travailleurs de la mer.*

But however productive his exile, Hugo was known to be wretchedly lonely. All his official mail was opened by the French police; he was starved for uncensored news of home and eager to enlarge the small network of committed friends who forwarded clandestine mail. It was after she had received his response to her letter of thanks concerning the Académie prize that Louise volunteered her services as one of Hugo's "mail drops."

Eventually she sought the help of Flaubert, even though he remained as apolitical as he had been in 1848, when he observed the revolution from Paris's best restaurant. At first reluctant, Flaubert was swayed by the adulation he had had for Hugo in his youth and agreed to help. Louise and Gustave devised stratagems to evade state censors: The "Crocodile," or "le Suprême Alligator," as Flaubert referred to Hugo in an early instance of Franglais, was to send his mail to London, to a former governess of Flaubert's dead sister, Caroline. The Londoner placed each letter in a new envelope and addressed it to Gustave, who sent it on to Louise in Paris. Louise, in turn, readdressed Hugo's letters to his various correspondents in France. The system worked equally well in reverse, with Hugo's friends sending letters to Louise, who sent them on to Gustave, who sent them on to London.

The Colet-Hugo correspondence, some 240 pages, conveys the depth of Louise's political commitment and the liveliness of her epistolary style. Throughout her missives to Hugo, their mutual nemesis Louis Napoleon Bonaparte, who in 1853 crowned himself Napoleon III and created the Second Empire, is referred to as "that man."

. . . How can we even make our voices heard? Not one newspaper, not one publisher, has stood up for freedom of speech! The Church and the police keep us enchained in double bondage. . . . Meanwhile our youth smokes its time away, keeps company with call girls, and forgets that there is a motherland and a French literature. . . . And that man

enjoys his horrible triumph; while those of pure, elevated, spirit remain in deep suffering.

The "Suprême Alligator" begged Louise for more such letters, "long, beautiful, noble, powerful pages. . . . Continue to be the proud, great, indignant woman you have been. In the midst of such men, your attitude is the honor of your gender and suffices to console all honest souls." There is much tenderness and gallantry in Hugo's greetings. "Has God created an artifact more ravishing than you? I open your poem, it is a ray of light. I receive your letter, it is a bouquet."

Eager to console Hugo, Louise often cheered him with news of his growing circle of fans.

I have just spent some days with two young writers, Mr. Bouilhet . . . and Mr. Gustave Flaubert, a young man of genius who is destined to be one of our greatest prose writers. Well, here are two noble young men, proud, independent, passionate lovers of art, who would gladly give up their life for your glory; they look upon you as the first and finest in-carnation of our France. . . . They touch your letters with respect and read them in tears; and their cult for you is important, for as you will someday see, their names will be famous; they truly have genius.

As for Flaubert, his initial wariness of the clandestine correspondence with Hugo soon turned into solicitude. He fretted much about the safe arrival of Hugo's letters from England, informing Hugo when envelopes were torn and handwriting exposed. He fussed to Louise about achieving just the proper tone in his own letters to "le Suprême Alligator." "He has afforded me so many fine hours of enthusiasm, given me so many splendid erections . . . that it was hard for me to strike a balance between constraint and adulation." Flaubert sent Olympio "all my admiration for your genius, the assurance of my entire devotion to your person."

There is an amusing sidelight to Flaubert's correspondence with Hugo. Although Flaubert treasured the memory of having met the famous writer at the Pradiers' when he was studying law in Paris, Hugo, understandably, did not remember the obscure young provincial, and for the first months he thought that "Gustave Flaubert" was just another pen name for the famous poet Louise Colet.

Louise and Gustave's complicity in support of Hugo was one of the many aspects of their liaison that gave it a novel peace. For the next two years, until the end of 1853, there is a tone of marital felicity in Gustave's letters to his mistress and confidante; compared to the tempests of their previous correspondence, reading these exchanges is like sailing on a calm lake on the sunniest evening of the year.

Both lovers, after all, had learned a few lessons. Louise was honest enough to regret her past impatience and tactlessness, her fits of temper. She also had grown more skeptical about love. Curiously, she seems to have become less physically passionate and was frequently frigid with Flaubert. "I had no pleasure with him, I had tenderness," she recorded in her Mementos a few months after they resumed their liaison.

As for Gustave, his trip to the Near East had made him feel more secure in his vocation and untied a few of his mother's apron strings. He was no longer the fearful schoolboy who had to look for excuses in order to go to Paris. He now came to visit Louise, if not as frequently as she wished, at least every month, and for longer stays.

The confidences he shared with her concerning his progress on *Madame Bovary* made her indispensable to him. There is a mood of delectation in his letters reached only by novelists who have found a way to shuttle between their real and fictional egos, to heal the painful division between life and art. Louise provided that vehicle: She was Flaubert's principal contact with reality, his warrior's repose from the continual conflict with words, a dynamic presence—both erotic and sisterly—that reenergized him.

Flaubert had set conditions for Louise's behavior: "I love your company when it is not tempestuous." And for a while Louise struggled valiantly and successfully in keeping her temper and moderating her demands. Her self-control may have been helped by the fact that a painful thorn had been removed from her side: Gustave's friendship with Maxime Du Camp had foundered after their Egyptian trip.

Since returning, Du Camp had become publisher of the distinguished literary magazine *Revue de Paris* and was writing Flaubert graphic letters describing his trysts with the beautiful, mid-fortyish Valentine Delessert ("I'm fucking the woman of advanced age with much pleasure"). In a letter sent soon after their return, Du Camp sharply derided Flaubert's lifestyle at his family home in Croisset.

"Your present way of living," he wrote Gustave, "thrusts you right back—feet and hands tied—into your mother's hands." No comrade had ever been so blunt with Gustave; Du Camp was striking at Flaubert's central obsession, challenging the elaborate tactics of seclusion that he had evolved years earlier to protect himself from epileptic seizures.

If he were to lead Du Camp's kind of "passionate, intriguing [Parisian] life," Gustave retorted in an angry letter, he would become "a man like any other." "Why do I preach chastity? Why do I stay mired in my provincial swamp? Don't you think I get as many erections as the next man? . . . [I live as I do] because I am simply not destined to remain a beautiful waltzer. . . . You talk about the 'breath of life' you enjoy in Paris. I think it rather smells of rotting teeth. . . . The laurels one plucks there are covered with shit."

Many other actions of "Bel Ami" were proving that Louise's former accusations of Maxime's deviousness were well founded. Visiting Louise on many an evening after she had resumed her liaison with Flaubert, Du Camp attempted once more to destroy their relationship. He told her that Gustave was "weak and cowardly," that there was "nothing worthwhile in [Gustave's] heart or his intelligence," that he had "no literary future." Having pretended to Gustave that he was enchanted by the outline of *Madame Bovary,* he predicted to Louise that it would be "a tremendous fiasco." It is a sign of Louise's new self-control that she never breathed a word to Flaubert about Du Camp's treacheries. She allowed her lover to come to his own conclusions; and a few months after their return, Flaubert himself was referring to Du Camp as "a triumph of dementia and vanity."

The result of this falling-out was that the timid, reclusive Bouilhet (nicknamed "Monseigneur") now replaced the cocky Du Camp as buddy number one in Flaubert's life. Bouilhet, too, would eventually betray Louise out of jealousy over his cherished Flaubert, but he would be slower about it. The harmony between Louise and Flaubert would last far longer in the second phase of their relationship—two years, this time, rather than four months.

And so in the fall of 1851, as the formal *vous* that marked the resumption of the Colet-Flaubert correspondence was again replaced by the familiar *tu,* Eros returned fully winged to Gustave's letters: "I kiss your breasts and your mouth," "a thousand kisses on your lips," "I kiss those beautiful eyes of yours, which I've so often caused to cry," "a necklace of kisses all about your neck," "I kiss you from the soles of your feet to the top of your hair." "My flesh loves yours, and when I look at myself naked every pore of my skin yearns after you," "I kiss you in every part of your heart and soul," "I kiss you, you old savage who remain in a constant state of inebriation." (He means the spiritual kind: Louise never touched a drop of spirits, a matter of some concern to Flaubert, who loved his wine and thought her habit of drinking plain water extremely unhealthy.)

There were many sexier endearments as well: "To you, all on you and in you." "I hope to soon be at your side and *on* your sides." "I kiss you on all your lips. . . . I place my finger in a secret place . . . which is full of your being, and go to sleep on your image, sending you a thousand kisses." And always, "I kiss you everywhere."

Some of Flaubert's warmest words to his mistress were now tinged with contrition: "To you who love me the way a tree loves the wind, to you for whom my heart is moved by long, gentle feelings, by emotions of gratitude which will never perish, to you, poor woman whom I've so often caused to weep and whom I'd so wish to bring gaiety, to you, good soul who tends to the leper even though the leper needs no tending and is often angered by it."

And more! "It's to you that my thoughts turn when I have completed the cycle of my musings; I lie down upon you as a tired traveler would lie on the grassy side of the field that adjoins his road. I think of you when I wake, and your image at daybreak is entwined with the phrases I search for."

How grateful Flaubert was for Louise's keen insights into the workings of his talent! He let her read his early failures—*Novembre,* written while he suffered through law school; *The Temptation of Saint Anthony,* so brutally attacked by Bouilhet and Du Camp; and the first draft of *Sentimental Education,* written when he was nineteen, which had received equally negative notices from Poittevin and Bouilhet. With marksman accuracy, Louise told Flaubert that *Novembre* did not have any great potential and that the book on Saint Anthony might be hard to rework into a marketable book, but that it "proved his genius." She reserved her highest praise for his *Sentimental Education,* which, in her view, revealed him as "a great artist." (It may have been due to Louise's encouragement that years later Flaubert worked hard on revising *Sentimental Education,* which to many literary historians is a greater work than *Madame Bovary* and the first truly modernist novel.)

Notwithstanding the serenity of her relations with Flaubert, Louise still suffered her share of torments and jealousies. One night, when she was expecting Flaubert for one of their Paris trysts, Louise felt certain that he was being unfaithful to her, back in Croisset, with the British governess of little Caroline. She dressed herself in black velvet and hid a knife in her bed, determined to kill the philandering villain. (Shades of her favorite heroines—Lady Macbeth, Charlotte Corday, Lucrezia Borgia? Of her melodrama with Alphonse Karr? But this time it was not a kitchen knife; it was the most ornate, elegant utensil she could find.)

These histrionics had been triggered by Flaubert's mere mention in a letter that "the new governess arrived ten days ago," even though he indicated that the young woman's physique did not impress him and that he had never felt "less venereal."

"Horrible night of Sunday to Monday," Louise confided in a Memento the morning after she had conceived the plot of knifing Gustave to death, "obsessed with the idea of killing him rather than knowing that he has gone on to another woman. . . . The most sinister projects went through my head. . . . Attired in a velvet dress; the knife. Finally at 9 P.M. he rings the doorbell. I try to compose myself. . . ."

After a few caresses, Flaubert seems totally to have dispelled Louise's suspicions. He returned to her bed the next night, and the next, and the next. They spent one of their most delightful weeks together, and that entire season remained unmarred by any of Louise's former faux pas or outbursts. She recorded in a journal entry:

> *"Oh my good Louise," he said, "if you knew how I continually thank God for your existence!" We embraced. . . . He was more passionate than ever, he told me that he has never loved me more.*

So they had to worry about the British Redcoats again and exulted at each of their "landings." Flaubert reiterated his terror of begetting life:

> *I begin with devouring you with kisses, I'm so happy. Your letter of this morning lifted a terrible weight from my heart. Yesterday I could not work all day. . . . I was feverish and completely despondent; once or twice I actually saw stars before my eyes. The idea of bringing someone into this world fills me with horror. I would curse myself if I were to become a father. A son! Oh, no, no, no! May my flesh perish utterly! May I never transmit to anyone the boredom and the ignominies of existence! My soul rebelled against this possibility. . . . Well, now there is nothing to fear, thank God. Blessed be the Redcoats. . . . May the god of coitus grant that I never again go through such agony.*

One should emphasize that this time round, Louise truly earned all of Gustave's endearments. Never had she been more tactful and delicate. Her most diplomatic move, in her reconquest of Flaubert, was to ingratiate herself with the man who would remain Flaubert's closest friend to the end of his life, the colleague he called his "alter ego," his "left testicle"—Louis Bouilhet. Since the cooling of Flaubert's friendship with Maxime Du Camp, Bouilhet had begun to spend every weekend at Croisset, engaging in meticulous line-by-line editing of the pages (or page) Flaubert had written that week of *Madame Bovary.*

During Flaubert's absence in the Near East, Bouilhet, whose aspirations to literature were as serious as his friend's and who earned his living teaching classics in a Rouen lycée, had written a very long poem, *Maelanis,* set in ancient times. Its visual details were much inspired by Flaubert's letters from Egypt, and Flaubert, who was often blinded by his love for Bouilhet, considered it a work of genius. But it was as hard for a poet to break out of provincial obscurity and publish his work in the nineteenth century as it is now. The essential first step toward recognition was to have one's work read in a prominent Paris salon to a select group of intellectuals, which is precisely what Louise set out to do when she "launched" Bouilhet by holding a party in his honor at one of her weekly salons.

To this special occasion Louise invited the most influential literati she knew. She was careful to include her friend Edma Roger des Genettes, who within the year would become Bouilhet's mistress. Edma, known as "Sylphide" for her narrow waist, was a prominent literary hostess and was noted for her great talent as a reader of contemporary verse.

At the time of this special occasion, Louise was as always struggling to make ends meet. To accommodate the unusually large crowd, she borrowed plates and spoons from the headmistress of Henriette's school. She discarded the dried tea leaves carefully recycled for a month of salons and bought enough for a fresh brew. She talked the best *patissier* of the Rue de Sèvres into giving her credit for an assortment of petits fours, and the merchant on the Rue de Grenelle for a few bottles of wine. (She stated proudly in her Mementos about the evening: "My careful *toilette,* notwithstanding my suffering, my *recherché* dinner, notwithstanding my penury.")

As her guests arrived, Louise was totally self-effacing, focusing the limelight exclusively on the two handsome young provincial visitors, Bouilhet and Flaubert, who were still quite unknown to her Parisian guests. After refreshments had been served, Bouilhet, on Louise's cue, handed her his poem. The hostess passed the manuscript to Edma des Genettes, who read from it for an hour with emotion and eloquence.

The poem was a great success with the guests, who announced they would praise it to all their literary acquaintances. The poet, congratulated by all, was smitten with his reader, the shapely thirty-four-year-old Edma. In all respects, the evening went off like a dream.

"The next day Gustave talked happily with me about that evening," so

Louise recorded the evening's aftermath in a Memento. "He thanked me, kissed me, he loves me; I think he can no longer do without me, as I cannot do without him. We are at a level where we should understand one another, and we are alone enough to feel that we are necessary to each other. . . . "

Flaubert's gratitude for Louise's generosity to his friend made it as happy a week as they would ever share in Paris. This most demanding of women ("No letter from Gustave for three days in a row!" she sometimes fumed in her journal) was more satisfied than ever with her lover.

His arrival at half past two, our reading my poems and those of Mme Valmore, his telling me the outline of his novel Bovaris *[sic]; our embraces, his passion, his tender words, our dinner at Restaurant Durand on the Place de la Madeleine, our return to all our old haunts of years ago! . . . Our two hours of delirium. . . . I found his handkerchief in my bed! And he left me his Egyptian ring!*

(When Louise does not have "the Brits"—occasions that seem to heighten her lover's physical ardor—Gustave apparently continues his former habit of ejaculating into his handkerchief as a measure of birth control and leaves it in Louise's bed as a keepsake.)

Flaubert reiterated his gratitude in the letters he wrote Louise after returning to Croisset:

Yes, how happy we were, poor dear woman, and I love you in all kinds of ways. Your kindness to Bouilhet went directly to my heart. It was all so good of you (and so agile!). You have given poor Bouilhet his first success. He will remember that evening for his entire life, and so will I. My interior Muse blesses you for it all and sends you the most tender kisses. —No, I shall never forget you, whatever the circumstances, and I shall always return to your affection through all kinds of storms. You will remain my principal shelter and refuge. . . . I swear that I love you . . . and that if I ever come to love another, I shall continue to love you to the end of my days.

Louise having provided him with a much-needed mistress as well as with his first literary success, Bouilhet, too, showered her with affectionate and grateful letters, and he inquired into the possibility of her finding a lodging for him in the capital. "What fun it will be when three true friends can all live in Paris!" Bouilhet wrote Louise, referring to Flaubert's plan to move to Paris when he had made enough progress on Bovary. And Louise was thrilled by the fact that she was finally being accepted into Flaubert's circle of intimates.

But Louise's new contentment with Flaubert did not allay her uncertainty concerning any future with him and her sense that this mama's boy had no understanding of or concern for the many vicissitudes of her life.

> *Not a word in Gustave's letter concerning my paragraph on Croisset and his mother. Certain areas of his soul are inaccessible. Why do I open all of mine to him?*
>
> *I am nothing in his future, I who only think of him, I who am ready to say to him, "Allow me to live near you, with my daughter and your mother!" Oh! I am mad! My sorrow is such that death would bring relief.*

Louise experienced great sadness at the Cimetière Montparnasse, where she visited the tombs of her former husband and her two infant sons, often bringing young Henriette. "In sorrow before these graves. Poor children, poor man! . . . and my daughter beside me, in tears," she jotted in a Memento after such a visit. "Henriette wished to place on {Hippolyte's} tomb the flowers he loved best. . . . If I were to design my own tomb . . . I would like my bones to be buried on some deserted beach, or rather under a rock in Servanes."

Louise's frequent depressions were aggravated by her penury. Her Mementos are filled with phrases like "Ten francs left in the house. Desperate," or "Not a cent left to live on." Repaying loans from friends—borrowing was painful to such a proud woman—instantly depleted each quarterly installment of her tiny government pension.

Louise continued to endure a humiliating relationship with Victor Cousin, who tried hard to remain (as his last resort) her principal adviser, admonishing her with gems such as: "Renounce forever this unnerving literature which constantly corrupts you with notions of love and sensuality." ("While he writes such things, the decrepit old lecher entertains strumpets at his home," Louise scribbled on the margin of that letter. "The wretch! the wretch!")

The former lovers' relationship was all the more troublesome because Cousin, a curious blend of loyalty and stinginess, often threatened to withhold the stipend he paid for Henriette's education when he felt that

Louise was involved with another man. He had warned of particularly severe financial retaliations after Flaubert's return from Egypt, when Louise was again seeing "the gentleman from Rouen."

"Now that Gustave is back, if I could only sell enough work to free myself from the philosopher, I would be almost happy," Louise wrote in a Memento. "Avarice blinds that man." And: "Necessity may force us to anything, but it will never force me to live with that man."

Her Mementos in the 1850s were filled with increasingly bitter observations on the universality of women's suffering. "Oh my God, my God, how I pity, how I love women! The drama I could write, and will write, about their destinies!" Such notations reflect the plight of any self-supporting woman writer those beauty turns her into sexual prey, whose vocation is at the mercy of powerful, lecherous men.

> A visit from Villemain this afternoon . . . his declarations, his tenderness! How vile men are! He threatens that if I enter the Académie contest again, he will block any award to me! I'm desolate. I'm penniless this month. That miserable [Cousin], who already cut my daughter's pension in half, is threatening to cut all of it because I don't want him to see her without me. And Gustave never even gives a thought to my distress! I am totally alone, alone!
>
> The doorbell rang at 10 P.M. It was Villemain. His new gambit is to seduce me with the promise that he will press the Académie to give me its award next year. Vile cad! What a charming world we live in! He knelt before me, I treated him roughly, he left early, he'll return.

(She sent all such suitors packing with scathing verbal abuses which only deteriorated her relations with the literary establishment.)

It was to avoid more such humiliations that Louise resorted to yet another genre of literature, fashion journalism and social chronicles; writings in the latter vein described such events as a children's birthday party she had once attended at the home of Madame Récamier and a costume ball given Teresa Guiccioli—two particular articles Flaubert edited meticulously and that, to his vast amusement, she sold to his hometown newspaper, *Le Journal de Rouen*.

As for her fashion reporting, Louise published it in *La Chronique de la mode,* which described itself as "a journal of good society—fashions, home furnishings, theaters, new books, social chitchat," and *La Gazette des femmes.*

Her work in this genre reveals an extensive grasp of haute couture:

Fashion was brilliantly displayed at the latest reunion of the Académie Française. The Comtesse de Salvandy wore a dress of black taffeta with valances of black lace spread out in waves down the sweep of the skirt. . . . Her daughter's dress was of pearl-gray taffeta, with nine little flounces cut on the bias, and a low-cut bodice embellished with a vest of white jaconet bristling with pink bows.

Madame Fould, the wife of the minister, wore a dress of sky-blue china silk cut in three tunic-like layers. A beautiful shawl of white Chantilly lace covered a corsage adorned with a large taffeta bow. . . . The five flounces of the Maréchale Vaillant's brilliant green dress were embellished by wide festoons of green silk; a shawl of white crepe de chine embroidered with multihued flowers and birds covered her corsage. . . .

Louise signed her fashion articles "Cleophée." However subconsciously, this pen name might well have expressed her longing to be accepted by the Flaubert family: Flaubert's father's name was "Achille-Cléophas."

Louise was devoted to Guerlain products—both vestments and scents—and became especially noted for her coverage of the hat industry. Milliners rewarded her for her chronicles by offering her scores of the plumed and fruited headgear she so eloquently described. She kept them in a large bookcase in her living room and became renowned as one of the best-chapeaued women in Paris. More to the point, she often sold them for a little extra cash, finding eager customers among members of her literary salon.

The *Figaro* correspondent Baron de Platel, a fashionable young Parisian, described Louise's little flat on the Rue de Sèvres and the disarming manner in which she persuaded him to purchase several hats at one of her weekly salons:

Her apartment was on the second floor. The entrance hall gave onto a small dining room and a living room with two windows. . . . The most curious piece of furniture in her salon was a large glassed-in book cupboard, locked under key and carefully veiled with green curtains. On its shelves, instead of books, she kept a score of women's hats of the latest vogue, gifts from merchants, which explains why the Muse was one of the best-coiffed women in Paris. She had a great mass of heavy, very beautiful hair, by the way, which had not been purchased. On a day of particular "impoverishment"—her word—she offered to sell me two pretty women's hats, which I successfully peddled in the Latin Quarter.

Yet Louise, a committed activist who engaged in the most serious political struggles of her time, a self-taught scholar who had translated Shakespeare and obscure Italian Renaissance texts, was bound to be humiliated by her need to grind out harebrained fashion chronicles. "I apologize for the insults and anguishes imposed in France upon women who write," Louise raged in a later memoir, explaining why she had to resort to fashion journalism,

> *for the flippancy and injustice of the big media critics, for the caddishness and calumnies poured out every morning by hack journalists in the small-fry press. . . . Struggling to find some place in this literary horde, overworked and battered with insults, ailing in body and soul, a woman finds that at the end of a year her killing, humiliating labor has barely earned her two or three thousand francs. That is not enough for herself and her child. . . . So she turns to a certain kind of honest, stupid, obscure, banal commercial literature to earn a few hundred francs a month. She goes from boutique to boutique exploring trinkets—furniture, jewelry, lace, cashmere, from Lyons velvets to Indian burnooses, from handkerchiefs to collars, from mesh gloves and candy to pots of pomade and rouge. In the life of such a woman writer, department store owners replace journalists and bookstore owners: She must please them, satisfy them, create copy which, as they say, "promotes" their inventory. Every week we recommence our perusal of their merchandise and again scribble, at a fixed hour, inanities which we can't even recognize the next day as ours.*

P.S. THE TRIBULATIONS OF NINETEENTH-CENTURY WOMEN WRITERS (OR, THE DIFFI-CULTIES OF BEING LOUISE COLET)

Many nations have died through the corruption brought them by courtesans, but courtesans are a natural phenomenon, and blue-stockings are not! They belong to a civilization whose depravity and degradation have no precedents in human history. . . .

Women's rage to write is the cholera epidemic of the nineteenth century.

Barbey d'Aurevilly

We would regret to see the more beautiful half of humankind adopt Louise Colet's overly solid and pedantic education.

Eugène de Mirecourt

Knowledge is what is most dangerous to women. The useful monotony of custom, honest mediocrity, sweet obscurity, there is women's lot.

Joseph de Maistre

In his novel Sentimental Education, *Flaubert limned a vicious portrait of intellectual women in the character of Mademoiselle Vatnaz. Like Louise Colet, Vatnaz is a literary jane-of-all-trades with very progressive opinions ("In olden times Gaul was ruled by women; so were the Anglo-Saxons. . . . All women must stand for political office."). Flaubert takes his satire of the "New Woman" one step further because, unlike Colet, Vatnaz is ugly and doomed to perennial spinsterhood.*

What is most interesting about Flaubert's depiction of Vatnaz, however, is that although she is too homely ever to have snared any man herself, she makes ends meet by moonlighting as a pimp, arranging liaisons between high-class whores and wealthy men. In this savage pastiche Flaubert expresses one of the most disturbing prejudices of mid-nineteenth-century France—that educated women are morally suspect, the same phobia that led Louise's siblings to scorn her intellectual achievements.

In a long essay on the theme of "Women Poets," published in the early 1840s in France's most prestigious magazine, Revue des deux mondes, *a periodical equivalent to our* New York Times Book Review *in its influence, the author elaborates on this notion of "learned" or "literary" woman as promiscuous.*

> In such a woman's youth, what should be vague curiosity becomes an insupportable desire to learn. . . . As she shuts herself into a library, she evokes imaginary voices, which confound her mind and trouble her senses. . . . She searches for powerful emotions and gives herself to scandalous loves.

If a woman's desire for education imperiled her morals, then putting a pen to paper was downright sluttish: "To be ready to draw thoughts, like precious stones, from the most mysterious depths of her soul . . . to dream of humankind when her only duty is to God and to nature—nothing is more sacrilegious, more inspiring of disgust."

Censuring the most prominent women poets of her generation, the critic singles out Madame Louise Colet as particularly reprehensible because of her use of personal memories and emotions. Savaging poems dedicated to her mother and father in her volume Penserosa, he rigorously denies women any right to that autobiographical impulse which inspired hordes of male Romantic poets throughout Europe: "When {Madame Colet} links sacred memories of a dying parent to the ambitious thoughts of her poetry's artifice, when she depicts the death agony of her father or the icy lips and closed eyes of her dying mother—that is a true profanation."

In the finale of the critic's invective against Louise and her peers, he implores all females to keep their inner emotions chastely veiled:

> A woman who wears a helmet and a sword, spurs on her horses, goes into battle . . . is less chimerical and monstrous than a woman who interrogates the depths of her soul, plumbs her pain, penetrates the sorrow . . . so cruel for the spirit and offensive to modesty, that the poet is forced to explore.

Such biases against educated women, already evident during Louise's youth, had grown even more extreme in midcentury: The general misogyny bred in France by a communal fear of the French Revolution's unleashed female militants was further exacerbated by the uprisings of 1848. Women participated in those rebellions as vigorously as they had in the upheaval of 1789. Throughout the 1840s, large groups of working-class French women, allying themselves with the newly powerful labor unions or using the network of their own "political clubs," had already demonstrated for suffrage, more humane working hours, and day care centers. A new class of professional women—schoolteachers, postmistresses, journalists who proclaimed the same ideals as Flaubert's Mademoiselle Vatnaz—also campaigned for divorce laws and equal access to secondary education, and stated their demands in many new women's magazines—La Voix des femmes, L'Opinion des femmes, Le Conseiller des femmes, Le Journal des femmes, La Gazette des femmes, La Tribune des femmes.

Within a few months, the republican government that overthrew Louis Philippe in 1848 repressed this wave of activism just as harshly as the revolutionary leaders of 1789 had. None of the requests of the "quarante-huitardes," as the female militants of 1848 were called, were granted, and the new National Assembly voted to close all of the women's political clubs founded in the previous decade. The alternatives offered by the socialist leader Pierre-Joseph Proudhon—"housewife or whore"—remained the order of the day.

> We have known the philanthropic woman writer, the republican poetess, the systematic priestess of love; and our eyes . . . have never been able to get used to all this stuffy ugliness, all these impious villainies . . . all these sacrilegious parodies of the male spirit.
> Charles Baudelaire

> If you made an autopsy of women writers with true talent, you'd find in them a clitoris similar to our penis.
> Jules and Edmond de Goncourt

> . . . an invasion of pedants not even capable, like barbaric women, of reproducing the human race. . . . Such women must be sent home to their proper places, like rebellious children who deserve to be whipped.
>
> Barbey d'Aurevilly

Seeing the prevalence of such views, no wonder the custom of taking on male pen names was more frequently resorted to in France than in any other culture. Beyond the obvious example of George Sand, who had devised her nom de plume from the name of her first lover, Jules Sandeau, here is a modest sampling of this popular survival tactic as it was used by some of Louise Colet's contemporaries:

Thérèse Karr, daughter of that same Alphonse Karr who incurred Louise Colet's lethal wrath, signed her writings "Pierre Rosenkranz"; the Countess Marie d'Agoult became "Daniel Stern"; and my own great-great-grandaunt, Madame de Saint-Aignan of Nantes, published her prolific fictions under the name "Jules d'Herbauges." Marie-Letizia Bonaparte Wyse, great-grandniece of the emperor, signed her books "Baron Stock." In 1840, the Parisian socialite Madame de Saint-Mars, broke and forbidden by her husband to use his name, signed her innumerable novels "Countess Dash," after her spaniel. And Sibylle de Mirabeau, great-grandniece of the revolutionary leader, also emulated the mode for all things British by signing her fabulously popular novels "Gyp" or "Scamp."

Thus Louise Colet was one of the few women writers in nineteenth-century France who refused the protection of such masks, who chose to publish, as one of her French chroniclers put it, "dans la nudité de son patronyme." Louise's self-exposure tells us a lot about her insecurity, expressed in numerous letters to lovers, about being treated as "a woman of low rank" and her constant attempt to rehabilitate her public image. And yet she was too forthright to fabricate any camouflages; she continued nakedly proclaiming her rebellion and her appetites for sex and knowledge.

The literary and economic survival of this woman whose beauty and warmth, in Flaubert's words, "could make a dead man fall in love" was all the more precarious because she did not inherit the prestige or personal fortunes that helped Germaine de Staël, George Sand, and Marie d'Agoult survive society's prejudices. In fact, it is hard to think of a literary woman as deprived as Louise Colet was of any personal resources beyond good looks, monumental determination, and a modest talent. She had to invent herself from scratch, seizing every opportunity that came her way: working the room exhaustively at every literary gathering she attended, seeking the protection of the few decent men (Cousin, Béranger, Hugo) who were willing to do her favors without tainting her integrity. In a culture obsessed with female decorum and "modesty," she paid a high price for her bravado and sass, and was often accused (as can still happen to such women today) of being an abrasive hustler.

And so this impoverished daughter of provincial gentry who had the gumption to re-create herself as a celebrity remained a thicket of contradictions: rejecting the silence imposed on her female peers but incensed when she was accused of immodesty; avid to seduce yet denouncing those suitors who offended her bourgeois sensibility; proclaiming her lust and yet shouting her outrage when it was satisfied in ways she considered indecorous. Alienating most of those she loved by her impatient and frequently self-destructive behavior, seeking "glory" in her often sloppy, sometimes powerful writings, channeling her aggression into reformist ardor and masochistic love affairs, Louise was the model of a woman driven to near hysteria by her society's dual prejudices against her sex and her vocation.

Pride, that male vice, has descended into the heart of woman, who has stood up to show that she is our equal, and whom we have not yet put back in her place!

Would it be possible that humanity is finally entertaining the idea that with the aid of science and education, one can draw dogs and monkeys out of the mire of their animality and allow them to enter—on the same level as men—into the idiotic travesty of Universal Suffrage?

Barbey d'Aurevilly

Women hold their pen the way they would hold a sewing needle, they write as if they were mending trousers.

Frédéric Soulié

Imperious, without respect for work, insatiable, [Louise Colet] persecuted Flaubert. . . . I have never understood how Flaubert, a distinguished intellectual, a solitary worker, a man of chastity, did not turn away from this literary androgyne.

Maxime Du Camp

You women, sisters in sorrow, you whom I so love / Oh! Pity me!

Louise Colet

12.

Fantasio and Stello

Louise's recklessness was in great part responsible for the end of her second affair with Flaubert. For at the height of his love for her, she plunged into an affair with France's most dissolute celebrity.

The prodigiously talented poet Alfred de Musset, "Prince Charming of Romanticism," was a man who squandered most every gift and privilege he was given. The spoiled child of aristocratic parents, Musset was brought up in an unusually loving and close family. By his late teens he had become as famous for his beauty and debauchery as for his precocious, pleasing verses. In the 1830s, Parisian youth so worshiped his image as profligate Romantic rascal—he was a drunk, a whorer, and generally outrageous—that they fought in the streets over his discarded cigarette butts.

In 1832, at the age of twenty-one, "Fantasio," as Musset was called for one of his popular early plays, began a notorious love affair with George Sand, then twenty-eight, which he would later document in his novel *La Confession d'un enfant du siècle,* "Confession of a Child of the Century."

On a trip to Italy, Sand attempted to cure Musset of his bad habits, but in her demanding company he only grew more dissipated. And after his liaison with Sand, his talent and his health declined as he became addicted to absinthe.

Musset met Louise Colet in 1836, the year she arrived in Paris, at the famous literary salon at the Bibliothèque de l'Arsenal. He was at the height of his glory, a French Beau Brummell, with flowing hair and "pink cheeks that retained the bloom of childhood, eyes come from heaven," who dressed in sky-blue tights and rakishly tilted top hats. He had been captivated by Louise's beauty, though he complained that the prim, long-sleeved garments her husband made her wear made her look "too puritanical." Louise had also been taken with Musset but had refused his invitation to a waltz because of Hippolyte's jealousy.

When they met again sixteen years later, in 1852, the once dashing Musset was a wasted semi-invalid in threadbare clothes. His eyes shone with fever in his gaunt face. But he still had the cachet of fame, and Fate led him to Louise at the Académie Française. Louise had been told that Musset, who was about to be inducted into the Académie, would be the perfect person to recite her verses on the Colonie de Mettray at the awards ceremony. She introduced herself to him and again provoked his desire.

Musset began to court Louise, whom he referred to as "a Venus, a fury of hot marble." He visited her daily, arriving disheveled, reeking of absinthe, demanding more to drink; Louise, who belonged to a temperance league, firmly rebuffed him. He celebrated his feelings for her in a sonnet inspired by their visits to Paris's zoo, "Une Promenade au jardin des plantes."

Antilope aux yeux noirs, dis, quelle est mon amante? . . .
O lion, tu le sait, toi, mon noble enchainé;
Toi qui m'a vu palir lorsque sa main charmante
Se baissa doucement sur mon front incliné.*

Louise remained aloof from the poet's advances, infuriating him. She told him that like the exotic Oriental and African animals he enjoyed visiting at the zoo, he "stank of that which he consumed." Musset then tried to woo Louise with gallantry. He rescued her when a lion tried to bite off her hand, almost collapsing from her weight as he carried her to safety.

*Dark-eyed antelope, tell me, who is my mistress?. . . .
O lion, noble beast in chains, you know who she is;
You saw my face grow pale when her charming hand
Gently brushed my inclined head.

Louise as a young girl at Servanes, the estate in Provence where she spent most of her first twenty-four years. The fountain, great trees, and antique statuary are still in place today. The artist is thought to be her cousin Pierre Révoil.

Louise Colet soon after she had arrived in Paris from Provence, portrayed by the fashionable society painter Franz X. Winterhalter, ca. 1840.

A contemporary view of Louise Colet's ancestral domain, Servanes, a half-hour's drive from Avignon. It has recently been converted into a hotel and golf resort.

4

Mr. Paul Révoil, Louise Colet's great-great-grandnephew, present proprietor of Servanes.

5

Portrait of Louise Colet by her friend James Pradier, the most popular sculptor of nineteenth-century France. Known to his friends as "Phidias," Pradier referred to Colet as "Sappho."

6

7

Medallion profile of
Louise Colet, ca. 1840, by
F. Woltreck.

Bas-relief portrait of
Louise's husband, the
moody musician Hippolyte
Colet, a fellow Provençal
from whom she separated
after seventeen years of
marriage. By Hippolyte
Ferrat, 1851.

8

Victor Cousin by Maurin. Cousin
was the preeminent philosopher
of nineteenth-century France,
Louise Colet's lover for many
years and the father, probably, of
her daughter, Henriette.

Louise Colet is said to have been the model for sculptor James Pradier's *Ville de Strasbourg* (1838), one of eight heroic sculptures on the Place de la Concorde representing France's most important cities.

Portrait of Louise Colet and her daughter, Henriette, by Adèle Grasset, probably painted in Aix-en-Provence in 1842.

Portrait of George Sand, the feminist colleague with whom Louise had a contentious correspondence.

David's famous portrait of Madame Récamier, who in the last years of her life looked on Louise as a cherished friend and confidante.

Flamboyant, high-living James Pradier, who befriended Louise soon after her arrival from Provence and sculpted several portraits of her.

Louise "Ludovica" Pradier, the libertine wife of James Pradier, ironically idealized by her artist husband in this Madonna-like pose. Ludovica, a childhood friend and occasional lover of Gustave Flaubert, would cause the breakup of Louise's first affair with the writer.

Louis Bouilhet, Flaubert's closest friend from 1851 on and his editor during the writing of *Madame Bovary*. An inconsequential writer but an editor of genius, Bouilhet has traditionally been thought of as the "midwife" of that novel, and was referred to by Flaubert as "my left testicle."

Portrait by Delauney of Flaubert at the
age of twenty-four, the year before he
met Louise Colet.

Eugène Giraud's caricature of Flaubert's friend, the elegant and devious writer Maxime Du
Camp. Excessively jealous of Flaubert's affection for Louise Colet, Du Camp started a
defamation campaign against her which lasted well into the twentieth century.

A painting by Thomsen of the Flauberts' residence at Croisset, five miles from Rouen,
where the writer spent most of his life. Louise was never allowed to cross its threshold.

Pierre-Jean de Béranger was France's most beloved poet throughout much of the nineteenth century. A cherished friend of Louise's and her closest adviser, he shared all of her progressive political views.

A painting by Charles Landelle of poet Alfred de Musset, enfant terrible of the Romantic movement and a lover of Louise's in 1845, during her relationship with Flaubert.

Henriette Colet, Louise's beautiful, brooding daughter, age twelve, painted by Fanny Chéron, 1852. She grew up to be the radical opposite of her mother—a pious, conformist provincial housewife.

Poet Alfred de Vigny, Louise's lover after the end of her affair with Flaubert. His aloof, elitist character inspired the critic Sainte-Beuve to coin the phrase "ivory tower."

The "Olympian" Victor Hugo, another treasured friend and confidant of Louise's, was exiled for nineteen years in the British Channel Islands for his left-wing political views. Louise Colet acted as a "mail drop" for his correspondence to France, and visited him in Guernsey.

Gustave Flaubert, photographed by Nadar in 1864, ten years after the end of his liaison with Louise. "How ugly he's become!" Louise exclaimed to her daughter the one time she saw him in public after their breakup.

Gustave Courbet's *L'Amazone,* ca. 1856, said to be a portrait of Louise Colet.

LE BOUFFON

Caricature of Louise Colet in 1867, after the publication of her satiric book on the decadence of Paris society in the last years of the Empire, *Ces Petits Messieurs* (*These Little Gentlemen*), by Edouard Ancourt.

L'art de se faire aimer de sa femme.

La femme émancipée, répandant la lumière sur le monde.

glimpse of the misogynous world that confronted Louise Colet. (*Left*) A view of women, ca. 1824, by anglumé. The caption reads, "The art of being loved by one's wife." (*Right*) A view of women, 1871, y Eugène Giraud. The caption reads, "The emancipated woman enlightening the world."

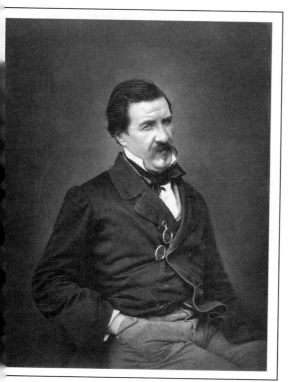

The eminent art critic Champfleury, who coined the term "Realism" for the movement pioneered by Flaubert in literature, and by Gustave Courbet in the visual arts. Champfleury and Louise had a brief, stormy affair—her last—the year she ended her relationship with Alfred de Vigny. The photograph is by Nadar.

Last known photograph of Louise Colet, 1874, two years before her death. It was probably taken in San Remo, during the last of her many stays in Italy.

Musset would return dozens of times to Louise's flat, turned away each time at the door because of her disgust for his drunkenness. But whatever Louise's initial repulsion, a central facet of her character—a reverence for that "glory" she so desired for herself, so admired in others—led her ultimately to succumb. Was it an impulse to self-destruction that induced her to spoil her new happiness with Flaubert? He never learned directly of Louise's affair with Musset, but after it had ended, Louise relapsed into her foolhardy former behavior and made a series of terrible mistakes that permanently alienated the love of her life.

Musset finally bedded Louise by staying sober for an afternoon (he was shaking visibly when he appeared at her flat). After returning from one of their visits to the zoo, Louise invited him to stay for dinner.

"His one sensation," Louise remarked laconically the next day in her journals, implying that Musset had had only one erection that night and could not come to orgasm. "Oh Gustave, Gustave, what a contrast!" she also jotted in her Memento (in that respect the Muse was very spoiled).

Musset was drunk again the following day, and Louise once more spurned him. He left in a fury, cursing that since she was not available he was going to the bordello.

The next afternoon he returned relatively sober, and Louise acceded again. "Impotent!" she scribbled that time in her journal. Eager to save his honor, Musset invited her to the Théâtre-Français to see Voltaire's *Oedipus.*

It is a stiflingly hot late evening in June 1852. Louise puts on her coolest attire, a vaporous white muslin dress that bares her shoulders and arms. Musset goes out to drink at every intermission, rants so loudly about the actors' performances that he is nearly ejected from the theater.

When they hail a carriage after the play, Musset asks to return to Louise's flat, but she refuses. He insults her. He calls her a cock teaser, he accuses her of having dressed in that wispy dress to excite him, to lead him on. Grasping her shoulders, he then claws at her dress, rips its muslin bodice, starts biting her breasts. Louise is enraged. As their hansom cab is passing the Place du Carrousel, nowhere near Louise's home, she decides to jump out. Louise described the incident in her Mementos:

I told him I was about to lunge out of the cab. . . . "Crazy threat, mountebank's comedy," Musset answered. "It'll be like your knifing incident with Alphonse Karr! Try, just try, the cab is going too fast!" He was humiliating and terrifying me. I opened the door of the cab and jumped. I landed on my side on the sidewalk. I had hurt my knees, I was afraid of being badly hurt, I had terrible inner cramps. Yet I didn't falter, I got up and tried to hide. . . . It was on the Place de la Concorde, right in front of the Chamber of Deputies. The cab stops just ahead, the driver comes toward me. "The gentleman sent me to ask you if you are hurt," he says. "Tell him you never found me," I answer. "I can see that he's a wretch and you're an honorable woman," the cabbie says. "May I abandon him right here and now and take you home?" "No," I repeated, "tell him that you never even saw me."

The cab left, drove on. What a coward! Or rather, what a brute! He was dead drunk. Beauty of the night, splendor of the moon! At this very moment, half past midnight, Gustave was writing me. I think of him, of my daughter, I resolve to never see that man [Musset] again, to not even answer his letters. I could have died on the spot. And my poor child! And Gustave! I try to go home on foot. . . .

She limps home across the Pont de la Concorde, stumbling, her clothes in shreds. It is long past midnight. Thank God the streets are nearly empty; there is no one to see her disarray. When she gets home, she is greeted by her maid, who is in a panic: Monsieur de Musset dropped in half an hour ago, looking more haggard than ever, and upon hearing she was not home stumbled down the stairs, shouting, "She is dead, she is dead!"

Louise runs into her daughter's room, kneels by her bed, and without waking the child swears she will never disgrace herself this way again.

As dawn approaches, she sits down and writes Gustave about Musset's recent advances. She has a habit of prodding Gustave to be more attentive by recounting each of her conquests of famous men, sending him their amorous letters. Of course, she sketches only selected aspects of those days with Musset, omits the brutal end of their cab ride and some other crucial details: ("Delete moment of forgetfulness," Louise scribbles in her Mementos while writing that letter to Gustave, by which she means that she never mentioned her tumble in bed with the impotent poet.)

The following morning, a note arrives from Musset: "Did you get hurt yesterday? I'm worried to death. May I come to see you today?" Louise sends him a message at the Café de la Régence, where he does most of his drinking, saying that she is not well and cannot receive him.

In the past weeks, Louise has received a flood of letters from Gustave, mildly berating her for associating with the debauched poet but focusing his attack, in his habitual Olympian tone, on Musset's poetics.

The substance of Musset is nothing but Pose! And for Pose everything goes—himself, others, the sun, cemetery graves, etc., he stews sentiment out of it all, and three fourths of the time you poor women are taken in by it. That poor boy probably can't even satisfy his laundress. . . . So it's only to seem manly that he says, "I'm a jealous type, I could kill a woman, etc." One doesn't kill women, one fears the tribunal too much; he didn't kill George Sand. . . .

A few days later, Flaubert rebuked Louise more bluntly for her "imprudences" with Musset: "Convention has it that one doesn't go for a moonlight drive with a man for the purpose of admiring the moon."

Louise must have written another letter to Flaubert, telling him in detail about the violent end of the cab ride, the dreadful hours alone in the night streets: In their next exchange, Flaubert is outraged and displays a very bourgeois sense of decorum.

You made me suffer much this morning, and in a totally new manner. . . . I felt as if I'd been slapped. One of these days I'll make that man pay for that insult! With what delectation I'd give him a whipping. . . . Ah, my poor Louise, for you, you, to have come to this! For a moment I envisioned you lying dead on the sidewalk, with the wheels of the carriage whirring on top of you, a horse's foot mangling your face, lying in the mud, where he should have been. Oh! . . . If he ever writes you again, answer in a monumental five-line letter: "Why do I want nothing to do with you? Because you disgust me and you're a coward."

. . . You lacked tact in this whole incident. Women's heads are as filled with hot air as a cello's casing. Instead of jumping out of the cab, you should have stopped the cab and told the driver, "Do me the pleasure of throwing out Monsieur A. de Musset, who is insulting me."

Louise must have been alarmed in turn. Fearful that the two men would come to a duel over her honor (a recurring fantasy with her), she must have begged Flaubert to spare Musset. Flaubert's response, for the first time, expresses guilt concerning his neglect of his mistress.

May I speak to you frankly? You're going to explode again, but too bad! You told me the truth, and I owe it to you in return: All this saddened me greatly. I said to myself: "Indeed, I spend so little time with her! And so rarely! And after all I'm not what one might call an agreeable man. And so, in one of her empty hours, another man came along, a very famous one for a change, begging, putting on his childlike charm. . . . Would it be better for her to abandon me? Wouldn't he make her happy?" And I saw you spending time together.

Musset and Louise would never resume their affair, but they continued to see each other a great deal in the next year. There were many intimate suppers à deux at which the poet revealed confidences about George Sand; dinners with friends like Edma Roger des Genettes at which Musset remained sober, enchanting everyone "with his beauty, distinction, and wit." There were dinners at Louise's flat with Victor Cousin when both men were "charming and most interesting" as they talked about Goethe's poetry, and Musset would recite Byron. There were nights when at one A.M. he would rent a private dining room at the elegant Café Anglais, sit down at the piano to sing after a few absinthes, and repeat, "My voice is gone, I am finished, finished." "He closed his eyes, I told him I would take him home," Louise reported on one such evening. " 'We're so comfortable here,' he said, stroking his hand through my hair. He sat down on the couch and kissed me. I burst into tears. Ah, the poet, the poet, I said to myself, to have fallen this low!"

There were also more moonlight cab rides in the Bois, during which Louise was again overwhelmed by the love of one of France's most famous men and by the Romantic stereotype of the *poète maudit* doomed to early death ("The idea that he might die soon obsesses me painfully").

As he spoke [so she described one of these moonlight rides], the brilliance of those stars he was pointing to caressed his inspired forehead. In that light his face was superb; his frail little body seemed to reach to the sky; he took on the proportions of genius. . . . I turned my face to his and felt his lips, rapid, frenetic, caressing my forehead, my eyes, my lips. I struggled out of his arms and escaped into the alleys of the Bois. . . .

And there were other outings that did not go so well. "As soon as we were in the Bois he started drinking again and resumed his ravings. As I tried to flee him or bring him back to the cab, he insulted me again. 'You wretch!' I said. Then, his furor; he grabbed my arm and shook me violently and called me a bluestocking. . . . I told him he was a villain, a coward." (The term "bluestocking" was clearly the ultimate insult in nineteenth-century France.)

The morning after such incidents, Musset would appear at Louise's door, bringing flowers, saying, "We'll never fight again; our caresses will reconcile us when you'll truly become my mistress." "Certain that he is nearly impotent or that he has only very transient, painful erections," Louise reflects in a Memento after refusing Musset's advances for the umpteenth time that month.

Along with this alternating attraction and repulsion, Louise felt maternal solicitude for Musset. Panicked by each of the poet's illnesses, she would call on him at all hours. "I found him seated in his large armchair, reading Dumas novels by his worktable, on which lay thimble and scissors; his maid was mending his flannel waistcoat. He was still covered with a cold sweat and was extremely feeble. I kissed his forehead; he told me to stop because he smelled so of fever. . . ."

And well into the following year, long after they had ceased to see each other alone, a week didn't go by without Louise inquiring after Musset's health, telling her daughter to find gifts to cheer the poet. ("Henriette persevered in finding Alfred a white camellia plant to bring him out of his despondence; we chose a beautiful, robust little tree covered with pale pink camellia blossoms and buds. I was asked ten francs for it, and bargained the price down to five.")

"How could this man, with his egotism, his vices, have cast a pall on my love for Gustave—so great, so true, my life's only passion?" Louise mused in her Mementos toward the end of her stormy relationship with Musset.

> . . . how curious that this man, when I'm not in his presence, exerts a fascination on me which verges on vertigo; I'm in love with his genius. Whatever I read of his inebriates me. Yet as soon as I see him again, I'm filled with disgust, even disdain.
>
> Ah, it's because Gustave neglects me too much [she added, attempting to justify herself]. It's because the doors of his mother's house never opened to me, it's because . . . I'm totally unsure about the future of his love.

Louise would remain deeply troubled by the poet's spell over her, as if it had tainted her feelings for Gustave. And even after the affair had ended, Louise constantly courted danger in her relationship with Flaubert. One particular incident recalls a vaudeville stock-in-trade of cuckolded lovers. Musset came to call on Louise a few minutes before she was expecting Flaubert for dinner. He carried two large cages with canaries and parakeets as gifts for her. When Louise told him that she was rushing out for an appointment, Musset put the cages down on the buffet, started kissing her hands and her forehead, begged her to cancel her engagement. Louise, staring frantically at the clock, barely managed to hustle him out of her flat before Flaubert's arrival. As the imprudent hostess anxiously looked out the window, she saw Gustave emerging from a cab two yards away from Musset, whose back, mercifully, was turned. . . . The two men had missed crossing each other on the stairwell by a few seconds.

Flaubert's passion for Louise was doubtless heightened by suspicions—never expressed—that he had a rival. His Paris stays grew longer—a week or two at a time—and he made earnest promises to Louise that he would move permanently to the capital as soon as he finished his *Bovary*. He demonstrated new levels of chivalry, buying her an amber bracelet she had admired, booking a private dining room at the Café Anglais for supper (by coincidence, it was the same room she had shared with Musset the previous week). And Louise remained enough of a bourgeoise to be responsive to such gallantries. "We went to bed after dinner notwithstanding the Brits," Louise confided in a Memento the same night Flaubert almost encountered Musset on her stairs. "Never was he more splendid, never did he make love better. 'In a year we'll be constantly together,' he said, 'patience, courage, pride.' I'll follow his advice, I'll steep myself in silence and solitude. . . ."

In those months Flaubert's expressions of tenderness and gratitude increased: "I'll never forget that you're the one who wove my first literary crown, who placed it on my head with your best kisses." "You are the blanket on which my heart lies down to rest, the commodious chest in which my spirit opens."

He arranged further meetings in Mantes, some of them as long as a week, with never a mention of Maman Flaubert's disapproval. In July 1852, their stay in Mantes's Hôtel du Grand Cerf was marred by news of the death of their old friend James Pradier. Pradier's end was fittingly sybaritic: He died while making love with one of his models during a picnic in the forest of Bougival. His last salon success had been a sculpture for which Louise was the model that showed her seated on a rock in a girlish dress, her head leaning on her hand. Flaubert, Louise, even Bouilhet immediately wrote eulogies to the memory of the friend who had been responsible for Louise's greatest happiness.

In the summer of 1852, soon after she had ended (in the physical sense) her "affair" with Musset, Louise nursed Gustave through one of his epileptic seizures. It was the first fit he had suffered in five years—his first, in fact, since February 1847, when he had collapsed in Du Camp's flat after his confrontation with Louise over Ludovica Pradier. Louise described the paroxysm in a Memento:

> *His seizure at the hotel, my terror. He begs me not to call anyone. His convulsions, his rasping breath. He foams at the mouth; my arm is bruised by his clenched hands and nails. In about ten minutes he comes to himself. Vomiting. I assure him the attack lasted only a few seconds and that there was no foaming. Deep sympathy for him on my part, great tenderness. I return home at one o'clock, exhausted by fatigue and sadness. He spent the entire next day with me, more amorous, more passionate, than ever; tired, but looking very well.*

This passage is of some value to Flaubert scholars, who have never had any precise proof of the nature of his lifelong ailment. Seeing the shame connected with epilepsy in the Flauberts' bourgeois circles, the writer's family persistently denied that he suffered from the disease; his niece and literary executor, Caroline Commanville, continued the cover-up for decades after his death. Maxime Du Camp's description, in a letter to Louise, of the writer's 1847 seizure is the only other firsthand account of Flaubert's recurrent crises, but Du Camp did not specify that Flaubert "foamed at the mouth," which is a possible symptom of petit mal epilepsy. So Louise's mention of this medical detail adds to the evidence that Flaubert was epileptic. And her great delicacy in hiding the "foaming" from Flaubert reveals that she knew how crucial this symptom was.

In their frequent letters, Louise and Gustave continued to discuss their current reading—Tacitus, *Uncle Tom's Cabin,* Molière, Shakespeare's *Pericles, Don Quixote,* Stendhal (unreadable, they agreed)—and Flaubert sent Louise a week-by-week chronicling of *Madame Bovary*'s composition: "I'm drafting a conversation of a young man and young woman on literature, the ocean, mountains, music, all poetic subjects. —One could take it seriously, and yet it is intentionally grotesque. I believe it will be the first time that a book mocks its hero and heroine. . . . Irony never takes away from pathos. On the contrary, it can enhance it."

Flaubert also discussed plans for future books with Louise. He described the structure of his projected *Dictionary of Accepted Ideas (Dictionnaire des idées reçues),* a massive collection of bourgeois platitudes: "*France:* Must be ruled with an Iron Hand. *Negresses:* Hotter stuff than white women. *Erection:* Should only be said of monuments."

Writing of his monastic dedication to Art, Flaubert frequently employed metaphors now beloved by many Western writers:

"I love my work with a love that is frantic and perverted, as an ascetic loves the hair shirt that scratches his belly."

"The true poet, for me, is a priest. As soon as he dons the cassock he must leave his family."

Flaubert's encouragement of Louise's writing in this phase of their liaison was wholehearted. Though tending to misogynous stereotypes (he constantly censured her for writing "with the breasts of her heart"), his estimate of her true talent was dead-on accurate, and one only wishes she had heeded it better:

> There are two strains in [your talent], your superior sense of drama, your instinctual sense of color, detail, texture—such gifts are innate. They are sullied, however, by two major weaknesses, one of which is acquired, the other inherent to your gender. The first defect is your tendency to sociodemocratic polemic . . . all the slobber inherited from Voltaire, from which even Father Hugo is not exempt. Your second weakness is that vague feminine "tenderomania." Once arrived to your level of quality, linen cannot smell of milk anymore. So do me a favor . . . show us your muscles and not your glands.

Flaubert was particularly supportive of what he called Colet's more "virile" work, such as "La Paysanne," which he considered a masterpiece and edited for days on end, polishing it with the same fastidiousness he brought to his own *Bovary*. In a letter of 1852, he dedicated a dozen pages to a word-by-word revision of the poem. A brief sample of his corrections:

In

> Oh, d'ou vient qu'aussitot que notre âme,
> D'une sublime idée au génie echappée*

> You have two que in the same line, both harsh in sound and weak in effect.

Instead of

---

*Oh, Why does our soul, as soon as it
grazes genius with a sublime idea

*Trop d'impures vapeurs ternissaient sa beauté**

"ta *beauté*" [your beauty] would be better, continuing the apostrophe for movement and clarity.

As for

Sceptre que façonnait la mort et l'esclavage†

la mort [death] is not clear enough; la guerre [war] would be better.

Flaubert lavished some thirty-eight pages of corrections on "La Paysanne." His editing of "La Servante," a poem he did not even like, was equally thorough.

"The past year has been the sweetest, the best year of my life," Louise wrote in her Mementos on New Year's Day, 1853. "Gustave loved me well and I tasted art and love with him as I never have before."

Due to Louis Bouilhet's machinations, their felicity would barely last another year.

Louise had been extraordinarily generous toward Flaubert's best friend. She had been the first person, along with Flaubert, to recognize and praise Bouilhet's modest literary talent. She had been his foremost promoter, single-handedly launching him into Paris literary society, introducing him to his first Parisian mistress, commending him to the most important critics. When he was penniless, she fed him at her own modest table. She finagled tickets for his theater outings, wrote praise-filled essays on his work, arranged writing assignments and Latin tutorials to help him make ends meet. She found him lodgings when he came to Paris from Rouen (a disastrous move for Louise, since it allowed Bouilhet to meddle more actively in her relationship with Flaubert).

For the first two years of their friendship, Bouilhet's expressions of gratitude were expansive. "We clasp hands in Gustave's heart," he wrote Louise, "and form an indissoluble trinity." He addressed her as "Dear sister" (as Du Camp had), signing himself "Your devoted brother," and entrusted her with details of his courtship of "Sylphide" (Edma Roger des Genettes) that he did not even disclose to Flaubert. Flaubert, accus-

---

*Too many impure vapors tarnished his beauty
†Scepter forged by death and slavery

tomed to sharing all sexual particulars with his male buddies, had taken a voyeuristic delight in tracking the progress of the affair: "Has the Roger broad been stuffed yet?" he queried Louise. "Or has Bouilhet sent her off to be laid by someone else?" "God, have you ever reflected on the importance of the cock to Parisian life? The Phallus is the lodestone of all navigation."

When Bouilhet finally did seduce Sylphide, he confided the details to Louise (three times in a row between three and five P.M., right on Sylphide's living room carpet) and implored her not to tell Gustave. So Bouilhet did his share in establishing a relationship of trust with his protector.

But in the autumn of 1853, when he moved to Paris, Bouilhet began to undermine Flaubert's liaison with Louise by feeding him bits of malicious gossip. Flaubert, often depressed that fall because he so sorely missed his friend's company, was incited by Bouilhet's anti-Louise campaign (and perhaps also by his suspicions concerning Louise's relationship with Musset) to start a bout of philandering of his own. In the winter of 1853–1854, he began an affair with an actress named Beatrix Person. He may also have been having an occasional fling with his old friend Ludovica Pradier. Though Bouilhet was reticent about his amorous adventures, Flaubert continued to be generous in the telling of his.

"I notice that the poor Muse falls ill right after each of our meetings. I'm doubtless too talented; however, that's not the case with Ludovica," he wrote to Bouilhet, implying that a recent performance had not been up to snuff. "I feel ashamed concerning her. I would like to have recaptured my honor, but that estimable wench didn't come to our last appointment."

Bouilhet's impending treachery would be all the more contemptible because it seems he may have had a brief affair with Louise himself, at approximately the same time (fall 1853) that he dedicated a poem to her, celebrating her "flaming gaze," "white arms," and "golden tresses." There is evidence of a romantic encounter in a Memento entry: "Bouilhet just couldn't contain himself anymore; he needed a woman. . . . If I had not loved Gustave, would I have started a liaison with him? None of this is clear in my mind." Jean-Paul Sartre and the prominent literary historian Enid Starkie feel that Flaubert may have actually encouraged his friend in this seduction. There is even stronger evidence of Bouilhet's fling with Louise, and of Flaubert's approval of it, in a letter of Flaubert's dated December 1853, the same week Louise hinted at Bouilhet's advances in her journal.

"It seems to me that you're forgetting . . . Ludovica," Flaubert wrote Bouilhet. "You would be wrong not to frequent her, for *entre nous* you might fire your shots more superbly with her than you ever could with the Muse."

It appears the two comrades were now assigning Louise to the collective trash bin of shareable, disposable women—and far more disdainfully than they might dismiss Ludovica, since Louise, as a member of that "bluestocking" class so loathed by their generation, was more contemptible.

In retaliation for Bouilhet's divisive tactics, Louise once more made the fatal mistake of denigrating Flaubert's best friend. Directly after his mention of Ludovica, Flaubert wrote Bouilhet:

> *Do you know that in her second-to-last letter [the Muse] insinuated . . . that you might well abandon me one of these days, and "prefer other friends"? (For God's sake don't open your mouth about all this.) I was so indignant that I didn't even answer directly. . . . I simply put her back in her place with a joke. But what do you say about a woman's cunt threatening to separate us? And of this little menace of hers, "Ah, you see . . . Bouilhet is abandoning you . . . ta ti ta ta . . ." This meddling shocks me greatly. There are coituses in which the presence of a third party makes you impotent. Elephants couple in the shade. Great vulvas are puritanical.*
>
> *The poor Muse much saddens me. I don't know what to do about her. I assure you that this all pains me greatly. . . . I sense she is very tired of me. Who is to blame? Destiny. . . . As for her being tired of me, so would anyone else be, in her place. There is nothing lovable about me. . . . She is indeed the only woman who has loved me. Is that a curse sent her from heaven?*

At that point Gustave, his ego perhaps ruffled by the cooling of Louise's passion for him, still seemed rather eager to retain her. In that same letter to Bouilhet, he mentioned that he might make the ultimate sacrifice and introduce the Muse to his mother!

So on the one hand, he was preparing to give her up; on the other, he couldn't afford to. She seemed to have a talismanic significance in his life; the singularly liberated stream of consciousness he had let loose in their correspondence, its uniquely detailed chronicling of his process of writing, had some crucial therapeutic effect on his work, and he was terrified of letting her go.

In the last months of 1853 (as in 1847), Flaubert's ambivalence about breaking up with Louise led him to play on her most tender chords, recalling the first days of their passion:

Your letters, dear love, fill an entire carton. They're all set aside with your little mementos: I've just been fingering . . . the slippers of our first night of love, and a handkerchief of mine soaked in your blood. —How I yearn to kiss you tonight; I put my lips on yours and embrace you from my deepest depths. . . .

Yet at the same time he was belligerent about their personality differences:

You persevere at Life, you do, you want to keep on pounding on that drum which at every moment sinks under our fists, and whose music is bearable only when it is muted. . . . —You love existence, you do; you're a pagan and a meridional, you respect passions and you aspire to happiness. . . . Whereas I detest life. I'm a Catholic. My heart is coated with something resembling the green moss of Norman cathedrals. . . .

Flaubert also resumed his delaying tactics of five years earlier. He was timing their meetings to his progress on *Bovary,* scheduling them two or three months apart. "This time I can't see you until the end of January," he wrote her in October 1853, "when I hope to finally have my fornication scene finished."

There were also tensions between them concerning Flaubert's continual criticisms of the Romantic nature of Louise's writings. His growing hostility to her work was all the more intense because it was linked to the crises of his own development as a writer and to the crisis of Romanticism itself, which by the late 1840s had run its course. After the failure of his *Temptation of Saint Anthony,* Flaubert had turned his back on the Romanticism of his early work, embracing instead the credo of the new literary zeitgeist—Realism—which would inform *Madame Bovary. Bovary*'s style is one of glacial impersonality, austere elegance, sparse irony, "precise as the language of the sciences," as he put it in a letter to Louise. All these precepts ran counter to Romantic confessionalism, which neither Louise, nor any other French woman poet of her generation, was ever able to transcend.

"Why do you continually return to *yourself?*" Flaubert wrote Louise in the spring of 1854. "You're your own worst enemy. Once in your life you wrote a masterpiece of genius ["La Paysanne"], because you forgot yourself, because you steeped yourself in the passions of others and not your own."

Louise's Romantic clichés about art and human behavior had begun to remind Flaubert of the bromides he was collecting for his great satirical work, the *Dictionary of Accepted Ideas.*

"You demand gallantries, you complain that I don't send you flowers? Ah, to hell with flowers! For that, take up with a sweet guy with rosy cheeks, a man with fine manners and accepted ideas." "You like all that is normal, deliberate. I do not behave 'the way a lover should.' . . . You love me the way others would, with the same prosaic obsessions and harassments." "You're always defending banalities, platitudes that drown out all thought, wretched assonances, banal turns of phrase."

Few works of Louise's incited Flaubert's rage more than "La Servante," the second installment in her cycle *Le Poème de la femme.* This text, in its denunciation of men's perverse impulse to corrupt women, was the most vehemently feminist of her writings so far. Her depiction of the narrative's principal villain, a debauched aristocrat and poet who ruins the life of a pure-hearted peasant girl and drives her to madness, was a barely disguised portrait of Musset. However deep his revulsion for Musset, Flaubert, who read the manuscript of "La Servante" in the first months of 1854, reacted violently against this transposing of life into literature, against what he considered an outrage to Art and to general decorum.

This work is not publishable as it stands, and I beg you not to publish it. Why insult Musset? What did he ever do to you? Is it any of your business? What right do we have to be censors? . . . That poor boy never intended to harm you. Why injure him more than he injured you? Think of posterity and the pathetic image that the detractors of great men have in it. . . . This poem is a bad action, and you will be punished for it because it is bad art. . . . You wrote it with a personal passion, which fuzzed out all vision; it totally lacks aesthetic. . . . You've turned art into a slop pail for passions, a kind of overflowing chamber pot; it does not smell good: it stinks of hate!

Remember that unfortunate incident with the knife and how much that harmed you. . . . You're constantly confusing art and life, your passions and your imagination, elements that are highly harmful to each other.

Flaubert's reference to the Alphonse Karr knife enraged Louise as few passages of their correspondence ever had. She lost all the control she had cultivated in the previous three years and again began to heap Flaubert with abuse. He was a man of "sepulchral detachment"; while he wallowed on his *maman*'s estate like a *grand seigneur,* she lived in constant penury; instead of taking pity and encouraging her, he was demolishing the work she produced to earn her daily bread. . . . And that invisible book "Bovary" was nonexistent, a myth and a lie, another excuse not to see her! And again, why wouldn't Flaubert allow her to meet his mother? He was an egotist, a monster. . . . Louise's sense of injury was so extreme that it induced Gustave to offer an apology.

"How violently you reacted, dear Muse, at my mention of Karr! Do you think I'm enough of a *cur* to remind you of such things with an intention of causing you pain?"

There were other issues in their growing dissension.

How could the committed feminist Louise Colet not have chafed, over the years, at Flaubert's repeated deprecation of women, his coarsely stated remarks concerning their bodies?

"I know where I could find a [woman] with a waist more slender than yours, but I don't know one with a more elevated spirit—elevated, that is, whenever your cunt (which I also appreciate) doesn't get the better of your mind."

"I love you precisely because there's very little woman in you, because you have neither their hypocrisy nor their weakness of intellect."

"You write verses the way a hen lays eggs."

"Don't you feel everything is currently dissolving into the humid element—tears, chatter, breast-feeding. Contemporary literature is drowning in women's menses."

There was also Flaubert's appetite for prostitutes in general and for the Egyptian almeh Kuchuk Hanem in particular. In an attack on the prudishness of Louise's friend Leconte de Lisle, a puritan who professed disgust for bordellos, Flaubert denigrated all men who claimed that they had never been attracted to whores. "Well, let me declare that *I* have, and often! All these disgusted people disgust me profoundly. . . . How many nice young men I have known who had a pious horror of 'houses' and yet picked up the most beautiful cases of clap from their so-called mistresses!"

At Louise's insistence, Flaubert had allowed her to read his Egyptian travel notes. She was horrified by what she read.

You tell me that Kuchuk's bedbugs degrade her in your eyes [he responded]; for me they were the most enchanting touch of all. Their nauseating odor mingled with the scent of her skin, which was dripping with sandalwood oil. I want a touch of bitterness in everything— always a jeer in the midst of our triumphs, desolation even in the midst of enthusiasm.

But the catalyst to Louise and Gustave's final estrangement was Louis Bouilhet.

In the last months of Louise's liaison with Flaubert, Bouilhet, having ended his brief affair with Edma Roger des Genettes, had taken up with an actress, Marie Durey (there would be many double dates in subsequent months with the comrades' "two angels," Marie Durey and Flaubert's new actress friend, Beatrix Person). Bouilhet wrote Flaubert derisive descriptions of Louise's Thursday gatherings, her "menagerie," as he called her weekly salon.

Last night I dined at Durey's, and at nine we went to the Muse's. . . . A numerous crowd was assembled there. Musset, Vigny, Mignet, a throng of academicians and habitués, Antony Deschamps (who spoke much about you and adores you), Captain d'Arpentigny, Roger des Genettes and his spouse, fearsome in her hideousness, attired in a very gauche toilette of pyramidal pretension . . . the dour Leconte de Lisle, and an honest gallery of females, atrocious and immobile like Egyptian divinities, minus the firmness of form. . . . There were ices, punch, tea, pastries, sweets, two waiters, a soirée du grand monde. . . . The Muse looked okay, but extravagantly, maladroitly painted up. . . . I think she's taking on grand airs, O Democracy!

The letter that follows shows the full extent of Bouilhet's possessiveness of Flaubert, his insistence on an exclusive relationship with his treasured friend. One now knows that Flaubert's buddy network is again ganging up to purge Louise from his life.

I have just had to suffer through [the Muse's] impossible, desperately long dialogues: '[Gustave] is an egotist, a monster, etc.' Beyond the deadly boredom of such confidences, I'm afraid of looking like a fool. The Muse's intentions strike me as neither sincere nor disinterested. Her display of sentiments masks an egotism that disgusts me. For the sake of the physical pleasure she receives with you, she has compro-

mised the future of her daughter, of her tender daughter, of her charming daughter . . . etc.

(There is indeed evidence that in 1854, Victor Cousin, with the intercession of Béranger, made a last-ditch proposal of marriage to Louise. For the sake of Henriette, Louise at first accepted. A contemporary who knew her well states that "the future spouses had packed their bags for a honeymoon trip to Great Britain," but Louise once more demurred at the last minute, "out of conscience.")

Shall I give you my honest opinion [Bouilhet continues in his letter to Gustave] of the ultimate goal of . . . [Louise's] invitations and dinners, her long-desired visits with your mother? She wishes, she believes, she is about to become your wife! I've long thought so without daring to say so, but the word has been spread to me, not directly by her but by another source, who quotes her. That is why she refused the Philosopher. . . .

Bouilhet then taunts Flaubert with even more pernicious tattling: Louise has asked him to inform Madame Flaubert of her consuming love for her son.

I told her that I would do nothing of the sort and that I didn't want anything to do with such errands.
    So, dear old adored one . . . at this point I don't think I can continue to see the Muse as I have in the past. She has been most charming to me, but it had such an obvious goal that I feel ashamed. I'll acknowledge through some suitable present the help she gave me with finding a lodging, and little by little, quietly, I'll drop her.

In the Christmas season of 1853, Bouilhet maliciously advised Louise that Madame Flaubert had just completed an extensive stay in Paris with little Caroline. Upon learning that Gustave had never arranged a meeting with his mother, Louise's reaction was predictable. The plaintive letter that follows—again, a first draft she wrote in her Mementos—is the third and last of Louise's letters to Flaubert to have survived. It begins with a mention of a five-hundred-franc loan that Flaubert made to Louise the previous year (a loan she felt he had made very grudgingly).

Paris, January 6, 1854
Let's hope that [circumstances] will allow me to send you the money I owe you before your return to Paris; notwithstanding my misery, you've so often stressed your own penury that you've made me understand that this debt is constraining to you; this, joined to the discussion we've had concerning your mother, suffices to create that "cloud" in our relations which you mentioned in your last letter. . . .
All my flesh and intelligence are drawn and dominated by you. But I must admit that such a lack of delicacy represses the impulses of my heart and makes me wonder what lies in yours. . . .
I learn through Bouilhet that your mother just came through Paris without even thinking of paying me a visit, a visit that she might well have officially made, seeing the self-abnegating love I've had for you in the past three years, the hospitality I've offered you, the friends I've shared with you. . . .

Gustave had already told her that he did not see the sense of "linking two very different kinds of affection"; but since it meant so much to Louise, he had recently written her: "It shall be as you wish. I promise, I swear, that I will explain your reasons to her and ask her to arrange a meeting."
Yet Flaubert never acted on that promise. And Louise must have continued complaining about it; and she must also have nagged Flaubert about his projected move to Paris—would he *ever* finish that "Bovary" book? Flaubert felt pressed to set her straight on both issues.

In your note that came this morning, you ask me to reply to your letter of last Friday. . . . I will be categorical, explicit:
About my mother. Yes: your guess is correct. It is because I am persuaded that if she were to see you she would behave toward you less than politely that I prefer you not to see one another. Besides, I dislike this confusion, this bringing together of two very dissimilar kinds of affection. . . . Now once again I beg you: leave this issue alone.
. . . As for finishing Bovary, I have already set myself so many dates, and been mistaken so often, that I refuse not only to speak of it but to think of it. I no longer have any idea, and can only trust in God. It will be finished in its own good time, even if I die of vexation and impatience—which might very well happen were it not for the fury that sustains me. Meanwhile I will come to see you every two months, as I promised.

Here comes the crucial paragraph of Flaubert's letter:

Now, poor dear Louise, do you want me to tell you what I really think, or rather what you really feel? I think that your love is wavering. Your dissatisfactions, the sufferings I inflict on you, can have only that cause. . . .

Flaubert and Colet had read each other uncannily well over the past seven and a half years. Louise's love for Gustave may well have been wavering. Why else, after two years of self-control, had she resumed that strident demeanor which was bound to alienate him?

Moreover, in the early months of 1854, Louise became involved with yet another writer who some decades earlier had achieved as great a measure of "glory" as any man in France, a poet whose reputation, over the next century, would be equaled only by those of Hugo, Baudelaire, Rimbaud, and Verlaine.

A liaison between the flamboyant populist Louise Colet and the aloof, ultraconservative poet Alfred de Vigny, thirteen years her senior, was not at first glance a likely one. Yet no lover courted Louise more gallantly or waited more patiently for her to return his passion.

Comte Alfred de Vigny was born in 1797, the child of embittered *ancien régime* aristocrats. His rigorous education included the services of a British tutor who made him translate Homer from Greek into English, then compared his version to Alexander Pope's. After several years of military service, Vigny became a hero of the Romantic movement for his pioneering translation of Shakespeare's *Othello,* which was played at the Comédie Française. He won equal recognition for his novels *Cinq-Mars* and *Stello,* his austere verses, and his play *Chatterton,* which expressed more poignantly than any other work of his generation society's heartlessness toward poets.

Vigny maintained a haughty distance from the newly powerful middle class and all forms of popular culture (it was for Vigny's scornful detachment that the term *tour d'ivoire,* "ivory tower," was originally coined, in the 1830s, by Sainte-Beuve). Without the heroic facility of Hugo or the unctuous ease of Musset, Vigny struggled far more over his poetry than his peers, but his verse may survive the centuries better than that of any other French Romantic. In the decades before World War II, every French schoolchild had to memorize this quatrain:

J'aime le son du Cor, le soir, au fond des bois,
Soit qu'il chante les pleurs de la biche aux abois,
Ou l'adieu du chasseur que l'écho faible accueille
Et que le vent du nord porte de feuille en feuille. *

Louise Colet met Alfred de Vigny—known to his friends as "Stello" for his early novel—in the summer of 1846 at James Pradier's studio. Vigny had been instantly entranced with Louise, and they had talked at great length about poetry. She had sent him a selection of her works— *Charlotte Corday, Madame Roland,* and a little collection entitled *Les Femmes de Shakespeare.* Within a few days Vigny wrote her an effusive letter: "Bless you, Madame, for being as beautiful and courageous as your French heroines and as those Shakespearean women whom you love and understand like a sister. . . ."

Sadly for Vigny, at the time of this correspondence Louise was falling in love with Flaubert and did not give Vigny's love any chance to flower. "You're in a position to worry the shit out of Vigny," Flaubert had written Louise in one of his first letters, exultant that she was choosing him over the famous poet. That fall Vigny returned to his family estate near Angoulême to nurse his wife, an indolent British heiress—in twenty years she had never learned a word of French—with whom he had made a pragmatic marriage in his youth. (Her father, a merchant, had so disapproved of his daughter's marrying a poet that he unexpectedly withheld all dowry beyond a barren, abandoned Polynesian island.) Vigny remained in rural seclusion for seven years, tending his invalid spouse with an unfailing sense of duty and writing some of his finest poetry. In 1853, he returned to the capital because his wife needed the care of Parisian doctors, and he resumed his courtship of Louise.

"What a great vengeance for a woman to wrench the pen out of our hands and write the truth about us," he wrote Louise in early 1854, referring to "La Paysanne." "What a fine war to wage with your beautiful talent!"

Louise was hatching a plot to get her protégé, the impoverished poet Leconte de Lisle, some kind of award from the Académie Française. In her response to Vigny, she communicated this wish, and "Stello" graciously agreed to help.

---

*I love to hear the hunting horn, at night, deep in the woods,
When it rings with the weeping of the hunted doe,
Or the farewell of the hunter greeted by faint echoes
Carried leaf to leaf by the North wind.

"Will you excuse the continuation of my fierce attention?" Vigny wrote Louise, reporting on his mission. "Tomorrow night, somewhat before nine, I hope to have good news to bring you. Never fear that something which touches you might be indifferent to me. I even find charm in the distress which your tormented beauty causes in me."

Some weeks later, growing bolder, Vigny sent Louise a statuette of Venus, accompanied by more compliments: "You are admired and loved beyond measure; no one has yet placed you on a sufficiently high pedestal. . . . Saturday night at nine, I shall come to see if your door might open for me. . . ."

Louise's door, and much else, was indeed open. Vigny stayed until after midnight, and the new lovers made an appointment for two days thence. Stello was so thrilled by his conquest that he wrote Louise directly upon coming home that first night, using the giveaway *tu.* "Never has a Tuesday been longer in coming than this one. Loving, admiring, learning—such are the delectations of the hours spent with you. Retain for me this triple happiness, that triple consolation. Raise up your beautiful white arms. Do you dream, as I do, that tomorrow night you will spread them on my head and through my hair?"

Louise treated her romance with Vigny with far more circumspection than any previous affair. We have no record from her of her growing commitment to Vigny or the concurrent disintegration of her affair with Flaubert; only half a dozen of Louise's Mementos dated later than 1853 survived destruction, and few of the extant ones relate her emotions in depth. So her state of mind during the last months of her liaison with Flaubert must be traced exclusively through his correspondence.

Throughout March of 1854, Flaubert's letters to Louise—his last—are holding actions; they refer benignly to her many mentions of Vigny. "I'm so happy that you ferreted out Vigny! May that old nightingale's strains distract you!" "I count on Vigny, who sounds like a good fellow though he terms himself to be your *slave,* which is a bit Empire in taste." (It is probable that Bouilhet had advised Flaubert of Louise's new affair.) "He sounds like an excellent man, that good de Vigny . . . he's one of the few honest writers of our time: a great compliment! I'm grateful to him for the enthusiasm he evoked in me with his *Chatterton.* There were also lovely pages in *Stello.* . . . After all, his is a pleasant and distinguished talent, and he comes from the good epoch, he had Faith! He translated Shakespeare, gave hell to the bourgeois, understood history. Let's never mock that generation of fellows; they'll long survive all those who come after them."

In his fourth-to-last letter to Louise (April 12, 1854), Flaubert reiterates his ambivalence about her body, his disappointment that she has remained "too female" for his taste. "I've always tried (but it seems I've failed) to turn you into a sublime hermaphrodite. . . . I would wish you to be a man from the waist up. Going downward you encumber me and trouble me and damage me with your femaleness." (What remains of Louise in Flaubert's metaphors of mutilation?)

In this third-to-last letter, Flaubert lashes into her poem "À Ma Fille," and into her overall attitude toward literature and art.

"As for your stanza 'Of your pretty body,' I find it *atrocious!* in every way. . . . 'Of your pretty body under the blanket,' is obscene . . . 'blanket' is ignoble in its realism, besides the fact that the word in itself is ugly . . . all this is truly porcine . . . totally false in sentiment and expression. . . ." "The worst thing about it all is the subject matter. . . . I detest verse written to my daughter, to my father, to my mother, to my sister. These are prostitutions that scandalize me. . . ."

In his second-to-last letter, Flaubert once more castigates Louise's subjective writings: "I refuse to look on art as a slop pail for our passions, like a chamber pot barely cleaner than a confidence. . . . No, no! Poetry must not be the foam of the heart . . . Your daughter deserves better than to be depicted in verse lying *under her blanket,* etc." Flaubert even criticizes Louise's intrusion of the personal into their social life: The last time he was at her salon, he complains, she addressed him as *tu* in front of Leconte de Lisle, and it made him uncomfortable.

On April 29, 1854, in the last full-length letter Flaubert wrote to Louise, he tells her that he is coming to Paris in a few days. He promises to bring her the corrections he has made on a recent prose piece of hers, an essay that he predicts will be "a chef d'oeuvre of bad taste and chic."

Then a brief note, hastily penned in Paris, postponing a previously scheduled appointment for the following evening:

Dear Muse, it is impossible for me to come see you today; I'm exhausted and overwhelmed with work. Moreover, I'd forgotten that I must go to Braudry's to do some research concerning music for the Bovary. I've already made three fruitless attempts to get this information, I hope the fourth one will be more successful.

So adieu, or rather à bientôt—perhaps I'll see you Wednesday night, but certainly early Thursday.

Mille tendresses, G.

And then silence. Nothing more.

It must have been right after Louise received that note on an early-May weekend, that their last stormy encounter took place: the meeting at which Gustave stared at the roaring fire in Louise's little living room and carefully measured the distance between the flaming logs and her forehead. . . . "I was really quite ready to kill her," he would tell his friends years later."

Flaubert's last note to Louise, what historians call "the definitive letter of rupture," was written in 1855, a year after the scene by her fireplace.

In spite of her serene liaison with the famous, faithful, ever gallant de Vigny, the obscure provincial scribbler Gustave Flaubert remained the center of Louise's life. She would never resign herself to losing him. He moved to Paris in October of 1854, to finish his *Bovary* in a little flat on the Boulevard du Temple, where she left notes with his concierge, pleading with him to see her one more time. On many occasions she spied him out, and Flaubert felt so harassed by Louise's pursuit that he would draw down the shades of the hansom cabs he rode about in to avoid the possibility of her ever tracing his path.

Flaubert's cruel last note to Louise, which was intended to put an end to her quest for him, was written in the very weeks during which he was describing, in his novel, the ruthless manner in which Emma Bovary's first lover abandons her. And there is much that is reminiscent of the cowardly Rodolphe in Flaubert's harshness toward his mistress.

In breaking with Louise Colet—a woman whom he had loved and esteemed above any other, who had healed the self-doubts inflicted by his philistine family and offered him a unique self-assurance about his vocation, who, tempestuous and possessive as she was, had served as the catalyst for his genius—he was very curt.

Madame: I was told that you took the trouble to come here to see me three times last evening.

I was not in. And, fearing that your persistence might provoke me to humiliate you, wisdom leads me to warn you that I shall never be in.

I have the honor of saluting you.

G.F.

"Lâche, couard et canaille," "Coward, poltroon and scum," Louise scribbled in her gigantic, irate hand in the margin of Flaubert's last missive.

Louise had only one more glimpse of Flaubert—in 1863, at a crowded reception in Paris. She was shocked by his corpulence and his general physical deterioration. "God, he's ugly! Just look how ugly he's become!" she exclaimed to Henriette.

After Flaubert exited from Louise's life, the author ceased his fastidious chronicling of his progress on *Madame Bovary*. There is no extensive record of the last third of the novel's composition. We know far less about the sequence in which Flaubert plotted his scenes, which sections gave him the greatest anguish, what discrepancies exist between original intent and final execution. We know only of the ruthlessness with which he dedicated his life to his mother, and to his art.

"Art, like the God of the Jews, feasts on holocausts": Gustave Flaubert to Louise Colet, August 21, 1853.

13.

Stello and Olympio

As they began their affair in the spring of 1854, Alfred de Vigny found in Louise Colet many of the qualities he had longed for in other women. This aloof intellectual had always resented having to educate his mistresses "in order to make them capable of conversing with me," and in Louise he found an equal. He had always had a reverence for melancholia; in the "Goddess of the Romantics" he appreciated a streak of sadness which he thought to be innate, and whose true cause (Flaubert's defection) Louise never revealed to him.

A model of self-control, a man of sternly ingrained habits, Vigny had an uncanny gift for calming Louise's frequent fits of bad temper. He had the custom of placing his cane in precisely the same place each time he entered her flat. One day, exasperated by Vigny's rigid ways, Louise threw his cane out the window. Without saying a word, Vigny put on his gloves and hat, went down the three flights of stairs into the street, retrieved his cane, and calmly put it back in its habitual place. Louise was disarmed.

Vigny lived across the city from Louise, on the Right Bank, with his reclusive British wife, Lydia Barnsbury. Though Lydia was a stout, childless, dim-witted invalid, he treated her with solicitude. He took pride in having "sacrificed all my desires for liberty in order to dedicate myself to her welfare, as a mother world to her daughter" and wished to spare her any suspicions concerning his affair with Louise.

So within a few weeks Louise's liaison with Vigny assumed a ritual punctuality, radically different from the erratic schedule she had endured with Flaubert. On Tuesdays and Thursdays—the days members of Académie Française convened—he walked from the Académie's building on Quai Malaquais to Louise's flat on the Rue de Sèvres, to spend the evening and a good part of the night with her.

One of the most interesting aspects of Vigny's relationship with Louise was the close paternal bond he formed with Henriette, who had become a beautiful, very bright, very difficult fifteen-year-old. Henriette's complex character—conformist yet mercurial, pious yet vain—perplexed all who were close to her, especially her mother. Henriette's correspondence with Victor Cousin, who continued to look on her as an adopted daughter even after he had totally ceased to see her mother, reveals some of the difficulties she faced:

"I hope that the painful confrontation [with your mother] is behind you," Cousin wrote Henriette after she'd had a particularly distressing blowup with Louise. "and that you're back to your sweet, cheerful self." Despite his notorious stinginess, Cousin would literally bribe Henriette to get her out of her dark moods: "Can I send you flowers, books . . . a coat . . . a little piece of jewelry?" Indeed, the willowy, blond-locked Henriette must have been as captivating as her mother had been in her youth; for Cousin, a fastidious judge of women, looked upon her as "my only happiness on earth," "the consolation of my solitary last years."

A man with a strong sense of family ties who would have enjoyed educating a large brood of offspring, Vigny seemed to be as entranced with Henriette as Cousin was; and he was all the more devoted to her because propriety had kept him from formally acknowledging his daughter by his former British mistress, Augusta Holmes. Vigny's letters to Louise concerning the "little husband," or the "little blond devil," as he referred to the assertive Henriette, reveal his gifts as an educator.

Spoil her as much as you can, I shall do as much as I can to help you in that task. It is essential that she believe, for a few years, that life is a very happy thing. We shall deceive her together and we'll let her retain all the illusions she's learning in her boarding school. Let them last as long as possible. . . . One blow to her house of cards, and we'll build others for her. [When dealing with the young] one must always ward off the enemy—the boredom and inevitable sadness of human existence.

Vigny enjoyed accompanying mother and daughter to the theater. And a sizable amount of his correspondence with Louise, in that first year, is dedicated to which of the dramas being performed at the Théâtre Français were most suitable for an impressionable teenager (notwithstanding his active love life, Vigny had a puritanical streak and detested any depiction of adultery). He vetoed Henriette's attending of one of Molière's most entertaining comedies, *George Dandin; or, The Deceived Husband.*

> *Dear friend [he wrote Louise], How can we allow your Little Husband to hear the Deceived Husband cry out "My children will be gentlemen and I shall be [a cuckold]—"*
> "What's that word, Mommy, what does that mean?"
> *Dear God, what could we answer? I tremble at the very prospect of these abysmal difficulties.*

Vigny chose other dramas suitable for Henriette:

> *The play* Louis XI *will suit us ideally. . . . There'll be brand-new characters there, and other, more ancient, better-known ones. During the intermission we can show Mademoiselle Henriette charming sculptures that she may not yet know. . . . You should teach her, ahead of time, the names of those great Poets and dramatists whom she'll see there.*

He was also good at soothing the quarrels between mother and daughter, which were growing increasingly violent.

> *It was painful for me to leave you last Thursday night, poor dear little Mommy, your maternal tears remained heavily on my heart. . . . Have you forgiven those harebrained, childish outbursts? . . . When she becomes more reflective, peace will be regained. But reflection is the enemy of all young people. They interpret every advice as a sermon— that's inevitably what schoolgirls call any serious talk. All that comes from their parents and their teachers seems suspect even before they've heard it. One must wait until serious feelings arise spontaneously in*

their gay, cold little hearts, which remain volatile because they still look on all of life as a game.

Vigny's insights into adolescent psychology were astute, and he often warned Louise to curb her own quick temper when confronting the "little blond devil" Henriette.

How could her blood, the same that runs in your own veins, not boil when she feels your pain? How could she not share your sorrows? In my opinion, her tenderness is hidden under a kind of false pride that forbids children to speak out their true feelings. They don't know how to show affection and even laugh about it with a true cruelty, trying to preserve a front of cold gaiety. . . . Feel certain that your Ondine does have a soul but does not wish it to be seen yet, and fears to even admit it to herself. She will show it entirely one day, with a big hug.

Vigny also understood, as no other lover had, Louise's grief over the death of her last infant son. She kept his sculpted likeness on her desk. "I've often seen you grow tearful at the sight of that mysterious little plaster bust standing in your study; your heart still bleeds, and you're rechanneling all of your tenderness upon your pretty little novice."

So Louise could not have found a more perfect companion. Not only was this glamorous writer an ideal surrogate parent for her child, he was as supportive as any man had ever been of her career. He praised her "virility of soul" and even urged her (an impulse rare among his male peers) to relish her freedom. "Why haven't you get gotten accustomed to the pride and dignity of your independence?"

Vigny was also the most passionate lover Louise had ever had. "It's very hot under his ermine," Sainte-Beuve once quipped about him. Vigny himself had described his temperament as "powerfully voluptuous." His letters to Louise are as explicitly sensual as any she received from Flaubert:

On your beautiful neck your plaits of blond hair constantly cover and uncover the little pink marks my kisses left on your breast. As long as we are still able to reason, we'll let our lips follow their passions without a word and I'll leave you lying all pale on your large pillows. . . . Your beautiful arms hugging my neck, your naked shoulders, whose grace I keep constantly in mind—the very memory of all that makes me tremble.

Why was Louise not more taken with this exemplary suitor, who so perfectly combined, in his own words, "a savage heart and a civilized spirit"? Beyond the mystery of sexual chemistry, two things come to mind. One has to do with Vigny's reclusiveness: He could not stand sharing Louise with anyone but Henriette, and he particularly hated her salons, which she considered crucial to her literary career. "I don't like your Sunday salons because I had to say *vous* to you," he wrote her, "and because you become a *lady* again, with nothing left of the woman who loves and feels loved, who waits for my passionate adoration."

The few times Louise convinced Vigny to attend one of her soirees, he stayed in the corner, surveying the crowd with a glacial, contemptuous air. He looked down his nose at famous scientists and men of letters, with the air of a "constipated swan," a "steely-haired mummy," as acquaintances described him. He barely listened to other poets read their verses and found pleasure solely in the company of Leconte de Lisle. A contemporary journalist described Vigny's aloof behavior.

"Although he was one of her intimates, Alfred de Vigny was seldom seen at these occasions," the eyewitness wrote. "Madame Colet used to tell us that Madame Dorval, Vigny's former mistress, had never once seen him eat. One guest claimed that he had to change his teeth for dinner. . . . Alfred de Vigny rarely talked. When he did, it was with the slowly grave timbre of a huge town clock, his axioms falling like the strokes of a hammer."

But there was an even more important reason why Vigny could not totally captivate Louise: Her obsession with Flaubert remained undiminished.

Soon after their last stormy meeting by her fireplace, Louise, in a characteristic display of punctiliousness and pride, struggled hard to return to Flaubert the eight hundred francs she owed him. Borrowing from friends, within a few weeks she sent the money, enclosed in a little red purse, via Louis Bouilhet. The receipt of the cash was acknowledged by Bouilhet: "Do excuse, *chère Madame,* this tiny note, this tiny piece of paper. I am officially announcing to you that Gustave received the eight hundred francs." ("Chère Madame?" For the two previous years, all communications from Bouilhet to Louise had been addressed to *"Chère Muse"* or, even more often, *"Chère soeur."*)

Bouilhet accompanied the note with a letter he had just received from Flaubert: "I must tell you that I threw myself on this money *with the avidity of a savage"* (the emphasis is Flaubert's). "Thank her for the purse, of course, which is charming."

"*Avidity of a savage*"—*Flaubert's emphatic phrasing, and the insensitivity with which Bouilhet deliberately exposed Louise to it, are amazing.* ("*Keep that money or return it to me, it's fine either way,*" *Flaubert had written Louise only three months earlier.*)

In one of the rare surviving Mementos of 1854, written soon after Bouilhet's note, Louise recorded the pain caused her by this most recent instance of Flaubert's churlishness.

> Horrors, what egotism! He knows of my privations. . . . He's even worse than all the others, being more intelligent.
>
> It all fills me with disgust. . . . No memory could enable me to regain any feeling for him. The notion of asking him to return all my souvenirs and letters, a prospect which once seemed impossible, now returns. . . .

(If only she *had* asked him to return her letters, as she intended to do back in the summer of 1851!)

The journal entry culminates in an outburst of emotional violence.

> I would like to reject him from my life like excrement. What a low nature! . . . How vile men are! . . . Today I feel no desire ever to see him again, and I think that void of feeling will last.

Louise's obsession with Flaubert remained unabated. In the hope that he might help to effect a reconciliation, she continued to pursue Bouilhet with notes, querying him about Flaubert's state of mind. Bouilhet responded by opening her wounds, underscoring Flaubert's indifference to her. Here is another note from Bouilhet, ostensibly written to acknowledge two books Louise had just sent him (her poem "La Servante" and her new collection of poetry, *Ce qu'on rêve en aimant*) but obviously intended to emphasize Flaubert's disaffection. (The emphases are Bouilhet's.)

> I mentioned Stello's name to him many times without him making any response. *I've already passed on to you his opinion of your volume: he very much likes "Appaisement" but is less impressed by the other pieces. Notwithstanding our reading of your verse, he never mentioned you in any way whatsoever.* . . . *His mother is well again; he is coming to live in Paris* at the end of October. *You can imagine my surprise at his sudden change of plans.*

Bouilhet seemed very pleased with that particular letter. He wrote Flaubert a few days later to say that he was "gracefully getting rid" of

Louise. "I've told her that I had absolutely nothing to say concerning you . . . in other words I sent her packing." A few weeks later, in October, Bouilhet must have shot a few more poisoned darts in Louise's direction, for the last of the Colet Mementos that survive for that year, dated October 1854, reads as follows:

> Bouilhet's arrival, my grief, my tears. His first visit Tuesday; he returns Wednesday. A scene concerning the Durey woman. He finds the courage to tell me that F. had wished to break with me for six months. I am convinced that he has been devious toward me. My sorrow, my rage, imperious desire to see F. just one more time. Anguish, irritation, barely the courage to see my daughter. . . . Stello is sick, heartache.

She concluded her entry with these pathetic verses: "Oh! Miserable woman / You will never be loved / Poor condemned one, lie down to die."

Louise sent Flaubert a few more notes during his winter's stay in Paris. He was living at 42 Boulevard du Temple, near the Place de la République, where he would stay for many more winters. Only one of these futile missives has survived, dated March 3, 1855:

> Paris, Saturday morning. I leave tomorrow for a trip abroad. . . . I may be away for a long while. It is absolutely essential that we see each other and talk a bit before I leave. It would be childish for you to consult with anyone about this meeting, and boorish to refuse it. So I shall wait for you tonight with confidence, from eight P.M. to midnight.

It is the persistence of such letters that caused Flaubert, two days later, to write his famous last communication to Louise ("wisdom leads me to warn you that I *shall never be in*").

Flaubert's boorishness toward Louise did not cease with his final note. Until he received news of her death, which preceded his by four years and seemed to affect him deeply, Flaubert derided Louise publicly. "I'd say about her what Danton said about Marat," he quipped to friends. "She was not sociable." He generally led his acquaintances to think of her as meddlesome (which she was to a degree). "She always came too early and left too late. . . . She wouldn't have left Flaubert alone with his pedicurist," Théophile Gautier reported.

But by far the most cruel remark on his one great love was Flaubert's report to the Goncourts that he had feigned desire for Louise at the beginning of their affair. Even during that memorable first cab drive they had taken in the last days of July 1846, Flaubert told the Goncourts, he had only simulated passion. "In his first lovemaking with Louise, which occurred right in a hansom cab," the tattling brothers wrote, Flaubert had "repeatedly leaned out of the carriage to hide his derision of her and have a good laugh."

There was at least one note of decency on Flaubert's part regarding the manner in which he chronicled his relationship with Louise: He admitted to friends that his mother had always criticized the harshness with which Flaubert had treated his mistress. He told them that Madame Flaubert had referred to his conduct with Louise as "an affront to her own sex" and had particularly resented his merciless refusal ever to let her into their home (Louise was obviously the last person to whom Gustave would have admitted this). "It's been the only troubled issue in my relations with my mother," Flaubert told the Goncourts.

Far greater malice toward Louise permeated the gossipy writings of Maxime Du Camp. In his *Souvenirs littéraires,* Du Camp made many biographical errors in his portrait of Louise; he unwittingly flattered her by making her five years younger, and he garbled her family history: "She was born in 1815; her father had been a professor of drawing in Lyons. . . . Her husband, who has always been maligned, was an excellent man, passionate about his music, of gentle and pleasant character." (The petty, irascible Hippolyte?)

Describing Louise's liaison with Flaubert, Du Camp did all he could to minimize her importance in the author's life: "He had hoped that it would be an adventure of no consequence, one of those agreeable and vulgar accidents that have no future."

And in a passage probably as inaccurate as his account of Louise's family, one that would be quoted by generations of literary historians, Du Camp dismissed Louise's good looks with the following remarks: "The opinion she had of her beauty ended up making her uglier. Her eyes lowered, her lips pursed like a heart, she used to ask candidly: 'Do you know where the arms of the Venus de Milo were found?'—'Where?'— 'In the sleeves of my dress.' Bouilhet used to say: 'She has a natural lack of naturalness.' "

Du Camp also asserted that upon their last meeting, Louise "threw a flaming log" at Flaubert's head—a detail Flaubert would surely have used to great humorous effect in his own table talk if it had been true, and an interesting garbling of Flaubert's stated impulse to throw a log at *Louise's* head. "Her epitaph would not be long," Du Camp concludes his portrait of Louise. " 'Here lies she who compromised Victor Cousin, ridiculed Alfred de Musset, vilified Gustave Flaubert, and tried to assassinate Alphonse Karr. *Requiescat in pace!* ' "

In spite of the great cooling of their relations, Du Camp had a very proprietary attitude toward Flaubert, and he continued until his last days to slander Flaubert's one acknowledged mistress. If Louise Colet, until the past few decades, has been maligned as few women authors have, it is because the influential Du Camp pioneered a tradition of Colet-bashing which was perpetuated by several generations of French literary critics.

As it happened, Du Camp's estimation of Flaubert's talent was as inaccurate as his portrait of Louise was malicious, and equally tinged with jealousy: "Gustave Flaubert was a writer of rare talent," Du Camp wrote in his memoirs. "If he had not suffered from a nervous disease, he would have been a man of genius."

It is ironic that the period of Louise's deepest personal unhappiness—those months in which she began to realize that Flaubert was irretrievably lost to her—coincided with her greatest literary success. In 1854, she won her fourth poetry prize from the Académie Française. Louise now had the distinction of having received the award more times than any other woman in French literary history.

The theme of the contest was "The Acropolis of Athens." It was a politically impeccable topic, for under the patronage of Napoleon III, who was fascinated by archaeology, France was entering its golden age of classical studies. The Acropolis was also a subject suited to Louise's Mediterranean origins and her pride in the Greek antiquities of Provence. "As a child and a young woman I meditated amid the ruins of Arles's temples and its theater," she wrote in a memoir. "Nîmes's Maison Carrée long ago made me dream of the Parthenon. I had literally lived in an Athenian colony, and this mother country had always obsessed me."

Louise submitted her entry anonymously, as she had the last time round. Upon winning, she received the additional honor of having Alfred de Vigny, to whom the poem was dedicated, read it at the Académie's ceremony.

Only a few weeks later, Louise published one of her loveliest collections of poems—*Ce qu'on rêve en aimant,* "What We Dream of When We Love." The volume drew praise from Victor Hugo. She was also composing the third section of her *Poème de la Femme,* "La Religieuse," whose epigraph was boldly feminist: "From the Word of God came Creation / From the Word of Man came Liberty / From the Word of Woman will come her liberation." And in 1855, Louise must have found some therapeutic relief in writing her first book-length fiction, a roman à clef entitled *Une Histoire de Soldat.*

This book, Louise's desperate final appeal to Flaubert, was the talk of Paris for some months. It was conceived in the "framed narrative" form then fashionable in French fiction, its tragedies recounted by the virtuous servant girl Madeleine to a small circle of Paris literati (among them a "sensitive poet" and a "famous sculptor" closely resembling Alfred de Musset and James Pradier). Madeleine is the girlfriend of the wholesome peasant boy Pierre and serves as personal maid to the beautiful young widow Caroline de Lorme. Caroline (the baptismal name of Flaubert's darling sister and his niece) has "ringlets of blond hair," lives in an apartment "all painted and furnished in shades of sky blue," and is courted by "the richest men." She has refused them all, for she is in love with Léonce, a fellow of "tall height, most beautiful of face," who lives in a château some hours from Paris and is constantly rushing back to it because he is urgently expected there by his mother.

Every detail of *Une Histoire de Soldat* is painfully true to the particulars of Louise's last decade: Caroline is often visited by Léonce's "false friend"—undeniably modeled on Bouilhet—who will eventually turn Léonce against her. Like their real-life originals, Léonce and Caroline meet for their rare trysts in a little riverside town "with a pretty church belfry," as there had been in Mantes, at a local inn named Auberge du Chevreuil (Louise and Gustave used to meet at Mantes's Hôtel du Grand *Cerf,* another word for *chevreuil,* "deer").

A tearful evening quarrel incited by the wiles of the "false friend" disrupts this idyll, and many months go by without Léonce coming to Paris. Caroline decides to call on Léonce at his country estate, her devoted maid Madeleine in tow. The expedition proves to be her "Calvary and Mount of Olives." It is pouring rain. From within the dark, forbidding dwelling, which "looks like a cemetery," Madeleine hears a clamor of voices and Madame Caroline's sobs. She then sees her mistress emerging from Léonce's house, "whiter than a shroud, her eyes looking like two spots of blood." Hark, who is that "dour, cantankerous-looking lady" ushering Caroline out?

A woman dressed in black was walking behind her, silently lighting the way. . . . This woman's tall, cold form resembled a funerary statue in

some church. *Her austere black wool dress made one know that she
was a widow who had never once smiled since her husband's death.*

There's an interesting Oedipal touch in Louise's fictional portrait of
Madame Colet: Despite the old lady's harshness, Caroline embraces her
"as if she were her mother" (my italics).

*The old woman looked startled [Madeleine relates] and said "Cour-
age!" after she had opened the door which gave onto the courtyard.
   The rain was pouring so hard no one would have put out a dog, yet
not a word was said to retain us. What kind of a mother and son were
these, leaving a poor, desperate woman to go out into that kind of
night?*

Caroline is so shocked by this rejection that she takes to her bed for
months. Finally, her doctor and her friends persuade her to go to the
theater in the company of the faithful Madeleine. Whom do they see
there, in a loge opposite theirs, but Léonce and his "false friend," in the
company of two strumpets, one round-faced and dark-haired, another
snub-nosed and red-haired—miniportraits of the actresses who were
Bouilhet's and Flaubert's lovers that season, Marie Durey and Beatrix
Person. (Person, who would remain Flaubert's mistress for another two
years, was currently acting in Paris in a play called *Le Juif de Vérone*.)
Madeleine describes the strumpet-actresses:

*Their dresses were so décolleté that they looked undressed. They dis-
played their teeth, laughing out loud and eating candy. . . . Monsieur
Léonce . . . was very changed: his red face was swollen as if with too
much drink, his body was bursting out of his white waistcoat; he had
lost the brilliance of his eyes, their gaze now thickened and clouded.*

Madeleine resolves that for the sake of her health, Madame must not
see Monsieur Léonce; she must immediately leave the theater. . . . But
alas, she can not wrench her mistress out of her seat in time. At the sight
of Léonce and his moll, Caroline de Lorme cries out and falls into a faint.
She never recovers consciousness and dies within a few hours. It is the
faithful Madeleine and her Pierre, about to enter into a blissful lifelong
marriage, who hold Madame's wake and bury her (compare the fidelity
and happiness of virtuous lower-class folk to the fecklessness and degradation of the upper crust).

Louise began this dark, confessional fantasy in the spring of 1855, soon after receiving Flaubert's last note, and finished it that fall. It was published the following February, and *le tout Paris* had a wonderful time guessing about who was who. Alas, instead of being moved to pity, Flaubert found the novel hilarious. "I split my sides laughing," he wrote to a friend. "That's what you get for having———with Muses" (Flaubert's elision).

Less biased readers also found it naive and sloppily written. Yet its melodramatic effects were in vogue, and some fans of Louise's found it wonderful. "What natural, genuine, and naive grace in this overly brief work!" Béranger exclaimed.

Louise received an equally warm acknowledgment from her pen pal Victor Hugo: "Your *Histoire de Soldat* is making the rounds of our group . . . everyone is fighting to read it and reread it. . . . Emotion, love, life are all there. The naive narrative voice enhances it all. It is ravishingly written. There's an exquisite sensibility under each word and a great sorrow throughout the book. . . ."

Sorrow there was—raw, undigested sorrow, for which the book was an attempted exorcism as well as a last plea for compassion. Did Louise truly believe that Flaubert, moved by her story, might return to her? Given her monumental capacity for self-delusion, it is quite possible that she did.

Since so few of Louise's Mementos for these years have survived, she can live for us only as in an echo chamber, her emotions glimpsed through the letters of a few friends. No surviving correspondence evokes her anguish in that decade more poignantly than the one she shared with the Olympian Victor Hugo.

In 1855, three years after he was exiled from France, Hugo, in the company of Juliette Drouet, moved from Jersey to the equally barren isle of Guernsey. By then a formidable entourage of relatives and friends had joined him: his wife Adèle, who still made frequent trips to Paris to look after the family's finances; his daughter Adèle, or "Dédé"; the family acolyte, Auguste Vacquerie, the brother of the Hugos' deceased son-in-law, who served as a glorified secretary and would become a good friend of Louise Colet's; Hugo's two sons, François-Victor and Charles-Victor, both in their late twenties; and a large assortment of domestics. Drouet lived in a separate house with her maid, within walking distance of the "Holy Family" 's residence.

Once settled in the Channel Islands, this clan had immediately become a kind of Hugo factory. Olympio began to write masterpieces at an unprecedented rate, his exile having spared him the most debilitating elements of his Paris life—no more debates in the French parliament, no more women sapping him dry. A volume composed at the beginning of Hugo's exile, *Contemplations,* in which philosophic essays mingled with lovely verses addressed to his daughter and to Juliette Drouet, received unprecedented acclaim. His tirade against the French monarch, *Napoléon le Petit,* sold a million copies in a dozen languages.

Every member of the Hugo tribe documented a different aspect of the genius's exile. His wife, Adèle, wrote *Victor Hugo raconté par un témoin de sa vie,* "Victor Hugo, by a Witness of His Life." His sons took up photography and left posterity innumerable daguerreotypes of their old man walking, writing, dressing, and bathing. In addition to socializing with the hundreds of other French political exiles living on Guernsey, who looked on the author as the symbolic head of the French émigré community, the Hugo family engaged in numerous ritual pastimes. For two years they practiced spiritualist table tipping, a fad that was currently the rage of Paris: They shared talks with Hugo's dead daughter, Léopoldine, and they conversed with Molière, Shakespeare, Dante, Racine, Marat, Charlotte Corday, Mahomet, Jesus Christ, Plato, and even with some animals—the dove of Noah's ark and Balaam's ass.

There were also numerous epistolary conversations with fellow dissidents in France who were courageous enough to correspond with the exiled giant, such as Louise Colet. Fully aware of the risks she was taking (a schoolmate of Flaubert's had been sentenced to a year's jail term for distributing Hugo's pamphlet on Napoleon III), Louise was steadfast in the correspondence she had begun with the writer in 1852. The same empathy and literary acumen that had seduced Flaubert into writing Louise his most self-probing letters led Hugo to open his heart to her. "What startles me is the stormy pace of life that has continued right into my exile," he wrote Louise from Jersey in the spring of 1854.

> *After all, I have won the right to a bit of solitude. Well, no, the mayhem of bustling incidents and speeding events—this mayhem seeks me out right into my hole, finds me in all possible forms—visits, questions, quests for advice, solicitations for aid, etc., etc.; and my hours and days and weeks are spent giving audience to all this make-believe business, to all these embryonic happenings, which are continually pulling this outlaw by the sleeve. . . .*

"Where will the wind carry me next?" he wrote her the following month.

The Spanish papers announce that their government offers me hospitality. I'm tempted by that beautiful sunshine, being a native of blue-sky regions. But alas, how sad to go even farther away! From here I can see the shore of France, and to see France is to see Paris, and to see you. The sea, and France on its other side—it would be sad to lose that horizon.

The following fall:

Women like you (so rare) appear to us from afar like the last halos of our poor dead motherland. I thank you for having so much heart, so much talent and soul, for writing such beautiful verses, for emitting such a soft and proud glow; I thank you for embellishing and crowning my France, which a bandit is stifling and sullying.

Hugo's affection and admiration for Louise were genuine. Along with Béranger and, later, Zola, he would be the only major nineteenth-century French writer to cherish her kind of aggressive female independence and to admire women's capacity for intellectual achievement. Yet Hugo's flatteries to Louise must have been at least occasionally motivated by his desire to retain her loyalty as a correspondent: "You write me the world's most ravishing letters. Make them as long and as frequent as possible, please. Thank the gentle, tender soul who writes them. . . . Exile whitens my hair, which does not keep me from throwing myself at your feet." "Your writing has a true, grave, powerful touch and yet remains gentle. Dare, dare try everything. It is your right and your duty. You are Muse and goddess. Do not fear to go naked."

And Louise responded with accounts of Paris's political and literary life under Napoleon III—some of them worthy of Saint-Simon or Sévigné in their vividness. She still referred to the emperor as "the man" or "that December man" (for his December 1851 coup d'état). Here is an interesting passage of Louise's concerning a hunt at the royal residence of Compiègne:

One hears that the man's wife, to whom I deny all capacity for feeling since she agreed to lie down in that red bed of December, affects a great sensitivity and weeps to excess . . . at the last hunt at Compiègne, when a stag was forced, the entire pack of hunters invaded the courtyard of a forest farmhouse; the hunted animal went to the wall to escape the swords, the December man adjusted his rifle; tears were streaming from the stag's eyes; Theba [Empress Marie Eugénie] cried out: "Oh, Sire, do not kill that poor weeping beast!" The lady herself was on the verge of tears as she spoke, the entire court was moved, the man let his rifle drop and said, like a well-trained opera escort, "Your will be done, Madame; we'll ask Maréchal Ney to kill the animal."

M. Ney rushed forward with his hunting dagger; he misses the beast, which is merely wounded and furiously charges the horses and carriages crowded into the courtyard; [Minister of Finance] Fould is knocked over; Madame Tayer, thrown against a wheel, breaks a leg; Theba weeps and loosens the lady's laces. All this was told to me by an eyewitness, who agreed with me that such sensitivity regarding a stag was juvenile, seeing all those humans whom they are killing or allowing to die. . . . Catherine de Médicis, after seeing the Huguenots burn from the terrace of the castle of Amboise, would also perhaps be lachrymose at the sight of a stag! Ah! please . . . dear master, brand this enthroned harlot with the imprint of your indignant verses!

Incited by his praise ("We read your letters *en famille,* and you make us weep, and sometimes you make us laugh. And that is a triumph, to make exiles laugh"), Louise also wrote Hugo some malicious passages of literary gossip.

Solitude, passion for art, and your encouragements, cher maître, are sorely needed among us. What is now missing in France, in poetry and literature, is patience. In all domains one is hasty, precipitous, noisome: what an example that poor Alexandre Dumas offers! Certainly he has imagination and a kind character, but his boasting and ostentation shock and revolt me. . . . Only this defect could explain Dumas's love for that poor Madame Waldor, . . . a pathetic woman so bereft of all qualities that through sheer pride she should have renounced love for her entire life. . . .

"Write me, write me, write me!" the exiled Hugo pleaded in response. "Your letters are the world's prettiest blondes. They graciously chatter and smile while showing charming teeth, which could well bite. I love the maliciousness that escapes from you. Like your cries of anguish, it comes from the nobility of your heart. Your letters' only flaw is that they're too short, even when you think they're long. . . ."

It was inevitable that Louise and Hugo would eventually meet. In the spring of 1856 (shortly after she had published *Une Histoire de Soldat* and was more despairing than ever of moving Flaubert to pity), Louise wrote Hugo that she was thinking of coming to pay him a visit in Guernsey. "Life is short," she wrote. "Death annihilates us after a few days of struggle, and we pass by those who are made to understand us, and whom we might have loved, without even shaking their hands."

Hugo responded enthusiastically, though he warned her of the political risks. "The Guernsey excursion has its particular perils. Have you weighed them? Have you decided to brave them? I know your courage is equal to your talent. . . . However, I must warn you that 'those people' are capable of all cowardice and vengeance. . . . My wife looks forward with joy to receiving you."

A few weeks later, Hugo outlined specific plans for Louise's venture. He had initially invited her to stay at his own residence, but upon further reflection he decided that it would increase her risk.

I shall not come to meet your boat, for my presence would alarm Bonaparte's entire spying system. Upon arriving, ask to be driven to the home of a Madame Rénier, at the Crown Hotel. The other hotel (Hotel de L'Europe) is haunted by the so-called French police. . . . You exude glory, and halos are treacherous.

The steamer's schedule allows you to arrive on a Tuesday, Thursday, or Saturday. Try to arrive on Tuesday.

The Hugo clan in Guernsey occupied a vast residence named Hauteville House, whose eccentric trappings had been paid for out of the author's royalties for *Contemplations* and which would remain his home until his return to France. All at Hauteville House was dark and foreboding. It was filled with gothic hangings, medieval doodads, armchairs dating from the time of the premedieval French king Dagobert. In the drawing room, amid a bizarre medley of the French Middle Ages and the Far East, a large canopied bed of Venetian origin was supported by six life-size Negroes in painted wood.

The first floor of this large, very English folly was occupied by the Hugo women, the second by the poet's sons. On the third floor Hugo had constructed a belvedere, which dominated the sea and from which, on a clear day, he could see the French coast. He wrote by the window, standing at a small, flat-topped desk, and slept in a small adjacent attic. Maids and other servants occupied the rooms next door, and the genius did more than sleep in his tiny chamber, for his diaries are filled with appreciative notes in garbled Spanish and Latin relating to nocturnal visits with these young women—Fanny, Julia, Constance, Marianne, Rosalie, Co-elina: *"Visto y tomado Julia,"* "I saw and possessed Julia."

It had taken Hugo some maneuvering to make his wife accept the presence of Juliette Drouet. At forty-six, Juliette had become a fat dowager, but Hugo was true to their twenty-year relationship and could never forget the way she had saved his life during the uprisings that followed Napoleon III's coup in 1851. So Juliette endured the tedium of exile in a little villa a few hundred yards from the Hugos' residence. She could see her beloved "Toto" from her window but was forbidden ever to address a word to his wife. Every day at dawn, having had her daily letter to the genius delivered by her maid, along with the two boiled eggs she always cooked for him, Juliette was content to watch for Hugo's rising, feasting her eyes on the body of her lover as he stood on his terrace performing his morning ablutions.

Then Juliette would wait through the morning for the hour's stroll Hugo accorded her every day after lunch, during which she usually had to walk beside him in silence; on those rare days when she was allowed to speak, she poured out her concern for his health, gently berating him for the silence he had imposed on her during the previous weeks and for his philandering with all those maids. For some fourteen more years, until the overthrow of Napoleon III and the establishment of the Third Republic in 1870, when Hugo returned to France, this model of fidelity would be content with very small joys.

We have no notion whether Louise met Juliette during her week's stay in Guernsey with the Hugos. It is doubtful. It is more likely that Louise saw her from afar, puttering on her little terrace. We do know that Louise took long walks on the beach with the master and confided to him her most intimate sorrows about Flaubert. Hugo apparently offered to approach Flaubert and plead Louise's cause.

> *I'll never forget the last hours of my stay in Guernsey [Louise wrote Hugo upon returning to Paris] . . . the bounty of your heart when mine involuntary opened its anguish to it. I thought carefully about what you told me, the fraternal intervention you proposed making toward that perverse spirit; at first I wished for such a mediation, and then my courage failed me. What purpose would it serve? I have no more faith in him; he broke it; he would have to come back to me on his own, or I would not believe in his return. . . .*

Louise had conquered the heart of every member of Hugo's family; her warm friendship with Madame Hugo and her sons would bring her much consolation in the following years. "How kind, gracious, and thoughtful you were to us," Adèle Hugo wrote a while later, after Louise had entertained the master's family in Paris. "I'm in haste to see you here to return a bit of your touching hospitality. . . . A big kiss to your daughter."

During the weeks when Louise was traveling in the British Isles, Alfred de Vigny was taking solicitous care of young Henriette. This parental attention was the principal form of affection Louise still accepted from Vigny, for in the early months of 1856 their relations had been strained by Vigny's persistent illnesses.

In February, the poet had ripped the tendons in his foot when stepping out of a moving carriage. His leg remained swollen for some months, and he was unable to stand or walk. "I suffer and I work to forget you," he wrote Louise, who several times visited him at his home, along with Henriette, without evoking his wife's suspicions.

There were only three or four such visits, and Vigny did not find them sufficient. Throughout their relationship he had complained that Louise tended to neglect him in favor of her compulsive socializing. "How can you hope to write anything of scope while running about Paris all day long?" he scolded her. "The dissipation of a large city is a foreign country whose noise and language separate us from ourselves, from our ideas, from our very emotions. . . . Come, my angel, sit down the way I do, think carefully and write your beautiful verses." "For the past eighteen days you've been running about so many parts of Paris that it would have been easy for you to drop in on me," he complained another time.

The spring months of 1856 were filled with such remonstrances, most passion spent. In August, when Louise left to visit Hugo, she sent Henriette to a summer boarding school, where Vigny often went to see her. "I saw the pretty little Henriette again, quite saddened by your absence, but gentle, resigned," he wrote Louise in Great Britain. "She has a character far more serious than one would imagine it to be during her capricious moments. . . . I keep telling her that all is not pleasure during her mother's peregrinations, that she's doing it for a worthy cause. To which she answers by letting big tears run down her slightly paler cheeks. I'll go and see her again in a few days, with books and candy."

Louise's own illnesses deepened their estrangement. While Vigny nursed his foot, Louise suffered a number of severe colds and was generally in a morose mood. "Written in bed," she jotted down in 1855 in one of the last journal entries that survives from that decade. "For a long time I haven't written any Mementos. Why should I? Nothing in life but discouragements, illnesses, disgust with humanity. . . ."

A subsequent journal note is more cheerful, relating her most recent amorous adventure. "Champfleury" was the pen name of the fellow she set her cap for in 1856, and he, too, was very famous.

Born Jules Fleury, this popular writer was, like Flaubert, eleven years Louise's junior. By 1856 "Champfleury" had already published ten books under his pen name: several novels, a vast history of caricature, and a few important volumes of art and literary criticism. He coined the term "Realism" for the movement that succeeded Romanticism in literature and the visual arts, and that would include as its stars Flaubert, Zola, Courbet, and Maupassant. In private life, the burly, mustached, swaggering Champfleury, who had no more probity than the villainous Alphonse Karr, was famous for his sexual indiscretions ("Five mistresses at one go," he bragged to a friend). At some point in the 1850s Champfleury had been introduced to Louise's salon by their mutual friend Antony Deschamps. Well into her forties, Louise remained a very handsome woman—"majestic, a bit of a virago," so Anatole France described her, "with a majordomo's voice and eyes that she did not veil." Some kind of flirtation between Louise and Champfleury was already in evidence in a journal entry of Louise's dated November 1855: "Champfleury is pressing himself against me with intentions. . . . What will become of it?"

The relationship between the two writers is more explicitly defined in a knavish description this Casanova wrote in the spring of 1856. It provides an arresting view of dating etiquette between members of the French intelligentsia in the mid-nineteenth century. (Champfleury's vehement prejudices against women writers were characteristic of his male peers.)

For some two years I have kept company with a tall, buxom, blond, very virile Muse whose amorous adventures were the talk of the town a decade ago. For a long time I did not compliment her on her poetry, which did not interest me, and on the remains of her beauty, which did not move me. A year ago, she opened all her heartaches to me, and I opened up mine. . . . Notwithstanding my distaste for writers of the other sex, I began to believe that this particular one had been abused by public opinion.

Two years went by in this fashion; I developed a true friendship for this forthright person who caused no trouble in society, warmly welcomed her guests, knew how to make them shine in her salon—in sum, behaved most charmingly.

One night an extensive fire burst out in the boarding school of the

Muse's daughter; alarmed, she hurriedly left her own party, taking me with her in a hansom cab in the company of a young philosopher. . . . I was facing her in the hansom cab; by coincidence, our crossed legs lightly rubbed against each other; this somewhat troubled me. But it was only a transient feeling, which I found insignificant.

— "Swear to me that you'll tell me the truth when you have heard me out," she said {a while later} when we again shared a cab.— "I swear," I said, laughing.— "Well, do you remember that evening of the great fire?"— "Not at all."— "What, nothing at all?"— "Nothing."— "You forcefully hugged my knees," she said.— "Is that possible?" I asked, still laughing, for if anyone initiated the whole thing, it was she. "In effect," I added, a bit terrified of this duet in a hansom cab, "I thought I felt something."— "You've been obsessing me for a month," she said.— "Truly?" I replied. "It's by pure coincidence that our legs touched."— "Coincidence!" she sighed. "In that case let's not mention it anymore." The Muse then forthrightly shook my hand.

Fortunately, we'd arrived at the theater, but the conversation had so upset me that I fled after the first act without saying a word. The next day, a letter, an offer of solid friendship, a little gift with an invitation to return. [Gustave] Courbet was idle. I told him the tale. He agreed to accompany me. I asked her to receive him. She invited us for the following Sunday.

We did not go!

I who was lately asking for a passion! Alas! the occasion presented itself, but it was not the passion I'd wished for. Forty-six years old— strong health—a manly character—a character of no great refinement—and literature to boot! Pouah!

"It takes a literary woman to be that audacious," Champfleury added, exhibiting the prevailing "all bluestockings are trollops" prejudice. "Champfleury story without issue," Louise wrote dourly in a journal entry in those same weeks.

Whoever made the first advances, Louise and Champfleury ended up being arrested by the police as they lay together on a warm day in a field of poppies in the suburban forest of Meudon. This bucolic high-noon caper engaged in by portly intellectuals of middle age (the sight could not have been conducive to reverie; even the chronic bragger Champfleury never breathed a word about it to anyone) was disclosed to the world only many years later, by Maxime Du Camp.

In the very first, serialized edition of his *Souvenirs littéraires,* Du Camp, who had a summer home in Meudon, asserted that a sheriff came upon the heaving, sweating twosome "in a field of poppies," and took them off to the local police station on charges of indecent exposure, not even allowing them to rearrange their clothing. They were asked to show their identity papers and pay a fine of five francs. But neither Louise nor Champfleury had the proper documents or cash on them. In Du Camp's perhaps fanciful account, the shamefaced trysters had to call on the mercy of neighboring acquaintances and were eventually bailed out by Du Camp.

It is likely that this last flourish is false, for in the book version of his *Souvenirs* Du Camp left out the legal particulars of the episode. The incident itself, however, most probably occurred, and it is significant: It marked the Indian summer of our heroine's sexuality, the last erotic episode in the wonderfully uninhibited sex life of Madame Louise Colet.

Perhaps out of pride, Louise gave up the role of Romantic Mistress at a considerable earlier age than many of her peers: Germaine de Staël, George Sand, and Du Camp's mistress Valentine Delessert remained erotically active well into their sixties, and with much younger men.

There remains another interesting sidelight to the relationship between Louise Colet and Champfleury. It has to do with a painting by Gustave Courbet, *L'Amazone,* dated 1856, which depicts a pensive woman in a riding habit standing in a verdant landscape. For over a century, this picture, which is now in the collection of the Metropolitan Museum in New York City, has been said to be a portrait of Louise Colet.

Here are a few art historians' comments on the canvas:

"*L'Amazone* represents Louise Colet, the famous novelist," asserted a commentator at the turn of the century, who disputed Champfleury's contention that he and Courbet never kept that Sunday date they made with Louise. "Courbet no doubt returned to Louise's flat and painted this portrait, which is one of his finest. . . . It is a powerful and harmonious work, with an approach to light that is precursive of Impressionism."

The second chronicler identifies Louise as a central model for Emma Bovary but mistakenly assigns her number-one bête noire, Alphonse Karr, as one of her lovers. "The poet and novelist Louise Colet had attained a certain celebrity through her affairs with Alphonse Karr and Gustave Flaubert," this particular art critic wrote in the 1930s. "The author of *Madame Bovary* had taken horseback rides in the environs of Mantes with Louise Colet. Blond, dark-eyed, with a turned-up nose, she is depicted by Courbet as an Amazon, standing, riding whip in hand. . . . Emma Bovary has the resigned attitude of a pretty provincial lady; she is waiting for her horse, which is pasturing on grass near the little pond where she has taken Rodolphe."

As for the art historian Lionello Venturi, the most distinguished of these commentators, he suggests a flirtation between Louise and Courbet. "The sitter is Louise Colet," Venturi wrote in the mid-twentieth century. "In 1856 she was in love with Champfleury, who did not respond to her advances and introduced her to his friend Courbet. . . . [Courbet] knew that he was a handsome man and was very proud of it. One may guess that Louise Colet, after her disappointment with Champfleury, took a shine to Courbet. Courbet was an uneducated man, whose manners and experience were quite inferior to those of the literate Louise Colet. He admired her distinction, her elegance, her pretension to nobility. All this is well impressed on the portrait. . . . The romantic landscape betrays a lover's contemplation."

❦

The bronchitis that afflicted Louise in autumn 1856 turned into an almost fatal pneumonia, and she did not leave her bed for some months.

I'm suffering from an obstinate cough that much worries the doctors [she wrote to Victor Hugo at Christmas time]; the strongest constitutions are eroded by sorrow and overwork.

Our poignant and painful conversation of last summer [Hugo wrote back to Louise the same week] was interrupted by your departure and should have continued. In opening your heart to me you opened your soul, and I was profoundly moved. That emotion is still with me.

Your letter went straight to my heart and brought tears to eyes grown dry and arid by suffering [Louise wrote Hugo in response]. Do you know that I almost died following that great sorrow which I confided in you the night before I left you at Guernsey? First my soul was in deep anguish, then in the past year my health so deteriorated I was given up for lost. . . . But it was impossible to die, to leave my beautiful and serene child at the mercy of life's anguish. I wished to get better and I did, notwithstanding an incessant and dulling work schedule. . . .

*Adieu, great master, or rather au revoir. I place my lips on your
inspired forehead.*

That autumn and winter, while she was confined by her illness, Louise's affair with Vigny quietly reached its natural end. On Christmas Day,
Vigny wrote his "dear invalid" that he felt badly about not having been
able to fetch her a better remedy for her cough, whose dryness "terrified"
him. Louise's finances had also taken a bad turn that season: In the first
months of 1857, she learned that her government pension had been cut
from two thousand to twelve hundred francs—the new minister of public
instruction, obliged to economize, had severely lowered all pensions al-
lotted to artists and writers. Vigny tried to intervene at the proper ministries, but his efforts came to naught. In the spring, Louise was forced to
leave her beloved flat on the Rue de Sèvres, her home for eight years, for
a more modest one on the Rue Vaneau, where she valiantly continued to
hold her Sunday salons.

In the first months of 1857, as he turned sixty years old, Vigny was
experiencing his own share of emotional burdens. His wife grew weaker
and sicker by the week. His former mistress Mrs. Holmes, who had remained a close friend of the poet's and was the mother of his illegitimate
child, Augusta, died of cancer, and Vigny dedicated himself to consoling
his daughter. Vigny's own health was deteriorating fast. Harassed by all
his nursing duties, he worked into the late night hours, and in the spring
he suffered from an illness that kept him in bed until August. Both lovers
expressed a general sense of lassitude. Vigny felt that he had less and less
energy and could barely even "uncross my mandarin's arms and legs."
The last of his notes to Louise that has survived, written in the summer of
1857, is filled with end-of-liaison melancholy:

> *You're quite right to say that it's useless to tell me that you are ill again,
> for I would not believe it.*
>
> *A concert, the [actress] Ristori, the Théâtre Français—those are my
> distractions. I had less pleasant ones this morning at the cemetery.*
>
> *I'm very sad and tired. All sleep has left me and I'm going home,
> where I hope to find a bit of it. I'll come to see you on Wednesday if
> you're in.*

A far cry from the elation of two years before, when after a night of love
Vigny had written Louise: "I clearly see you by my side as you were the
other day in your bed, with your beautiful soft eyes and your child's

mouth and all the pearls of your teeth, and your words after all the night's love, and our forgetfulness of everything."

There was never a definitive rupture between Louise and Alfred de Vigny. There occurred, rather, a gentle fading away caused mostly by the brunt of advancing age—that inevitable of life which Louise found very hard to accept.

In the meantime, Louise was still battling old demons. In the spring of 1857, Victor Hugo again prodded her to transcend all personal sorrow in her writing—in other words, forget Gustave Flaubert.

You have sent me some superb poems. Purge them of all that is personal. They will be even more beautiful. Priestess of humanity, don't waste your time cursing out one man. Forget your personal pains, and see only the larger wounds. Climb, climb higher, ever higher; glide, that is your eagle's duty.

Forgetting Flaubert: easier said than done, particularly in the year when Louise's greatest rival, *Madame Bovary,* finally came to life and was published.

14.
Emma and Louise

❧

In view of its author's belief that art must remain impersonal ("Like God in the universe," the writer must be "everywhere present but never visible"), Flaubert's *Madame Bovary* left a startling amount of literary spoor. No novel of Tolstoy, Balzac, Melville, or Dickens had its progress as precisely documented as *Madame Bovary*'s was in Flaubert's letters to Louise Colet; and few nineteenth-century classics adhere as closely to the facts of real life.

Three women provided the principal sources of inspiration for the creation of Emma Bovary. Only one of them—Delphine Delamare, the adulterous wife of a Norman country doctor, who committed suicide after running up scandalous debts—is familiar to most Flaubert readers. The other two, whose influences deserve to be far better known, were Ludovica Pradier and, of course, Louise Colet. It is interesting to trace the manner in which each of the women contributed to the creation of Emma Bovary.

The correlations between Emma Bovary and Delphine Delamare, whose tragic story was published in the Rouen papers shortly before Flaubert left for Egypt, are striking. Both were married at the age of eighteen to a widowed *officier de santé* (a shade below full "doctor" status) who had previously been married to a much older woman; both Delphine and Emma had one child, a daughter; both went into debt as a result of illicit affairs; and both committed suicide before thirty. Both women's husbands—Eugène Delamare and Charles Bovary—died in poverty the year after their second widowerhood, leaving an orphaned daughter.

As for the fictional Yonville-L'Abbaye in which the major part of Flaubert's novel is set, it resembles the little village of Ry, fifteen kilometers from Rouen, where the Delamares lived. A decade after Flaubert's death, Ry began to be recognized as the principal model for Yonville: Flaubert's rough sketch of Yonville's main street, found in his manuscripts—"the length of a gunshot, lined by a few shops"—still bears a strong resemblance to the *Grande Rue* of contemporary Ry. (Many scholars have also noted the linguistic associations of the town and the novel's protagonists: Charles Bovary is a placidly bovine, plodding man who lives in Ry.)

But the site and characters of Flaubert's novel are complex amalgams of several villages and several women. Some of the most revealing new discoveries in Flaubert studies concern the second model for Emma Bovary—Louise "Ludovica" Pradier, Flaubert's profligate sometime lover. Details of Ludovica's recently discovered memoirs bear unmistakable parallels to the saga of Emma Bovary's financial downfall.

Having run up huge debts—money spent on her many paramours—that threatened to bankrupt even her affluent sculptor husband James Pradier, Ludovica was forced into a divorce that left her penniless. After a botched attempt at suicide (Emma's way out of her quandaries), Ludovica decided to dictate the account of her scandalous life to a confidante. The manuscript, a riveting document entitled "Les Mémoires de Madame Ludovica," was found only a few decades ago in Rouen's municipal library among the early drafts of Flaubert's last novel, *Bouvard et Pécuchet.* The writer's many annotations in the margins offer proof that he modeled the course of Emma's financial catastrophe far more on the rakish Parisian than on the provincial adulteress. There is even speculation that Flaubert, needing more details for his *Bovary,* himself commissioned Ludovica's memoirs in the late 1840s.

Here are only a few of the hundreds of passages of "Les Mémoires de Madame Ludovica" that Flaubert underlined and annotated in his copy of the manuscript (I offer the citations in the original semiliterate working-class French, with its misspellings, lowercase styling, and eccentric punctuation):

"Epuis ludovica etait genereuse pour ces amours, loin d'en recevoir elle aimait a leurs faire des cadeaux et comme si la nature n'avait pas assez donné a sa beauté elle cherchait a se rendre plus belle par ces capricieuses modes qui coute si chère. . . ." (And then Ludovica was generous to her lovers, far from receiving she liked to make them presents and as if nature had not given enough to her beauty she tried to make herself more beautiful by those capricious fashions which cost so much. . . .)

It is Emma's extravagant expenditures on her clothes and her prodigal gifts to her lovers that bring on her financial disaster.

". . . pas un des ces hommes ne mit meme de politesse dans le refus qu'ils fesaient." (. . . not one of those men even put any politeness into the refusals they made.)

On the margin of this text, which refers to Ludovica's futile attempts to borrow money, as Emma Bovary would, from her former lovers, Flaubert wrote a sentence that he emulated closely in his novel: "She left for Rouen the next day, in order to solicit all the bankers she knew."

But the crucial influences of Delphine Delamare's and Ludovica Pradier's stories do not diminish the importance of Louise Colet as a model for Emma. Like Emma, she was brought up in obscure provincial circumstances and aspired to big-city glamour and romance. Like Emma, Louise had hidden in the woods at sunset to read Lamartine, had gotten her first romantic delusions from second-rate Romantic literature, and had suffered disastrously from its fantasies. Like Emma, Louise was a highly-sexed narcissist, seldom satisfied with reality, seeking in others a glorified image of herself.

There are other telling details: the first costume Emma Bovary buys to seduce her lover Rodolphe is a sky-blue dress, Louise's trademark color. Most crucial of all, the motto *Amor nel cor*, inscribed on the signet ring Emma offers Rodolphe, had been on the cigar holder Louise gave Gustave at the beginning of their affair.

"If Madame Colet had not existed, Flaubert would not have written *Madame Bovary* . . . Emma Bovary was Louise Colet with her blue stockings off," a prominent French critic of the 1940s wrote. Flaubert's most eminent British biographer, Enid Starkie, thinks that the author deliberately resumed his affair with Louise in the fall of 1851 "because he needed the material of her character for the creation of his heroine." Francis Steegmuller, whose *Flaubert and Madame Bovary* remains the finest biography of Flaubert to date, feels that "No one who knows Louise Colet can read of Emma Bovary without having Louise before his eyes. . . .

Emma had begun, perhaps, as young Madame Delamare, but ... had subsequently taken on a resemblance to Louise Colet. ... The adultery scenes in particular contain whole phrases and passages of feeling that had been born in Paris or Mantes."

The correlations between Emma Bovary and his own mistress, portrayed in his novel as a witless, sex-crazed provincial, do not speak much for Flaubert's compassion. The pivotal hansom cab episode of *Madame Bovary* may have been the most cruel life-to-art transposition of all: Emma and Léon's first sexual encounter, like Flaubert's and Colet's, occurs during a ride in a closed hansom cab. What must have wounded Louise most is that this passage depicts the sexual act at its most comical and grotesque. The cab, "as tightly shut as a tomb and tossing about like a lost ship," hurtles frenetically through Rouen for six hours; Emma's lover, as in some taped vaudeville gag, occasionally yells to the driver, "Continue driving!" "Don't stop!" The scene communicates the burlesque pathos of a terrified, impatient male to whom any "stopping" of the cab's motion implies the loss of his erection.

One remembers how fondly Flaubert had recalled that cab in his early letters to Louise, even fantasizing that he might purchase it. What kind of rancor or meanness incited him to turn the ardent beginning of a long and inspiring relationship—his only true love affair—into a macabre nightmare? Jean-Paul Sartre, who devotes some eight pages to this cab scene, writes that "Gustave described the travels of the hansom cab—which brings no new information and is totally gratuitous to the inner logic of the narrative—to let us see this 'fucking' as the grotesque and terrifying frenzy of any pure matter ... the copulation which they wished to hide is transformed into an obscene exhibition ... the bourgeois see carnal love pass by in all its hideous nakedness, see the fucking couple in their most obscene nudity ... as they are metamorphosed into this strange and sinister object, a funerary carriage."

Sartre concludes that this scene denotes the "rage and hatred" Flaubert felt toward his own penis, and his general terror of a sexual involvement with Louise. "The aloof narrator who takes a sarcastic attitude while Emma makes love is the one Flaubert *would have wished to have been* to escape a tête-à-tête that terrified him." Sartre also brings up the possibility that the impotence Flaubert experienced in a Paris cab during his first lovemaking with Louise helped to incite the malevolence of this passage. And Sartre, hardly known as a feminist, harshly berates Flaubert for his meanness: "Flaubert must have taken the hansom cab ride vengefully to heart in order to have the inexcusable caddishness of limning, in the traits of a bitch in heat, a woman whom he loved and esteemed during eight years. This elephantine memory of rancor is the final proof that Louise's hansom cab is the model for Madame Bovary's."

Flaubert occasionally acknowledged his capacity for mental cruelty. In 1855, shortly before he composed his last note to Louise, he wrote these revealing sentences to Bouilhet: "Do you know that my mother, some six months ago, made a sublime comment to me (a comment which might have led the Muse to hang herself out of jealousy for not having invented it herself): here it is: 'The rage for phrases has dried up your heart.' "

From September 15 to December 15, 1856, before it was published in book form, *Madame Bovary* was serialized in Maxime Du Camp's *Revue de Paris*. (To Flaubert's outrage, the hansom cab episode was edited out as too obscene.) The novel was an immediate *succès de scandale,* evoking as much condemnation as praise, and it eventually led to a famous lawsuit. "Our subscribers wrote us letters ... accusing us of slandering France and disgracing it in the eyes of the world," Du Camp wrote. " 'What? Such women exist? Women who deceive their husbands, pile up debts, meet their lovers in gardens and hotels? Such creatures exist in our lovely France, in the provinces where life is so pure? Impossible!' "

Although some of the most influential people in France, including Lamartine and the emperor's cousin, Princess Mathilde, expressed their admiration for *Madame Bovary,* and hundreds of influential society ladies became *"Bovarystes enragées"* overnight, a work so explicitly sexual ran risks of persecution under Napoleon III's repressive regime. Sure enough, as the last installment of *Bovary* appeared, in December 1856, the government handed down an indictment against the novel's publication on grounds of "outrage to public morals and religion." Three persons were summoned to court: Flaubert; the managing editor of *Revue de Paris;* and one Monsieur Pillet, the printer.

As soon as the case came to trial, however, it was clear that the prosecution did not have any great chance of success. The presiding judge was a man of culture who welcomed the case as an agreeable change from the usual procession of thieves, pimps, and prostitutes that passed daily before his eyes. As a passage from *Madame Bovary* was read, his lips were even seen to form the word "charming." The prosecutor, on the other hand, was severely limited in his literary education and kept the courtroom in a state of hilarity with his faux pas. The court, while expressing a preference "for life as it should be rather than life as it is," exonerated Flaubert, the managing editor, and the printer. A few months later, in mid-April of 1857, *Madame Bovary* was published as a book, with a dedication to Louis Bouilhet. It sold 15,000 copies in two months (the equivalent, approximately, of 150,000 copies in our own decade in the United States).

The reviews were mixed. *Le Figaro* scathingly described *Madame Bovary* as the tale of "a simpleminded medic, an intolerable dolt . . . who kills his first wife through inertia and does all he can to be cuckolded by his second one." The most important critic in France was still Sainte-Beuve, and it was his qualified but ultimately admiring review that made the novel a best-seller. He regretted that "there is no goodness in the book, no character represents it," and that it gave a distorted view of the French provinces, where "there are also to be found good and beautiful souls, which have remained in a state of innocence." Yet *Madame Bovary* bore every evidence of careful craftsmanship, Sainte-Beuve wrote, and was "entirely impersonal"—a great proof of its strength.

Such praise, from a man known for the purity and severity of his tastes and his bourgeois habits, was a certificate of moral character for Flaubert's novel and exonerated it far more than any acquittal in court. So Flaubert's reputation was saved by Sainte-Beuve. Yet only one opinion truly mattered to him—that of a controversial young poet named Charles Baudelaire, whom Flaubert had often met in the company of Théophile Gautier. Baudelaire's criticism appeared late, not until September 1857, because that summer the poet was also being prosecuted on grounds of "immorality," for his volume *Fleurs du Mal.*

In his essay on *Bovary,* which remains one of the landmarks of nineteenth-century literary criticism, Baudelaire praised Flaubert for being the first to utilize female hysteria, "that physiological mystery," as "the base and bedrock of a literary work." "To accomplish the tour de force in its entirety," Baudelaire wrote, "it remained for the author only to divest himself (as much as possible) of his sex and to become a woman. The result is a marvel; for . . . Madame Bovary, in the most forceful and ambitious aspects of her character, and also the most pensive, remained a man."

Thus another side of Louise Colet's character—that "virility" which so fascinated Cousin, Hugo, de Vigny, Champfleury, and many other friends and lovers—was cannibalized by Flaubert for the creation of his heroine.

One last correlation of art and life, perhaps the most curious of all, was the portrayal of Charles Bovary's mother. Flaubert models that lady closely on Louise's perception of his own parent, as a woman "made oppressive by her rectitude of judgment and her gravity of manner." The serenity shared by Charles Bovary and his mother after Emma's death seems to emulate the calm intimacy of Flaubert's post-Louise life with Madame Flaubert. "Charles and his mother . . . talked of bygone days, and of the future. She would come to live in Yonville, she would keep house for him, they would never leave each other anymore. Madame Bovary was charming and affectionate, quietly rejoicing at the prospect of regaining an affection which for so many years had slipped away."

Indeed, after Flaubert's eight-year liaison with Louise ended, Madame Flaubert is said to have become far more cheerful and affable. Her one rival gone, she even began to go out visiting, and became generally sociable.

During the three months that Flaubert's novel was being serialized, Louise was as sick as she had ever been in her life, confined to bed with bronchitis. One cannot but wonder to what degree her affliction was worsened by her reading of *Madame Bovary*.

Far too much of a *grande bourgeoise* to discuss publicly the passage of Bovary that must have hurt her most deeply—the cab episode—Louise concentrated her pique on the *Amor nel cor* detail.

"Imagine my indignation, you who have a righteous soul," she wrote to a friend, "when in reading *Madame Bovary* I came upon this passage: 'Besides the riding whip with its silver-gilt handle, Rodolphe had received a seal bearing the motto *Amor nel cor*.' I did my best to keep from laughing, and the next morning, when I told the story to Sainte-Beuve, he laid his razor on the edge of the mantlepiece to avoid cutting himself, he was laughing so." (Both these laughs sound very strained: Louise laughs to preserve her public image; Sainte-Beuve laughs at Louise, as he has done for two decades.)

Commenting on Louise's fury over the similarities between herself and Emma Bovary, and her particular rage about the *Amor nel cor* episode, Jules Troubat, Sainte-Beuve's secretary and one of the most eloquent chroniclers of the mid-nineteenth-century Parisian literary scene, had this to say: "In antiquity she would have been a Medea, she would have done anything to revenge herself against Flaubert's disloyalty."

The first public evidence of Louise's rancor toward *Bovary* was a long poem published in the popular periodical *Le Monde illustré*. It ended with the following verses, in which the female narrator has spent the last cent of her meager fortune on a gift for her lover, a cigar case:

The silver setting, finely chiseled,
Had enameled flowers and gold chasing;

On its stone was engraved the phrase Amor nel cor,
A Tuscan verse filled with secret emotion.

It was for him, for him whom she loved like a god,
For him, callous to all human sorrow, uncouth to women.
Alas, she was poor and had little to give,
But all gifts are sacred that incarnate a soul.

Well! In a novel of traveling-salesman style,
As nauseating as a toxic wind,
He mocked that gift in a flat-footed phrase,
Yet kept the fine agate seal.

Eighteen fifty-seven, the year Louise's relationship with Vigny dissolved and *Madame Bovary* was published, was made all the more sorrowful for her by the deaths of two of the men she had most admired and loved—Alfred de Musset and her cherished Béranger. That summer Louise went on a long trip to Belgium and Holland to visit the many French political exiles who had sought asylum in those countries and also to oversee foreign-language editions of her work. She paid for her travels by putting together a series of essays, *Promenades en Hollande,* which Hachette published a few months later. Back in Paris in the fall, she was more depressed and restless than ever.

If I share my sentiments with you less often than usual [Louise wrote Victor Hugo that fall], it is from fear of bringing you constantly sorrowful news. I was already ailing when our friend Mr. Vacquerie came to Paris; now I am truly ill. I again have an obstinate cough that nothing can cure. I tried mineral water cures, and now I'm going on a diet of asses' milk. . . . The ailment has deep causes.

In the following year, 1858, Louise seemed to grow even more restless. She returned to Guernsey to stay with the Hugos and then went on to take cures for her lungs in a variety of spas in the Pyrenees, which had become popular with the Paris intelligentsia: Pau, Eaux-Bonnes—and Eaux-Chaudes, where her poor husband, Hippolyte, had sought to remedy his consumption.

During that depressed year, Louise, undecided about what to write, how to cure her ailments, or where to travel next, seemed to be living more in the past than in the future.

But in the winter of 1858–1859, she had a burst of inspiration for a new project, another book-length fiction.

Their pens liberated the previous year by Alfred de Musset's death, several Paris writers—George Sand was the first of them—had written much-publicized romans à clef about the dissolute poet. Louise, although she had been considerably grieved by Musset's death, decided to follow suit and set to work on a novel entitled *Lui*.

The first of the Musset-centered books to titillate Paris, George Sand's *Elle et Lui,* was a thinly disguised account of the frenzied love affair she had had with the poet a quarter of a century earlier. The spoiled dandy Musset, who had been as drunken, philandering, and generally insupportable in his youth as he was in later years, had painted a fairly scathing portrait of Sand in his epochal *Confessions d'un enfant du siècle;* three decades later, Sand still felt the need to settle accounts. *Elle et Lui*—a tedious, stilted fiction written in less than four weeks—portrays Sand and Musset in the guise of two gifted painters, Thérèse Jacques and Laurent de Fauvel, who fall in love. The industrious Thérèse has been abandoned by her husband, who absconded with her beloved son, and she now lives only for her art. She travels to Italy with the dissolute Laurent, who spends most of his time buying himself new clothes, chasing girls, and complaining that Thérèse will not party with him, yet is filled with "that particular charm of which Thérèse is fatally enamored—weakness!"

Musset's older brother, Paul, who since youth had been devoted to his sibling, immediately retaliated with his own book, *Lui et Elle,* which was serialized, in another periodical, a few weeks after Sand's work. Paul de Musset, originally trained as a lawyer, was a third-string litterateur who had written a series on nature entitled *Scènes de la vie privée et publique des animaux,* but he was mostly concentrating his energies on rehabilitating his beloved brother's reputation and editing his correspondence. His *Lui et Elle* vengefully corrected the negative image of Musset in Sand's *Elle et Lui,* depicting Sand as a manipulative, icy bitch. The Paris literary world immediately split into two camps, Mussetists pitted against Sandists. Friendships were altered, lawsuits and duels were threatened; one could barely invite members of the opposite factions to the same dinner party (the majority of literati took George Sand's side).

The trend to Sand-Musset scandalmongering took on a life of its own. A hack writer named Gaston Lavalley capitalized on the successes of *Elle et Lui* and *Lui et Elle* by writing a novel entitled *Eux* ("Them"). And a spate of articles and cartoons came out in the Paris press, which chronicled these various imbroglios under the title *Eux brouillés,* "They Have

Had a Falling-out," phonetically translatable as "Scrambled Eggs." This is the background for the considerable success of Louise Colet's novel *Lui*, which began to be serialized in the periodical *Le Messager de Paris* in August of 1859, some months after the publication of Sand's and Musset's books.

Whereas Colet's *Une Histoire de Soldat* is a psychologically interesting but sloppily written exorcism, *Lui* is a spirited, carefully crafted fiction of some originality; and it offers an entertaining portrait of the Paris intelligentsia at midcentury. Its box-within-box structure works on two levels:

The "frame" narrative concerns the Louise Colet–Alfred de Musset–Gustave Flaubert triangle; A handsome young widow in straitened circumstances with unmistakable similarities to Louise, Marquise Stéphanie de Rostan, is torn between her affection for the dissolute young poet Albert de Lincel (Musset) and an aloof, unfeeling novelist (Flaubert), once again called Léonce, who is frequently referred to but never seen onstage.

The "inner," "narrated" story line, set mostly in Venice, deals exclusively with the George Sand–Musset affair and is recounted to Stéphanie-Louise by Lincel-Musset himself.

More discreet in its vanity than *Une Histoire de Soldat, Lui* still offers a flattering portrait of golden-locked Stéphanie-Louise, who often places her arms "in the pose of Pradier's Sappho" and supports herself and her child by writing literary translations. Apart from the fact that Stéphanie has a seven-year-old son rather than a nineteen-year-old daughter, most other details are true to life. Stéphanie has been ruined by a disastrous lawsuit (the suit brought against Louise by Madame Récamier's heirs); and she is constantly the prey of lecherous men (Villemain and company), who vainly try to take advantage of her penury by offering her literary favors. Stéphanie-Louise, faithful to her love for Léonce-Flaubert, refuses Lincel-Musset's amorous advances (as in real life, the fictional Lincel tries to bite through the bodice of her dress in a hansom cab, then peevishly goes off to divert himself "with some beauty who will spare me metaphysics").

Dominating the novel's outer frame, of course, is the brooding, glacial, ever-absent lover Léonce, the "unknown genius" who lives at his faraway family estate, "working on a great book like a fanatic in a cult of art." "Every two months, when a segment of his book was finished, I again became his adored recompense," Stéphanie tells us. "[He] was so indifferent to anything that wasn't an abstraction of art and beauty that he acquired a special grandeur and prestige."

Stéphanie realizes that the famous Lincel's affection might be more genuine than that of the obscure Léonce, but she is irresistibly drawn to the mystery of that distant, unrecognized genius:

"Oh, poor Albert, in your apparent madness, you were the man who loved, it is you who were inspired by life! The other man, away out there, far from me, in his laboring pride and eternal self-analysis, he didn't love at all. Love for him was only the subject for a dissertation, a dead letter!"

Léonce's stinginess ("a blend of bourgeous cunning and Norman aloofness"), his delaying tactics, his paramystical dedication to art, are painfully akin to Flaubert's:

> Léonce had promised to visit in the spring, but now he wrote me that the first part of the great book he was working on would chain him to his lonely desk for another month. . . . He delighted in comparing himself to the Desert Fathers. . . . For him Art was the jealous god which can be possessed and assimilated only when you dedicate yourself entirely to him in solitude.

The lonely heroine is consoled by her dear friend René Delmart (a blend of the brothers Émile and Antony Deschamps), who tells her: "Yours is a credulous soul ready for all martyrdoms. . . . I fear that once [Léonce's] work is written he will totally belong to his book, however vulgar and shapeless it might be. An abstract passion, driven to excess, atrophies the heart."

The Deschamps brothers are among dozens of Paris literati who make cameo appearances in Colet's transparent fiction. The reader is also treated to the "philosophical poet" Albert de Germiny (Alfred de Vigny) and the popular bard Duverger (Béranger). Sand's all-powerful editor at the *Revue des deux mondes,* the prominent Parisian figure François Buloz, is satirized as Frémont, the "Danubian peasant" of publishing. The radical aristocrat Princess Cristina Belgiojoso, yet another former lover of Musset's, "an overly skinny beauty with ecstatic eyes," who "wrote books on dogma and went off to Asia to amuse herself with Arabs," is mentioned under the guise of Princess X. The male star of Princess X's entourage, "a little pianist, lively and self-confident, kind of like her cocker spaniel . . . one of those brainless virtuosos," combines traits of Liszt and Chopin. The Comtesse de Vernoult, "infatuated with one of the clavichord heroes," is Marie d'Agoult, who bore Franz Liszt three children during the decade of their affair.

And finally, first mentioned in the company of the fictionalized d'Agoult and Belgiojoso, there is the true star of *Lui,* the writer Antonia

Back (George Sand), whose affair with Lincel-Musset serves as the inner frame of the novel's narrative.

In spite of Sand's rebuff of Louise's offers of friendship, Louise's complex portrait of her is at times very flattering. "I admire her talent, her life's incessant labor, I believe in the kindness of her character," Stéphanie-Louise admits. However, there is one passage of Louise's novel that was bound to sting Sand—her critical comments on Sand's dissolute behavior in front of her children (however liberated she may have been in *her* private life, Louise was prudish concerning children's education, and she did not approve of Sand's bohemian poses):

> *We found the great sibyl still in bed, in a vast room littered with men's and women's garments [Stéphanie relates]. Her children played on the carpet. The pale pianist [Chopin], her lover of the moment, was lying on a couch. He had coughed a great deal during the night and could not sleep. While speaking to us Antonia Back chain-smoked cigarettes which she kept in a little purse of Algerian leather lying on her night table. She only stopped talking to offer tisane to the musician, whom she addressed as tu.*
>
> *This laisser-aller ["anything goes"] in front of children shocked me profoundly; one must not taint the purity and ignorance of children with this licentiousness of middle-aged lust.*

There is another passage that may have incited Sand's ire because it went to the heart of her sexuality, an issue she was very touchy about: "She was truly the best and the greatest of women," Lincel-Musset muses, "but . . . her sensuality was based on curiosity, ardent rather than truly erotic; which led me to find her indecent in her very frigidity."

What woman, indeed, would enjoy having her intimate life dissected with an eye as cutting as Louise's?

Most of the episodes based on Sand and Musset are set in 1830s Venice, and in these passages *Lui* takes off into a remarkable feminist narrative that quite reverses the stereotypical nineteenth-century images of hardworking man and light-headed woman. Antonia Back is depicted as an artist dedicated to her work; Lincel is a hopelessly weak-willed *enfant du siècle* playboy who is barely ever able to work because he looks on all life as one continuous party:

"If we took a gondola ride or enjoyed some fresh air on the Piazzetta," Lincel suggests. "Go ahead, if you want to," Antonia says, "but I've put myself on my honor not to allow myself any diversion until I've sent a manuscript off to my publisher." "This kind of language from a woman humiliated me a little," the hero reflects. "I felt she was usurping my place."

Or else:

She replied that . . . any distractions ran the risk of leaving her work unfinished. . . . "Imitate me," she advised, "and afterwards we'll have some vacation days."

"You well know," I replied, "that I can work only in spurts. What will happen to me in this solitude in which you let me suffer?"

And ignoring my outstretched arms, she locked herself in her work room again.

Alternately severe, sensuous, and maternal, and above all devoted to her writing, Colet's heroine Antonia Back is one of the first literary prototypes of the industrious female artist. Her austere probity is a foil for the self-indulgent decadence of Venetian life; her moral strength and commitment to art are contrasted with the shiftlessness of her male companion. Interestingly, Colet's Antonia Back—in her monastic dedication and the numerous tactics she devises to keep her horny paramour at bay—closely resembles Gustave Flaubert.

The more general subtext of *Lui,* deftly emphasized in its splendid English translation by Marilyn Gaddis Rose, concerns the trials of professional women writers in the male-dominated world of nineteenth-century Europe: Both the frame romances (the Stéphanie-Louise/Lincel-Musset/Léonce-Flaubert triad) and the embedded romance (Lincel-Musset's affair with Back-Sand) depict literary women's survival tactics in a milieu of exploitative, unfeeling, or feckless men. And in that sense *Lui* is a prophetic book. Its title refers not only to the object of the central heroine's affections but to men at every level of the narrative: "*Lui*" is an umbrella term to denote *all* men whom nineteenth-century literary women had to confront from a position of weakness.

How did *Lui* play in 1859 Paris? Obviously, with mixed results.

Would you like to be entertained? [Flaubert wrote to his friend the novelist Ernest Feydeau, father of the writer of theater farces]. Do me (and yourself) a favor, and go buy Lui, a contemporary novel by Mme Louise Colet. You'll recognize your buddy in it, beautifully transformed. . . . I come out of it white as the driven snow, but as an insensitive, avaricious boor, a somber imbecile. . . . All this once more confirms my theory concerning the profound immorality of women.

A while later, Flaubert wrote the following comments to another of his pen pals, a Mlle Bosquet, who had tactlessly questioned him concerning his relations to Louise:

"My liaison with Madame Colet did not leave me with any 'wounds' in the deep, sentimental sense of the word; it's rather the memory (and, to this day, the sensation) of a very long irritation. Her book *Lui* took the cake. Just think of the commentaries, queries, witticisms, allusions made concerning me since the publication of this work. . . ."

So although he came out of the novel, as he admitted, "white as the driven snow," Flaubert was too obsessed by his theory of aesthetic "impersonality" to tolerate any allusions to his life or character in anyone else's fiction. As for readers, they were titillated by Louise's portraits of Musset, Sand, and a dozen other Paris celebrities. Despite the great success of *Madame Bovary,* few noticed Colet's portrayal of Flaubert—he was not yet famous enough to have become part of the Paris gossip mill.

In fact, Maxine Du Camp offered the only reaction to *Lui* that focused on the portrait of Flaubert. "Léonce is Gustave Flaubert. —Ah! I know the story, I'm saturated with it *ad nauseum,"* he wrote in his memoirs. "I own over three hundred letters which Louise Colet wrote me because she used me, against my will, as confidant for the tenderness with which she persecuted Flaubert."

Even though George Sand had started the nefarious enterprise that ended with *Eux brouillés,* she complained about Colet's contribution. Writing to Sainte-Beuve concerning her own *Elle et Lui* the year after both novels were published, she had this to say:

This book of mine provoked two replies filled with venom and caddishness and imposture: a so-called novel called Lui et Elle and a supposedly fictional report called Lui, in which a woman of merit and talent forgot what she owed herself in order to satisfy some kind of hatred whose causes I can't begin to trace. I was never hostile to her; I am innocent of the impertinences she assigns to me; I have never even dreamed of being disagreeable to her. My only wrongdoing is to have refused forging bonds of friendship with her, a decision I made because I found her too literary, in a certain way, for my tastes and mental habits.

Sainte-Beuve himself, however, had a positive response to *Lui:* "It's a novel which scandalized timid folk and which will endure," he wrote Louise.

Parisian readers' reactions to this spate of romans à clef—Sand's, Louise's, Paul de Musset's—were aptly summed up in an amusing little book, published with great success a year after those three, called *Eux et Elles: L'Histoire d'un scandale,* by Mathurin de Lescure. It eviscerates Paul de Musset's contribution and dissects the other two with both severity and sympathy, expressing a slight preference for Louise's work.

Both novels are eloquent, subtle, and passionate, the critic wrote. *Lui* is an exhibitionist "coquetry," but Sand's *Elle et Lui* is more gravely flawed by being the calumny of a dead man and by "pridefully defaming a reputation which *Lui* merely compromises by vanity." Colet simply transgresses the rule that "one does not shoot at oneself." Sand's novel offends by "shooting at a tomb." *Lui* is "a book of gentle sadness which makes one smile, a book as sad as regret," whereas *Elle et Lui* is "as sad as hatred."

Of course, this would not be the French nineteenth century if the writer did not take a dig at both novels' implicit feminism: Sand's female protagonist, the critic declared, is unpleasantly turned into the true "hero" of the book, whereas the male protagonist, "destitute of his male superiority, is merely its heroine, a charming invalid." And both books, he complained, concern "the exploitation of Man by Woman."

Louise suffered new sorrows in the late 1850s and made headlines less favorable than those received by her novel. In 1858, the year after the death of her loyal mentor Béranger, Louise, hard-pressed as ever, succumbed to the temptation of publishing some works by both Béranger and Alfred de Musset.

In what she considered to be an homage to Musset, she sold a magazine a satiric poem of Musset's that caricatured some twenty of the "Immortals" of the Académie Française. The witty irreverence of the verses—which Musset composed at Louise's house and were alleged to be a collaboration—caused much controversy. (The Musset-Colet team's punning rhymes translate poorly.)

> *Debout, ruisselant comme un fleuve,*
>   *Sainte-Beuve,*
> *Dans un angle, le beau Mignet*
>   *Se peignait.*
>
> *Cousin cherchait d'un air tragique*
>   *Sa logique,*
> *Et tonnait, dévot éloquent,*
>   *Contre Kant.*

Chaque jour leur chantant matines,
   Lamartine,
Rappelle a ses chers souscripteurs
   Ses malheurs.*

*Standing, sweating like a stream,
   Sainte-Beuve,
In a corner, the handsome Mignet
   Combed his hair.

Cousin, with a tragic air,
   searched his logic
And fulminated, eloquent,
   Against Kant.

Daily singing their matins,
   Lamartine
Recalled to his dear readers,
   His miseries.

Too soon after Musset's death to publish his occasional verse, some said. Disrespectful to the venerable academicians, others complained.

Ferociously disputing these censures and ever pressed for cash, Louise a few months later published the letters Béranger had written her over two decades, prefaced with an affectionate introduction. Again, she thought of this publication as an homage. Again, she was rebuked for opportunism.

It was a blessing for Louise's morale that these setbacks were followed by the commercial success of *Lui,* which went into four editions in the space of a few months. However, she barely had time to savor this little triumph. Showing more wisdom than she had on earlier occasions, she left the country the week her book was published.

The former "Goddess of the Romantics" was off to Italy, where she was to spend a good part of the following decade, attending to a revolution.

She was once again reinventing herself, this time as a political reporter.

15.

Attending a Revolution

❧❧❧

In the late 1850s, the struggle for Italian unification, led by the diplomat Camillo Cavour and one of the greatest guerrilla fighters of history, Giuseppe Garibaldi, was providing the hottest copy in Europe. Alexandre Dumas *père,* the Continent's best-known historical novelist, was the first of many French literati who traveled to the Italian peninsula to report. In 1859 and 1860, Louise Colet and Maxime Du Camp were to follow.

A grass-roots movement for the Risorgimento, or "Resurrection," of Italy—which since the Congress of Vienna had been divided into a score of separate states subservient to the Pope, to Spanish Bourbon rulers, and to Austrian monarchs—had begun in the 1820s. Louise's interest in this cause, whose leaders demanded a unified Italy liberated from all forms of foreign rule, was deep-seated: Her father had spent his first twenty years in Naples, and his own parents remained there for decades after he returned to France. He had taught her fluent Italian and infused her with a passion for Italian culture. She had translated several important Italian texts, among them the verses of the nationalist poet Alessandro Manzoni. And Silvio Pellico, the greatest hero of the Risorgimento's first phase— the Carbonari movement—had been an idol of her youth.

Dissolved in the 1830s, the Carbonari nationalists were followed by the Giovine Italia faction, led by the visionary leader Giuseppe Mazzini. After several abortive rebellions against the Hapsburgs, Mazzini was sentenced to death, escaped to Great Britain, and spent nearly two decades in exile there. Working from London throughout the 1840s and 1850s, he rallied thousands of followers who helped him to plan many insurrections in his increasingly restless motherland, and he created the ideological ferment that would make Italy's liberation possible. Mazzini corresponded with liberal intelligentsia throughout Europe, including, of course, Louise Colet.

Mazzini and Louise met during the trip Louise took to Great Britain in 1851, just before she resumed her relationship with Flaubert. "Mazzini paid me a very long visit yesterday," she wrote a friend from London. "He has the eyes of a genius and is very eloquent." They continued to write to each other during the years that followed, Mazzini fanning Louise's enthusiasm for the Italian struggle. With her habitual largesse, she helped any colleagues of Mazzini's who passed through Paris. She also kept him well stocked with Italian journals and periodicals, utilizing the different "mail drops" he had to use in Great Britain (as Hugo did) to keep authorities from intercepting his mail. Mazzini's letters to Louise are filled with sentences such as "Tell our brothers from Italy that we must progress with greater speed toward establishing a republic." And he constantly thanked her for helping his fellow revolutionaries in Paris.

The pinpoint insurrections masterminded by Mazzini throughout the 1840s and '50s had been premature; by 1859, when Louise left for Italy, several political events—and the emergence of two other great nationalist leaders, Cavour and Garibaldi—had vastly diminished Mazzini's influence. The kingdom of Piedmont-Sardinia, which bordered Austria and had suffered the Hapsburgs' repressive rule since 1815, had assumed the leadership of the Risorgimento. The goal of liberating Italy, on the diplomatic level, was now in the hands of the Piedmontese monarch, Victor Emmanuel II, and particularly of his prime minister, Camillo Cavour.

This remarkable leader was as fervent a nationalist as Mazzini, but he wished to achieve unity through politics rather than guerrilla war. In 1858, at a secret meeting with Napoleon III, Cavour capitalized on France's traditional hostility toward Austria and on the French monarch's lifelong enthusiasm for the Risorgimento. (As a fiery liberal youth of nineteen, Napoleon III had taken part in a Carbonari uprising in central Italy and had lost his elder brother in that conflict.) So Cavour easily convinced Napoleon III that by helping Piedmont and other Italian states overthrow their hated Hapsburg occupiers, France could shift the balance of power and become the Continent's leading nation. Cavour and the French emperor struck a secret deal whereby France and Piedmont would provoke Austria, the following year, to go to war.

The alliance was a delicate one for Napoleon III. One of the principal goals of the Risorgimento was to abolish the secular power of the papacy, and since midcentury, France had been the official "protector" of the Papal States. So the French monarch was under formidable pressure from his conservative Catholic supporters to stay out of the conflict. However, in May 1859, before France's Catholic faction had time to organize, the cause of Italian liberation was saved by a monumental blunder on the part of Austria: Upon Piedmont's refusal to follow Austria's order to disarm, Austria invaded the little kingdom and was confronted by a powerful Franco-Piedmontese army, which immediately won a series of devastating victories at Magenta and Solferino.

By the time the war broke out, a new guerrilla patriot, Giuseppe Garibaldi, had come to the fore to both challenge and aid Cavour. While still in his twenties, Garibaldi, a sailor by vocation, born in the Piedmontese town of Nice, had been exiled for participating in insurrections throughout Italy. For the following twelve years he honed his combat tactics by leading local uprisings in South America, where he first began the custom of wearing the red-hued shirts that would remain the trademark of his troops throughout his career. By the mid-1850s Garibaldi had become an international idol, "the hero of two worlds." And Cavour, aware of Garibaldi's growing power, invited him back to Italy and made him a major general in the Piedmontese army.

This was the complex political situation Louise Colet confronted when she left Paris in the fall of 1859 for a long stay in Italy:

Napoleon III's powerful pro-papist compatriots had pressured him, in the summer of 1859, into signing a treaty with Austria. Italian nationalists, who needed France's support for their cause until full unification was achieved, were embittered by this premature peace; the peninsula's rebels were more restless than ever; and Garibaldi, whose forces were growing, was threatening to liberate the Kingdom of Sicily and Naples—a vast area under the rule of Spanish Bourbons—without any official backing from Cavour or his king, Victor Emmanuel of Piedmont.

Beyond Louise's commitment to Italy's liberation and her desire to escape the debates caused by *Lui*'s publication, two novel aspects of her life made her trip possible: The success of *Lui* had earned her enough money to live abroad comfortably for a few seasons; and her daughter,

Henriette, now nineteen, was old enough to be more on her own. Louise left her in the care of Sidonie Colet, one of Hippolyte Colet's sisters, who for some years had been asking to oversee Henriette's education, an education that in the opinion of the conservative Colet clan Louise had sorely neglected.

So Louise set off for Italy, a solitary woman approaching fifty. One could say that she had become more "ladylike," matronly, sedate. Her hair was now dyed brown, to hide her graying temples, and coiffed in a modest chignon. Her figure, never slender, had increased in corpulence. She was learning to live alone. It was natural that on her way to Italy she lingered for a fortnight in her native Provence. She had not set foot in southern France in fifteen years, not since that summer of 1844 when she journeyed there with Hippolyte and Henriette and was turned away from her family home by her own brother.

Louise began her local tour in Arles, where she stayed with the cousin she always referred to as "my only kind relative," the distinguished archaeologist Honoré Clair, who was directing the restoration of his city's antique monuments and had written several books. Though it is a bare twenty kilometers from Arles, Louise made no further attempt to visit Servanes. Her pride was too great and her wounds too deep; she did not risk being rebuffed again by her bachelor brother, who still managed the family estate.

Instead, Louise went to visit her old nurse, Reine Picard, who was living in Marseilles. "My nurse's ancient, wrinkled face, still beautiful of expression, was framed by the white lace cap traditional to Marseillaises," Louise later recalled. "She sprang to me and hugged me in her arms as if I were her own daughter. She rekindled in me memories of my earliest childhood, she evoked recollections of my mother, who had remained her idol. . . . During the days I spent in Marseilles my friends were startled by the sight of this joyous, rustic old woman who followed me like a shadow in all my excursions. . . . Together we visited the length of the old and new port, chatting in Provençal patois and recalling the melodious Provençal songs with which she had lulled me to sleep as an infant; it was a primitive Italian dialect we had already shared."

After this tender reunion, Louise traveled to the Italian border. She reached the frontier at midnight and had to wake the chief customs man. "He was a Frenchman who had read my verses in the papers," so she wrote of this emotional crossing. "Draping himself in his dressing gown, he exclaimed: 'Muses pass freely; they have wings.' " The next morning, Louise rejoiced at the great political drama that was about to unroll before her eyes: "To go and judge for myself the resurrection of Italy—this became my most imperious desire," she exulted in the opening of the four-volume work that resulted from her long stay on the peninsula. *L'Italie des Italiens* took its title from a speech of Victor Emmanuel II's that Louise heard a few months after her arrival. "When the barrier fell behind me at the frontier, I trod at last upon Italian soil, which for so long had been the promised land of my dreams, the land of poetry, of art, and, today, of liberty."

An impassioned tract for Italian unity, *L'Italie* is a curious blend of political reporting, travel essay, social chronicle, and autobiography, laced with poetry dedicated to Louise's distinguished Italian hosts, meditations on six centuries of Italian painting, and digressions on Catullus and on Montaigne, whose *Souvenirs d'Italie* was the author's bedside book during her voyage. Comparable, on a primitive level, to Mary McCarthy's books on Venice and Florence, Louise's work is also a kind of Baedeker of the Italian peninsula, recording her impressions of most every notable work of art and architectural landmark of Verona, Naples, Pisa, Padua, Siena, and a dozen other cities. It offers no less than 240 pages alone on the churches and museums of Florence, 260 pages on those of Venice. It is distinguished by a keen political sense, a fluent command of Italian, and a remarkable eye for good art. She dismisses the Salvator Rosas or Sebastiano del Piombos and zeros in on Veronese, Giotto, Cimabue, and Duccio, masters who were only beginning to be given their due in the mid-nineteenth century.

L'Italie des Italiens would be an utterly engrossing book if it had been edited to one fourth of its present length. A few highlights:

Milan, November 1859. When she arrives, Louise visits the grave of the Italian idol of her youth, the patriot fighter Silvio Pellico. Another nationalist leader, the great Italian writer Alessandro Manzoni, author of *I promesi sposi,* receives Louise at his home. She appears for their meeting with a copy of his novel *Hermengarde,* a long passage of which she has translated into French. During her three-hour visit with the gallant seventy-four-year-old Manzoni, she records, he expresses great disappointment that France signed a peace treaty with Austria long before the liberation of Italy was achieved: "[The continuing subjugation of] Venice is one of my life's great sorrows," the gentle silver-haired poet tells Louise. "The peace treaty [enforced by your emperor] was a terrible blow; I tried to not believe it; I still hope that France will not abandon us."

*   *   *

Lake Garda, November 28. Louise crosses the border to Venice, which is still under Austrian occupation. She hears hundreds of Italian men on her train defy a cluster of Austrian sentries with the shouts *"E viva l'Italia! Siamo liberi! Siamo Italiani!"*

"Vive l'Italie!" Louise shouts in French. *"E viva la Francia!"* the men shout back to her. *"Sono i Francesi che si fanno liberi!"* they add ("It's the French who liberated us!").

Venice, December 1859. Louise contrasts the gloom of Venice, which is still under Austrian occupation, with the pride and elation of democratic, Piedmontese Milan. "This fish is just like our city, German of skin but Italian of heart," an old fisherman tells her as he cleans a sturgeon on the docks of the Rialto. Louise offers him her wishes for the liberation of Venice. "A Frenchwoman!" the old man says, hearing her accent. "We're eagerly waiting for the French to return!"

While the Adriatic, tossed by winter storms, "howls like a beast about to pounce on Venice," Louise often sits at the Café Florian in Piazza San Marco, enjoying its memorable *zabaglione.* She is particularly entranced by this venerable city, which she described in her last novel, *Lui,* before she ever set foot in it. While writing her hundredfold pages on Venice's churches and museums, she makes numerous forays in search of the site where Musset and George Sand held their stormy idyll three decades ago, the Hotel Nani.

Louise learns that Sand and Musset lived in the very hotel in which she is staying—it has recently been renamed after its owner, Signor Danieli. Signor Danieli indeed recollects "a beautiful young Frenchman with blond hair who was very sick in this hotel." Louise asks her host to look up his 1833 registers, and they find the room in which the couple stayed. It is not far from the room Louise is occupying. She is led to the large communicating chambers, looking out toward the church of Santa Maria della Salute, in which the two writers wrote and fought.

"I stared with tenderness at that bed where he had suffered so much, at that mirror where his pale, noble face was once reflected," she reports. "I began to weep, prey to that anguish wrought by our inability ever to resurrect the past. . . . I touched the walls of his room, leaned at his windows, he seemed ready to reappear before me, young, beautiful, inspired." Louise suggests to her host that he put up a plaque on the door of the apartment. "Many women will make pilgrimages here," she predicts.

*   *   *

Back in Milan, February 1860. It has been a glorious month, Louise records, for the patriots of Piedmont. Tuscany and several other regions have voted to be united with Victor Emmanuel's kingdom. Great Britain's desire for a strong, unified Italian state whose power might balance France's has impelled it to support Piedmont. In a trade-off that provokes the fury of the more radical patriots, Cavour manages to retain France's backing by ceding it the territories of Savoy and Nice.

Louise watches King Victor Emmanuel II, whose family has ruled Piedmont for several generations, make a triumphant entry into Milan. At his side is Count Camillo Cavour, the shrewd diplomat who inherited many of his enlightened ideals from his Swiss-born Calvinist mother.

From early morning on, all of Milan's streets were filled by a dense crowd swarming into the Via del Corso, where the king's procession was scheduled to take place.... The entire soul of Italy was on holiday.... The drum roll began, the regimental band played the hymn of the House of Savoy; but clarions and drums were overshadowed by the great voice of the people as a monumental Viva! announced the approach of the adored king. He passed in an open coach, M. de Cavour at his side. It was the first time I saw the glorious Italian minister; as he took off his hat to salute the crowd, I was stuck by the beauty of his large, powerful forehead; the great politician, every one of whose actions had assured the renaissance of his country, appeared to be radiant from the recent triumphs of the patriots' cause. : ..

I had already seen the king in Paris during the celebrations held for him in 1855. This particular day I found his bearing more martial and his physiognomy more proud. Victor Emmanuel is certainly the personification of a soldier-king; in the gesture of his arms one feels the sword more keenly than the scepter.... His warrior's head is stamped with a fierceness and sincerity that would frighten off any cowardice or disloyalty....

Never mind that Victor Emmanuel, to many biographers, was "a vulgar little man, obscene in speech and devoted to nothing much except hunting and fornication, and to extending his domains whenever possible." Never mind that he delighted in indecent expressions that shocked the most libertine members of French society, launched the famous Castiglione upon her career as courtesan when she was sixteen, and publicly boasted that he had bedded "every important woman of Turin." What-

ever Victor Emmanuel's personal drawbacks, his nationalism was heartfelt, so Louise was under his spell.

*His rather savage mustache veils the kindness of his very forthright
smile, which shines out pleasantly over his white teeth [Louise continues her star-struck portrait of the monarch]. His gaze is direct, as audacious as his character, tempered by the purity and calm of his face;
all of his powerful head shines with health and heroism.*

A few days later, the Muse is invited to a ball at court, where she encounters one of Paris's most celebrated hostesses, the Italian-born intellectual Princess Cristina Belgiojoso, whose pallor and memorably
mysterious eyes were attributed by many to a morphine addiction. Louise's jealousy had long been piqued by the glamour of Belgiojoso's progressive rival salon and by Musset's great affection for her; and now the
women were competing again. "There appeared the phantom of a princess whose great wealth and adventures had brought her fame thirty years
ago," Louise's scalpel portrait begins.

*The princess in ruins passed before us. Under the loose folds of a white
dress her bent body was horrible to behold: her spine vaulted promi-
nently under her parchment skin; her toothless mouth had an envious
smile; her hollow, haggard eyes flamed with greed; her hair sparsely
covered her denuded skull, where a few diamonds emitted their ironic
light.*

The savagery of Louise's portrait was by way of vengeance. An unscru-
pulous French publisher residing in Milan had offered Louise the editor-
ship of a French-language newspaper to be published in Italy but had not
yet raised the money for it. He approached the very wealthy, devious
Princess Belgiojoso, who immediately offered to put up the funds on the
condition that Louise Colet be dropped from the project. Louise, furious,
then obtained an interview with Cavour to raise funds for a rival magazine
of her own, which she planned to call *L'Annexion*.

"Poor lady, I hear that the princess stole that journal from under you,"
Cavour quipped as Louise arrived at his office. But to his visitor's surprise, the suave fifty-year-old Cavour, a short, plump, balding man with
an enormous forehead and metal-rimmed glasses, immediately switched
the subject to Louise's last novel, *Lui*.

"I found one of your heroines rather ridiculous," Cavour commented. "No woman would spend two months waiting for an icy-hearted man who loves her so little."

"Are you denying women's hearts an element of idealism?" Louise asked.

"It's a totally unnatural romantic situation," the minister replied, laughing. "One might find women of such blind fidelity in France, but not in Italy."

The rest of the interview was a trifle disappointing. Cavour gave his approval and "platonic blessing" to the successful founding of Louise's journal yet could not suggest any ways of funding it. But he did offer her a special pass to attend the first session of the Piedmontese parliament.

Turin, April 2, 1860. The Piedmontese parliament is convening for the first time in its brand-new form, representing a vastly enlarged democratic monarchy comprising territories recaptured from Austria, most notably Lombardy and Tuscany. It is as emotional a session as any political assembly held in Europe in decades. The stars of the show, again, are Emperor Victor Emmanuel and Camillo Cavour. "Escorted by his military staff, Victor Emmanuel entered the senate room, dressed in his general's habit," so Louise begins her description of this historic gathering.

Then all handkerchiefs waved, all voices shouted out Viva! A frenetic enthusiasm swept all observers and was echoed by the patriots standing in the street below. . . .

At the last phrase of the king's address, "Italy must henceforth be the Italy of Italians," the euphoria of the crowd surpassed all imagination. . . . The two shouts "Long Live the King!" and "Viva Italia!" were emitted by all. What jubilation! What force! . . . What security for the future of the renascent fatherland!

Louise is wonderfully skilled at cornering the men in power. She obtains another long interview with Cavour the morning after the opening of the senate. He tells her that Rome's reactionary papal government, which suffers from "the somnolence of theocracy," worries and saddens him far more than the Austrian occupation of Venice, which he predicts will rise autonomously against Austria. "The Roman nobility is the most passive and cowardly in Italy. . . . The memory of antiquity stifles Rome," Cavour tells her.

That same week, the shaky alliance between the superdiplomat Cavour and the guerrilla fighter Garibaldi had moved into open enmity. Protesting the cession of his hometown of Nice to France, Garibaldi was threatening to invade the territories of Sicily and Naples without Cavour's support. Louise questioned Cavour about the wisdom of bribing France with Nice and Savoy.

"What could I do?" Cavour answered, looking somber as he expounded on the numerous pro-Austrian and papist French leaders who were lobbying Napoleon III to cease all support for Italian unity. "If your daughter were near death, wouldn't you cut off her finger to save her? The emperor is our only ally; only he has given us an army. . . . Look at all the groups in France opposing the emperor and us. . . . What can one think of Thiers, Guizot, Lamoricière, becoming our enemies and supporting Austria? . . . We're being treated as revolutionary apostates by the very same men who made the Glorious Revolution of July 1830!"

Louise's question was timely. The next week, Garibaldi made one of his rare appearances in the new Piedmontese parliament to protest Cavour's ceding of Nice to France, and Louise was on hand to cover the confrontation.

This is where I saw, for the first time, the hero who a few months later would startle the entire world. . . . When he appeared in the parliamentary chamber, all spectators acclaimed him; they also rose to salute Mr. Cavour. . . . These two men symbolized the diverse elements which would soon blend and merge to reconstitute the Italian nation: In Garbaldi—inspiration, impulse, courage, audacity; in Cavour—wisdom, firmness, perseverance.

Garibaldi's attack was impassioned, angry, and highly personal, based on purity of purpose and absolute patriotism.

Cavour's response was as calm as necessity, as impersonal as sacrifice, as incisive as any reality which does not allow for personal emotion or grief.

Reports of this session startled and alarmed many persons in France. Cursed be our nation when its leaders have lost concern for such displays of abnegation, devotion, and audacity! It is a sign of our public numbing and decadence.

A fortnight later, Louise braves a high fever and terrible bronchitis (as she gets older she is increasingly plagued with lung ailments) to go to Victor Emmanuel's inaugural ball at the Borghese Palace. Her friend Princess Marie Bonaparte beckons her to her side as she stands next to the monarch, and Louise's description of the meeting has a modesty quite new to her: that of a former beauty openly admitting her advancing age.

> *The king, who was speaking with the princess, saw the affectionate smile with which she looked at me, and asked her who I was; he accompanied this question with flattering epithets, which I wouldn't have had the right to receive at any age. . . . Princess Marie told the king my name and asked him if she should introduce me to him. Fixing me with his piercing eyes, he answered with a kind smile: "What could I say to a Muse? I'd rather look at her than talk to her."*

In those spring weeks of 1860, Louise is happy because her daughter has joined her in Italy for the summer months. In Henriette's company, Louise spends a month visiting Florence's treasures, writing over one hundred pages on the city's art and architecture, with particular reverence for Giotto and Cimabue.

On May 11, Louise and Henriette hear that Garibaldi and his "thousand men" have landed in Sicily. A popular insurrection had swept through the island in previous weeks, and Garibaldi, without his government's official approval, took advantage of this new wave of unrest. He sailed from Genoa to Sicily with his red-shirted volunteers—principally recruited from the liberal bourgeoisie of Lombardy and Venetia—and landed in Marsala, where he set up a provisional government and proclaimed himself "Dictator in the name of Victor Emmanuel II, King of Italy."

"Every city throughout the peninsula rang with the phrase '*Garibaldi é sbarcato a Marsala!*'" Louise reports from Florence. "News vendors shouted out the phrase throughout the streets, huge crowds echoed it. . . . I wished I had a son in order to tell him, 'Those are true men! That is the true way of belief! That is the true model of behavior!'"

June 1860. Louise and Henriette leave Tuscany and cross the border into the Papal States, whose mercenary armies, she notes with rage, are still headed by the conservative French general Lamoricière—"a stigma of shame. . . . Under what right does a stranger fight to maintain the slavery of a people that is not his?" In Perugia, she witnesses the ruthlessness of Austrian occupying troops toward local citizens. On the days when they did not indulge in outright massacres, "they daily insulted the citizenry, with any pretext for brutality. They even whipped young school-girls for carrying a portrait of Victor Emmanuel." Louise calls on the archbishop of the city, who leaves his palace only in the protection of Austrian soldiers and tells her that "Garibaldi is a man possessed by the devil."

Turin, mid-August 1860. By this time, Garibaldi, "the hero of two worlds," has shown his mettle and has almost completed his conquest of Sicily for the Risorgimento. Aided by Sicilians' long-seated hatred for the Bourbons, his barely armed "thousand men," whose principal gunrunner is the French volunteer Dumas *père,* sweep through the island in a matter of weeks. And in August his troops are reinforced by thousands more guerrilla fighters from all over the Italian peninsula.

> *Despite the complex political scruples he had to maintain toward the European powers, Count Cavour facilitated the convoys of men and of arms to Garibaldi [Louise writes]. It took all his genius of conciliation and audacity to lead this double-edged strategy. . . . Privately, he was swept by the powerful enthusiasm of the nation; on the level of international diplomacy, obstacles confronted his every move.*

Garibaldi's next plan was to cross to Calabria and invade the Kingdom of Naples, directly defying orders from Cavour and Victor Emmanuel. "Sire . . . Allow me to countermand your orders this time," Garibaldi wrote his monarch in late August, in an exchange of letters that Louise includes in Volume II of *L'Italie des Italiens.* "When I shall have accomplished my duty by delivering all our people from the yoke that oppresses them, I shall deposit my sword at your feet and obey you until the end of my days."

It was during these turbulent weeks of late August 1860, just before Garibaldi's redshirts crossed the Strait of Messina and invaded the Kingdom of Naples, that Louise had her third interview with Prime Minister Cavour. Though grieving over Henriette's return to the south of France, where the young woman was to spend the fall with her paternal aunt, Louise was now free to undertake more hazardous missions. She was determined to receive permission to leave for Naples on a military convoy, and went about it shrewdly: During her visit with Cavour, she expressed the hope that he would promulgate a law on civil marriage, and other legislation favorable to women, in Italy's forthcoming constitution. Cavour replied that the new constitution would offer women many new freedoms.

"Since you're concerned with the general destiny of women, the plight of one particular woman must also interest you," Louise said, "and I'm going to ask you for a favor."

"What can I do for you?" Cavour graciously asked.

"I'd like to cross to Naples on a government ship."

"Ah, ah!" Cavour exclaimed, laughing, "You're going to rejoin Garibaldi! But he's still on the Sicilian side of the Strait of Messina."

"He'll cross imminently," Louise replied, "and I'd like to witness his triumphal entry into Naples in order to write about it."

"As soon as Garibaldi sets foot in Naples, I'll send troops there to support him, and if the company of a regiment of men doesn't frighten you, I'll get you passage on a military ship."

August 20, 1860. Louise, impatient to get to Naples, pays yet another call on Prime Minister Cavour.

"Ah!" he said, laughing, as soon as I entered his office. "I think you'll leave soon. Prepare your red costume."

"Garibaldi has disembarked!" I exclaimed.

"I don't have the time to tell you any more about it," he replied as he prepared to go to an emergency meeting of his cabinet. "I gave Admiral Sera orders to let you leave Genoa in a beautiful ship. And I'll send you a letter for the governor of Genoa once you're there."

"In this great maelstrom that surrounds you, you'll forget all about me, Monsieur le Comte."

"I never forget any of my promises," the minister retorted. "Adieu. Sing your praises of Garibaldi, and continue to love Italy as you love it now."

While waiting for her orders, Louise goes to spend the night in Venice. At the train station, she buys the local newspapers, which announce Garibaldi's triumphant landing on the Italian peninsula and his capture of Reggio di Calabria. She begins to spread the word the second she steps off the train, for Austrian censors will prevent the news from reaching Venice for several days.

At my arrival in Venice, an old gondolier who had often taken me to the Lido during my last stay here met me at the station. His two sons, who had been drafted into the Austrian Army, had defected to join Garibaldi. I told him the good news and gave him my Milan newspapers. The happy tidings were immediately transmitted, in whispers, from gondolier to gondolier. The words "É sbarcato, il grand'uomo" [the great man has landed], were repeated rhythmically from laguna to laguna, and within a half hour all of Venice was ringing with the phrase. How electric is glory, when that glory is that of an entire people!

The first two volumes of Colet's *L'Italie des Italiens,* summarized above, focus on northern and central Italy. Volume III, dedicated to southern Italy, begins with her departure for Naples.

Genoa, September 8–10. Thanks to Cavour, Louise is given passage on the Sardinian military vessel *Constitution,* on which she is given the most beautiful room on the ship and treated like a queen. The vessel stops briefly at the island of Elba, whose governor sends sherbets, fruit, and flowers to her cabin and gives her a guided tour of Napoleon's site of exile.

After a two-day crossing, Louise's ship arrives in the Bay of Naples, where Garibaldi landed just two days earlier. Casting anchor, the captain shuttles to a large Piedmontese frigate to take orders from an admiral, and upon his return tells Louise that Garibaldi is about to cross the bay. Here is Louise's first sighting of Garibaldi, the "Liberator."

I hasten into a launch, which soon crosses the one carrying the Liberator; calm and contemplative, dressed as ever in his red shirt and scarf, he stands next to the admiral. Guiding my dinghy alongside his, I give him the verses I wrote upon his entry into Palermo. He shakes my hand. I say to him, "Permit me to say au revoir, General." At that moment, salvos of artillery come out of all the Sardinian vessels and drown out my voice; my dory is lost among numerous others, from which shouts of "Viva Garibaldi!" are echoed throughout the bay.

Louise would never forget the patriotic ecstasy that spread through Naples as Garibaldi's redshirts—"these clouds of dazzling red vestments which glowed as brilliantly over the city's pavements as Vesuvius's red flames gleam over the gray rocks of the mountain"—liberated the city in September 1860.

*   *   *

The last substantial Bourbon resistance to Garibaldi's troops was overcome at the battle of Volturno, near the town of Caserta. Wishing to make herself useful, Louise visits the hospitals of Caserta, "still ablaze with the blood of the wounded, of amputated limbs." "I went from bed to bed amid the moans of pain, gleaning the soldiers' names and addresses, their family particulars, in order to write brief reassuring letters to their parents." (This modest act of charity would earn Louise yet another mean epithet from the polemicist Barbey d'Aurevilly: He called her "Garibaldi's canteen manager.") That week, military authorities try to restrain Louise from coming straight into the battlefield, but at Capua and Sant'Angelo she insists on venturing onto the scene of action while the artillery is still shooting and touches the hot, still-smoking metal of the cannons without a trace of fear. "If those grenades had reached me, such a death would have been less somber than a death in Paris on a foggy day," she muses.

But the elation of Garibaldi's conquest was drawing to a close. On October 27, Victor Emmanuel arrived in Naples with his own army, trying to steal Garibaldi's thunder and pretend that it was his own Piedmontese troops, rather than Garibaldi's volunteers, who had conquered the city. He persuaded the Liberator to call off his plan of invading Rome, which would threaten a total cutoff of French support. Submitting to the pressure of public opinion, after months of distancing himself from Garibaldi, Victor Emmanuel reluctantly agreed to have him join a triumphant procession through the city. (In her description of that event, Louise greatly idealizes the relationship between the two men, obscuring Victor Emmanuel's glacial treatment of the Liberator.)

The Piedmontese forces took over from Garibaldi's heroic redshirts, and Garibaldi went home to his estate in Sicily, brokenhearted from his emperor's callousness. Order had been reestablished in Naples, but like many other champions of the Risorgimento, Louise missed the poetry of revolution. With Garibaldi's guerrillas gone, Naples no longer had that "visible palpitation of a blissful, liberated people."

16.

Increasing Solitude

❧◦❧

Tarrying in Naples in the autumn of 1860, with no revolution to chronicle, Louise reverted to art history. It was a welcome distraction for her, for she still grieved over her "cruel separation" from her daughter. Hippolyte Colet's family had wished Henriette to leave Italy to be spared, in the Colet family's words, "her mother's stormy disposition and impieties." It is obvious that this archconservative Catholic clan had dreaded the notion of their young niece's being further exposed to Louise's revolutionary ardor.

In the next few months, Louise documented the churches and artistic sites of the Naples region as fastidiously as she had chronicled the treasures of Florence and Venice. She visited the superb Chiamonte Palace, awarded by Garibaldi to Alexandre Dumas in return for his support of the Risorgimento; she saw the celebrated writer editing his newspaper dispatches by the seashore, seated under a trellis of climbing roses. (The fifty-eight-year-old Dumas had participated in Garibaldi's campaign in the company of a large and exotic Parisian entourage, which included a Russian valet, resplendent in the gold and silver court uniform of Georgian princes, and a nineteen-year-old beauty called "the admiral," who dressed in a nautical costume of gilded violet velvet and was pregnant by the novelist.)

Visiting Pompeii, whose archaeological excavations Dumas was directing—another reward for his support of Garibaldi—Louise dropped in on the so-called secret museum. It already housed one of the world's great collections of pornographic art; and Louise, who in her middle years was growing increasingly puritanical, was thoroughly shocked by its profusion of sculpted phalluses ("Art must not lower itself to depict such turpitudes").

But she was generally pleased with her life in Naples. Her hotel room had a superb view of Capri, Sorrento, and Vesuvius, and she decided to spend most of the winter there. Louise felt a very special relationship with this city because her father's youth was spent there. Memories of her father visited her constantly during her stay in Naples, and in a moving passage of *L'Italie des Italiens* she offers an emotional tribute to him: "I owe [my parents] all of what I am. . . . The flower that they brought to bloom is not as worthy as the branch that bore it. When I evoke in my prayers my splendid memories of them, I'm humiliated by the insignificance of my own achievements, and I humbly ask them, 'Forgive me for being so unworthy of you.' "

Seduced by the sight of Vesuvius from her window, Louise elects to climb to the top of the volcano, which she does in the company of some native guides and two other European tourists. The excursion is made perilous by her high-heeled shoes and fashionable hoop skirt. "My guides did not warn me about the dangers of the metal rods built into my stupid skirt," she writes in warning to future female climbers. "A pair of bloomers, a plain straight dress, and hobnailed shoes are indispensable to any woman who undertakes this perilous climb." When she reaches the top of Vesuvius, Louise, clinging to a rock, is frightened by the sight of its seething crater: "Flames rising into incandescent vapors light up the vast funnel of the mountain; formidable rumbling sounds and a strong odor of sulfur emanate from the pit; my lips and eyes are on fire, I turn away from the vertiginous abyss; to fall into the pit and be engulfed in its mystery must have tempted more than one visitor."

The tourists cook their dinner on hot volcanic ash; eggs and tea water boil in two seconds. In her middle age Louise has begun to enjoy wine, and the tourists accompany their meal with a notable local vintage, Lachrymae Cristi. They come down the mountain after nightfall, and in Louise's description of the terrifying descent, hampered by her chronically weak lungs, she again warns women to abandon their female attire when undertaking such a journey. "The metal hoops of my skirt constantly cause a cascade of large stones to hurtle against my legs; the soles of my shoes, already burnt by the lava, come right off; my lacerated feet are bleeding, my ankles black and blue. . . ."

Despite her weakened health, Louise remains the fearless, adventurous tomboy she has been since youth. Loving all extremes of emotion, she does not regret a minute of the hazardous excursion: "Among the most cherished sensations of my life—vertiginous during their duration, poignant in their aftermath—this one will survive as particularly superb and memorable. Even a lingering death would not be too high a price for it!"

Naples, December 1860–January 1861. Louise joined in the elegant social life that was revived in Naples after Garibaldi's victory, when Piedmont officially annexed the city. Members of Naples's aristocracy referred to her as *la buona Francesa,* and she was very popular with them. Louise loved to hobnob with nobility. She sought out high society in any country she visited, and was capable of extravagant name-dropping. Often asked to the home of the Marquis de Villamarina, the new Piedmontese governor of Naples, she read her poetry and passages of her work in progress, *L'Italie des Italiens.*

By coincidence, these Neapolitan evenings were also attended by Maxime Du Camp, who had just served a stint as a volunteer with Garibaldi's troops. The two crossed paths only once, and although Louise never recorded their encounter, Du Camp did. This meeting of two old enemies offers an interesting insight into the diverse impulses that drew French literati to Italy during various phases of the Risorgimento.

Maxime Du Camp, an apolitical opportunist who had been decorated for fighting on the conservative side in the 1848 revolution, was drawn to Garibaldi's campaign out of disappointed love. In the summer of 1860, his mistress of nine years, Valentine Delessert—whose sexual exploits he so graphically recorded in his letters to Flaubert—left him, and he suffered a severe depression. "In 1860 I had climbed Jacob's ladder," he wrote to a friend. "It was shaken; I fell and hurt myself badly. . . . [Garibaldi's campaign] was like a wake-up call." So the forty-year-old Du Camp joined the Liberator's redshirts to "change air" and to have an adventure that might result in good copy. He left for Palermo on August 13, 1860, the week Garibaldi completed his Sicilian campaign, ten months after Louise had gone to Italy. Because of his connections in French government circles, he was given the rank of major in Garibaldi's troops. Within a few weeks, Du Camp's friend Flaubert, who was struggling at Croisset over the composition of his novel *Salammbô,* was writing him anguished letters. "Send me *one* word to let me know what has become of you, for God's sake! Whether you're dead, alive or wounded!" Du Camp wrote back to Flaubert within a fortnight, giving him an amusing account of an experience in the field of battle:

> *I was on the firing line from 5 A.M. to 6 P.M. . . . A literary detail: In the late morning the position we were defending was surrounded on two sides. My baggage was in our headquarters, about to fall into the enemy's hands. I thought: "My notes, my notes." I recklessly went to get the two thick folders and clutched them over my stomach; one of them was so huge that it beat against my penis each time my horse made a high leap. The Neapolitan imbeciles, not guessing that I was a man of letters protecting his copy, shot out a great burst of gunfire, which only harmed my poor horse, whose ear was torn off. . . . I saw many other amusing things, and good spectacles. . . .*

The next lines reveal Du Camp's derision of the leader he had come to support and his continuing malice toward Louise:

> *I thought for a while that that imbecile Garibaldi was going to forge right on and attack Rome; what a beating he would have taken, and how it would have advanced the cause of liberty. Thank God he renounced that project, and this amazes me, seeing that his brains are minimal. . . . Take heart,* cher vieux, *I hope your next book will exasperate the bourgeois. You may know that the Muse is here and recites. her verses in local salons; it's a good spectacle, and if she once gave you a lot of grief you're avenged, for it's difficult to be more ridiculous.*

As for Du Camp and Louise's encounter at the Naples soiree, it is briefly dismissed in Du Camp's memoirs with the following phrase: "I saw Louise Colet at the Marquis de Villamarina's, and turned away."

There was one last irony concerning Colet's and Du Camp's involvement in the Risorgimento. When George Sand, who was not yet personally acquainted with Du Camp, read the book that resulted from his Italian adventure, *L'Éxpedition des deux Siciles,* she praised the author for his courage and "political convictions." "He gave his will and his life to the most beautiful of causes, the salvation of Italy," Sand exulted. "He enrolled in Garibaldi's troops. . . . One is struck by the seriousness of that act and of the text that arose from it." Thus Du Camp was credited for a political idealism that, in reality, far better characterized Louise Colet.

During the subsequent months of her stay in Italy, Louise had two more brief encounters with Garibaldi. On one of these occasions, she was returning to Naples after visiting wounded soldiers in Caserta and found that Garibaldi was on the same train. For once, she exercised great tact: Although her reserved seat was in the same wagon as Garibaldi's, she decided that "he who bore the weight of the destiny of Italy deserved the respect of solitude." She left discreetly after offering him a bouquet of flowers and took a second-class seat in another wagon. Her courtesy was returned: When Garibaldi got off the train, one of his aides-de-camp went to Louise and offered her the seat the Liberator had just vacated.

Their last meeting occurred at a palace in Naples where Victor Emmanuel, just arrived in the city to play the role of conqueror, was holding a reception. Louise approached Garibaldi, clutched his hands, and asked him if it was true that he was leaving Naples. With a look of sadness, the Liberator replied that he was. "No, no," Louise replied with anguish, "that cannot be." When he left a few days later, he took with him, in her words, "all the poetry of the revolution."

In February of 1861, after visits to Sicily that inspired many more pages of art history, Louise Colet left Naples for Rome. Victor Emmanuel had vastly diminished the Papal States the previous autumn when he occupied the Marches and Umbria, as Garibaldi had wished to do. The papal territory was reduced to the city of Rome, where the entrenched conservative factions had grown more bitter. The city was rife with secret police that kept watch on antipapist elements; one of its targets, in the first months of 1861, was Louise Colet. As soon as she had settled at the Hotel Inghilterra—a lovely hostelry still standing today on the Via Bocca del Leone, two blocks from the Spanish Steps—she was warned by one of her compatriots, a bookstore owner, that she was under police surveillance.

The warning left her undaunted. She was determined to remain in Rome—whose antiquities thrilled her as its religious artifacts horrified her—to continue her campaign against the Catholic clergy, which she considered to be the principal enemy of human progress.

Louise's anticlericalism was fanned by a pope who was one of the more repressive Catholic leaders of the post-Reformation era and whose pontificate was the longest in the history of the papacy (1846–1878). Although he had begun as a fairly liberal reformist, Pius IX became an archconservative in the 1850s, when Cavour attempted to limit his temporal power. He militantly opposed every goal of the Risorgimento, and his reign was defined by two of the most regressive encyclicals of papal history, those that set forth the dogma of the Immaculate Conception and the doctrine of Papal Infallibility.

When she arrived in Rome, Louise immediately set off to visit the Vatican, where she assisted at a Mass officiated by Pius IX in the Sistine Chapel. She describes the obese little Pope, his thick head doddering over a swollen neck, his muddy eyes and weak lips, his blotched red face and powdered hair, the archaic pomp with which his chair is carried into the church by fourteen papal guards. She considered the basilica of Saint Peter a site "of glacial pomp . . . totally devoid of any mysticism or mystery." With the exception of the *Pietà* of Michelangelo, who "would have been a far greater artist if he had fawned less upon illiterate pontiffs," the basilica's "overabundance of riches" was "a monument to hypocrisy . . . catering to the taste of parvenus and bankers."

Louise was particularly disgusted with the opulent tomb of Queen Christina of Sweden—"a ruler more pagan in her mores than those of pre-Christian times"—whose recently published letters had revealed her to be "a thief, a violent, insolent and debauched strumpet." In the middle of Saint Peter's, Louise shouted, "I protest this sanctification of Christina of Sweden! As a saint, as one of the truly just, I far prefer Garibaldi!" Her outburst terrified a priest, who took to his heels and rushed back into the depths of the basilica.

Later that month, she wrote a burlesque of a Holy Week Mass at Saint Peter's, which re-created the Last Supper: The Holy Father himself served food to the thirteen beggars who were seated at the table as stand-ins for Christ and his apostles. At the end of the liturgy, a few seconds after the Pope had left the church, a group of fat monks rushed to the altar, chased out the beggars, and stuffed the food and wine into large baskets for their own use (Louise's descriptions of Rome's decadent religious mores occasionally strain the imagination).

Visiting the church of Santa Maria Maggiore, Louise was prompted to make her own profession of faith, in which she reveals a nonsectarian piety. She was, in fact, a Deist: She believed in a Supreme Being but maintained that the truths of this "implacable Unknown" could not be incarnated in any temporal sect or power. Her credo was a blend of the ideologies that had influenced her since youth—her maternal grandfather's Voltairian skepticism, Victor Cousin's eclectic mysticism, Alfred de Vigny's Stoicism, Victor Hugo's catchall pantheism:

Although I long ago left the Catholic faith [she wrote in the fourth and final volume of L'Italie des Italiens], *I enjoy meditating whenever I can in a great empty basilica. I do not feel as much communion with infinity there as I do when gazing on a beautiful starry night or the immensity of the ocean; but I cannot enter into one of these temples which a succession of religious sects erected to their gods without feeling a sorrowful compassion concerning our finitude.*

Within the obscurity which shrouds us in such sites there is a luminous spark that aspires to rejoin the hidden sanctuary whence it originally sprung; this luminous point is the soul; that sanctuary is the ever-hidden Godhead—a feeble but permanent radiance, and the only one which pierces the night that shrouds us. . . .

Religions alter God, modeling Him upon human passions; philosophers may create a purer, fairer image of Him, but it remains tenuous. To affirm God through our good works—that is the doctrine of philosophy; to believe in Him by intuition, and not through the dictates of a fallacious authority—that is the law of the true thinker. . . .

The spiritualism of antiquity was best expressed by philosophers— Socrates, Plato, Marcus Aurelius, Hypatia. . . . The message of redemptive love was even more intensely expressed in the Gospels than in these ancient philosophers, but the Gospels weakened the nature of Christ by proclaiming him to be God. . . .

Louise ends her credo with a blazing attack on the Catholic Church, whose excesses of bigotry she had experienced among her own kin as a young woman:

In our time the human soul is stifled by Catholicism, an antihuman doctrine whose architects suppressed all air and light. . . . Liberty, Justice, Charity, Science, and Chastity have been no more than ringing words in the mouthpiece of the Church; She has always aligned Herself with the forces of tyranny and darkness . . . and at this very hour, the forces of liberty and justice shout out against the Church through all the voices of the Italian fatherland: "Why do you deny our liberation?"

These are the opinions with which Louise assaulted Cardinal Antonelli, Prime Minister of the Papal States, one of the Church's highest-ranking prelates, when she cornered him at the Vatican in an attempt to obtain an audience with the Pope. It was a few days before her return to France, and Louise had a grand purpose in desiring to talk with the Holy Father: She wished to convert Pius IX to the cause of Italian liberation, to the side of Garibaldi and Cavour!

Sitting so close to her that his frock touched her dress, the cardinal, who wore immense rings of square-cut emeralds, addressed Louise as *"cara mia"* and heard her out but was not in the least swayed. "The Church," he told her, "cannot recognize the people's novel claim to emancipation, which of course is no more than the right to rape and murder. The meaningless concepts of 'patriotism,' 'liberty,' or 'universal suffrage' can only be brought about by violence." Nor did the prelate rush to get Louise an audience with Pius. She had given him three days to arrange the meeting, and the cardinal explained that the Holy Father did not accept ultimatums. Thus were we deprived of a colorful episode—Louise Colet preaching revolution to the most reactionary Pope of modern times.

Louise left Rome for Paris in the spring of 1861, after a year and eight months in Italy. She would soon grieve over Camillo Cavour, who died suddenly, at fifty-one, a few weeks after she returned to France. But the revolutionary goals Cavour pursued had been fulfilled. All of the Italian peninsula, with the exclusion of Rome, had voted to be annexed to Victor Emmanuel's kingdom. In March, at a parliamentary session in Turin, Victor Emmanuel II proclaimed the birth of a united kingdom of Italy.

"I wept from the sorrow of returning to all these indifferent, bustling, distracted crowds," Louise wrote on her return to Paris, in the closing pages of her fourth volume on Italy, "some of them only desiring material gain, others only wishing to parade their wealth." "It would be good to die before this century comes to an end," she wrote in a final passage, "for the century that follows will be marked by the leveling of the entire globe into one single country scattered with identical, monotypical cities."

There is much anxiety and loneliness in those words; and *L'Italie des Italiens* is as interesting for what it reveals about Louise in middle age as it is for her account of the Risorgimento's triumphant last phase.

The venom in Louise's pen, and the biting social satire that Flaubert considered to be her greatest literary talent, increased in her later years. ("Please accept the assurance of my most perfect disdain," she signed letters to some of her antagonists.) In her tart portrait of Cristina Belgiojoso, Louise takes off on the radical chic of the princess's political role-playing. " 'Let's go for patriotism; it's a new fad I've got to try out,' " she has Belgiojoso say to herself when her days of Parisian glory fade.

[Belgiojoso] went from Turin to Milan, from Rome to Naples, saying, "I'm Joan of Arc!" Everyone stared at her, searching for the naive

maid and finding only a decrepit adventurer who dove toward army camps like a scavenging bird. A patriot smiled at her and advised her to choose retirement and the home. "I, dear man, abdicate?" she retorted to that biting criticism. "Disappear into the crowd, when I've reigned so well, no, no! I still have many years of éclat and adventures! Changing scenes renews the actress; I shall be transfigured on a new stage. . . ."

But the most poignant insight we have into Louise's state of mind in the sixth decade of her life is her complicated and difficult bond with her daughter.

Until a few decades ago, the daughters of prominent women noted for their liberated mores have tended to have tormented relationships with their mothers. Conformism is a necessary aspect of a young girl's psychic growth; and mothers such as Louise did not provide comfortable models, since they were experimenting with new roles, pioneering novel modes of female identity. Three eminent women writers with impossible daughters immediately come to mind in the French culture alone, all of whom Louise much admired: her predecessor Madame de Sévigné and her contemporaries George Sand and Marie d'Agoult.

Madame de Sévigné's love for her cold, unresponsive daughter—the Countess de Grignan—was such that her confessor warned her that it amounted to idolatry and threatened her relationship with God. Yet the Countess de Grignan remained from adolescence haughty, arrogant, and utterly unfeeling toward her mother; their relations were so strained that they often communicated by letter from room to room, across closed doors, rather than risk violent confrontation; and although they were in the same house during the two final weeks of the illness that carried her mother away, Madame de Sévigné's daughter never once set foot into the sickroom; she did not even attend her mother's funeral.

After an adolescence spent defying most of her mother's decisions concerning her education, George Sand's daughter, Solange, married a man of bad reputation, whom her mother detested. Solange divorced him and to her mother's horror, entered into the life of a demimondaine, supported by a succession of wealthy lovers. The two women became so estranged that four years went by without their once communicating with each other, even in writing. Solange's final act of filial enmity was to insist, against Sand's explicit wishes, on giving her mother a Catholic burial.

Marie d'Agoult's two daughters by Franz Liszt, Claire du Charnacé and Cosima von Bülow Wagner, also defied their mother. (D'Agoult, like Louise, was a famous beauty and a prolific writer; the two had a brief correspondence, but it is probable that they never met.) The conformism and bourgeois ways of Cosima Liszt, her tendency to subject herself totally to the men she married—Hans von Bülow, Richard Wagner—were as deplored by her independent mother as her sister Claire's aloofness. For many years the three lived in a maelstrom of disputes, pallid reconciliations, and renewed estrangements.

So the strained relations between Louise and Henriette Colet are not unique. And they may have been made more difficult because of the Colets' poverty and isolation—the daughters of Sévigné, Sand, and d'Agoult were protected by their parents' independent means and a network of families ties.

So far, Henriette Colet has remained a cipher for us, for there are few direct references to her in Louise's writings. As a small child, we can imagine her shuttling from a series of boarding schools to Louise's apartment, perhaps overhearing her mother's tempestuous arguments with a succession of lovers; we sense a girl who must often have wondered who her father was and was probably resentful of her mother's unorthodox behavior. In the one school-day letter that has survived, we detect an urgent need for her mother's attention and approval. "I'm working hard, Maman darling, and doing everything I can so that you will be pleased with me." Later we see Henriette through the eyes of Victor Cousin and Alfred de Vigny, as an entrancing, rebellious teenage beauty, disputing her mother at every turn. And we read allusions to Henriette in Louise's journals. She is often praised as "ravishing," and one of Louise's poems celebrates her intellect: "that God-given light which one calls intelligence / Was poured into you the very day you were born."

As Henriette reached her late teens, we begin to see her more clearly through the eyes of friends. She was a tall, lanky, good-looking girl with a pale face, melancholy eyes, and her mother's abundant wavy blond hair. Like Louise, she was short-tempered and tended to hopeless infatuation. At sixteen she fell in love with the poet Leconte de Lisle, thirty years her senior. Her mother's close friend commemorated Henriette's loveliness in his verses, describing her as *"L'Aube adorable qui se lève,"* "The adorable rising dawn." Despite his admiration for Henriette, de Lisle was a strict family man with an unwavering belief in marital fidelity. He had to write the lovelorn teenager several tactful, cool, paternal letters to subdue her passion.

L'Italie des Italiens is the only book of Colet's in which Henriette comes occasionally to life; and one lingers on every detail, trying to imagine the only being Louise may have loved more than Flaubert.

When Henriette joined her mother in northern Italy in the spring of 1860, she was almost twenty. In Ravenna, the two women share a room in a seedy hotel, where they spend much of the night fighting an invasion of bedbugs; and while Louise blames this indignity on the general decadence that prevails in the Papal States, Henriette tackles it with spunky humor. "This will be a good episode for your book," she tells her mother. "Call it 'Desperate night's vigil of two Parisians hunting foul animals for which there is no suitable name in academic circles.' "

There is pride in Louise's descriptions of her daughter, and great concern for her often fragile health. In Ravenna, making a round of social calls, Louise records that the young Countess Rasponi is instantly charmed by the beauty of "frail, suffering" Henriette, who much reminds her of her own sister. Later that month, Louise cuts short her stay in Turin to take Henriette to Genoa, because she is "under doctor's orders" to take sea baths.

Henriette repeatedly proved that she was as spunky as her mother. One day in Genoa, an old boatman was teaching Henriette to swim by making her wade into increasingly deep water, holding a rope around her waist. Louise describes how the boatman, an admirer of Garibaldi, asks Henriette to echo the "Viva Garibaldi!" being shouted from all the boats in the bay:

> *"I can only shout* vive la France," *Henriette replied, laughing. "Without France you wouldn't have gotten anywhere."*
>
> *The boatman's face reddened with anger. He immediately let go of most of the swim-training rope, only holding on to its very end. My daughter sank into the water and disappeared for a few seconds.*
>
> *I shouted out and ran into the water. "Briccone! che questo?" I asked the boatman in a rage, seizing his arm. —"Signora," he answered with a terrible coolness, "senza voi che amate molto l'Italia, l'avrei affogata" [if it were not for your great love of Italy, I would have drowned her]. While speaking those words he pulled in the rope, and my daughter returned to the surface, reassuring me with a great laugh.*

Beneath these affectionate episodes a darker drama was unfolding. Understandably, Louise did not publicize the disputes that had marred her relationship with Henriette ever since her daughter's adolescence.

But by the late 1850s, the growing tension between the two was often hinted at in her letters. "At this very moment there is peace in the house," she wrote to one of her friends, "for [Henriette] seems to have disarmed herself, and so here we are in a period of calm until the next storm."

In 1859, on the eve of Louise's departure for Italy, the conflict between mother and daughter was heightened by the intervention of Henriette's aunt Sidonie, a devout Catholic whose narrowness recalls Louise's own kin. Sidonie Colet, the childless widow of Hippolyte Colet's brother, a navy officer, had always taken a keen interest in her niece. As Louise was about to leave for her first long trip to Italy, Sidonie Colet began to write to Victor Cousin, complaining that Henriette was suffering dreadfully from her mother's short temper and asserting her right to oversee the young woman's education. Cousin had continued to correspond with and visit Henriette regularly. And since he still doled out a modest yearly stipend for Henriette's education, his opinions had weight. Sidonie Colet's letters to Cousin described the fractious relations between Louise and Hippolyte's family:

I love Henriette like a sister, but I'm not allowed to show my affection. Her mother resents me and accuses me of having stolen her daughter's heart from her. What course of action should I take? She can't go on living the life imposed on her; yet I know too much about her mother's hostile feelings toward my family and me not to realize that any intervention on my part would only irritate her further, without sensibly improving Henriette's plight. Henriette admirably fulfills the difficult fate which God dealt out to her, trying to avoid confrontations with her mother and bearing her sad life with fortitude. . . .

Another letter showed Sidonie Colet's devious attempts to estrange Henriette from her mother:

What a life for poor [Henriette], to find happiness and calm only when she's far away from her mother, who is doubtless killing her. I pity them both. . . . [Madame Colet] has incurable delusions concerning herself, as she has concerning everything on earth.

During Louise's stay in Italy, Sidonie tried to profit from her new bond with Henriette by asking Cousin to intercede on her behalf with various ministries to improve her pension. Yet despite Cousin's pleas that she allow Henriette to live with her in Nîmes as a paying guest until "a good marriage" was arranged for her, Sidonie refused to put Henriette up for more than a season in the apartment she shared with her father and sister. She complained that Henriette's continued presence would create overly crowded housing conditions, which would pose "a threat to our health"; neither could she lodge Henriette alone in a neighboring apartment, as it would be considered "of the utmost indecency" unless they hired a maid to live with her, a luxury they could not possibly afford.

So: What to do with poor Henriette, who seemed to have no inclination to spend more than a few months a year with her nomadic mother? Sidonie Colet judged that the only solution was to have the young woman board in a convent, where she would be "sheltered from the adventures which her unfortunate mother will inevitably fall into" and "admirably protected from all criticism . . . until her marriage." (The ardor of Sidonie's piety is such that whenever Cousin offered to send her one of his books of philosophy, she had first to get permission from her confessor.)

In 1862, Sidonie Colet moved to Paris with her father and sister and placed Henriette in a convent school run by Benedictine nuns in Verneuil, Normandy. The assistant prioress was a sister of Sidonie's. By that time Louise had been back in Paris for a year. She was working on her fourth volume of *L'Italie des Italiens* and planning a second long trip to Italy. The militantly anticlerical Louise was vehemently opposed to convent life for her child. And the situation between mother and daughter, who saw each other at home during infrequent holidays, seems to have further deteriorated.

Victor Cousin, who continued his solicitous care of Henriette after she entered the convent, received several alarming letters from the confessor of that institution. One of these was written as Louise was planning her second trip to Italy, on which she wished Henriette to accompany her.

> There has been a truce between mother and daughter. Her mother's departure [to Italy] seems to be once more postponed. . . . Henriette can return to Paris to live with her mother; but in the case of a too violent confrontation between them, if the situation becomes unbearable, I've arranged shelter for Mademoiselle H. in a family with which I have close links. She will be assured of a refuge, and that is important. . . .

The correspondence suggests that Henriette was so enjoying the tutelage of her aunt Sidonie, of whom she had grown too fond for her mother's comfort, that she refused to accompany Louise on another of her excursions. For from her late teens on, Henriette's letters reveal that despite her intelligence and wit, she was growing into a highly conformist young woman; she refused to see her mother as any kind of role model, instead hanging on to the affection of the few other kin she had. Writing in those years to her cousin Honoré Clair, Henriette explained that she was enjoying "the severe but tranquil life" she shared with Sidonie's family and revealed why she refused to join her mother in Naples: She did not feel up to sharing "the fatigues of Mother's nomadic life." She also complained to Monsieur Clair that Louise was living abroad far too much for her comfort: "Mother promises her return to France for May; I hope that this delay is the last one."

After a few years of convent life in Normandy, Henriette turned twenty-three, an age at which even the independent Louise had dreaded becoming an old maid. Her aunt and her mother started to search independently for potential suitors. Louise's candidate was a young writer noted for his liberal, anticlerical opinions, who frequented her salon. He had often spoken of his admiration for Henriette's beauty and sassy wit, and addressed her teasingly as "Satan": "Bonjour, Satan, rebellious angel, I place my hand in your fiery claws." But the young man revealed that he was tubercular and wrote Louise stating the impossibility of such a union. "My health is profoundly and fatally stricken. . . . Your Henriette is an exquisite *chef d'oeuvre* and merits a far better life than the one you destine her for."

Ultimately, the influence of the Colet family and convent life seems to have turned "the little blond devil," as Vigny had also called her, into a model of middle-class decorum and Catholic piety. Henriette's fate was settled by the appearance of a very proper suitor, twelve years her senior, who had been found by Sidonie Colet. She married Doctor Émile Bissieu, scion of a fairly prosperous, devoutly Catholic family from Verneuil—the site of her convent—whom she had met during a Sunday outing. It was "not a brilliant marriage, but a solid one," Henriette explained to Honoré Clair. Louise, who had already left for Italy, did not attend the wedding.

During these years of maternal concerns, as she worked on her four volumes on Italy, which she finally completed in 1864, Louise consoled herself for a few seasons by resurrecting her literary salon. Many of the old familiars returned to her little flat on the Rue Vaneau: Leconte de Lisle and Antony and Émile Deschamps. They put her in touch with the members of the new "Parnassian" school, whose thrust was to purge poetry of "the lyrification of one's own emotions, the public disclosure of the mysteries of love, the poetic use of private passions." The movement had been pioneered by Leconte de Lisle in the 1850s but flowered only in the 1860s. For the next few years the ever hospitable Muse served as prominent hostess to the movement whenever she was home from Italy.

Louise contributed her poetry to a short-lived publication, *La Revue fantaisiste,* which was founded by the poets Catulle Mendès and Théodore de Banville to serve as a mouthpiece for the Parnassians. She appeared in its pages alongside Baudelaire, Barbey d'Aurevilly, and other celebrated younger talents. Her enthusiasms unabated by advancing age and failing health, she expressed her fervor for the Parnassian movement in the last pages of *L'Italie des Italiens:* "One senses the imminence of some kind of renaissance. . . . I want to live long enough to see it flower. I shall wholeheartedly follow those who are preparing it; my faith will never leave them."

The first Parnassian journal, *La Revue fantaisiste,* was followed by *Parnasse,* a distinguished periodical that would last for a decade. Colet's verse was represented in several of that magazine's early issues alongside the work of Gautier, Sainte-Beuve, and Champfleury. Louise's participation was crucial to the last phases of her work because the Parnassian school's credos were so very contrary to the Romanticism that had long permeated her writings. Few contemporary poets had more lavishly indulged in the "lyrification" of personal emotion, banned by the Parnassians, than Louise Colet. But her enthusiasm for the Parnassians stirred, Louise began to rid her verse of its Romantic excesses. Ironically, she seems finally to have taken to heart Flaubert's exhortations to a more "objective" style. "God destined you to equal, if not surpass, your most powerful contemporaries," he had written her in the first months of 1854. "No one else was *born* with your talent, and yet with the best goodwill, you're capable of producing detestable works. . . . Reread your writings carefully, and you'll notice that there is a built-in enemy within you, a *je ne sais quoi* which, despite your excellent qualities and fine sentiments. . . . makes you seem to be the very contrary of what you should be."

Flaubert was often in Louise's thoughts during the last months of 1862. His novel *Salammbô,* a colorful narrative set in the first century in Carthage, was published to wider acclaim than *Bovary.* By this time he had received a Legion of Honor, had developed a taste for Parisian social life, hobnobbed with the imperial family, and visited London from time to time, where he was probably having a secret affair with his niece's former governess, Juliet Herbert. Louise had not been impressed when she read the serialized *Salammbô*, but she changed her mind when she read the entire book.

"It's very beautiful, very grand, of irreproachable style," she wrote to Edma Roger des Genettes, Bouilhet's former mistress. "The African horizons, the mercenaries' camps, Amilcar, Hannibal, are extraordinary pages. What a work! The vulgar will prefer *Bovary,* that coarse pastiche of Balzac; in my judgment its author is only a great writer and thinker in *Salammbô....* Those who prefer the filthy *Bovary* to this great and serious book are indeed pathetic."

After this praise, Louise confessed her revulsion for the author.

I tell you this as if I were dead, as if he were dead also. He would be incapable of inciting in me any movement of the heart, any stirring of the senses. I find him ugly, common, and as far as I'm concerned profoundly evil ... but I recognize the very great, the very true talent of his book. Since I know that you still see him, you can tell him all this, not for his sake, which concerns me little, but for mine, for I make a point of never committing an injustice.

Edma passed on Louise's praises to Flaubert and wrote her by return mail: "I do believe your praises were far more precious to him than the lyrical effusions of Mr. Gautier."

"If you passed on my praise to the author," Louise answered emphatically, "in all truthfulness you should also let him know the absolute disdain I have for his character and the incredible repulsion I feel for his premature decrepitude.... My heart is as void of emotion for him as Pompeii is of inhabitants."

Louise went on to make a curious comparison between Flaubert and her other bête noire, Emperor Napoleon III:

I'll offer an analogy: In politics, Napoleon III waged a war in Italy, a luminous and great action, which I praise and admire, and which casts an imposing radiance on an otherwise accursed life. Does this make him into a great and honest man, and would any loyal person wish to shake his hand?

To love everyone, to forgive willfully committed crimes, treasons, or base actions—these are aspects of Christian charity that I repudiate! I wish to die as a whole person, with all my hatred for evil and my passion for the beauty of goodness....

A decade after the end of the affair, Louise was still obsessed by Flaubert: Her passion had simply taken a negative turn.

In the fall of 1863, as she was finishing her fourth volume on Italy and looking forward to returning shortly to Rome, Louise moved out of her flat on the Rue Vaneau, which she could not afford to keep up anymore, and took a modest room at the Hôtel du Louvre. She parked most of her furniture in a friend's apartment and put up some of her more valuable possessions for auction. A note to her friend Edma des Genettes reveals her state:

> I have put up for lottery my two Chinese vases and my two large Baccarat vases. All my friends have taken out tickets to the raffle—there are only a hundred tickets, only four remain, and I've committed the indiscretion of sending them to you, thinking that you could use those objects in your home. The drawing will be held on Sunday night. . . .

Volume IV of *L'Italie des Italiens* appeared in April 1864. Louise received the money due her on publication and immediately left for Italy. She stopped off at Lake Geneva, trying to improve her health and her morale by reading Hugo's huge volume on Shakespeare.

"I left the city broken in spirit and in soul," she explained to Hugo in a letter from Geneva. "Having departed alone, at random, leaving my daughter with strangers, I arrived in Geneva quite ill and feared I would never leave it. Finally, a month of medical treatments and pure air have revived me."

Since Louise, over the next two years, would send frequent and affectionate letters to Henriette and her new husband from Italy, it is striking that she was absent from their wedding. Was the marriage proposal made after she had already left for Italy, and did her fragile health prevent her from returning to France? Or did she choose not to attend, upset by the prospect of seeing her daughter married in a traditional Roman Catholic ceremony?

Perhaps Louise was coming to accept that her daughter took far more from the Révoil and Colet lineage than from the freethinking maternal Le Blanc de Servanes ancestors. If so, she must have begun to feel that Henriette, too, was becoming something of a "stranger."

17.
Taking on the Vatican

❧

Louise spent the summer and fall months of 1864 in Venice and the surrounding countryside, suffering frequent depressions. She no longer had the energy to see all of a city's museums in a few days, pay courtesy calls on local luminaries, and spend consecutive evenings in high society. In December, she left for Rome, even though she had been warned that the anticlericalism of her volumes on Italy might cause her to be expelled from the Papal States. She paid no attention. "The notion of danger has never stood in my way, or stifled my voice, or chained my pen!" she exclaimed to a friend. She quietly crossed the Papal States' frontier at Civitavecchia by tipping a guard, and settled again at the Hotel Inghilterra.

In Rome, Louise had another of those encounters that fed her growing penchant for satire. She spent an evening with Franz Liszt, whom she had first met twenty-five years earlier at the Conservatory of Music in Paris and later portrayed, in *Lui,* as a "brainless virtuoso." By 1864 Liszt had ended the amorous adventures of his youth and embraced an ascetic life. He was grief-stricken over the loss of his son with Marie d'Agoult, who had died in his early twenties. His third child, Cosima, the wife of his favorite pupil, Hans von Bülow, was having an affair with Richard Wagner, of which Liszt greatly disapproved. When he and Louise met again in 1865, he was living in Rome, where he dedicated himself to playing concerts and writing religious music, and had taken the four minor orders of the Church. Accompanied always by his new alter ego, Father Hermann, Liszt had become an abbé, a lay brother. He lived in a convent, from which he occasionally emerged at night, attired in gold-braided vestments, to entertain high society with his virtuoso performances. Louise portrayed Abbé Liszt giving a recital at the Colosseum:

> In the penumbra artfully contrived about his person, the virtuoso with pale flowing blond hair shook his doddering head like a delirious tomcat taunting mice. As his body balanced from left to right and his hands ran convulsively over the strident keyboard, his eyes were made grotesque by the expression of ecstasy he strove to achieve.
>
> Then, as he stood under the luminous arches of the Colosseum, hair flowing in the wind, looking as fanatic as the archangel Michael exorcising demons, the ecstatic pianist, his waist arched, leaning on the fat Father Hermann, seemed to be saying, "Here I am, anointed a great man!"

Louise thinks back to Liszt's past as a freethinker, his friendships with most of the idols of her own youth—George Sand, the radical priest Abbé de Lamennais, the socialist thinker Louis Blanc. She doubts the sincerity of this once militant progressive who now hobnobs with the Vatican hierarchy and goes into society with decorations plastered on his chamberlain's uniform, resembling a "sommelier" at a fancy Paris restaurant. And she disdains this extravagantly gifted man who has used his aristocratic connections to boost his ego and further his career as a performer.

Shortly after she saw him perform at Rome's Colosseum, Louise was invited to dine with Liszt at the home of a German baroness who was determined that they reconcile. (The baroness had winced at Louise's portrait of Liszt in *Lui*.) Liszt, his haggard face now framed by long, unkempt graying hair, offered Louise his arm to escort her to the dining table, where they were seated next to each other. Although he had most probably read her unflattering portrait of him in *Lui*, and her anticlerical volumes on Italy, he treated her with great gallantry as he downed quantities of Marsala wine. He remembered her well, he told her; Abbé de Lamennais had often spoken to him of her; how were all his old Paris friends faring—George Sand, Victor Hugo? Louise assured Liszt that his old friends "have not reneged on their lifelong political convictions and have remained valiant fighters for liberty of thought." The pious Abbé Liszt seemed not to notice the disparagement. "I hear they fight a great deal among themselves," he mumbled. After warmly shaking her hand, he offered her any aid she might need during her stay. "Count on me as a friend!" he said as he left. "How can I help you in Rome?"

"I only desire Rome's enmity," Louise retorted sharply. "You know perfectly well that we belong to different camps, and you also know that I've recently portrayed you in such a way that you can't forgive me."

"No matter! I'm now a Christian!" Liszt replied, deadpan, before returning to his convent.

"O buffoonery! O decadence of the *derniers abbés!*" she wrote about their dinner together, having found a title for her last book. "They are now recruited among performers!"

Louise started researching *Les Derniers Abbés,* "The Last Clerics," during the spring and summer of 1865, which she spent in a rented cottage in the Campagna, observing the local population's relationship to its clergy. For the first time ever, Victor Hugo tried to discourage her from a work in progress. France seemed "less and less like a republic," he warned her, and the conservative factions that were controlling French culture were far too powerful for such a book to have an audience. "Don't expect your publisher to ever support such a courageous book," he wrote Louise from Guernsey. "Right now there's panic among Paris editors. You must reserve your militancy for a braver time. Louis Bonaparte controls and organizes our literature as if it were an army. Liberal scribblers are using all their powers of flattery just to survive. It is currently in bad taste to miss out on the Bible. Such is the power of the Bonapartist and Catholic cliques."

Louise forged ahead anyhow, and wrote a text that may be one of the most ferocious anti-Church polemics published in the nineteenth century. "The vicious influence of monks and priests is the most degrading force in the life of the Italian peasantry," she noted in her early pages. "Obscenity and falsehood, cynicism of daily mores, disgusting filth, have undermined the strength, audacity, and natural beauty of the Italian rural character." Describing the implacable and sinister influence of the papacy, Louise compared it to "a putrefying limb which threatens to decompose the entire body social."

Priests inculcate a "debased polytheism" in the Italian peasantry, which is far more pernicious than atheism, Louise continued, revealing her own streak of Deism in a startling phrase: "Priests obstruct and hide the image of the one true God."

Louise's strongest accusations concern the Italian clergy's sexual mores. Priests are the first to violate vows of chastity. Deprived of family ties, members of the clergy infiltrate others' families through "debauch and intrigue." The Italian peasantry, who live in close daily communion with the clergy, sharing with them their cafés and their local boccie and card games, also "share their wives, their daughters, and their sisters."

Sexual licentiousness, Louise claims, is only one of many cardinal sins through which the clergy debases the Italian population, who are afraid to reveal the priests' debauchery and crimes. "In each theft, in each murder or rape committed by brigands, a priest was involved," Louise asserts outlandishly.

The clergy's political influence is also deplorable. They have "indoctrinated" the Italian people against nationalism by representing their foreign oppressors—the Bourbon and Hapsburg monarchs—as more favorable to their interests than a national, democratic government. The Church has predisposed its flock to "a love of lucre rather than a love of fatherland" and has preached "worldly immorality rather than divine morality."

One can not read *Les Derniers Abbés* without wondering how it would have played back home with her daughter, Henriette, or with her son-in-law, a pious Normandy doctor. One can not read the following poem—a Juvenalian satire on Rome, which is included in *Les Derniers Abbés*—without thinking how it might have increased the alienation between mother and daughter.

This poem, whose terse, caustic style was clearly influenced by the Parnassian school, is spoken in the voice of the ancient spirit of the Tiber River. A few stanzas:

Depuis qu'ils ont régnés, les pontifes romains
Ont si bien pollué leurs mère de leurs mains,
Courbant, pillant, vendant cette Rome immortelle
Qu'ils ont rendu honteux ce qui serait d'elle.

N'est ce pas un spectacle à navrer la raison
Qu'un peuple qui pour code unique à l'oraison,
Et pour roi éternels les exploiteurs d'un culte
Tartuffes endurcis par la débauche occulte.

. . . .

Basilique de Saint Pierre—Bazaar a la splendeur vulgaire—
Saint Paul, se pavanant comme un débarcadère.
Le Gesù! Chargé d'or, revoltant le regard
Comme une courtisane au luxe du hasard.

L'Hospice Saint Michel! une immense masure
Renfermant les bâtards qu'engendre leur luxure!!
Rome! Mieux vaut pour toi l'inanité des morts.
Je suis humilié de te voir sur mes bords.

Cadavre fastueux, dissous-toi dans ta bière
Et que mon dernier flot soit bu par ta poussière.

Une voix répondit au vieux Tibre irrité:
*"Silence, écoutes! écoutes! Voici la liberté!"**

Before being published in Louise's book, this poem appeared in several Italian newspapers and served to expand the dossier on Louise Colet that papal authorities had been assembling since the publication of *L'Italie des Italiens.* Louise's militancy was increasing with age, and this passage of *Les Derniers Abbés* might well serve as the leitmotiv of her last

*Ever since they have reigned, Roman pontiffs
Have so polluted their mother city,
Pillaging, humiliating, prostituting immortal Rome,
That they have shamed all of her progeny.

Doesn't this spectacle offend all reason:
A people whose only ethic is to pray,
Whose rulers—Cynics hardened by arcane debauch—
Do nothing but exploit a cult.

. . . .

Saint Peter's basilica—bazaar of vulgar splendor—
Church of Saint Paul, flaunting its wares like a marketplace.
The Gesù! Laden with gold, as revolting to gaze on
As a strolling whore.

Hospice of Saint Michael! An immense barrack
Housing the bastards engendered by clerics' vice!!
Rome! You'd be better served by the stillness of death.
I'm humiliated to see you on my shores.

Lavish cadaver, be dissolved in your bier
And let my last wave be absorbed by your dust.

A voice answered the angry old Tiber:
"Silence! Listen! Here, finally, is freedom!"

years: "Wherever I see an injury, a lie, a hypocrisy, I attack it. . . . When I discern some hidden cowardice, injustice, indecency, I unmask it, I publicize it, I loyally shout 'Look!' "

Louise began shouting "Look!" shortly after arriving at the island of Ischia, just south of Naples, where she settled for the autumn months. She lived in a tiny wing of the Palace of Villareale, a summer retreat built a century earlier for King Ferdinand and Queen Caroline of Naples, the Bourbon monarchs whose decadence and brutality had provoked the first stirrings of the Risorgimento in the early nineteenth century. The palace was now a property of the state, a museum of sorts; an acquaintance of Louise's, the director of antiquities of the Naples region, had arranged for her to stay there.

At Villareale there was a superb vista from Louise's window—"an animated nature, which exhales pantheism"—and a particularly magnificent view of Vesuvius. "I enjoyed there an abundance of fruits and flowers of delectable scent, a clement and healthy climate vivified by sea breeze. Oh, those warm and gentle hours! I savored them with love! Short of happiness, they offered me inexhaustible serenity."

At first the islanders looked favorably upon the plump, grandmotherly Louise. Rumors had it that she was the widow of the prince of Syracuse, traveling incognito, and the locals called her *Su Altezza,* "Your Highness." Louise's troubles began when one of the villa's caretakers brought her a message from the local priest, offering her a pew in a place of honor at his church. Louise politely replied with a no thank you, saying that she never went to Mass. "Gesù Maria! She never goes to church!" she heard the servants whispering from then on.

Nor was Louise's reputation helped by her strange hours: She worked every night until at least two A.M.; in fact, hers was the only light seen from the sea beyond those of Ischia's lighthouse and its prison. The villagers began to think that there was something eerie about this woman who, while the rest of the island slept, paced continually on her terrace, contemplating the fiery volcano glowing over the Bay of Naples. What spells was this "solitary one" casting? The Naples region is rife with some of the most archaic superstitions to this day; and most of the traits that primitive societies have traditionally assigned to witches—advancing age, unclear social origins, a predilection for night hours—increasingly branded this heathen foreigner.

Louise had a few loyal friends on the island: the subprefect of the region, who was often away on business on the mainland; the commander of the local garrison; and the tax collector of Ischia. Within a month of her arrival, the three men, all of whom were ardent republicans, began to warn her that there was malicious gossip going around the local cafés about *"la signora della casa reale."* The local clergy in particular, whose sympathies were militantly pro-Bourbon, criticized her to the local population as "a friend of the new regime" because she was often visited by government officials. By coincidence, Louise's friends warned her, Ischia's seminary had been closed by government decree the month after her arrival, and Ischians were wondering whether Louise might have instigated that.

"She is charged with a mission against us," the prefect quoted the villagers as saying, "she is *veramente molto potente* [truly very powerful], so she must be feared and watched." "She is surely a friend of Garibaldi's and a heathen," the local priest was overheard to say, "for she never sets foot the church." Other locals had spread the rumor that she was a sorceress, that she evoked the ghosts of Ischia's ancient kings in order to insult them.

The threat of cholera was widespread in 1865 throughout Western Europe. In the spring it had decimated the cities of Marseilles, Toulon, and Arles. The epidemic had been so vicious during the previous summer that Louise, wishing to return to France to tend to her daughter upon the birth of her first grandchild, was forbidden the trip by Henriette, who considered it far too dangerous for her mother's health.

When the cholera epidemic reached Naples in November, some three months after Louise had moved to Ischia, she suddenly felt totally isolated from the world. Her few companions—the subprefect, the tax collector, the garrison commander—were attending to crises on the mainland or on neighboring islands. Ischia's priests began to proclaim from the pulpit that the cholera epidemic was a punishment from God incited by the presence of a heathen. Louise was not the *buona signora* among the villagers anymore.

Louise stayed in touch with the world solely by corresponding with family and friends. She wrote that she was beginning to feel like a prisoner, and the late-autumn rains increased her sense of isolation. Her only distraction was the daily afternoon arrival of the steamer from Naples, which occasionally brought her a mainland newspaper.

When the steamer arrived on November 10—a bleak, stormy day—a huge crowd of villagers, aroused by their dread of the epidemic, demonstrated on the beach against a government official who had brought anti-cholera medications from Naples. The crowd chased him back into the steamer, shouting that he had brought poison. Emperor Victor Emmanuel was expected to visit the island that weekend, and in the mounting hysteria of the crowds, a peasant woman standing next to Louise cried out that the liberal monarch was coming "to poison us." *"Siete pazza!"* "You're mad!" Louise laughed in the woman's face, accusing her of ingratitude to the ruler who helped liberate Italy.

The woman responded with a curse. After the steamer had headed back to Naples and the crowd had dispersed, Louise walked back to Villareale through the main piazza of Ischia. She sensed that the villagers stared at her with heightened malice and distrust. Moreover, at the corner of the next piazza she heard a pious doctor haranguing a large crowd, telling them, as were Ischia's priests, that the cholera epidemic was "a punishment from God" sent to the islanders for harboring "foreign heathen."

From the beginning of her stay in Ischia, Louise had the habit of giving a little money to some of the village women who came to draw water at the well that stood halfway up the avenue of her villa. "When I saw them pass by me," she wrote in *Les Derniers Abbés,* "their backs bent, their foreheads running with sweat under the large copper vessels they carried on their heads while their husbands smoked or slept by the seashore, I gave alms to the poorest of them. . . . I gave them little, having little to give." This custom, Louise realized that evening as she went to her books, might have helped to instigate the villagers' now ferocious hostility toward her. They suspected her of spreading the cholera epidemic by poisoning their well!

The following day, as rains and high winds still raged, the tax collector, just returned from the mainland, came to Villareale on an urgent mission: He had been delegated by the mayor of Ischia and the head of the local national guard unit, which had strongly pro-Bourbon sympathies, to warn Louise that she must leave the island immediately to escape the fury of the population.

Accusing Ischia's mayor of capitulating to the "medieval ignorance" of the crowd, Louise adamantly refused to leave. "I barricade myself here and wait for death," she said, laughing. "France and Italy will demand an account of my bloody end."

The mayor himself arrived in the late afternoon. He found Louise writing telegrams to the French counsul, to the prefect of Naples, and to other powerful friends on the peninsula. He pleaded with her not to send the messages. She threatened to send them, and to add the sentence:

"Mayor is a coward; immediately send carabinieri to the island." The mayor left in a panic. It was a Saturday afternoon, and the situation was increasingly perilous: Ischia's telegraph connections had been severed by the storm, the telegraph office at the neighboring island of Procida was already closed; and although the tax collector—now Louise's only friend on Ischia—had promised to take her messages to Procida the next morning, the villagers had reportedly assembled in large groups all over town, their anger against the "foreign heathen" growing apace.

In a somber mood, Louise stared at the tempest howling outside her window, breaking trees on her terrace. She sat in front of her daughter's portrait, longing to see her first grandchild, three-month-old Raymond Bissieu; she feared that Henriette's frail health, weakened by recent childbirth, "could not stand to be further harmed by the death of her mother." She had recently dedicated a militantly feminist poem to her daughter:

Oh, divine grandeur des femmes
En elles s'incarnent les âmes
Qui palpitent dans l'infini.
Dante, Goethe, Homère, Shakespeare,
Ces dieux, à l'immortel empire,
C'est de nos flancs qu'ils sont sortis
Et c'est l'essence maternelle
Qui dans l'humanité ruisselle
Des plus grand jusqu'aux plus petits.

Et la création, au grand souffle éternel,
Nous berce avec amour sur son sein maternel.*

In her villa, listening to the storm snapping branches outside her windows, fearful but resigned to the violence about to be unleashed against her, Louise compared herself grandly to Hypatia, the Neoplatonist phi-

---

*"Oh, divine grandeur of women,
In whom are incarnated the souls
That throb throughout infinity.
The most immortal bards—
Dante, Goethe, Homer, Shakespeare—
Emerged from our wombs.
For it is the maternal essence
That imbues humanity
From the highest to the humblest.

And the eternal breath of creation
Holds us lovingly on her motherly breast.

losopher and teacher of fourth-century Alexandria, who was the first woman to make notable contributions to mathematics and astronomy. It was a time when Christians identified learning and science with paganism (as did the population of contemporary Ischia). At the age of forty-five, Hypatia, who was a pagan, was murdered by fanatical Christian monks, her mutilated limbs dragged through the streets of Alexandria. . . . What irony, Louise mused, if she were to die a similar death at the hands of this rabble, considering how much energy she'd given to the liberation of Italy! Were there no more bold crusaders who dared to denounce the obscurantism of the papacy, men such as Giordano Bruno, Luther, Rabelais, Voltaire?

Louise had a fitful night. Despite the storm, the following morning, Sunday, the tax collector arrived at dawn, as he had promised, to take Louise's telegrams to the neighboring island. He was demanding, in his own messages, that authorities on the mainland immediately send the carabinieri to protect Colet. Meanwhile he advised her to lock her doors.

"I dressed, getting myself up like a true Parisian who would wish to die well coiffed, carefully groomed so as not to displease death too much," Louise wrote in *Les Derniers Abbés,* describing this day. As she put the last pin into her hair, she heard shouting at the bottom of her carriage drive. A crowd of Ischia's citizens, fresh from church, where the priest had whipped them to a new furor against "foreign heathen," had come to demonstrate at her gate.

The shouts became howls; Louise's faithful young servant told her that a priest was haranguing the crowd in front of her gate. *"Si la signora non parte, l'amazzaremo questa sera* ["If the signora does not leave, we'll kill her tonight"], he reported some locals as saying. Louise continued to read her newspaper, write her letters. In the early afternoon, she heard a rush of footsteps up the marble stairs. It was the mayor, his face deadly pale. The crowd was calling Louise a "poisoner," claiming she had been sent by Victor Emmanuel to poison the cistern of the island. For the time being she was being protected by a single assistant of the loyal subprefect, who stood at her gate with revolver in hand, preventing the villagers from breaking into the villa.

While Louise calmly offered him dinner, the mayor expressed his fears of an international incident, for the mob was attempting to force Louise's gate open. . . . But later in the afternoon, Louise's servant rushed in to announce that a detachment of carabinieri had just arrived on the island. Upon the appearance of the feared guardsmen, the crowds dispersed, the priests disappeared. Sixty demonstrators were arrested later that evening.

The brand-new technology of the telegraph machine and the loyalty of the young government functionary who guarded Louise's gate with a revolver had saved the day.

The following morning the subprefect returned from the cholera-stricken mainland and visited Louise at Villareale. They spoke of progressive contemporary literature—Renan's life of Christ, John Stuart Mill's essays, "all books that must be read to cure people of the ignorance and superstition in which the clergy maintains them." "If Rome has ceased to legally *burn* philosophers, it is due to the justice of laymen," Louise preached to her visitor.

Louise went on to read her friend passages from the "Declaration of faith" that she had published in the final volume of *L'Italie des Italiens:*

"The Church has obscured each light with a shroud. The guillotine, death by fire at the stake, the varied tortures of the inquisition—all were deemed proper to abolish science. . . . So man's soul, to this day, is stifled by the Catholic Church, an inhuman structure whose architectures suppress all air and light."

"Well, I understand why Rome is persecuting you," the prefect said. "The clergy certainly instigated the rebellion against you—hardly had the soldiers arrived than they vanished, and at this very hour they're hiding in the mountains."

The following day, the wives and sisters of the imprisoned villagers came to see Louise at the villa, asking her if they might resume drawing water from her well (the well they had accused her of having poisoned!). Louise maintained an aloof manner toward them, "because they had flouted legitimate authority," but gave them access to the water.

Louise's confrontation with Ischia's clergy and its superstitious population was immediately chronicled in the French press:

We have heard that Madame Colet has liberal ideas, which she expresses freely, and the clergy of Ischia announced that she was drawing the wrath of God. There was only one more step to accusations that she was responsible for spreading cholera throughout the island, and it was swiftly taken.

On Sunday, November 12, the wrathful and menacing population assembled around her lodgings. The French consulate received news of the menacing events by telegraph. . . . It acted decisively. The prefect of Naples commanded that fifty policemen be sent to the island, and order was finally restored.

A letter from the prefect of Naples to the French consul made even more blunt reference to the clerical powers that incited the anti-Colet riots: "The true culprits must be apprehended, whatever the nature of their *vestments*" (the emphasis is the prefect's).

Louise had been determined to remain in Ischia throughout the winter, but in December the first case of cholera was reported on the island and she packed her bags. She spent a year on the island of Capri, where she finished working on *Les Derniers Abbés* and wrote preliminary drafts of two satirical novels on Italian life, which she intended to title *Cybele* and *The Courtesans of Capri*. At the end of 1866 she returned to Rome. Her stay there was a far cry from the spirited conversations and energetic touring she had chronicled five years earlier. Again falling ill with severe bronchitis, she spent several months in bed in her hotel room. Once she was well, she was able to visit only a few of her favorite antique sites.

Louise's one source of cheer during her last stay in the Eternal City was that her detested antagonists—Pope Pius IX, the Vatican government, the Church hierarchy—were finally facing defeat and were being forced to confront modern times. "An enormous upheaval is presaging the overthrow of that theocratic power which has oppressed Italy for so many centuries," Louise wrote in her last chapter of *Les Derniers Abbés*. Indeed, the French garrisons that had protected the papacy for over a decade, and had been the principal supporters of its temporal power, would leave Rome in the fall of 1867; a few seasons later, Victor Emmanuel's troops conquered Rome; and in 1871, after an overwhelming plebiscite concerning the site of Italy's capital, Rome would become the governmental seat of a unified Italy.

In the spring of 1867, Louise decided to return to Paris. It was clear that her dislike of the ecclesiastical authorities was returned in kind. As her train reached the frontier of the Papal States, a captain of the Vatican police, with twelve men, burst into her train compartment with a warning: "We know who you are!" he shouted. "Never set foot in our territories again!"

When she arrived in Paris and unpacked her bags, Louise found that she was missing all the manuscripts she had worked on in the previous year, except for *Les Derniers Abbés*. She decided that there could be only one culprit—the papal police. A tall, cadaverous man had appeared at her hotel every day under the pretext of recording the number of guests registered there. . . . She had been warned that he might be one of the

Pope's plainclothesmen. . . . The Hotel Inghilterra had such a distinguished foreign clientele that there were no locks on any of the doors or desks. . . . The missing manuscripts—the drafts of her satirical novels on Italian mores—had been kept in a desk drawer in her hotel room. They were there the night before her departure. How easy it would have been for the Pope's spy to open the drawer during her last morning in Rome, as she was paying a farewell visit to the Forum.

Louise was desperate. With her health and energies so diminished, it was especially painful to lose two years' work. She sent letters to the French press bemoaning the loss of her manuscripts, "my very soul's children." Moved by her plight, her publisher, Dentu, offered a one thousand franc reward for the return of the documents. "Priests denounce me and menace you," Hugo wrote Louise from Guernsey. "A century or so ago, we would have been burned side by side on the same stake."

Louise settled in the humblest lodgings she had lived in since her earliest days as a young bride. She took her family silver out of consignment and retrieved the few pieces of furniture she had left with friends. Her new home, on the Rue Vavin, close to the Luxembourg Gardens, was not the elegant little flat on the Rue de Sèvres where her literary salon had flourished, not even the cheerful bohemian meeting place of Parnassians that she had enjoyed on the Rue Vaneau. It consisted of two very modest rooms, in which she bathed in a white metal tub behind a curtain drawn across a corner of her bedroom.

Henriette Colet Bissieu and her growing family now had a pied-à-terre in Paris on the Rue des Écoles, a few blocks from her mother. Her marriage appeared to be a happy one—her husband adored her and compared her blond beauty to that of "a Correggio madonna." During her mother's stay in Italy and in the two or three following years, Henriette's letters to her Provençal relative Honoré Clair concentrated solely on the joys of motherhood and her unswerving piety. She chronicled the sewing of layettes, her babies' teething pains, her husband's absorption with a growing clientele, her fear of "the bed of misery" that her next childbearing would bring. She urged Clair, the godfather of her second child, a daughter, to come as swiftly as possible to the baby's baptism, since "the Church gives us only three months' dispensation." She continued to express her disapproval of her mother's nomadic life: "My mother is still in the Naples region—she still writes us, but not enough to my taste. How different our lives are!" "Mother writes that she will leave Italy soon; I hope that this time she won't once more delay her return!" "Since my mother keeps postponing her return from month to month, I can't even expect her anymore . . . wouldn't you think she'd be eager to see her children and grandchildren?"

Nevertheless Louise's reunion with Henriette was not without affection: her second grandchild, born in the spring of 1867, had been named Louise; and this very infant's future offspring will be a heroine of the following narrative.

P.S. ON LOUISE'S TRACES: THE LOST SUIT-CASE, AND A FEW OTHER CONFUSIONS

At the turn of the century, there lived a distinguished French biblio-phile named Paul Mariéton. A member of Provence's cultural elite, he was an enthusiast of French Romantic literature and was a particular fan of Louise Colet, whom he considered to be "a central figure" of the Romantic movement. He owned copies of all her works and collected every shred of information about her life. His goal was to establish a "Fonds Colet," or "Colet Archives," at the Musée Calvet in Avignon, one of Provence's most distinguished museums.

In 1906, Monsieur Mariéton went to visit Louise's daughter, Hen-riette, then 66 years old. He described her as "an ingratiating lady, touchingly attached to her mother's memory." It was a high point of Mariéton's career. "I've finally put my hands on Louise Colet's per-sonal papers. What a nest of treasures!" he wrote to a friend after his first meeting with Henriette. "What great studies in Romantic psychol-ogy I'm finding there!" "I've dug up an intimate diary of Louise Co-let's, opened many envelopes left sealed for half a century," he wrote a few weeks later. "My work on the Romantics will be extraordinary. . . . This will be a book of global interest!"

Dealing with her mother's papers, Henriette Bissieu-Colet (as she began to call herself in her middle years) had tried to sanitize Louise's image. In the 1890s, she had sold the more conservative portion of the Flaubert-Colet correspondence, "those [missives] that pertained strictly to literary history and aggrandized my mother's image," to the distinguished editors Conard and Charpentier, who had published the first collection of Flaubert's letters. Such was Monsieur Mariéton's enthusiasm that he charmed Henriette into selling him the passionate, controversial remainder of Flaubert's letters to Louise. Henriette also sold him her mother's Mementos, an unfinished autobiography, and much of Louise Colet's correspondence with the greatest figures of the century, from Garibaldi, John Stuart Mill, Victor Hugo, Alfred de Vigny, Victor Cousin, Manzoni, Mazzini, and Alfred de Musset to Delacroix, Gérôme, Meyerbeer, and George Sand.

Elated by his acquisition, Mariéton returned to Provence and made notes for a three-volume biography of Louise Colet. "I was increasingly taken with the desire to rehabilitate the beautiful woman who was the Muse of Victor Cousin and of Flaubert," he wrote in the outline of his work in progress, "[this woman] whose beauty, talent, character, courage, and greatness of heart were celebrated by the most illustrious men of that century. . . . For she was shamelessly executed in Maxime Du Camp's venomous, odiously prejudiced Mémoires littéraires . . . and since then, a harmful and unjust reputation as a bluestocking and an amorous virago continues to defame her memory." Mariéton went on to praise "the proud independence of Colet's life," "a vigor and firmness of literary style unusual, almost unique among women," and the "virility of her poetic talent," which he judged to be "incontestably superior . . . to that of George Sand and Delphine Gay."

Sadly, in 1911, before he had finished the first draft of his book, Paul Mariéton died of injuries suffered in an automobile accident. It was shortly after he had been awarded the Legion of Honor for his contributions to French literature. He had bequeathed to the Musée Calvet all his manuscripts, including a Fonds Colet, which was meant eventually to comprise his entire collection of Coletana. Mariéton also left a good part of his Colet documents to the executor of his will, a close friend named Marc Varenne, with the proviso that before turning the "Coletana" over to the Musée Calvet, Varenne would finish the biography of Louise.

Alas, Varenne, who seems to have been somewhat of a literary dilettante, apparently never did a stroke of work on the book, and after World War II he moved to Belgium and was not heard from again for many years.

Flash forward a few decades to the 1960s: In those years there lived in Paris yet another Colet fan, Henri Chavet, a bank employee with a summer house in Avignon. Having discovered the Fonds Colet at Avignon's Musée Calvet, he was chagrined to find that most of the papers were still in the possession of Mariéton's legatee. Chavet made many inquiries concerning Varenne's whereabouts, but his quest came to naught.

Then one day in the mid-1960s, Chavet met a woman named Suzanne Savalle, who worked in the very same Paris bank. Madame Savalle, then in her fifties, was a great-granddaughter of Louise Colet, the daughter of Henriette's second child, Louise Bissieu. In the course of their acquaintanceship, Chavet learned that his colleague knew all about the derelict Marc Varenne; the following day she brought him Varenne's address in Belgium.

Chavet immediately communicated this information to the director of the Musée Calvet, Georges de Loÿe. After many unsuccessful efforts to reach Varenne by mail, de Loÿe simply took a train to Brussels, where Varenne finally delivered to him a valise full of Louise's manuscripts.

"I just barely made it; Varenne was approaching ninety," Monsieur de Loÿe, the retired director of the Calvet Museum, told me as I visited with him recently at his home in Provence. "But only about half of the Colet documents collected by Mariéton were in that valise.... Varenne had obviously been an idler; he gave me all kinds of folderol about how Nazis occupied his house during the war and absconded with many of the Colet manuscripts, including many of her Mementos.... Who'll ever know what really happened to them?"

Was Monsieur Chavet still alive, I asked, did Monsieur de Loÿe know of anyone else who might possibly help me in my search for unpublished Colet documents? My host, who himself was approaching ninety, proudly shook his head. "Chavet died years ago. I'm the only one still alive who knows anything."

"In Paris, there's a family by the name of Bood who're related to Louise Colet," he murmured as he accompanied me to his door. "They might have a few documents lying around...."

The name Bood was familiar, for I had read a brief biography of Louise Colet by Micheline Bood (the author died from Hodgkin's disease before finishing the book, so it was completed by her editors). Micheline Bood was Louise's great-great-grandniece by marriage: Madame Bood's maternal grandmother was a sister of the wife of Raymond Bissieu, Henriette's first-born, that first grandchild over whose birth Louise had so exulted during her hazardous stay in Ischia.

Seated amid purring computers and fax machines in the offices of the late Madame Bood's husband, a very gracious man who directs a prosperous public relations concern on the Rue Saint-Honoré, I studied a large black box that contained all the documents that Louise's grandson, Raymond Bissieu, had given his grandniece Micheline Bood shortly before he died, at the age of ninety. What treasures I found in this box: that curious note of Louise's asking the head of Henriette's boarding school to have her child say her prayers twice a day; unpublished letters from Hippolyte, Bancel, Bouilhet, Du Camp, Cousin, and various other friends and lovers; Louise's note to Flaubert, perhaps never sent, in which she stated her painful realization that he wished "to break off all relations."

As I copied documents in Monsieur Bood's office, my host came to ask if I needed anything. I thanked him for his graciousness and told him I was fine.

Did I know that there was a very curious poem of Louise Colet's in the guestbook of a small Vietnamese restaurant on the Left Bank? Monsieur Bood asked before returning to his desk. It was an extremely erotic—if not downright pornographic—example of Louise's writing, he added delicately.

In a Vietnamese restaurant? I asked incredulously. Yes, yes, a charming place, Monsieur Bood said.

Baffled, I continued to copy—Cousin, Du Camp, Louise's own huge scrawl. A pornographic poem of Louise's in a Vietnamese restaurant. . . .

As I was finishing my copying Mr. Brood returned to my post and asked: "Louise Colet did live in the Palais-Royal, didn't she?"

"No," I said. "You're probably thinking of Colette."

"Oh, then that poem might not be by Colet, but by Colette," he said, looking a bit confused, "but do go to that restaurant anyway—I recommend it highly."

On the remote chance that I might find a new Colet document after all, I went to dine a few evenings later at the restaurant, in question, Le Lotus Blanc, 45 Rue de Bourgogne. I asked the restaurant's young patron if he could show me "a certain poem" in his guestbook. He nodded knowingly, brought me a large volume bound in red leather, and turned to a page on which a poem—indeed outlandishly pornographic—had been written out.

It was not signed "Colette" at all, let alone "Colet." It was signed "George Sand."

As I read this standard S-M trash—who was this joker pretending to be the progressive but rather puritanical George Sand?—my eyes wandered to the top left of the page, where the title of the poem was inscribed: "Invitation à Verlaine." Sand was born in 1804, Verlaine in 1844. Whoever had indulged in this literary prank had not done his research very well. Sand had many younger lovers, but not that much younger.

These bizarre episodes can be read in one of two ways, or in both: They relate to the chronic neglect of Louise Colet's documents over the past century—Flaubert's bonfire, Du Camp's distortions and defamations, Marc Varenne's slothful loss of her manuscripts, the elegant Monsieur Bood's confusions.

But these incidents might also serve as a fable for history's generally careless approach toward literary women. Could it be that the communal male psyche, particularly in France, still retains a trace of the nineteenth-century prejudices against women writers? That in the minds of many men, female scribblers remain barely distinguishable from one another—part of an anonymous, lascivious, somewhat threatening collectivity?

18.
Dueling with
Phantoms

❧❧❧

In early 1867, as Louise was preparing to return to Paris from Italy, Victor Cousin passed away in Cannes, where he had spent his last retirement years.

The obituaries reported that Cousin had designated Louise Colet and her daughter as his only heirs. Henriette took pains to deny this hearsay and with the help of her confessor wrote the following letter to the editors of all major French newspapers: "The entire press is stating that Monsieur Cousin bequeathed a sizable portion of his fortune to my mother and to me. I have no need to remind you how uncivil these rumors are. I would be very grateful if you could deny them with as much delicacy as possible."

Cousin's last will and testament was quite complicated. It stated that he wished to leave a significant sum of money to Louise, who was the first legatee mentioned in the document; but it did not stipulate the sum. Brazenly attempting to clarify the extent of Cousin's involvement with Louise Colet, a few of his nephews and nieces asked her to give them all the letters Cousin had sent her during their twenty-year correspondence.

Louise was not about to buy herself a handsome inheritance by sharing the details of her love life. She declined to give up any of the letters and refused to specify the amount of money she desired to receive, leaving it to the discretion of Cousin's relatives, who awarded her a puny few hundred francs. For once, Louise was unanimously praised for her "abnegation and admirable high-mindedness."

"Indignant, the poetess sent [Cousin's relatives] packing," stated one article concerning Louise Colet's handling of the philosopher's will. "She accepted only that which Cousin's family was willing to offer her with no strings attached. . . . in doing so Madame Colet evidenced a notable dignity and decorum."

Louise would still need to publish at least a book a year to make ends meet. This became more and more difficult, for her writings became increasingly caustic as her physical energies waned. Like *Les Derniers Abbés,* the books she published after returning from Italy—*Ces Petits Messieurs, Les Dévotes du grand monde, La Satire du siècle*—not only were vehemently anticlerical but also savagely condemned Napoleon III's lavish "Belle Époque." *Ces Petits Messieurs,* for instance, ranted against the Parisian tradition of "gigolos" living idly on the charity of lonely older women, often absconding with their money. "How to do away with such scum? That is the task of mothers," Louise wrote like some ascetic commissar, her belief in family growing stronger every year. "Only mothers can shape their sons' characters through doctrines of austerity, the sole guarantee of honest and healthy mores in the family and the state."

Louise had always had a strong bourgeois streak, but as she approached her sixties she became a militant born-again moralist. Her rage against the Church patriarchy was equaled by her disgust with the opulence and loose morals of the Second Empire. Like most social reformers, she now based her worldview on political dedication, Spartan austerity, and a chaste personal life (she had even come to believe in marital fidelity).

Her position was hardly in tune with the extravagance of the Second Empire years, during which Napoleon III offered the Countess de Castiglione a pearl necklace worth half a million francs and a monthly stipend of fifty thousand, while Parisian workmen earned four to five francs a day. At her lavish soirees, the famous *grande horizontale* Cora Pearl was carried to her dining room by four valets as she lay quite naked on a huge silver platter garnished with beds of violets. Compared to the Paris she had known under Louis Philippe, in which such extravagances were kept relatively tame or discreetly hidden, Louise saw Napoleon III's Paris as "a shameless steeplechase of a city, filled with *hetaira,* in which regal dress, diamonds, horse and carriages, palatial residences, have become the reward of the most dissolute strumpets. . . . This infection of material luxury is sullying the entire nation."

Louise's attacks against every aspect of the glittering Belle Époque, from the courtesan trade to the haute couture industry being pioneered by Worth, were so excessive that even the newspaper that had been most supportive of her work, the progressive *Le Siècle,* refused to publish her articles without extensive cuts. And even though the government had cut down her pension over the last decade because of her growing radicalism, Louise refused to bend to what she called "censorship." "I know perfectly well that my pension may be totally withdrawn," she said to the editor of *Le Siècle,* "but you know what? Lies disgust me! I must speak out loudly, very loudly, against whatever burdens my conscience."

The most vehement of Louise's texts, in the late 1860s, was a verse pamphlet entitled *Paris matière: La Satire du siècle.* Throughout its couplets, the materialism and moral pollution of the French capital are compared to the Roman Empire just before its downfall. Louise refused to cut *Paris matière* for publication in the mainstream press; it finally appeared in *Le Nain Jaune,* a combative progressive publication. The first segment is dedicated to Victor Hugo, whose recent writings, in Louise's judgment, had been too kind to Napoleon III's capital. "Oh, generous master, you flatter Paris too much," Louise began. Her castigation of the capital is severe. In a tone reminiscent of Hogarth's "The Rake's Progress," the author cites several instances of Parisian courtesans destroyed, along with their protectors, by their extravagant lifestyles:

Aux missives d'amour succèdent les factures;
On ne les lit jamais, ne pouvant les payer;
Alors les créanciers commencent d'aboyer;
Leur meute est implacable; elle traque sa proie.
*La menace, l'insulte et sans pitié la broie.**

But Louise does not wish her conversion to moral rigor to be misunderstood:

"Oh!" diront les railleurs sceptiques
(Sans doute il en est parmi vous?):

---

* Bills and debts succeed love letters.
  Unable to pay them, one leaves them unread;
  Then creditors start their barking;
  Its pack of hounds is implacable; they stalk their prey.
  Menace, insult it, and pitilessly crush it.

"Les femmes ne sont ascétiques
Qu'a défaut de plaisirs plus doux!"

Eh bien, non!—Sans qu'on m'humilie
Du mot sinistre: "Il est trop tard!"
J'ai compri l'horreur de la lie
Qui se cache au fond du nectar.*

A prominent Paris critic called Louise's *Satire du siècle* "one of the most virulent satires that, since Juvenal, indignation has inspired a poet to create." He praised her for having written "her most *virile* work,"—the highest accolade offered nineteenth-century women writers.

Curiously, the radical writings of Louise's last years found enthusiastic support from one of her most acerbic critics of the past, Sainte-Beuve, who also compared them to the great tradition of Roman satiric verse.

"Dear Poet, be assured that you've done yourself proud with that satire," Sainte-Beuve wrote after reading excerpts from *La Satire du siècle*. "The portrait of Aurelian is magnificent! How many verses are struck in a most *virile* manner, worthy of Juvenal. . . . My admiration and homage."

Sainte-Beuve had always kept his distance from Louise because he feared her aggressiveness, and he remained terrified that she would press him to write about her. ("I ask you only one favor," he had written her some years earlier. "Allow me to admire you in silence, without being obliged to explain the point at which I cease to admire you.") But after Louise returned from her first trip to Italy, they had had a reconciliation. Sainte-Beuve was sympathetic to Louise's growing anticlericalism. On two occasions in the early 1860s he had even intervened with Princess Mathilde, the most liberal and enlightened member of the royal family, to ensure that Louise's pension not be reduced further because of her attacks against the Church.

Like similar intercessions undertaken decades earlier by Victor Cousin, Sainte-Beuve's attempt to help Louise was complicated by her

---

* "Oh!" The skeptics will gibe
 (Surely some of you, dear readers, are such?):
 "Women become ascetic
 When they lose sweeter pleasures!"

 Well, no!—Before being shamed
 By the somber words "It's too late for her!"
 I perceived the horror of the poison
 That hides under the nectar.

extreme pride. The generous Princess Mathilde, moved by Louise's plight, offered her a stipend of five hundred francs a year from her own purse. Louise rejected this offer of personal charity, wishing to receive such a stipend only from the government in recognition of her accomplishments. It took an entire year, and numerous subterfuges on the part of Sainte-Beuve and Princess Mathilde, to disguise this gift as a new form of state subsidy, which Louise finally accepted.

When Louise finally returned from Rome in 1867 and moved into her tiny flat on the Rue Vavin, she became a neighbor of Sainte-Beuve's, and the two met often at his home in the Rue Montparnasse to talk culture and politics. They had aged considerably since they had last come face-to-face: The debonair dandy with wavy red hair, now an elected senator, had become a stooped old man with craggy features and a mottled potato-like nose. Louise had become a plump, gray-haired old lady who wore stark black vestments and panted painfully as she climbed the stairs to his flat. But they shared a consuming passion for literature which Sainte-Beuve had found in a very few women; and Louise continued to delight Sainte-Beuve with her relentless attacks against the clergy.

"When I left Italy," she wrote him, "the convents were being closed. As I returned to France, it looked as if they had all been transported to our shores. In Nice, Marseilles, Lyons, everywhere, I saw newly built monasteries; I saw an unprecedented number of monks swarming about Paris, more omnipotent than ever. Protected by the court, owning princely mansions in all parts of the capital, they insolently defy civilization, science, truth, morality, love of motherland and family. . . ."

For a year, a lonely Sainte-Beuve, whose closest friends had all died, listened raptly to this impassioned survivor. Then Louise, ever imprudent, committed another of her impulsive mistakes.

Two occasions led to the final falling-out between the two writers. The first was an essay Sainte-Beuve wrote in 1869 about Louise's old friend, the late Marceline Desbordes-Valmore, in which he said: "I would give all of Madame Colet's poetic baggage for that one poem" by Desbordes-Valmore. Needless to say, Louise felt betrayed and communicated her wrath in intemperate terms.

An equally important factor in their last dispute was the reappearance of Alphonse Karr. For a decade, the former editor of *Les Guêpes* had been living in retirement in Nice, where he supported himself as a gardener and flower merchant. In 1869, he arrived in Paris, ready for mischief.

One of Karr's first pranks was to resurrect what he called "The Assassination Attempt of June 1840." He wrote an essay describing Louise's attempt to stab him in revenge for his remarks on her affair with Victor Cousin. It appeared in the influential periodical *L'Opinion nationale,* and Louise, though anonymous, was easily recognizable. Sainte-Beuve was forthrightly named: Karr alleged that the critic had intervened on Cousin's behalf and been rewarded with the directorship of the Bibliothèque de l'Arsenal. (Karr got his libraries wrong. Cousin offered Sainte-Beuve the equally distinguished Bibliothèque Mazarine as his reward.)

The Colet-Karr affair had remained popular with the reading public, and Karr's article was immediately reprinted in several French dailies and periodicals. Sainte-Beuve was appalled. "Thirty years ago, no one would have dared to so distort these facts," he protested in an open letter to the French press. "Not only has all delicacy left our literary mores—most probity has equally disappeared."

Louise wrote an eleven-page letter to Sainte-Beuve defending her actions of 1840 and announcing her intent to present a public defense of her case. Karr had resurrected the story, she told him, because he was "envious of your noble literary reputation, which only keeps on growing, even envious of my modest one, which in its probity far surpasses his mediocre spirit."

Sainte-Beuve begged Louise to desist from any further public mention of the episode. Such publicity would not restore her reputation, he warned her, or undo the injustice that had been done her; and his own health was too frail to endure the turmoil. "It is impossible for me to tolerate any more such storms in my life," he pleaded.

But Louise was not one to remain silent. The following week, her thirty-page letter appeared in *Le Figaro,* "rectifying" Karr's allegations; and such was the public's appetite for the ancient scandal that it was shortly after published as a little book, under the title *Réponse aux "Guêpes" de M. Alphonse Karr.*

Although Louise claimed that she had intended the pamphlet to be printed posthumously, the publication of the document put a definitive end to Louise's three decades of correspondence with Sainte-Beuve. He died a few months later.

In those years, Louise was fast losing her friends (and old friends turned enemies) to the force of age: Marceline Desbordes-Valmore had died in 1859, alone and destitute; Alfred de Vigny had died in 1862, having spent his last years in a liaison with a pretty young governess. Adèle Hugo died in 1868, a year after Cousin. Louis Bouilhet, and Louise's devoted colleague Antony Deschamps, came to their ends in the later months of 1869; in 1870, Paris would mourn the death of Ville-main—the lecherous literary historian who had been a great supporter of Louise's in her youth—and of another devoted member of Louise's salon, the scientist Jacques Babinet.

But no loss was more painful than the death of Reine Picard. Louise's old nurse passed away in January 1868 in her late eighties, in the Provençal village where she had spent her last decade. There is a moving correspondence between Louise and a cousin of hers in Aix, Hermance Révoil, which documents the various gifts of money Louise sent to Reine Picard every two months in the preceding years; the letters make it clear that this was a kindness she had performed for decades, throughout her own most impoverished moments. When Reine Picard died, Louise sent her cousin additional money to have her beloved nurse photographed on her deathbed, a frequent custom in the nineteenth century. And notwithstanding her anticlerical views, a few weeks later Louise commissioned a memorial Mass in her nurse's honor at the village church.

One of the few remaining friends to offer Louise solace was Victor Hugo, who still wrote her warm letters from his Guernsey exile. "You're suffering, that is women's lot," he wrote, "the most inspired ones are the ones most sorely tested. . . . Continue to pen fine and noble verses, enjoy some more beautiful voyages, and save a little love for me."

There was indeed a very fine voyage forthcoming, one Louise had dreamed of all her life—her first trip to the Near East.

In 1869, there was a great fuss in France over the inauguration of the Suez Canal, which had been conceived and designed by the French engineer Ferdinand de Lesseps. Louise was exhilarated by the venture: "The prodigious reunion of two separate seas, long declared impossible, was being accomplished by the tenacious will of a single man." Louise was delighted when France's leading progressive daily, *Le Siècle,* assigned her to cover the opening.

On October 7, 1869, a large crowd of Parisians—artists, writers, scientists, members of high society—assembled at the Gare de Lyon to say farewell to the French delegation. Henriette, that "adorable being," her "beloved and only child," as Louise described her daughter on this occasion, came from Normandy to see her off. That year the two women's relations must have been warmer. In the book that resulted from this expedition, Louise proudly describes the solicitude with which Henriette, standing by her side at the station, asked several of Louise's colleagues to take care of her often ailing mother.

In Marseilles, as Louise boarded the ship that would take her to Cairo, she noted that the great majority of the French delegation was snubbing her, making her feel "like an embarrassing witness who must be held at a distance." Even Théophile Gautier, who had frequented Louise's salon in the 1850s in the hopes that her distinguished friends could help get him elected to the Académie Française, pretended not to recognize her. Most of Louise's male colleagues represented conformist pro-imperialist publications; she ascribed their aloofness to their conservative views and to the fact that she had just published the most scathing anti-imperialist polemic of the decade, *La Satire du siècle.*

There was no "feminist" rationale yet that might have enabled Louise to perceive the true source of their hostility: She was the only woman officially assigned to the Suez-bound delegation, and an old woman at that. Louise was now particularly prey to double standards of judgment because she transgressed the stereotypes assigned to "proper old ladies"—she remained combative, dynamic, and aggressively assertive. Just as Freud criticized his fifty-three-year-old mother-in-law for precisely the same traits, complaining that her energy was unnatural for her age and calling her "an old man," so Louise's male colleagues thought her forcefulness aberrant, if not downright threatening.

The maliciousness of several accounts of Colet-in-Egypt make these bigotries clear. A fellow journalist in the delegation noted: "She was a rather vulgar fat woman with a virile voice and masculine manners, with a free and vain conversation. . . . It was hard to recall that she had once been an ornament of Madame Récamier's salon and that she had gathered in her own salon Récamier's most illustrious recruits."

Another French colleague wrote, adding a few years to Louise's age: "She who in her youth had been called the tenth Muse and who boasted that her charms were capable of returning the world to pagan idolatry was then sixty-two years old [sic]; her virile face recalled that of Catherine the Great. . . . On the moral level she had the most intolerable fanaticism of all, that of impiety."

Radically progressive views, "impiety," the great beauty that had once protected her now faded, failing lungs that occasionally inconvenienced others when she could not continue walking, a "virile" character that refused to conform to current stereotypes of old age, an aging "crinolined reporter" usurping a vocation heretofore reserved to men—how could Louise Colet *not* alienate that male club? There were several fellows in her group far more dilapidated and demanding than Louise—Théophile Gautier was a case in point. As Louise described him, "His swollen lids and bloated features turned his face into a waxen mask; he never wrote, he never spoke, and his lips barely seemed strong enough to hold on to a cigar." But he were a man, and his decrepitude did not arouse derision.

Gautier eventually decided to recognize Louise and talked to her kindly, and there were just enough liberals and gentlemen on board ship to keep her from being isolated. The son of the canal's creator, young de Lesseps, was particularly charming to her.

For reasons unclear, Louise sent only two dispatches from Egypt to *Le Siècle,* but the trip provided material for the book *Les Pays lumineux: Voyage en Orient,* in which she set out to document "the most beautiful monuments of Egyptian art" and give a report on Egyptians' "religion, their ways of life, their sentiments, their passions."

In Cairo, Louise did her Baedeker-style chronicling of the Mosque of Tulun, the mosques of Sultan Hasan and of El Azhar, and the caliphs' necropolis in the suburbs of Cairo. Folk customs interested her equally. Louise was in Egypt at the same time of year that Flaubert had made his journey there—it was precisely twenty years later, to the week—and the memory of his fascination with one of Egypt's most renowned courtesan-dancers, the almeh Kuchuk Hanem, made her particularly interested in documenting that kind of woman. In a portrait as vivid as one by Flaubert, though more derisive, Louise describes the "bee dance" performed by the most famous almeh of 1860s Egypt:

> As enacted in the homes of the pashas and beys of Cairo, the bee dance consists of a voluptuous pantomime: the dancer languishes at first, her eyes heavy with weariness; then a feverish trembling seizes her body; her entire body shudders, her throat undulates, her hips begin to make brusque frenzied movements. The music and chanting double in vigor; the dancer's strident metal castanets clink with furor in her convulsive fingers, her sensual inebriation reaches its limit. But then she is slowly appeased: the upright almeh . . . arches her chest, straightens her head, then collapses, simulating a faint; but she instantly springs up again; her clenched lips imitate the buzzing of a bee which might have just stung her. Where did the lethal animal hide? —Perhaps in her vest. —She rips off her vest and throws it away; the invisible insect continues to buzz under her trousers and her shirt; the courtesan-almeh takes them off in turn and, left quite naked, throws herself into the arms of whatever spectator she has judged to be the wealthiest.

Louise deplored the Westernization that seemed to have swept Egypt and that she feared would increase with the opening of the canal. In her first dispatch to *Le Siècle* she used the pseudonym "Mohammed el-Akmar," pretending she was a proud native of Egypt censuring this ancient culture's current vogue for Europeanization.

> . . . *Cairo has become a corner of Paris. I have to rub my eyes to convince myself that the Mosque of Amur is not the Théâtre des Variétés and that Shepheard Hotel is not our Grand Hôtel de la Paix. . . . In the streets and the bazaars, everywhere, I saw only Parisian gentlemen and cocottes sporting short jackets and long trains. . . . Civilization is overflowing here, civilization for the next fifteen minutes is our big business. We absolutely insist, we Africans, on being civilized, and we play at civilization with a brio, a gusto, that leaves nothing to be desired. . . . Do you remember the story of Potemkin, who erected cardboard villages by the side of the road that Catherine the Great planned to travel on? At this moment all of Egypt is Potemkinized.*

The editors of *Le Siècle* waited in vain for another letter from this intrepid spokesman of a new Islamic nationalist movement; but Louise had said her anticolonialist piece and may have been fearful that further criticism of her Egyptian hosts would hamper her journey. And as she traveled on the Nile toward Luxor in the company of her compatriots, her polemical zeal may have been softened by the enchantment of the scenery.

Even in the relatively luxurious accommodations provided for distinguished foreign guests, in those years a cruise up the Nile was an arduous journey. Gautier declined the trip and returned to Paris, fearing he did not have the strength to withstand it, and Louise was not sure whether her own health would survive the expedition. "My throat is on fire, and I have no voice, but never mind," she wrote Henriette from Cairo just before boarding her ship. "I count on my strong constitution, and above all on my moral energy. The powerful attraction of the unknown sustains me, as it will help me to confront death—that other unknown—when my hour comes. . . . I kiss all of you, and bless you with a tender heart."

The ship, *Gizeh,* provided to the French travelers was a filthy vessel with "garbage bins" for cabins and a pervasive smell of latrines. The first night Louise spent on board, on the eve of departure, was one of the most tortured of her life. It was over ninety degrees inside her squalid cabin; she had developed a fever; and that very night she was haunted by the most disturbing phantom of all—that of Gustave Flaubert.

For many hours [she wrote of the experience], I was prey to a strange and indefinable hallucination. The defunct image of a being whom I had loved in my blind youth, buried in my heart for over twenty years, was suddenly resurrected in dominating and brutal form. His giant's body bent toward me as if to seize me; and his specter spoke to me, with a quiet voice as icy as the air that comes from a tomb closed centuries ago:

"Take care! You don't have the strength anymore to suffer through the tribulations which I once imposed on you. You might well lose your body this time, in the same manner in which you injured yourself trying to soften my heart, that tough metal compressed in the double carapace of science and debauch."

My voice, stifled by suffering, answered him with indifference:

"What do you want of me? What do I care about the nature of your heart? You have no more power over me. Your phantom is vanished in the void of time."

As Louise continued her conversation with this ghostly vision of Flaubert, the phantom took on the form of a vampire. . . .

The larval spirit weighed upon my burning chest, heavy and opaque as some brutish animal. The round porthole, through which two large stars shone, seemed to be his haggard-eyed face, at times blazing, at times dimmed in a penumbra. I closed my eyes. . . . As I ceased to see him, I still felt his crude, obtrusive presence. Weren't those his hands, trying to strangle my wheezing throat? Wasn't that his mouth, biting at my languishing body?

Over my head, I heard a continuous noise similar to those of footsteps on a wooden floor. The biting was succeeded by a raw, intolerable itching, as if I were clawing at my body with my own hands; I shouted out in pain more than in fear, for I do not believe in ghosts; sitting up, I lit a candle I had by my bedside. . . .

Louise discovered that it was not Flaubert's ghost after all that was harassing her. "It was the plague of nineteenth-century tourists, cockroaches! I saw, climbing up my white nightshirt, ceremoniously ambling across the woodwork of the cabin, a dozen of those horrible insects. . . . Brushing off the animals that were on me, I crushed them under the soles of my bedroom slippers."

Two A.M.: four more hours before the *Gizeh* would raise anchor. Louise decided that the only way to exorcise the feverish vision was to jot down her impressions of that painful night.

Why the reappearance of that forgotten being? [she scribbled in her journal]. Ah! it's quite simple. . . . Yesterday I realized that the motives inciting me to take this excursion to Upper Egypt had to do with my desire to encounter—perhaps in the form of a living mummy—one of those seductive almehs who so revolted and upset me in [Flaubert's] accounts of his Egyptian journey. The nightmare of this night may have arisen from that prospect. . . .

It was twenty years ago [she continued, comparing her love for Gustave to a "sacred temple"] that this man shattered and sullied with his uncouth hands the dazzling pedestal which I built to him in a temple which he ignored. . . . He chased himself out of the sacred precinct by sullying it with fleshly debauch and, worse, with a corrupt soul and ignoble vanity.

Then she turned her analysis on herself.

You who have retained, over the years, all your youthfulness and vigor of spirit, how could you fear the apparition of this specter? Is it the memory of him which batters you and gives you this spectral air? No! It's the enormous sadness of having your most sacred beliefs lost, destroyed, profaned by him. . . .

The next lines are Louise's final curse upon Flaubert, the "assassin" of her youth. (The vocative "you" still refers to Louise, the "he" to Gustave.)

Victim, you have been heaped with outrage; executioner, he has been glorified; but the hour of reckoning is sure to come; he will not escape punishment. . . . Remember that great Arab proverb: If a man has secretly killed, the grass of the fields will tell you so. . . .

And feminist militancy pervades her last coda:

A tear is sometimes a more powerful weapon than a knife! Reveal your emotions, and you will be the victor! Woman is forever the sacrificial lamb at the mercy of love. But the lamb so bestially stabbed in secret

can heal its wounds, it revives and becomes a young lion, it can attack
the unpunished murderer and become the instrument of eternal jus-
tice.

After writing those lines, Louise was seized by such a violent cough
that she had to take opium to alleviate her chest pains. She drank three
times the prescribed amount and fell into a heavy, dreamless sleep. She
was awakened in the early morning by the moaning voices of two of her
male colleagues, who were standing in the hall outside her cabin; these
Parisian journalists had spent as wretched a night as she had in their
cockroach-infested cabins. "I don't want to die on this boat!" one was
complaining. "How could I sleep when I was bitten into blindness?"
groaned another, whose eyes were almost shut tight by insect bites. The
boat was beginning to move, and Louise went up on deck to see the
sights.

Louise was obsessed by her desire to find Kuchuk Hanem, to see her
aged and decrepit. When the travelers alighted at the courtesan's native
village, Louise scoured its red-light district, searching for a house resembling Flaubert's descriptions . . . but there was no trace of such a house,
or of a woman with such a name.

So Louise returned to her chaste Baedeker of Upper Egypt: the temples of Dendera, Karnak, and Edfu, the colossal statue of Ramses lying in
the stone quarries of Aswan, the obelisk of Luxor, twin of the one in the
Place de la Concorde.

Louise's book *Les Pays lumineux* was left unfinished (it was published
posthumously). It documents many preliminary festivities but does not
include the actual opening of the Suez Canal. Besides the letter she wrote
as the "Egyptian nationalist," the only other article Louise published in
Le Siècle was an attack on the poverty and bondage that still prevailed in
Egypt. A monologue to Ismail Pasha, the ruler who had supported de
Lesseps's plan to build the Suez Canal, it was written right after she had
had an audience with him.

Prince, you dominate a people of slaves who have been debased, tor-
tured, and despoiled for centuries. This is the great Arab people whose
genius is attested to by the monuments it left in art, science, and liter-
ature. . . . Well, Your Highness, with that decisiveness and prompt-
ness of all inspired reformers and heroes, you must rehabilitate this
dispossessed people. . . . I have seen with my own eyes your henchmen

flagellating the bodies of miserable Arabs whose flaming eyes protested against this barbarism and the agony of this torture; and many of my traveling companions have visited areas of your holy city in which men and women are still sold like vile cattle.

If it is true, Your Highness, that your love of civilization is sincere, put an end to such atrocities. . . . Have the pride to reign over men and not over slaves. This people redeemed by you will champion your most ambitious enterprises; with its support you will be able to liberate yourself from Turkey, which is nothing more than a cadaver threatening to corrupt the body of a resurrected Egypt.

Do not treat this glorious endeavor as a utopia. If the advice is grand, does it matter that the voice which gives it is humble? Isn't it fitting that it should be offered to you by a woman, a mother? . . .

It is clear that by the end of her voyage Louise was not only impatient with the "moral and political decadence" she had witnessed throughout her trip; she was exhausted.

I've been so ailing in the past three days that I'm filled with fury [she wrote her daughter toward the end of her trip]. Take care of your own cold, darling; one needs much strength to live and to age. Who would have guessed that I, once so robust, would suffer from such feeble lungs. . . . My larnyx is so irritated that there are days when merely holding a pen is a martyrdom. . . . Alexandria is populated with Europeans whose mores are as torpid and infamous as those of Cairo; one constantly sees aged men following young boys in the street, adolescents preying on children. . . . The moral sense does not exist here, either among men or women.

From Egypt, Louise went on to Greece and then to Istanbul, where she accepted an invitation extended to very few Western women—she visited several harems, which she planned to describe in the second volume of her book on the Near East. Since that volume was never finished, we know only from her working notes that these encounters moved her deeply, that in these rigidly segregated female enclaves she found "the most exalted souls, the most delicate, loving hearts . . . comparable to those deep, limpid lakes hidden on the heights of the Alps, immeasurable diamonds which radiate all the more brilliantly because of their inaccessible solitude."

It was also in Istanbul, in July 1870, that Louise heard of the outbreak of the Franco-Prussian War, a conflict that would tragically mark her last years and the lives of all her compatriots.

By the mid 1860s, Napoleon III, whose power had been weakened by his ill-fated intervention in the Mexican-American war, was becoming concerned with the increasing power of the Prussian Empire under the leadership of Kaiser Wilhelm II and his prime minister, Otto von Bismarck. When Prussian victories over Denmark and Austria began to threaten the European balance of power, Napoleon tried to block the accession to the Spanish throne of a Hohenzollern prince who was a nephew of the Kaiser. This offered Bismarck an excellent opportunity to arouse Germany, and to goad France, in July 1870, into declaring war.

Few French or foreign observers anticipated the military disasters that ensued. The French army, slow to mobilize, suffered crushing defeats at Metz and at Sedan. Some 83,000 French soldiers, including thirty-nine generals and the emperor himself, were taken prisoner and deported to Germany; Empress Eugénie fled to Great Britain. "I am dying of grief," Flaubert wrote to George Sand, who was to be the most cherished correspondent of his later years. "I curse women; they are the cause of all our woes," he added, perhaps in reference to the empress, who had alienated her subjects by her extravagance and her nefarious influence on her husband's foreign policy.

Flaubert was not alone in his rage. Napoleon's regime could not survive the humiliation of military defeat. Two days after the tragedy at Sedan, on September 4, hundreds of thousands of citizens converged on the National Assembly to demand the emperor's abdication. They encountered little serious resistance. Not a shot was fired. And in the most bloodless coup of French history, that very day the Third Republic was founded, temporarily headed by the radical deputy Léon Gambetta.

Louise was still in Istanbul when she heard street vendors call out the headlines: "Capitulation at Sedan! Downfall of Napoleon! Proclamation of the French Republic!" Rather than celebrate, as did many of her progressive colleagues, she worried about the tragedy that the defeat would bring France, and decided to head home. She boarded a boat on the Danube bound for Vienna, in which city she spent a week nursing yet another bout of bronchitis, and then went on to Geneva. There she heard that the Prussians had begun a blockade of Paris. Thousands of her compatriots—mostly members of high society who supported Napoleon III—had sought refuge in Geneva, "abandoning France at the hour of its greatest disasters," as she put it.

"So you've come to join us!" one of the émigrés greeted her. "You're afraid of the anarchy about to sweep through our poor France?"

"Let's not confuse our purposes," Louise answered. "You've just left France, and I'm about to return to it."

An hour later, unable to get back to Paris because of the blockade, Louise left for Lyons, her father's native city, where she hoped to give some lectures to encourage local women to patriotic action. But Lyons's more radical factions had declared an independent commune, and the city was on the verge of civil strife. So Louise went instead to Marseilles, where she was warmly greeted by the prominent socialist deputy Alphonse Esquiros, whom Gambetta had just put in charge of that region of France, the Bouches-du-Rhône. Esquiros, a popular poet of the Romantic movement who had just spent two decades of exile in Great Britain for his opposition to Napoleon III, was enthusiastic about Louise's plan to address Marseilles's women. He offered her the amphitheater of the Faculty of Sciences.

Louise's conference was advertised throughout the city on large billboards. On the assigned day, November 1, the fifteen-hundred-seat amphitheater was filled to capacity, and an equal number of women stood in the streets outside unable to find a place. Half of them were *femmes du monde* (society women), the others were working women—shopkeepers, bakers, and grocers. (In one of his outbursts against Louise, Barbey d'Aurevilly would suggest that her Marseilles audience was composed of "local fishwives.")

We do not have the texts of her speeches, but we know that they dealt with the patriotism that was needed at this time of national crisis, and that she again attacked "the clerical spirit and those superstitions which, in Marseilles as throughout France, stifle the love of country in women's hearts." She had an immense success. "It was the first time in my life that I spoke publicly," she reported in one of her last memoirs. "My voice, trembling at first, became increasingly firm as the applause grew. The clapping was repeated outside the lecture hall by a crowd of women twice as large as those who had found seats in the amphitheater."

Louise's talk provoked such enthusiasm that a group of several dozen women, "my improvised sisters," rushed up to the podium to embrace her and accompanied her back to her hotel. She must indeed have done well. A second address was scheduled for the following day, to be held, this time, in the city's largest lecture hall. "To persuade, to move through spoken word, is the highest sensation available to the spirit," Louise wrote about that evening. "I [finally] tasted the intellectual inebriation reserved to the orator. Oh! Why didn't I know of it earlier in life! My waning strength may not allow me to feel that elation again."

At the age of sixty, Louise, who throughout her life had idolized the French Revolution's greatest orator, Mirabeau, was finally receiving the kind of instant popular acclaim she had coveted. She was modest about this achievement.

"The seriousness of the political events gave me that night a force of persuasion quite foreign to my nature. I heard, in turn, indignant cries and desperate appeals for the help which we must all bring to our outraged communal motherland, who was being less humbled by the Prussians . . . than by the base cowardice of our own generals."

Louise's second address was so controversial that it provoked street violence; outraged conservatives rioted outside the conference hall the morning after her talk, accusing Colet of fomenting revolt and demanding that the regional administrator, Esquiros, be put on trial for having sanctioned her lectures. And the clerical establishment got in a swipe as well. Misquoting a passage from her first address, France's most conservative Catholic paper, *L'Univers,* cited her as saying that "Bismarck, Napoleon III, and the Pope should be locked in the same cage and allowed to devour each other." (According to Louise, she had merely quoted a young citizen of Lyons; it was not her own figure of speech, as the Catholic paper implied.)

Shaken by this series of powerful emotions, Louise fell ill again. A fever confined her to her Marseilles hotel room for the three months that coincided with the siege of Paris. The city was reduced to near famine, all correspondence in and out of the capital had to travel by balloon, and the provisional government was forced to move first to Tours, then to Bordeaux, before settling in Versailles.

"What humiliation, my poor Carol, what ruin! What sadness! what misery!" Flaubert wrote about the German occupation of Croisset to his niece Caroline Commanville, who was living in Dieppe with the lumber merchant she had married a few years earlier. "When we are not running errands for the Prussians (yesterday I was on my feet for three hours getting them hay), we spend our time . . . weeping in a corner."

By January 1871 it was clear that the French effort to resist the Prussian invasion would fail. Through the machinations of the nation's conservative factions, over the angry protests of Gambetta and French progressives, an armistice was signed with the Prussians the following month. Its terms were severe: Beyond paying huge indemnities, Alsace and half of Lorraine were to be annexed to the German Empire; the

German Army, which was allowed to stage a victory march down the Champs Élysées, was to occupy a fifth of Paris until the indemnities were paid. The greatest humiliation of all, symbolically, was that Kaiser Wilhelm II insisted on being crowned Emperor of Germany in the great hall of Versailles, ancient emblem of national glory, where the government of the Third Republic had settled. "I could hang myself with rage!" Flaubert wrote Caroline upon that event. "I regret that Paris wasn't burned to the last house, leaving only a great black void. France . . . is so dishonored, so debased, that I wish she could disappear completely."

After months of illness, Louise returned to the capital on March 10, 1871, a week before the outbreak of the massive popular rebellions that established the Paris Commune and brought about civil war. Those few of her friends who were still alive greeted her with tears at her little flat on the Rue Vavin. Why such emotion? Louise asked. Because the newspapers, her friends replied, had announced that she had died in Marseilles. The source of the rumor? The Catholic newspaper *L'Univers,* which had stated that Madame Colet, "famous for her revolutionary impulses and for her raging hatred of priests, of the Pope, of all that refers to God and to religion," had died. The cause of death, the newspaper report added, was an ulcer on her tongue, a divine retribution of her "sacrilegious discourses."

19.
The Last
Barricades

෯෨෮ඁ෮෨෯

The Paris Commune of 1871 is one of the more complex and elusive events of French history. Right-wing factions throughout Europe looked on it as a savage revolt staged by bandits. Karl Marx saw it as a heroic step in the dialectic of history, "the antithesis of the empire," the first great uprising of the proletariat against its bourgeois oppressors. To the Russian insurgents of 1917, it was the archetypal insurrection that made their own revolution possible.

But to the French, it was, more simply and tragically, the most fratricidal of all the civil wars—1789, 1830, 1848—that had plagued the nation in a short span of eighty years. "Our Republic is debilitated, exhausted, bled to the bone," Louise Colet mourned that year, "our sinister divisions are displayed to the world by martyrdoms whose frightening number and variety have turned us into barbarians."

The principal factor in the formation of the Commune was the Parisians' outrage at the conservative nature of the National Assembly that ratified the "heinous and cowardly peace" with Germany. Voted into power in February 1871, headed by the aging royalist Louis-Adolphe Thiers, the Assembly was dominated by monarchists. And to the further rage of the overwhelmingly republican citizens of Paris, it transferred the capital of France to Versailles, archaic symbol of royal power. On March 21, when Thiers, sensing Parisians' rising unrest, sent troops into the city to disarm the national guard—a fiercely republican unit—there was a bloody encounter on the Buttes de Montmartre. Two of Thiers's generals were captured and lynched by the mob. As civil war raged, Parisians went to the polls and elected a municipal council whose ideological spectrum ranged from radical republicans to militant socialists. It promptly declared its independence from the national government reigning in Versailles, and called itself, in emulation of 1789, the Commune of Paris.

In order to form a siege army that might efficiently assault and dissolve the Commune, Thiers asked Bismarck to release French prisoners of war. During the two months it took to assemble these troops, as the Versailles army's cannons pounded at Paris, the Commune evolved a Jacobin rhetoric that resurrected much of the spirit of 1789. The capital's ruling body was called Le Comité du Salut Public, and its citizens addressed each other as *"Citoyens membres de la Commune."* Months were renamed according to the calendar of the Great Revolution—"Fructidor" for September, "Frimaire" for November. Paris's churches were closed and many of its clergy arrested on grounds that "priests are bandits, and churches are enclaves where they normally assassinate the masses." "France is currently engaged in completing the Revolution of 1789," the radical republican leader Gambetta declared.

Louise's romantic nostalgia for the Revolution of 1789 was certainly a factor in her ardent support of the Commune; and she was the only writer of renown who unequivocally espoused its cause, for the French literary community was almost unanimously on the side of the Versailles government.

Where were the other liberals? That national emblem of antigovernment opposition, Victor Hugo, had returned from exile in September of the previous year, the day after the downfall of the empire, and had been met at the Gare du Nord by several hundred thousands of cheering, weeping compatriots. So as not to be suffocated by the worshiping crowds, he had sought refuge in a building adjoining the train station and had addressed them from its second floor. "Citizens, I told you I'd return when the republic returned. *Me voici!*" However, though he would offer shelter to Communards and vigorously campaign to grant them amnesty, Hugo spent most of the months of the Commune in Belgium, dismayed by the Commune's excesses. Émile Zola, too, advocated the Commune only intermittently and halfheartedly.

As for Alexandre Dumas *père,* recently Garibaldi's chief gunrunner, he militantly opposed the Commune. So did Théophile Gautier, who described the Communards as "furious iconocolasts, entrenched enemies of the Beautiful, misshapen beings filthy with mud and blood, diabolically perverse natures committing evil for the sake of evil." Even George Sand judged the Parisian insurgents to be "uncouth and stupid mules, lowlife riffraff leading a crowd in part duped and crazed, in part ignoble and evil."

The Commune was equally reviled by traditionalists. Maxime Du Camp saw it as "a case of social epilepsy," and alleged that "those unfortunate ones who fought on the side of the Commune were *ill* in the medical sense that is used in insane asylums." And Flaubert would declare, not unpredictably, that all those "bloodstained imbeciles" who had supported the Commune should be "sentenced to hard labor . . . chained by the neck like common criminals and be forced to rebuild the ruins of Paris." Thus Colet was the only writer of note siding with the greatest painters of her time; unlike the literati, the artists Courbet, Corot, Manet, Monet, and Daumier were united on the side of the Commune and even joined a five-hundred-member federation that described itself as "a government of the art world led by artists."

So there was Louise, quite alone among her colleagues, writing to her friends in Provence about "the cowardice of the government and the Assembly, which rules in Versailles instead of taking its rightful place in Paris and brings to our poor nation tragedies and shames which break my heart. . . . Paris is being bombarded by the generals of our former Empire far more brutally than it ever was by the Prussians. . . . The National Guard are fighting with very great courage, and the Versailles troops will enter Paris, if they ever do, at the cost of immense bloodshed."

Louise's predictions were right on target. As she would realize some months later, internal divisions not only prevented the Commune from achieving any coherent experiments in social reform but also impeded the organization of an effective armed force. And although their acts of bloodshed were far less despicable than those of the "legitimate" Versailles government, the Communards were indeed responsible for many outrageous or just plain absurd actions: Several dozen members of the clergy were executed, all churches were closed, and school prayers were forbidden. At the instigation of Courbet and a few other leaders, the Communards, in a daylong extravaganza attended by thousands of cheering citizens, tore down the column of the Place Vendôme, a symbol of Bonapartism and militarism, and they even flirted with the notion of destroying Notre Dame Cathedral. The Communards demolished the Paris home of Louis-Adolphe Thiers, the president of the "official" government established at Versailles, and only at the last minute were persuaded by Courbet that its precious art collection, instead of being sold to Great Britain to buy more guns for the Commune, should be stored at the Louvre. The most publicized of the Communards' reprisals was their holding hostage, and later executing, the archbishop of Paris, Monsignor Darboy.

As the siege wore on, and as the power of the Versailles troops increased and the hopes of the insurgents waned, Paris was plunged into a state of panic akin to that of the Terror of 1794 or of the Nazi occupation of the 1940s. Denunciations of neighbor against neighbor proliferated. In this revolution that ended up devouring many of its own children, the Paris police's roundup of "saboteurs" and "public enemies" included not only innocent bystanders but also a good many former leaders of the faction-ridden Commune. Exhausted by the famine and terror caused by five months of Prussian siege, Parisians made constant slips of the tongue, saying "Prussians" when they meant "Versaillais."

"We're confused, we don't know who the enemy is anymore," lamented Malvina Blanchecotte, a friend of Louise's and one of the Commune's most eloquent chroniclers. "Brothers fight brothers, neighbors kill neighbors, Versaillais and Parisians refer to each other as enemies." Edmond de Goncourt wrote in his journal on the eve of the "Bloody Days" that ended the Commune: "In our streets one meets only persons indulging in perpetual monologues, like the inmates of asylums, persons from whose mouths come only the words 'desolation, misery, death, ruin'—the entire vocabulary of despair."

The Versailles government, its forces strengthened by sixty thousand French soldiers released by the previous enemy, Germany, made a massive onslaught on the capital on May 21, 1871, the eve of the violent conflict that has gone down in French history as the "Bloody Days." Parisians were apprised of imminent invasion. Church bells rang throughout the city, barricades went up at every street corner. The size of Versailles's armed forces—130,000 men—took the Communards by surprise, and so did its viciousness. The invading army began systematic massacres of Parisian insurgents from the day they entered the city. The Versailles troops would lose some 870 men. The death toll on the Communards' side was between 20,000 and 25,000 citizens, slaughtered by their compatriots. And 43,000 prisoners were taken. "The laws of war!" protested The Times of London. "They are mild and Christian compared to the inhuman laws of revenge under which the Versailles troops have been shooting, bayonetting, ripping up prisoners, women and children. . . . There has been nothing like it in history."

From the twenty-third to the twenty-fifth of May, as the Versailles troops pressed on, the Communards resorted to the only retaliation left to them: They set fire to Paris to slow their enemies' advance. The Tuileries Palace, the Hôtel de Ville, the Palais-Royal, the Ministry of Finance, the Palais de Justice—these were only some of the thousands of buildings destroyed, or gravely damaged, by the Communards. The city was illuminated day and night by the fires and by the government troops' shelling. The streets were filled around the clock with ambulances and buses carrying the blood-soaked bodies of wounded and dead. At noon of the twenty-fourth, a huge explosion shook Paris. Houses trembled as in an earthquake, windows shattered, doors came off their hinges, as one of the city's largest ammunition storehouses exploded in the Luxembourg district, two blocks from Louise's flat on the Rue Vavin. Among the numerous accounts of the "Bloody Days," Louise's are among the most eloquent, for she remained at the center of the conflict.

The Versailles troops had just seized the barricades of the Rue Vavin. The boom of machine guns and of executions still rang out in the adjacent streets; the glare of many fires intersected under my windows. I took refuge in a room that looked out upon the Luxembourg Gardens, not knowing that the peril was even greater on that side. Suddenly I was thrown to the floor by the explosion and wounded in my hip and arm by masses of debris. Voices shouted out that the house was on fire. I steeled myself against the pain and rushed down the stairs. . . .

The rumors of fire in Louise's house were false, but five other buildings on her block were burning. Louise packed up all her manuscripts into metal boxes, not knowing where to find shelter next.

I ran down the bloody sidewalks, as hot under my feet as the walls of a crater. . . . Blood ran down my mangled wrist. . . . Many women as innocent as I were randomly shot that day for merely looking suspicious. But I was known in my part of town, and as they offered drinks to the conquerors, many of my neighbors said. "Let her pass, she's a lady." I reached the Rue Montparnasse and stopped before the cortege of generals—Mac-Mahon, Vinoy, de Cissey—parading on horseback in their most gleaming uniforms, as if they had triumphantly entered

Berlin. *They chatted gaily among themselves, heads held high. . . . And yet Paris, at that hour, could have moved even those hearts most habituated to carnage. . . . One still heard the whistle of shells arching over the city's roofs, ear-shattering volleys followed by long, rumbling clamors. The blue sky disappeared under the red lights which rose like spouts of blood over the fire of monuments, as if all of Paris was about to go up in flames. . . .*

Louise was particularly shocked by the sight of a priest who greeted the occupying troops with kisses and embraces and "outbursts of ecstatically merry laughter."

Indignant, I went up to him, shook his arm, and asked, "Who are you, sir, to rejoice in this manner. Might you be a foreigner, a Prussian? . . . Don't you know that Paris is burning, that French blood is flowing in streams, that the unfortunate hostages are being slaughtered? That on both sides thousands of persons are dying, and that it is vile to laugh at this kind of tragedy?

He looked at me disdainfully and said, "We are saved! We are triumphing! And you, Madame, who are you not to applaud the triumph of religion and civic order?" "I am a broken soul whom a priestly heart could never understand," I answered. "I mourn the ruin of our motherland and of our humanity, two entities that are foreign to you."

In the following days, teams of Versaillais soldiers went house-to-house, routing out those who looked suspicious. Anyone with a gun was shot, anyone wearing any part of an army uniform, even men with watches were shot, on the grounds that they must be Communard officials. Other suspects were marched to prison in Versailles, and many were summarily executed on the way, in the Bois de Boulogne, without so much as a hearing in court. Louise registered her indignation at the reprisals in which thousands were executed in an attempt to "sanitize" the city of insurgents.

Shots rang out right under my window, in the Luxembourg Gardens, where thirteen hundred insurgents, women and children among them, were executed on that day alone. At one A.M., I saw carts filled with cadavers being led to the Cimetière Montparnasse. . . . The resistance was not totally vanquished until Sunday at noon. Then a deathly silence spread over our ruined capital, a silence occasionally interrupted

by the volleys of rifles that continued to slaughter insurgents throughout the city's streets, squares, gardens, cemeteries. . . .

Horrendous details reached me from all parts of the city: At the
Champs Élysées, a great number of vanquished insurgents were shot
down en masse with machine guns; a few of the survivors stood up on
top of their companions' heaped bodies and shouted to their executioners: "Shoot! You're forgetting us!" Some Paris newspapers attest
that "many wounded persons were buried without any definitive proof
of death in the Cimetière Montparnasse." Have there been any more
lugubrious episodes in the most barbaric wars of antiquity?

An estimated thirty thousand insurgents have either perished in the
combat or been shot in reprisal. Forty-three thousand prisoners, including women and children, have been taken to Versailles on foot and
put in chains, to await trial.

I well know that in expressing such piety, even in limiting it to those
innocents who were among the accused, I'm exposing myself to suspicions of moral complicity with the abominable criminals who dishonored the sacred cause of the republic; such a fear could never curb
my words. In the midst of this white terror which reigns today and
seems to drive most of France to madness, I would be ashamed to stifle
my feelings and have any selfish fear in my fate. . . . The two hundred
thousand insurgents supporting the Commune were not all monstrous
scoundrels; the majority of them, I believe, were part of those heroic
citizens of Paris who proved their patriotism and abnegation during
the previous five months' siege by Prussian troops. Exhausted by pri-
vation and moral suffering, humiliated by a ruinous peace, overly stim-
ulated by the appeals of the capital's press and political clubs, by the
handling of arms, and by the abuse of alcohol, which for ten months
has been the only palliative of this unfortunate people, still, I think,
they had attributes of energy and courage which a great statesman
might perhaps have succeeded in putting to profit for the salvation of
France.

However tortured she was by the horrors that surrounded her, Louise's experience of the siege of Paris had its ironic moments. On May 22,
the day after the Versailles troops entered Paris, the young writer Jules
Troubat, who had served for some years as Sainte-Beuve's secretary and
had inherited the writer's flat on Montparnasse, came to call on her. The
two took a walk together to get a clearer sense of what was going on. After
half an hour, as bullets whistled about them, they decided to return to

Louise's flat and found a new barricade going up on that street. Troubat, afraid of crossing the barricade, spent the night on her sofa. The next morning, when the ammunition warehouse exploded on Montparnasse, they decided to shift camp and moved on to Sainte-Beuve's old apartment on the Rue Montparnasse, where the fighting seemed less violent. Louise spent the following night in the room formerly occupied by the distinguished critic, and surely she noted the irony of finding herself, ailing and aged, in the bed of the man who had once desired her, and occasionally befriended her, and far more often attacked her. The incongruity would not be lost on Flaubert. A few days after the defeat of the Commune, he wrote to Edma Roger des Genettes, slightly distorting the facts: "The Muse spent three days in Sainte-Beuve's cellar! Is that not a wondrous vision?"

The aftermath of the Commune—the massive reprisals wrought by the "official" government against the Commune's sympathizers—was even more brutal than the consecutive sieges of Paris imposed by Prussian and Versailles troops. Throughout the rest of 1871, Paris suffered horrific events: "The sound of [Prussians'] mortar," Malvina Blanchecotte wrote, "had been but an innocent music compared to the most tragic, most unforgettable sound of all—the incessant nocturnal din of firing squads." Denunciations—neighbor reporting on neighbor in exchange for a paltry government sum or some bureaucratic favor—reached new heights after the legitimate government had recaptured the city; they rose to the astonishing number of 350,000 in the four weeks that followed the Commune's fall. Some of the Communards killed during the conflict, or executed in the Versailles troops' reprisals, had been so hastily and haphazardly buried that after heavy rains their corpses often reappeared in public parks or thrust through the very pavements of the city. Colet's book *La Vérité sur l'anarchie des esprits en France,* a memoir of the Commune and a commentary on its causes and consequences, communicates the sense of terror that continued to grip Parisians in the Commune's aftermath: "Denunciations—cowardly and hideous homicides in which assassins can strike in full security—have succeeded massacres. . . . Certain newspapers are preaching denunciation as a public virtue. . . . The day is won by those who can describe in utmost dramatic detail the capture of some unfortunate person tracked down during his flight or betrayed by a friend with whom he had sought shelter."

In August 1871, twenty-six courts-martial were founded to render judgment on some forty thousand prisoners. Only a few dozen citizens were actually executed, but ten thousand were sentenced to prison terms or deported to New Caledonia. A striking number of the detainees were women, who had played as great a role fighting for the Commune as they had in the Revolution of 1789, using weapons, fighting on the barricades beside the men. The ancient French fear of the unleashed, armed virago of 1789 was once more awakened among conservatives and found expression in the myth of the *pétroleuses:* Working-class women who had carried wine or milk bottles in their shopping bags as they scrounged for food in the starving capital were accused of having carried petrol to fling firebombs throughout Paris.

"The victors continue to wage, in cold blood, all the furors of the struggle," Louise wrote in *La Vérité sur l'anarchie,* describing the tens of thousands of Communards brought to Versailles on foot in chains, like convicts, to await trial. "In Versailles, crowds spit in the face of women and old men, and lacerate their faces with their hands. Our newspapers delight in describing the rags, the fright, and the exhaustion of these victims, who are reduced to begging for a little water in order to continue walking, and receiving nothing but blows from their jailers. . . ."

And so Louise Colet lived on for a few more seasons in the city that had once incarnated all her aspirations to happiness and glory ("Paris! Bazaar of the world, immense capital!"), a city now ravaged by shelling, blackened by fire, soaked in fratricidal blood, and shamed by the baseness of citizens denouncing one another for profit.

A few months after the defeat of the Commune, Louise went to the country to stay with a family that she refers to anonymously in a memoir as "they," but which the reader readily understands to be the family of her daughter, Henriette Bissieu. She describes herself sitting on the flower-strewn lawn of a pastoral country house where two young children play. The youngsters' mother, "young, beautiful, happy," plays alongside the children. One giveaway line reveals Louise's affectionate, grandmotherly attitude toward the young ones: "I caught them in my arms when they ran by and kissed them with all the tenderness of my heart. They returned my kisses with the fugitive tenderness of childhood."

But in the middle of this pastoral scene Louise starts reading her newspaper, which gives daily accounts of the trials of Communards being staged in Versailles. This particular day, the accounts focus on the judgments being meted out against hundreds of alleged *pétroleuses.*

Louise reads the indictments against the women, the "heartfelt emotions and maternal despair" with which they responded to their accusers, and finally she reads that a few of them received the death sentence. She imagines their pathetic cries: "We have been hungry and cold, we have lived in the streets without shelter, we are victims of society and are being exterminated like monsters. What will become of our children!"

The prisoners' voices alternate poignantly in Louise's mind with the gaiety of the children playing at her feet. She fingers the silk of her dress, the warm shawl wrapping her shoulders. "These pathetic convicts evoked innumerable holocausts of other women . . . who have died in ignorance and silence without their despair having any effect on the emotions of others. . . . I would have wished to uplift those souls, purify them with my consolation, offer whatever clothing I owned to cover those poor wasted bodies. . . . My impotence in helping them led me to burst into tears."

Louise's hostess (Henriette, of course) comes to Louise's side and expresses concern for her tears. Louise shows her the newspaper. The young woman skims absentmindedly through the report.

"I can't think of these women's fates without compassion," Louise comments to her hostess. "Their lives, already tormented and pitiful, will end with a horrible death."

"What, you pity those monsters?" the masked Henriette replies with a laugh. "One could never kill too many of them to assure our peace."

Louise glares at the young woman and goes to her room. It is evident, in this moment, that she wished to veil the identity of her hosts in order not to criticize her daughter publicly. But if there was any doubt that Louise's rigid, elegant hostess was Henriette Colet Bissieu, it is dispelled by the following sentences: "Experience had taught me the futility of trying to nurture any pity, generosity, devotion, in this superficial and flighty person. An extreme volatility, a vain and insecure personality, rendered her hostile to any communal, civic sentiment. She enjoyed only that which flattered and gilded her well-being and her limited pleasures. . . . She obstructed all moral law with the allegedly divine, exclusive right of the Church, which consists in adhesion to dogma and to puerile practices void of all sentiment. . . . Her provincial mores reinforced her spiritual sterility and the narrowness of her passions."

The Colet clan's indoctrination, the years in the Benedictine convent, had paid off; Louise felt more estranged than ever from her only child, from the only love left to her. She knew that her political convictions horrified her hosts, and she prepared to return to Paris, to leave the house where she had hoped to find "the sympathy which would have given me the wish to live." With a sense of "added mourning," she noticed that her hosts seemed relieved by her departure, and upon leaving them she did her best to repress her tears.

* * *

After the fall of the Commune, France's more thoughtful citizens suffered a severe crisis of conscience. There was much soul-searching concerning the flaws of national character that had led to the savage and tragic conflicts of the past century, much fear concerning the nation's future: "Among us a revolution is certain approximately three times per century," Malvina Blanchecotte commented. "What happiness to be a woman, to be a nothing! It will spare us from the task of judging and punishing."

"Not satisfied with the summary executions already imposed upon a miserable flock of humans led by unprincipled and dim-witted leaders, and treated by its conquerors like cattle for slaughter," Louise wrote of the courts-martial in Versailles, ". . . not satisfied, French soldiers, turned into executioners, are getting used to shedding yet more French blood."

Louise's book *La Vérité sur l'anarchie,* which she had to publish in Italy because its views were too condemnatory of the French government, was one of several to contemplate the larger historical reasons for the Commune's bloody debacle, for this "fratricidal war of which I was a witness and nearly became a victim." She attributed the Commune's failure to "a lack of homogeneity of vision rather than of troops." She traced the devastation of 1870 and 1871 to the fact that France had become "a Republic without Republicans": In each attempt to transform a monarchy into a republic—the upheaval of 1789, the "Glorious" revolution of 1830, the bloodbath of 1848, the coup of September 1870—the same pro-royalist functionaries had blocked all true reform and catered to the vested interests of wealthy bourgeois and proclerical monarchists in order to remain in power. In Louise's view, each resulting regime, rebuilt with "the debris of the preceding orders," had remained totally devoid of any "communal sense" and incapable of "collective action," and had manifested "a cold-blooded cynicism and disdain" toward the people's needs. "Each of our revolutions has sold out the hopes of our citizenry, each wasted effort has laid it low again, vanquished and bloodied, in a state of resignation."

What shocked Louise in the year that succeeded the Commune was the ease with which Parisians resumed the ostentation of the Second Empire. "In the shade of destroyed monuments, on lawns still wet with the blood of victims, down the streets still blackened by flames, gaiety sparkles, the air resounds with songs and joyous dances, prostitution spreads its wares. . . ."

She would expand on these renewed festivities in a castigating letter to a friend in Istanbul, which was circulated for publication in numerous European newspapers.

> *Know that our ruined Paris, our Paris still bathed in French blood, is filled at this hour with joyous strollers rushing to visit our still-smoking monuments. One goes then* en famille, *in a spirit of excursion! Orchestras play at the barricades, and one sings, one dances, with the liberating soldiers. Women in provocatively festive dress promenade as shamelessly as they did under the empire. . . . Gold-braided French officers are feted, applauded, embraced, crowned with flowers, just as if they had conquered Berlin! . . . Meanwhile the serious and enlightened part of the public moans in the shade and muses on the cruel uncertainty of France's future.*

With the exception of her friend from Marseilles, Deputy Alphonse Esquiros, and the faithful Jules Troubat, the members of Louise's little salon had been dispersed like so many autumn leaves by the tragedies of the Commune. Her solitude the following winter was aggravated by illness. In January 1872, Louise suffered painful surgery to remove an abscess from her head. As soon as she recovered, she was impelled to commit yet one more very imprudent act: She earned a bit of badly needed cash with an abrasive posthumous article on Sainte-Beuve.

Although he had praised some of her individual works, Louise stated with startling candor in her "Étude sur Monsieur Sainte-Beuve," she could not forgive him for never mentioning her in his studies of contemporary women authors. She wrote of the unhappiness suffered by Sainte-Beuve because of the "physical ugliness" that prevented him from ever making a happy marriage or coupling with a desirable woman, and drove him into the arms of streetwalkers. While praising the critic's "undulating and diverse" intellectual genius, she discoursed at length, with the full vigor of her new puritanism, on his venality, rapaciousness, and political opportunism, and compared his secret dissoluteness with the life of his devoted young secretary, Jules Troubat, a dedicated family man with two adorable children, in whose household she felt "a perfume of honesty."

Louise was thus drawn into another of those vituperative public debates with which she had continually poisoned her life. In an open letter to the press, Troubat pleaded that his fidelity to Sainte-Beuve was greater than his susceptibility to Madame Colet's flatteries. He expressed outrage at Louise's attack on Sainte-Beuve's private life and asked whether Madame Colet, "Victor Cousin's former friend and *pensioner,*" was the right person to accuse Sainte-Beuve of cupidity. Louise angrily rebutted, in an open letter to the press, that she had never been Cousin's "pensioner" (kept woman) and had received all her pensions from the French government in recognition of her achievements. She also pointed out that in 1871, Troubat, accused of writing an article favorable to the Commune, had sought shelter several times in her tiny flat, which hardly had "the opulence [displayed by] a minister's pensioner."

The upshot of this episode was that Louise lost one of the few friends she had left and became more isolated than ever. The following fall, she addressed a letter to Victor Hugo that was headed "From my bed of suffering." "Since you left, all has been effort and struggle, a ghastly struggle which I tried to finish through sheer persistence of will," she wrote the "Suprême Alligator," who had returned to Guernsey for a few months. "I put my entire soul into it, a soul torn by too many sorrows, which will end up by destroying the body. I had hoped to leave last September for Italy, but I wished to finish this book, of which each page has been a torture. . . . Each evening, I don't know whether my hand will be paralyzed the following day."

The book Louise refers to is *Les Dévotes du grand monde,* "Devout Women of High Society," another hodge podge text in which social satire alternates with philosophical musings, snippets of personal reminiscence, assorted poems, and diatribes on the renascent power of the Catholic Church over the lives of Parisian women. An excerpt of *Les Dévotes* was published in an antigovernment paper that Hugo received at his Guernsey retreat. "It is all noble, dignified, generous," he wrote her. "I read with growing emotion those beautiful pages filled with the fever of the Beautiful and the Good. Courage, valiant woman! You merit a great success, you will have it." (Upon this letter from Hugo, Louise commented, somewhat incongruously in light of her adulation of fame: "Success! That flattering concept has never been more than a mirage for me. . . . I write for those who suffer and grieve, for the eternal vanquished of the earth.")

Before leaving for the south of France and Italy, Louise supervised the publication of the entire text of *Les Dévotes du grand monde.* In this book, Louise once more affirms her Deist brand of piety and particularly upholds the philosophy of Marcus Aurelius, "a doctrine based on Reason and a faith in the perfectibility of Man, which is devoid of miracles and superior to that of the Gospel." And she again deplores the effect of moral laxness and marital infidelity on the lives of Parisian women, and of men's tendency to look on wives as nothing more than machines for childbearing.

Paris abonde en maris infâmes!
Dans leur mains que peut-on que deviennent les femmes?
Non! Les gallantes moeurs de ce monde futile
Après l'enfantement rend la mère inutile.*

Eventually Louise felt well enough to leave "this incandescent and gruesome city, which devours bodies and consumes souls," to move back toward the Mediterranean sun and heat she craved. "After two years of suffering," she wrote a friend, "the doctors have decided that I should flee Paris and go to live at least two years in the Midi to strengthen my weakened lungs. I leave next Saturday for a long while, perhaps forever."

The Provençal air Louise so eagerly sought was wretched that summer. The chill, violent mistral wind blew continually. In her native Aix, she took to her bed for several weeks, racked by fever, and then she went on to Milan, where she edited the proofs of her volume on the Commune, *La Vérité sur l'anarchie des esprits en France.*
She found one of her last refuges in a small, cheap boardinghouse in the seaside resort of San Remo, where she hoped to improve her health and finish the second volume of her book on the Near East. She lived there in desolate circumstances she described in a letter to a friend.

If I look out of my window I see the old Genoan fort which serves as prison to the French and Italian criminals arrested at the frontier; they're brought there in droves several times a day under police escort, their hands and feet shackled; some of these personages would terrify you on a forsaken road. The most sinister of them are not the ones in rags but the pickpockets in flowered vests and silk ties, arrested in the gambling houses of Nice and Monaco; these ruffians exchange salutations and smiles with the mountebanks in pailletted costumes who've set up their ambulating caravan at the seashore, by the prison's walls. Standing at the head of the caravan, a Pierrot in floured face blows on his trumpet, while his Columbine in torn maillot beats her drum.
At that signal all of San Remo's riffraff appears. Most of them emerge from the garbage-filled caves at the base of the prison walls. Squatting in these filthy nests, urchins of eight to ten years spend their

---

* Paris abounds in infamous husbands!
  What do you expect women to become in their hands?
  The gallant mores of this vain society
  Make a mother worthless after her childbearing years.

days playing with cards as greasy as old soup pots. Only the attraction della commedia, which inflames their imagination, can tear them away from that love of cards which has possessed them since birth. Their fathers and older brothers, themselves lazy gamblers, set this example of idleness and low life, while the community's unfortunate women do all the work for husbands and sons, carrying weighty loads. Brusque, savage, but courageous, these miserable creatures have no youth and become toothless old women at the age of twenty. Hideous spectacle! The ignoble, cowardly male versus the woman reduced to a beast of burden!

That is the invariable tableau offered to me at the marina di San Remo. To heighten this lugubrious mood, fate led me to live in a pensione that adjoins a coffin factory and a garage for hearses. On stormy days, when I can't go out, I would go crazy without the French and Italian newspapers and letters from a few friends who've not forgotten. As soon as the sound of wheels is heard, you desperately wish that one of those friends had sensed your anguish and come to the rescue; alas! it's only a hearse returning to the adjoining house.

Solitude, greater than ever; winter rain on the desolate little boarding-house; winter rain on this "sinister and burlesque settlement" decked with the mocking gaiety of flowered terraces; winter rain on the lugubrious Riviera, where thousands of aging Europeans are awaiting their end; several months of 1874 spent in bed, fighting another bout of aggravated bronchitis. Slow-moving, portly, black-gowned Louise occasionally emerges to go to the library, to buy some fruit; the malevolent urchins tumble out of their foul caves to run after her, call her Old Witch. The local doctors counsel Louise to "fortify" her health with old wine. The former teetotaler takes to drinking a little glass of port with her evening meal.

"Two winters spent in abandonment and oblivion": so the woman who was once Paris's Tenth Muse describes those last seasons spent in the melancholy village of San Remo. She retaliates with the dignity of silence. She speaks to no one. When the weather is fair, she shuttles slowly between her dingy boardinghouse and the little municipal library near the town hall.

It is there, on a chill day of January 1875, that Louise came upon a book, just published in France, that for a few months would restore her enthusiasm and vitality. It was the work of Edgar Quinet, whom she had greatly admired since her adolescence. "I read in one night, sitting up until dawn, that powerful work which blazingly sums up all of my own convictions," she wrote a friend in Paris. "Even my cough came to a stop, the spirit triumphed over the body, and once more I am reborn, I live, I work, I hope. . . ."

The poet and historian Edgar Quinet, one of the most eloquent thinkers of nineteenth-century France, was seven years older than Louise. His prose poem *Ahasuerus,* immensely popular with his generation of liberal Romantics, had provided epigraphs for her first collection of verse, *Fleurs du Midi.* He had become controversial in the 1840s for attacking the clergy and supporting Europe's oppressed nationalities. Following Napoleon III's coup d'état of 1851, Quinet went into exile in Switzerland and Belgium, where Louise visited him in the mid-1850s. Like Hugo and thousands of other left-leaning citizens, Quinet returned to Paris in 1870 when the empire fell. He was elected deputy to the National Assembly, where he fought for the enfranchisement of women and for legislation that would banish religious instruction from France's public schools.

Quinet's book of 1874, *L'Esprit nouveau,* was a summation of his life's thought—a declaration of his faith in the progress of science and in the possibility of establishing a secular, democratic republic in France. This was the book Louise discovered in the San Remo library. She decided to write her next book about Quinet, and the two began a correspondence.

Oh, if I were twenty years old [she wrote him], it's in Rome's Colosseum that I would proclaim [your] sublime epilogue, that winged ode filled with flamboyant phrases in which the human spirit so palpitates. . . .

Oh, why am I not a twenty-year-old Hypatia! Even if I were to be stoned to death, as she was, I would preach this book's radiant doctrines in a stilled amphitheater, and the New Spirit would revivify Rome and radiate into the depths of that tenebrous Vatican, still filled with pestilential vapors. . . .

Louise sent Quinet a copy of her own last book, *La Vérite sur l'anarchie.* "What energy! What variety! What courageous indignation!" Quinet wrote. "Madame, what a letter you wrote me! What a moment of happiness it gives me! So my book fought off your illness and was able to suspend your suffering? You couldn't have told me anything that moved me more. Get entirely well very soon, in order to make me truly happy."

Their correspondence lasted only a few weeks. In March of 1875, only a few weeks after Quinet had so miraculously revived her, Louise, picking up her Paris newspaper, read the headlines announcing his death following a brief illness. His last words were: "We shall find each other again in truth."

The newspaper trembled in her hands, her eyes filled with tears, she was barely able to regain her bed without falling. A fever seized her again, and another long illness ensued. Or so the emotional old woman related it: "I hung on to furniture to reach my bed. . . . A doctor was called the next morning. I listened to his prescriptions for calm and rest with a sad smile. How easily can one master such an emotion, resign oneself to the rupture of such a bond?"

Once the fever waned, Louise could no longer stand San Remo. She began to think of where she would spend her last days: Greece, where some friends had invited her to stay? Rome, Milan, scenes of better times? She chose Paris, the site of her greatest illusions, passions, deceptions.

She wound her way northward, spending a few weeks in Nice to rest. We have only one eyewitness account of Louise in her final year, from a sympathetic young journalist in Nice who served as her private secretary for a few hours a day. He published a little memoir of Louise fifty-three years later, wishing to do his part in rehabilitating "the 'dear muse' who was condemned by all of [Flaubert's] friends without ever having had a fair hearing."

She was then sixty-five years old. She was a former blonde, portly, quite tall. She lived [in Nice] in an airy, well-lit room where she prepared her breakfast and her tea on a little alcohol lamp.

Lying on her bed, Madame Colet scribbled in pencil on a schoolchild's notebook, day and night, the first draft of a new book. After having reread, shortened, or, more frequently, augmented her draft, she used to read the final text to me out loud, walking up and down her room and declaiming with dramatic emphasis the passages she had sketched out that morning.

The weather in northern France was miserable that summer. Louise spent a few days with Henriette and her family at their estate in Verneuil, Normandy, which was aptly named Fryleuse, "The Chilly One." But her pride, her independence, and perhaps the political disagreements that had estranged her from Henriette over the years, soon drove her back to Paris. Her letters of that summer are first written from the Hôtel d'Angleterre, Rue Jacob, and later from the Hôtel du Palais-Royal, Rue de Rivoli.

"The rain and the cold that assail me here are harming me greatly," she wrote to her compassionate young Nice secretary. "Although covered with blankets, I shiver constantly while writing you. Whatever happens, I shall return to Nice in September. . . ."

She was trying to fight on.

"Even if it kills me, I must finish and publish my volume on the Orient and my new collection of poetry. Paris is totally consumed by commerce, and above all by pleasure. . . . I've received the visit of Hugo and of a few other great spirits. . . ."

Aside from Hugo, the only friends Louise had left were a handful of militant reformers—Louis Blanc, the socialist historian and deputy who had been a leader of the 1848 revolution and, like so many other liberals, had returned in 1870 from two decades in exile; Alphonse Esquiros, the poet and progressive deputy who had sponsored her lectures in Marseilles; Alfred Naquet, the extraordinary scientist and humanist who was pioneering legislation that would give French women the right to divorce. This remnant of friends must have provided Louise with a saving measure of community and warmth.

"My health having improved, I'm at work from six A.M. to midnight," she wrote her friend in Nice at summer's end. "I hope to finish, before winter, not only my book on the Orient but also three volumes of my collected poetry. . . . I go out little, beyond an occasional dinner at the homes of Louis Blanc and Victor Hugo. He is full of hope for the foundation of a solid republic, though he does have fears, and storms mightily against clerical conspiracies. . . ."

In one of the last letters of Louise's we have, written to Esquiros, the sick, impoverished old woman still has the energy and the largesse to invite her friend and his wife to dinner in her shabby little hotel room and to organize a little social outing.

. . . If next Sunday you and your wife have the cordiality to share a modest dinner with me and M. Alfred Naquet, we could go on to end the evening at M. Hugo's, in the company of M. Naquet. . . . Answer me with a resounding "yes," and I shall return your visit at length in the week that follows. I shall be much pained if you refuse me; I shall expect both of you at six o'clock and embrace you with all my heart.

Louise Colet died at the end of the winter, on March 8, 1876, at her daughter's Paris flat on the Rue des Écoles. Louise's will stipulated a civic burial; but her daughter, countering her mother's wishes, brought her body back to Verneuil and buried her with the full rites of the Church in her husband's family enclosure at the municipal cemetery.

Louise's grave is still there, dour and green with the dank moss of Norman climes, as Flaubert had described his own heart. The large, unremarkable, blackened stone is engraved with her name and her years and, over that, Henriette's homage to her mother's gifts—a small wreath of laurel, the traditional symbol of the poet.

Although Henriette and her husband do not seem to be buried in the family compound, Louise is not alone in her grave: her grandson, Raymond Bissieu, is buried with her, as is her great-granddaughter Suzanne Savalle, the former bank employee who helped track down Louise's lost manuscripts and return them to the Fonds Colet in Avignon, thus making it possible, at last, to document Louise Colet's sad, joyous, tempestuous life.

Epilogue I

COSÌ FAN TUTTE

George Sand

She died three months after Colet, aged seventy-two, at her family estate, in Nohant, central France. Her last words were "Laissez verdure" ("leave the greenery"), perhaps a reference to her wish that no tombstone be placed upon her grave.

In attendance at her deathbed were her son, Maurice, and her daughter, Solange, who, like Henriette Bissieu, countermanded her mother's request for a secular funeral and insisted on having her buried with the full rites of the Church.

The spring of 1876 was also marked by the death of Sand's sometime friend Marie d'Agoult, who passed away on March 5, three days before Louise Colet.

The three great Romantic Muses of nineteenth-century France died within twelve weeks of each other.

Gustave Flaubert

In the mid-1870s, he started Bouvard et Pécuchet *but encountered difficulties. He published his superb* Three Tales *in 1877, to critical acclaim, and resumed the composition of* Bouvard et Pécuchet, *but it remained* unfinished at his death. His closest friend, in the years that followed the death of George Sand, was Guy de Maupassant, nephew of his favorite comrade, Alfred de Poittevin, to whom Maupassant bore a haunting resemblance.

Flaubert spent much of his last decade mourning Louis Bouilhet, getting Bouilhet's poetry published and his plays produced. His friendship with Maxime Du Camp remained cool after their return from the Near East, yet there is one enterprise on which the two men eagerly collaborated in Flaubert's last years. They agreed to burn the more "compromising" correspondence they had exchanged during their youth. This decision was in great part incited by the sensational publication, in 1874, of Prosper Mérimée's posthumous work, Lettres à une inconnue. These love letters to a woman of high Parisian circles titillated French society more than any other cultural event of the decade and led numerous literati to burn the evidence of their pasts. Flaubert had long believed that "the writer should leave nothing of himself except his works," and his panic was equal to that of the careerist Du Camp. After the two men had destroyed most of the bawdy letters they had exchanged in their youth (some of them, fortunately, survived), Flaubert indulged in several subsequent bonfires—such as the one described by Maupassant, during which he most probably destroyed Louise Colet's letters.

Despite his friendships with Maupassant, Sand, and a few other devoted colleagues, Flaubert's last decade was pitiful. He never recovered from the grief he suffered, in 1872, over his mother's death, or from his niece's subsequent treachery. Madame Flaubert had left the Croisset property to Caroline Commanville, with the proviso that Flaubert be allowed to live there for the rest of his life. In the mid-1870s, when the lumber concern owned by Caroline's husband, Ernest Commanville, went bankrupt, Flaubert sacrificed a large part of his modest capital in a vain attempt to stave off Commanville's business collapse. From then on he lived in Croisset in relative poverty, with little money to pay for the upkeep of his house and frequently threatened with eviction by his young relatives.

The sanctuary of his cherished family house, from which Louise had been so severely excluded, became a straitjacket that helped to speed his end.

On the morning of Saturday, May 8, 1881, on the eve of a trip to Paris, Flaubert took a hot bath and suddenly felt unwell. He shouted to his maid to fetch a doctor. "It's a good thing it's happening today," he told her. "It would have been a nuisance tomorrow, on the train." Those were his last coherent words. His legs gave way, and a few moments later he lost consciousness. By the time the doctor arrived, Flaubert's heart had stopped. The official diagnosis was apoplexy; but it could have been a final occurrence of the epilepsy that had plagued him much of his life and that his family, and Louise Colet, had so carefully concealed from the world.

Like Henriette Colet and Sand's daughter, Solange, Caroline Commanville countered her uncle's wishes for a secular funeral. Du Camp did not bother to come; but Émile Zola, Edmond de Goncourt, Alphonse Daudet, and the poet José Maria de Heredia were there, along with Maupassant, and after the church service they took turns holding the silver tassels of the coffin as the procession wound up the hill of Rouen's cemetery.

Flaubert was to be interred beside the tombs of his mother and father, his sister, Caroline, and other members of his family, but there was a mishap at the burial site. The funeral workers had dug a hole that was too short for the tall man's coffin; it got stuck on a slant, head down. The ropes slipped on the sides of the coffin. The gravediggers strained and cursed, but the coffin would not move. Caroline Commanville wrung her hands. "Enough, enough!" Zola cried out. It was decided that the task would be completed after the mourners had gone. A priest sprinkled holy water on the bier, and "the whole thirsty crowd made off down the hill toward the city"—Goncourt's description—"with eager, merry faces."

A festive dinner was offered at Croisset that night by Flaubert's relatives.

The first English-language edition of Madame Bovary appeared in London the following year. It was translated by a daughter of Karl Marx, Eleanor Aveling, who shortly after completing her translation attempted suicide by taking an overdose of opium. She was found unconscious, and revived, by her friend Havelock Ellis.

Ludovica Pradier

This lusty daughter of the aristocracy continued to carouse well into her fifties with some of Europe's most alluring rakes, traveling widely with her protectors. In the 1860s, she ran a hotel of suspect reputation in the sixteenth arrondissement. This establishment seems not to have lived up to her expectations, and in the 1870s, partially paralyzed, she spent most of her time with one of her married daughters in Brighton, England, and *then in a series of nursing homes. She was a devoted mother, and her children loved her. She died in 1886, aged seventy-two, and was buried in her family's vault at the Père Lachaise Cemetery, close to her father, former government minister Jean-Pierre-Joseph d'Arcet, who had invented gelatinous soups for the greater glory of France.*

The Daughter, Henriette

She survived her mother by forty years, dying in 1916 at the age of seventy-six. According to family chroniclers, at some point in her middle age Henriette chucked her docile, pious family life and eloped with a close friend of her mother's, the distinguished essayist and political activist Auguste Vacquerie, who was the brother of Victor Hugo's son-in-law and had shared much of the Hugo clan's exile in Guernsey.

There are two clues to support this version of Henriette's biography: her absence from the Bissieu family plot at Verneuil and the fact that in her middle years she frequently went by the name of Henriette Bissieu-Colet rather than Henriette Colet Bissieu. At least that is the way she signed her letters to the many literary historians she received in the decades after her mother's death.

Despite her often strained relations with her mother, Henriette proved to be a dedicated literary heir. She was devoted to Louise's memory, selling her manuscripts with shrewdness and with the sole aim of rehabilitating her mother's reputation. Beyond the portrait of Henriette left by the bibliophile Paul Mariéton in his personal notes, and her reputation as an avid theater fan who never missed the openings at the Comédie Française, there is little published information on Henriette aside from her obituary in the French press:

> *Many people had high esteem for this fetching old lady, always attired in a most original manner, whose gaze had remained most vivacious. . . . Those who knew her well said she was charming, very witty and cultivated. As soon as one gained her trust—which was not difficult—she talked volubly about her mother and the stars of her literary circle.*
>
> *In her account, she never lost a chance to deny the current legend that Louise Colet had martyrized Gustave Flaubert. She maintained that from the beginning of their liaison, Louise Colet had been a devoted friend and adviser to Flaubert, and even the best of collaborators. When they met, Flaubert was but an obscure provincial, ignorant*

of the Parisian literary life in which Madame Colet was already recognized and celebrated. He immediately benefited from the relations provided by this friend of Sainte-Beuve, Madame Récamier, Victor Cousin, Victor Hugo, etc.

Notwithstanding her filial piety, [Madame Colet-Bissieu] tried hard to be impartial and admitted that her mother had occasionally been unjust to Flaubert. "Poor Maman," she would say, "had a character which made everyone suffer."

The Niece, Caroline

Flaubert's niece grew to be very pious, puritanical, and rather cold. After the death, in 1890, of her first husband, Commanville, she married a prosperous doctor who had been in love with her for some years and became Madame Franklin-Groult. The Franklin-Groults soon moved to a beautiful house in Antibes, Villa Tanit (the name of the Carthaginian goddess in Salammbô), where Caroline spent the rest of her life reinforcing her uncle's reputation and drawing maximum financial profit from her collection of his manuscripts.

In the 1880s, Caroline tried to purchase from Henriette Bissieu-Colet her uncle's letters to Louise. Henriette refused to sell her the originals but allowed selected letters to be published on the condition that the tu be changed to vous throughout. Although the two women disliked each other intensely, they agreed to protect their families' reputations by deleting every hint of prurience from Gustave's letters and by disguising Louise Colet as "Madame X." It was not until the 1970s, in the Pléiade edition of his correspondence, that Flaubert's letters to Louise were published uncensored.

There is one accusation against the treacherous Caroline Commanville that I believe to be untrue: For decades, many biographers have assumed that Flaubert's prudish niece was the one who burned Louise's letters to Gustave. Recent research indicates that in her attempt to sanitize her uncle's image, Caroline, not finding any of Louise's letters among his papers, tried to purchase them from Henriette Bissieu and discovered that Henriette had never seen them either— they were quite simply missing.

Madame Franklin-Groult survived her second husband by a decade. She lived on in Antibes until her death in 1931, at the age of eighty-four. Her house, the Villa Tanit, became a shrine for Flaubertists from all parts of the world—including Edith Wharton, who visited Caroline shortly *before her death and found her alert, authoritarian, and highly opinionated.*

Victor Hugo

In 1883, the "Suprême Alligator" and Juliette Drouet, the once beautiful former actress who had shared his two decades of exile, celebrated the fiftieth anniversary of their liaison.

Hugo had survived the loss of most of his kin: the deaths of his older daughter, Léopoldine, and his wife, Adèle; the lifetime incarceration, in an asylum, of his daughter Dédé, who went insane after she eloped and left for America; the deaths of his two sons, Charles-Victor and François-Victor, the latter of whom he nursed through a long illness during the two years that followed his return from exile.

When he returned to Paris in 1870—he was then sixty-eight—Hugo resumed the frenzied sexual activity of his earlier years. Leaving Juliette Drouet at home in charge of his grandchildren, he went daily to a rented room, where several women of diverse milieus—from the basest streetwalkers to Paris's most illustrious grandes dames—awaited his sexual favors. "Through the window of his ground-floor room," so one eyewitness reported, "one could see, morning or night, naked bodies engaged in curious poses of coupling."

Hugo died on May 22, 1885, at the age of eighty-three, after a month of illness. To the immense delight of the French press, several hundred of whom camped in front of his house to report on every detail of his progress toward death, some of his last recorded words were "C'est ici le combat entre le jour et la nuit,"* a phrase he spoke repeatedly while pointing to his forehead and passing his hand over his brow.

Hugo received the most elaborate funeral in the history of France. Throughout the week preceding the burial, a major part of the citizenry wore black armbands in mourning for the poet. To the humiliation and fury of France's Catholic Church, the funeral rites remained strictly secular, according to his wishes. His body lay in state at the Arc de Triomphe on an immense catafalque designed for the occasion by Charles Garnier, the architect of the Paris Opera. To the accompaniment of Saint-Saëns's "Hymne à Victor Hugo," it was then carried in an eight-hour procession down the Champs Élysées, the Boulevard Saint-

---

* "It is here that the struggle between the forces of light and the forces of darkness is waged."

Germain and the Boulevard Saint-Michel to the Pantheon, thus restoring that building to the secular cult of "Great Men" for which the Revolution had intended it.

"The nineteenth century will be the century of Victor Hugo, just as the eighteenth was that of Voltaire," Le Figaro declared. Hugo's funeral was attended by some two million people, many of them coming from the provinces to witness the great man's last voyage. The event turned into a vast commercial enterprise: peddlers of wine and food, composers of popular songs, ambulating caravans of mountebanks, and carousing citizens gamboled throughout the day in the wooded alleys of the Champs Élysées; Paris residents whose flats looked out on the procession route rented standing room to the public, charging several hundred francs for a ground-floor window, several thousand for a balcony view.

Hugo's funeral transformed him, in the eyes of his contemporaries, into "a national symbol of the glory restored to France after the humiliation of 1870." But this magnificent, Dionysiac jamboree could also be seen as the definitive end of that libidinous epoch—the Romantic era— which had infused Louise Colet with so many of her illusions and delusions, her joys and her despairs, her fierce appetites and her modest glories.

Maxime Du Camp

Du Camp outlived most of his contemporaries, as cads often do. He continued to grind out volumes on his travels abroad, his travels in France, Paris's water systems, its transportation systems. A year before Flaubert's death, he was received into the Académie Française, an honor never awarded Gustave, who was thrust into "a state of limitless reverie."

There was an uproar in 1885 when Du Camp was asked by the Académie Française to pronounce its official funeral oration for Victor Hugo. A massive expression of outrage denied him that privilege: "We shall not allow . . . that cowardly and talentless wretch . . . to defile with his venomous eulogies the corpse of the man who saved our national honor," one newspaper warned in its editorial, referring to Du Camp's militancy against the Paris Commune. "We shall not allow . . . the greatest murderer in Paris after Thiers and Mac-Mahon to speak."

But Du Camp lived out the rest of his days in smug serenity. He died in 1894, at the age of seventy-two, while taking the waters in Baden-Baden, Germany. He had continued to revile Louise Colet at every opportunity, setting up the rules for Colet-bashing for a century to come—he even distorted the facts of Louise's death, as he had almost every fact of her life.

She came to die in Paris in 1875 [sic], a powerful spirit, denying everything, since she herself was a negation; wishing to surround her coffin with a renown she had never had while alive, she wrote out her last testament and demanded a civic burial. She was obeyed. Her body was transported to God knows what village of the Paris suburbs, and, at seven A.M., it was dumped in a corner of the cemetery; no one noticed it. . . .

Epilogue II

❧⚬❧

CONCERNING LOUISE

"*Madame Colet's agitated existence has come to an end,*" Le Courier de France *stated upon her death.* "*All one can say is that she was brilliant and that she was made pleasing to us by that rare attribute: sincerity in passion. . . .*"

Le Bien Public: "*After years of tragic ingratitude, now that [Madame Colet's] merits can be judged impartially, one begins to think that her champions were more astute than her adversaries.*"

La Gironde: "*The feverish life of poor Louise Colet has come to an end. Hers was not a banal soul, and all she would have needed to take her place among the highest rank of our illustrious women was a calmer spirit. But always tormented by the need to draw attention to herself, she dispersed herself in hasty and imperfect works. . . . [She] had the great misfortune to lack a sense of measure . . . yet one must never forget that she had a very strong dedication to noble causes and that at a time of shameful moral decadence, she was distinguished by her proud and independent spirit.*"

L'Illustration: "*[Madame Colet] had a militant intelligence, a versatile* talent which merits attention. . . . After a laborious existence, Madame Collet [sic] died without having made a fortune; but she at least left us works which merited her triumphs, and which without a doubt will remain in the canon of our recent literature."

From one of her colleagues, the popular poet Théodore de Banville: "Madame Louise Colet deserves to be counted among the fine lyric poets of our time. She had remarkable and singular poetic gifts which assured her a place of her own; and while other illustrious women sang of the bitterness of life, the deceptions of love, the sadness of bygone youth . . . Madame Colet . . . was exceptionally possessed with that supreme quality of all robust poetry, joy. . . . Her tomb merits a branch, however slender and frail, of the divine laurel."

And then a very private obituary from Flaubert, writing to Edma Roger des Genettes:

"You can well guess how affected I was by news of my poor Muse's death. The memory of her, thus revived, forced me to relive the years. . . . I trod on so many things in order to survive! One more end! Do you remember the little apartment on the Rue de Sèvres? And all the rest? Ah! Misery on us all!"

Notes

❧

In translating Colet's poetry, I have used several alternatives:

Since it is not a striking exemplar of French romantic verse, I render her earlier poetry directly into English.

The poems of her later years, which are more vigorous and terse, are rendered in both languages, for the French text is essential to communicate their satiric intent.

Unless otherwise specified, I have worked exclusively from the French originals of the manuscripts I have quoted from, and all the translations are mine.

Prologue

15 "chair and left": Flaubert studies abound with descriptions of this last meeting by Louise's fireplace. On this occasion, according to Flaubert, the poet's foot repeatedly hit her lover's leg while she accused him of having just visited "the red-light district," and he was flooded with fantasies of hitting her with a burning log but desisted because of his fear of a trial. One of the earliest, and most cogent, accounts of this encounter was published in Jules Troubat's *Notes et pensées* (Paris: Librairie Générale de L. Sauvaitre, 1888), pp. 128–29.

16 is nearly finished: The account of this letter-burning episode is by its witness, Guy de Maupassant. Collected in *Les Jours de Flaubert,* ed. Georges-Émile Bertrand (Paris: Éditions du Myrte, 1947), pp. 198–200. The only Flaubertist who seems to have taken note of this account of Maupassant's is Hermia Oliver, author of the excellent *Flaubert and an English Governess* (Oxford: Clarendon Press, 1980). Flaubert's other biographers—Enid Starkie, Benjamin Bart, among many others—do not seem to have been acquainted with Maupassant's memoir, for I have not seen it listed in any bibliographies outside of Miss Oliver's.

1. Provence

19 "rich in trade": Louise Colet, "Aix," in *Poésies complètes* (Paris: Librairie de Charles Gosselin, 1854).

19 it in 1831: Cited in Dr. Benassis, "Essais de clinique littéraire: Les Amis de Flaubert," *Les Alcoloides,* December 1950, pp. 5–15.

19 "die of boredom": *Histoire d'Aix-en-Provence,* ed. Marcel Bernos, Noel Coulet, et al. (Aix-en-Provence: Edisud, 1978), p. 336.

20 "thousand miles apart": Ibid., p. 344.

22 "her sisters' enmity": *Les Belles Femmes de Paris et de la province* (anonymous, Paris, 1847), pp. 368–69.

23 "sarcasm and mockery": Ibid. pp. 369–70.

24 "to her daughter": Colet, "Aix," in *Poésies complètes*.

26 "and pedantic education": Eugène de Mirecourt, *Les Contemporains, Louise Colet* (Paris: Gustave Havard, 1857), p. 10.

27 "soul wasted away": Colet, "Fleurs du Midi," in *Poésies complètes*.

28 "pain of reality": Colet, *L'Italie des Italiens*, vol. I (Paris: É. Dentu, 1862), p. 14.

30 "we bought peace": Micheline Bood and Serge Grand, *L'Indomptable Louise Colet* (Paris: Pierre Horay, 1986), p. 27. This biography was left unfinished at the time of the death of Micheline Bood, a great-great-grandniece of Louise Colet, and completed by M. Grand. Madame Bood owned an extensive file of documents concerning Colet, which was not available to any chronicler of Colet's life until her book's publication.

32 "soothing my sorrows . . .": Colet, "Paris," in *Poésies complètes*.

32 "and of friendship . . .": Colet, *Poésies complètes*.

33 "cultivated for me": Colet, "Le Legs," in *Ce qui est dans le coeur des femmes* (Paris: Librairie Nouvelle, 1852).

34 "loving friend, Henriette": Bood, *Colet,* p. 25.

34 "bit more selfish . . .": Ibid.

2. To Paris!

38 "victim of genius!": Jean Reboul, *Poésies* (Paris, 1840), pp. 170–72.

38 "crown your memory": Colet, "À Monsieur Canonge," Bibliothèque de Nîmes, ms. 492, fol. 258. Cited in Joseph Jackson, *Louise Colet et ses amis littéraires* (New Haven: Yale University Press, 1937).

39 "May 19, 1833": Ibid., fol. 252.

39 "ideal love: Orient!": Arsène Thévenot, "Souvenirs des Baux," in *Méridionales: Poésies intimes* (Arles, 1835).

42 "a young artist?": Bood, p. 32.

42 "unite our Loves": Ibid.

43 "honor and *glory*": Ibid.

45 "more to Hippolyte. . . .": Ibid., p. 34.

46 and golf resort: The Hotel de Servanes is given two stars in *Guide des auberges de campagne et hôtels de charme en France,* ed. Alexis Nabokov, Julien Bauer, and Colombe Schneck (Paris: Rivages, 1991), p. 359. "The two hundred hectares of this beautiful Provençal domain, which has remained in the same family for five generations, is planted with several thousand cypresses and olive trees," the editors tell us. "The hotel has a most entrancing old-fashioned aura. . . . The rooms have charm . . . and retain a seductive sense of antiquity."

48 "throughout her life": Colet, *Deux Mois d'émotions* (Paris: W. Coquebert, 1843), p. 106.

3. Her Conquest of the Capital

52 "of our institutions": Delphine de Girardin, *Chroniques parisiennes,* 1836–1848 (Paris: Éditions des Femmes, 1986), p. 224.

52 "relieve conjugal tedium": Dominique Desanti, *Daniel, ou Le Visage secret d'une comtesse romantique: Marie d'Agoult* (Paris: Stock, 1980), p. 20.

53 "many little troubles": Bood, p. 27.

54 "of early youth. . . .": Colet, *Italie des Italiens,* vol. I, pp. 107–20.

55 "have called Poetry!": Mirecourt, *Louise Colet,* pp. 17–21.

57 serene platonic friendship: Desanti, *Daniel,* p. 185.

57 "influenced by Lamartine": J. Bonnerot, "À la Poursuite d'un article; ou, Trente Ans de la vie de Sainte-Beuve et de la belle Madame Colet," *La Muse française* XII (October 15, 1933), pp. 429–46.

58 "to predict yours": Bood, p. 42.

59 "and uncommon facility": Ibid.

59 "a future life": Cited in [Émile] Auriant, *L'Envers d'une muse* (Paris: Oeuvres Nouvelles Libres, 1938), p. 209.

61 his wife's head: Barbey d'Aurevilly, *Les Bas-Bleus* (Paris: V. Palmé, 1878), p. 250.

62 "of my judges": Louise Colet, *Réponse aux "Guêpes" de M. Alphonse Karr* (Paris: Hurtau, 1869), pp. 5–6.

63 "of our parliament": *Les Belles Femmes de Paris,* pp. 362–66.

64 "and popular lies": *Revue de Paris* VI (1839), p. 68.

64 somber little musician: *Les Alcoloides.*

65 "in French philosophy": D. G. Charlton, *The French Romantics* (Cambridge: Cambridge University Press, 1974), vol. I, p. 35.

66 engineered her award: This slander was particularly elaborated by a fairly eminent Flaubertiste of the prewar era, Gérard-Gailly, in his book *Les Véhémences de Madame Colet.* It remained unquestioned by other literary historians until it was magisterially dismantled by Colet's first responsible biographer, Yale professor Joseph Jackson, in his *Louise Colet et ses amis littéraires.*

66 "a young woman": Colet, *Réponse aux "Guêpes,"* pp. 6–7.

67 "two P.M. Memory!": Louise de Wieclawik, "Victor Cousin amoureux et critique littéraire," *Revue des sciences humaines,* no. 140 (October–December 1970), pp. 531–40.

69 "his only justice. . . .": Louise Colet, *La Jeunesse de Goethe* (Paris: Imprimeries de Vve. Dondey-Dupré, n.d.).

69 "is not powerful": *Revue de Paris,* June 30, 1839, pp. 352–53.

69 "all this, Madame!": Guy de Molènes, "Simples Essais d'histoire littéraire," I. "Les Femmes Poètes," *Revue des deux mondes,* July 1, 1842, pp. 48–76.

70 *Gustave Flaubert:* cited in *La Femme au XIXe siècle,* ed. Nicole Priollaud (Paris: Liana Levi et Sylvie Messinger, 1983), pp. 194, 53, 237.

70 *Pierre-Joseph Proudhon:* Cited in *Misérable et glorieuse: La Femme du XIXe siècle,* ed. Jean-Paul Aron (Paris: Éditions Complexe, 1980), p. 227.

71 of both sexes: Maïte Albistur and Daniel Armogathe, *Histoire du féminisme français* (Paris: Éditions des Femmes, 1977), p. 227.

71 *"Girls to Read":* Ibid., p. 235.

72 "men and wine": Ibid., p. 236.

72 "of paternal justice": Pierre-Joseph Proudhon, *La Pornocratie; ou, Les Temps modernes,* 1875, cited in *Histoire de la vie privée,* IV. *De la Révolution à la Grande Guerre,* ed. Philippe Ariès and Georges Duby (Paris: Seuil, 1985), p. 122.

73 Alphonse Karr: Cited in Priollaud, *La Femme,* pp. 178, 17, 205.

73 "speaking of her. . . .": d'Aurevilly, *Les Bas-Bleus,* pp. 237–52.

73 Allusions to "bluestocking" women were so frequent and derogatory in nineteenth-century France that an etymology of the term is in order: As far as I've been able to determine, it was coined in England in the eighteenth century to emphasize the abundance of ink that stained the hands and clothing of women authors. But many nineteenth-century French writers gave the phrase overtones of bodily filth and general slovenliness. D'Aurevilly, for instance, tells us that the euphemism was coined to describe women who were so obsessed with improving their minds that they had no time to wash.

73–74 and to divorce: An amusing sidelight on the terms for separation or divorce in nineteenth-century France: The only time it was granted upon a wife's wish was for "perverseness" such as sodomy, an admission most women were reluctant to publicize with medical proof in courts of law. Certain male fancies, such as enforced oral penetration, may have been harder to prove; yet one of the more famous divorce cases of the nineteenth century concerned a wife who, upon her mother's advice, had savagely bit into her husband's penis and succeeded in obtaining an injunction that forced her husband to display his wound in court. Laure Adler, *Secrets de l'alcove: Histoire du couple de 1830 à 1930* (Paris: Hachette, 1983).

75 Alexandre Dumas, *fils:* Cited in Priollaud, *La Femme,* pp. 192, 93–94, 191, 238, 236.

4. Penserosa

78 "subject for poetry": Théodore de Banville, *Critiques,* ed. Victor Barrucand (Paris: Bibliothèque Charpentier, 1917), p. 146.

78 "my blond hair!": Colet, *Poésies complètes.*

78 "and sonorous touch": *Revue des deux mondes,* December 1, 1839, pp. 709–11.

79 Cited in Jean-Paul Clébert, *Louise Colet ou la muse* (Paris: Presses de la Renaissance, 1986), p. 263.

80 replied in outrage: André Maurois, *Olympio; The Life of Victor Hugo* (New York: Carrol & Graf, 1956), p. 173.

80 "man of letters": *Les Guêpes,* May 1840, June 1840, September 1840.

80 "its godfather. Well!": *Les Guêpes,* May 1840.

82 "into the world": Colet, *Réponse aux "Guêpes."*

83 "are terrible housekeepers": *Les Guêpes,* September 1840.

84 "in his soul!": Fonds Louise Colet, Bibliothèque Municipale d'Avignon, ms. 6.421, fol. 10. The *Fonds Louise Colet,* or Colet Archives, is a 6,000-page collection of Colet documents which was donated in the early twentieth century to Avignon's municipal library, whose holdings were then housed in the Musée Calvet. In 1984 all of the municipal library's collections were transferred to the ancient Collège des Jésuites d'Avignon, a superb fourteenth-century building which has recently been restored and renamed the Médiathèque Ceccano. The Fonds Colet contains, among other treasures, some 250 pages of Gustave Flaubert's letters to Louise Colet and an extensive correspondence with (among many others) Alfred de Vigny, Leconte de Lisle, Victor Cousin, several members of her family, and hundreds of her contemporaries. (See the last pages of my chapter 17 for a detailed account of the formation of the Colet Archives.)

The Fonds Colet is accessible only on microfilm. Since this medium often makes the folio numbers illegible, I have been able to note them only when I could read them, and have occasionally been forced to contain my footnotes to the manuscript number.

84 "soon as possible": Félix Chambon, "Deux Passions d'un philosophe," *Annales romantiques* I (1904), p. 41.

84 "of your claws": Cited in Mlle de Mestral-Combremont, *La Belle Madame Colet, une Déesse des Romantiques* (Paris: Fontemoing et Cie, 1913), pp. 71–72.

85 "us to comprehend": Jackson, *Louise Colet*, p. 113.

85 "works of Corneille. . . .": Fonds Colet, ms. 6.412, fol. 5.325–5.336.

86 "express my gratitude. . . .": Ibid., fol. 5.218–5.221.

89 "which bore me": George Sand, *Correspondance,* vol. V, ed. Georges Lubin (Paris: Garnier, 1969), letter of November 19, 1841.

91 "shall outdo you": All subsequent quotes from this play are cited from Colet's *Charlotte Corday et Madame Roland* (Paris: Berquet et Pétion, 1842).

92 "to their beliefs": Sand, *Correspondance,* vol. VI, letter of February 15, 1843.

93 "on their side": Ibid., letter of February 28, 1843.

93 "poor in spirit": Ibid., letter of February 18, 1843.

94 "lose without regret. . . .": Ibid., letter of February 19, 1843.

5. Three Great Friendships

96 "men's idiotic pretensions. . . .": Louise Colet, ed., *Quarante-cinq Lettres de Béranger* (Paris: Librairie Nouvelle, 1857), p. 41.

97 "for Mme Colet": Cited in Jackson, *Louise Colet*, p. 109.

98 "another careful reading. . . .": Colet, *Quarante-Cinq Lettres,* p. 42.

99 "a deaf woman": Ibid., p. 21.

99 "address a madwoman": Bood, *Colet,* p. 60.

99 "most docile lamb": Ibid.

100 "forewarned, Benedict Révoil": Ibid., pp. 57–58.

100 "the sun's heat": Colet, *Deux Mois d'émotions,* preface, p. vi.

101 "have received me": Ibid., pp. 163–71.

102 "tracks of Byron": Molènes, "Les Femmes Poètes."

104 "half an hour": Beth Archer Brombert, *Cristina: Portrait of a Princess* (New York: Knopf, 1977), p. 82.

106 "before making poets": Colet, *Quarante-cinq Lettres,* pp. 65–66.

107 "this proud genius!": Louise Colet, *Quatre Poèmes couronnés par l'Académie Française* (Paris: Librairie Nouvelle, 1855).

107 "of being beautiful": Charles-Augustin Sainte-Beuve, *Chroniques parisiennes* (Paris: Calmann-Lévy, 1876), July 28, 1843, p. 79.

107 "that is irremediable": Colet, *Quarante-cinq Lettres,* p. 47.

108 "to their limit": Cited in Jackson, *Louise Colet,* p. 112.

109 "Enslaved yet unconquerable": Louise Colet, *Réveil de la Pologne* (Paris: A. René, 1846).

110 "to my shoulders": All entries from Louise Colet's "Mementos" cited in this volume come from the Fonds Colet, Bibliothèque Municipale d'Avignon, mss. 6.416 and 6.417.

112 "a special gift": Raoul-Rochette, *Notice historique sur la vie et les ouvrages de M. Pradier* (Paris, 1853), cited in Douglas Siler, *Statues de chair: Sculptures de James Pradier* (Paris: Éditions de la Réunion des Musées Nationaux, 1986), p. 15.

113 "flights and inebriations": *Flaubert et Louise Pradier: Le Texte intégral des Mémoires de Madame Ludovica,* ed. Douglas Siler, *Archives des lettres modernes,* no. 145, 1973.
114 "flaws and modesty": Siler, *Statues de chair,* p. 358.

6. Lui
116 "with her father": Jean-Paul Sartre, *L'Idiot de la famille,* vol. I (Paris: Gallimard, 1971), p. 85.
116 "yet another cadaver": Letter to Louise Colet, July 7, 1853.
Unless otherwise noted, throughout this book all quotes from Flaubert's letters, and most of his friends' and relatives' letters to him, are cited from volumes I and II of Jean Bruneau's peerless edition of the writer's correspondence: *Gustave Flaubert: Correspondance* (Paris: Gallimard, Bibliothèque de la Pléiade, 1973 and 1981). The translations are mine.
116 "she is digesting": Caroline Flaubert to Gustave, November 25, 1843.
118 "torrent of flames": Flaubert to Colet, September 2, 1853.
118 "or firework explosions": Flaubert to Ernest Chevalier, June 7, 1844.
118 "to be *un*well": Flaubert to Alfred de Poittevin, May 3, 1845.
119 "removed the wound": Flaubert to Chevalier, late January 1846.
120 "as a trumpet": Excerpts from Maxime Du Camp, *Souvenirs littéraires,* in preface to Gustave Flaubert, *Oeuvres complètes,* vol. I, ed. Bernard Masson (Paris: Seuil, 1964), p. 19.
120 "To have erections!": Flaubert to Colet, July 15, 1853.
120 "exchange of letters": Jules and Edmond de Goncourt, *Journal,* vol. I (Paris: Laffont, 1989), entry of February 20, 1860.
121 "birth unto death": Flaubert to Chevalier, 1829–1830.
121 "and children survive": Ibid., April 22, 1832.
121 "write them down": Ibid., January 31, 1832.
121 "we call life": Ibid., August 29, 1834.
121 "embraced each other": Gustave Flaubert, *Bouvard et Pécuchet* (Paris: Laffont, 1981), p. 680.
122 of his poems: Cited in Sartre, *L'Idiot,* vol. I, p. 1005.
122 "and continual yawns. . . .": Flaubert to Chevalier, November 14, 1840.
122 "achievement of mankind": Flaubert to Colet, August 6–7, 1846.
123 "emotions toward you": Maxime Du Camp to Flaubert, October 2, 1844, vol. I, appendix I, of Flaubert's *Correspondance.*
123 "and socratize you": Unpublished letters from Poittevin to Flaubert, cited in Roger Kempf, "Le Double Pupitre," *Les Cahiers du chènevis,* October 15, 1969.
123 "like a man": Du Camp to Flaubert, May 15, 1844, vol. I, appendix I, of Flaubert's *Correspondance.*
124 "on your eulogies": Poittevin to Flaubert, July 15, 1842, vol. I, appendix IV, of Flaubert's *Correspondance.*
124 "to this woman": Ibid., August 6, 1842.
124 "your cock intact": Ibid., March 18, 1843.
125 "pile of shit": Flaubert to Chevalier, April 15, 1839.
125 *"which terrifies me":* Flaubert to his mother, December 15, 1850.
125 "her natural element": Cited in Siler, *Mémoires de Madame Ludovica,* p. 169.
126 "a mistress, etc.": Kempf, "Le Double Pupitre," p. 125.

126 "all our moderns": Flaubert to Colet, August 30, 1846.

126 "not entice me": Flaubert to Poittevin, May 16, 1845.

126 "I've tried it": Ibid., June 17, 1845.

129 *"a great deal":* Flaubert to Colet, June 1, 1853.

130 *"she afterwards kissed. . . .":* Du Camp to Flaubert, August–September 1851, vol. II, appendix I, of Flaubert's *Correspondance.*

131 *"prove her affection. . . .":* Ibid., October 6, 1851.

131 *"and the daughter?":* Ibid., September 22, 1851.

7. Love Letters

133 " 'will help you' ": Gabrielle Réval, *Les Grandes Amoureuses romantiques* (Paris: Albin Michel, 1928), pp. 30–31.

135 "of *The Tempest":* Both of the following translations are in *"Jules César et la Tempête,* traduction française en regard par M. Jay et Madame Louise Colet" (Paris: Bibliothèque Anglo-Française, 1839).

138 "like cello strings": Flaubert to Colet, August 15, 1846.

138 "speaking mad words": Ibid., August 13, 1846.

139 "old bear's skin": Flaubert to his sister Caroline, December 20, 1843.

139 "place my heart": Flaubert to Colet, August 4–5, 1846.

140 "arm, your face. . . .": Ibid., August 6–7, 1846.

141 "kisses, everywhere, *everywhere":* Ibid.

142 lock of hair: Sartre, *L'Idiot.*

143 "a thousand kisses": Flaubert to Colet, August 8–9, 1846.

143 "day to night": Ibid., August 9, 1846.

144 "one, till soon!": Ibid., August 11, 1846.

144 "to your visitors": Ibid., August 14–15, 1846.

144 "at the memory": Ibid.

144 "on, long night!": Ibid., August 18, 1846.

145 "down your breast": Ibid., August 20–21, 1846.

145 "a few times": Ibid., August 23, 1846.

145 "touch them again. . . .": Ibid.

145 "mother needs me": Ibid., August 30, 1846.

146 *"toi, sur toi":* Ibid., September 2, 1846.

146 "me at all": Ibid., September 5, 1846.

146 "me, Bite me!": Ibid., September 10, 1846.

147 "their moist pressure": Ibid., September 12, 1846.

147 "transports, demented passions": Goncourt, *Journal,* vol. I, entry of February 21, 1862.

148 "a great shudder": Gustave Flaubert, *Madame Bovary* (Paris: Classiques Garnier, 1961), p. 262.

148 "the entire hotel": Maurice Donnay, *La Vie amoureuse d'Alfred de Musset* (Paris: Flammarion, 1926), p. 182.

148 "take greater care": Flaubert to Colet, August 24, 1846.

148 "have any posterity!": Ibid., September 15–16, 1846.

149 "come to Paris": Ibid., September 4, 1846.

149 "rid of them": Ibid., September 24, 1846.

149 "other life lasts": Ibid., August 27–28, 1846.

149 "satisfy your desires?": Ibid., December 16, 1846.
149 "hearts of others": Ibid., end of December 1846.
149 of the page: Ibid.
149 "any great reward": Ibid., September 2, 1846.
151 "of the soul": Ibid., March 27, 1853.
151 "of blood lost": Flaubert to Louis Bouilhet, June 16, 1850. One should note that this concept of sexual intercourse as weakening and debilitating to the male organism was not particular to Flaubert, but prevailed throughout nineteenth-century Europe. In this view, any substantial loss of semen, whether through marital or extramarital sex, could lead to "languor of mind, confusion of ideas, and inability to control the thoughts"—a concept which could readily encourage male writers to opt for bachelorhood. These theories of spermatic economy are succinctly described in Steven Marcus's *The Other Victorians* (New York: Basic Books, 1966), pp. 25–28.
151 "me with life": Cited in the footnotes to the Pléiade edition of Flaubert's *Correspondance,* vol. I, p. 1011.
151 "illuminate their boudoir": Flaubert to Colet, April 24, 1852.
152 "of the strong": Ibid., December 28, 1853.
152 "died of rape": Ibid., March 11, 1853.
152 "in any need": Ibid., September 26, 1846.

8. Tempests

154 "in my arms": Flaubert to Colet, October 23, 1846.
155 "of the Beautiful": Ibid., September 14, 1846.
155 "second rank women": Ibid., end of December 1846.
156 "him too much": Du Camp to Colet, vol. I, appendix III, of Flaubert's *Correspondance,* December 18, 1846.
156 "for accompanying you!": Ibid., December 1846.
156 "already agreed on ": Ibid., January 3, 1847.
156 "trip to Brittany?": Ibid., before January 21, 1847.
156 "to be amused": Ibid., February 16, 1847.
157 "in violet silk. . . .": Flaubert to Poittevin, April 2, 1845.
157 "new these days": Ibid., May 13, 1845.
158 "another crisis today": Du Camp to Colet, February 21, 1847, vol. I, appendix III, of Flaubert's *Correspondance.*
158 old friend Ludovica: Flaubert to Colet, March 7, 1847.
159 "line, and sinker": Du Camp toFlaubert, July 31, 1847, vol. I, appendix I, of Flaubert's *Correspondance.*
159 "trip to Rouen": Du Camp to Flaubert, August 1847.
159 "with him seriously": Du Camp to Flaubert, December 26–27, 1847.
159 " 'shocking.' Poor Ludovica!": Flaubert to Du Camp, late May 1848.
160 " 'of you, adieu' ": Flaubert to Colet, July 7, 1847.
161 "the Bibliothèque Nationale": Ibid., August 16, 1847.
161 "others of pipes": Ibid., February 27, 1847.
161 "God knows what": Ibid., November 7, 1847.
162 "very platonic friend . . .": Colet to Flaubert, November 9, 1847.
164 "be more stupid": Flaubert to Colet, March 1848.
164 "you a kiss": Ibid., March 18, 1848.

165 "on his account": Flaubert to Du Camp, April 7, 1848.

166 "made people laugh": Gustave Flaubert, *L'Éducation sentimentale* (Paris: Bibliothèque Charpentier, 1922), vol. II, p. 106.

167 "memory. Yours, G.": Flaubert to Colet, August 25, 1848.

9. The Years Without Him

169 All of Victor Cousin's letters to Louise Colet are preserved at the Fonds Louise Colet, Bibliothèque Municipale d'Avignon, ms. 6.405 and 6.406.

This immense correspondence comprises some 1,500 folio pages, mostly undated. The year of these letters' provenance can only be approximated by their references to events in Louise's life. So unless they have been published in a periodical that establishes a precise date, I shall not attempt to provide footnotes for each of the many letters from Cousin cited in this text.

169 "bring her home. . . .": Musée Paul Arbaud, Aix-en-Provence, Dossier Colet 1160.A.1.

169 "terrible for women": The Fonds Colet at Avignon's Médiathèque Ceccano contains some 150 folio pages of Marceline Desbordes-Valmore's letters to Louise Colet, ms. 6.407, fol. 2.843–2.991. Like Cousin's correspondence, most of these missives are undated, and I shall not attempt to footnote them.

170 "our bond": Cited in Mestral-Combremont, *La Belle Madame Colet*, pp. 80–83.

170 "most sacred regrets": Colet, *Ce qui est dans les coeurs des femmes*, pp. 19–21.

173 "motion against you": Colet, *Quarante-cinq Lettres, Louise Colet*, p. 83.

173 "Christians accuse her": Jackson, *Louise Colet*, p. 158.

173 "Manzoni, Silvio Pellico. . . .": Ibid., p. 152.

177 "a homosexual's preference": Cited in Clébert, p. 192.

180 "your transparent teeth": Bood, *Colet*, p. 90.

183 "most serene glory. . . .": Ibid., p. 96.

184 "within our love": Ibid., p. 97.

184 "let you sleep. . . .": Ibid., p. 100.

10. Flaubert in Egypt, and Back

187 come back later: Flaubert's visits to Kuchuk Hanem, and all episodes relating to her, are reconstructed in great detail in [Émile] Auriant, "Histoire de Safia, dite Koutchouk-Hanem, Almée d'Esneh," *Les Marges*, June 26, 1926.

Spellings of "Koutchouk-Hanem" vary widely throughout Flaubert biographies. I have chosen Francis Steegmuller's transliteration, "Kuchuk Hanem." *Flaubert in Egypt*, trans. and ed. by Francis Steegmuller (Chicago: Academy Publishers, 1972). Throughout this chapter, I have also followed Steegmuller's translations of Flaubert's letters from Egypt.

187 "women of letters. . . ! ! !": In view of the derision with which Flaubert referred to "learned women" in general (and to Louise in particular) throughout his correspondence with his male friends, this is obviously a reference to Louise.

188 "to be present": Flaubert to Bouilhet, March 13, 1850.

189 "with the sound": Ibid., January 15, 1850.

189 times with delight: Excerpts from Du Camp, *Souvenirs littéraires*, in preface to Flaubert, *Oeuvres complètes*, p. 28.

190 "I enjoyed it": Flaubert to Bouilhet, March 13, 1850.

191 "to be repeated": Ibid., June 2, 1850.

191 "have a rival": Flaubert to his mother, December 15, 1850.

192 "grasping his cock": Flaubert to Bouilhet, November 14, 1850.

193 " 'count on me' ": Louise seems to have merged two different letters of Flaubert's (see pp. 140 and 164 of my text). Flaubert's phrasing, in his letter of August 6–7, 1846, had been the following: "I am devoted to you for life. . . . That is an oath, keep it in mind, use it." On March 18, 1848, in the second-to-last letter he wrote her before breaking off the first phase of their liaison, he wrote: "Whatever happens, always count on me. Even at the time when . . . we shall never see each other, there will remain a link between us that can never be dissolved."

196 "is much admired": *Gazette anecdotique,* "Lettres inédites de Louise Colet," vol. I (1881), p. 268.

197 " 'to you kindly' ": Flaubert's use of quotation marks implies that he is citing words from an earlier letter of Louise's.

11. Amor Nel Cor

199 "of seeing things": Flaubert to Colet, January 15, 1852.

200 "reach their culmination": Ibid., December 9, 1852.

200 "with our dreams": Ibid.

200 "rhythmic and sonorous": Ibid., July 22, 1852.

200 "of ancient literature": Ibid., April 24, 1852.

200 "reach to gibberish!": Ibid., July 6, 1852.

200 "like a demigod": Ibid., August 21, 1853.

201 "with each other": Ibid., September 19, 1852.

201 be officially acknowledged: Jean Bruneau, preface to vol. I of Flaubert's *Correspondance,* p. xviii, footnote 2.

201 "details I need": Flaubert to Colet, March 3, 1852.

203 "would an angel's": Victor Hugo to Louise Colet, September 29, 1852.

All correspondence between Hugo and Colet quoted throughout the rest of this volume is cited from the extensive collection of their letters edited by Gustave Simon, "Victor Hugo et Louise Colet," in *Revue de France,* May 15, 1926.

203 "in higher spheres": Hugo to Colet, December 12, 1852.

204 "Famous Childhoods": Louise Colet, *Enfances célèbres* (Paris: L. Hachette, 1854).

205 "our only grandeur!": Colet, *Ce qui est dans le coeur des femmes.*

207 "in deep suffering": Colet to Hugo, December 8, 1852.

207 "all honest souls": Hugo to Colet, March 17, 1853.

207 "truly have genius": Colet to Hugo, November 17, 1852.

207 "to your person": Flaubert to Hugo, June 2, 1853.

208 "your mother's hands": Du Camp to Flaubert, October 29, 1851, vol. II, appendix I, of Flaubert's *Correspondance.*

209 "covered with shit": Flaubert to Du Camp, June 26, 1852.

210 "and in you": Flaubert to Colet, June 23, 1853.

210 "*on* your sides": Ibid., July 22, 1852.

210 "a thousand kisses": Ibid., January 2, 1854.

210 "angered by it": Ibid., December 31, 1851.

210 "I search for": Ibid., September 19, 1852.

211 "through such agony": Ibid., December 11, 1852.

213 "of my days": Ibid., March 20, 1852.

214 "live in Paris!": Bouilhet to Colet, June 14, 1852.

Bouilhet's correspondence with Louise is so crucial to the denouement of her affair with Flaubert that a professor at the University of Rouen has devoted a 180-page book to it: *Louis Bouilhet: Lettres à Louise Colet,* edited and commented on by Marie-Claire Bancquart and a group of her students (Paris: Presses Universitaires de France, 1973). All future references to Bouilhet's letters to Louise will be cited from this volume.

214 "love and sensuality": Louise Colet copied this letter of Cousin's into a memento dated November 1852.

216 "covered her corsage. . . .": Cited in Hélène Frejlich, *Les Amants de Mantes* (Paris: Sfelt, 1936), pp. 23–24.

217 "the Latin Quarter": "Ignotus" (Baron de Platel), "Une Muse," in *Échos de Paris,* ca. 1857, Louise Colet file at the women's history center at Médiathèque Marguerite Durand, Paris.

217 "day as ours": Colet, *Italie des Italiens,* vol. I, pp. 113–16.

218 Barbey d'Aurevilly: Cited in Priollaud, *La Femme,* p. 222.

218 Eugène de Mirecourt: Mirecourt, *Louise Colet,* p. 10.

218 Joseph de Maistre: Cited in Albistur and Armogathe, *Histoire du féminisme français,* p. 244.

218 "for political office": Flaubert, *L'Éducation sentimentale,* vol. II, p. 133.

218 and wealthy men: The significance of Flaubert's Mademoiselle Vatnaz is elaborated in a superb book by the French scholar Luce Czyba: *La Femme dans les romans de Flaubert: Mythes et idéologie* (Lyons: Presses Universitaires de Lyons, 1983), pp. 187–97.

219 "to scandalous loves": Molènes, "Les Femmes Poètes," pp. 48–76.

219 "forced to explore": Ibid.

220 Charles Baudelaire: Baudelaire, *Oeuvres complètes* (Paris: Gallimard, Bibliothèque de la Pléiade, 1976). Quoted in *Displacements: Women, Traditions and Literatures in French,* ed. Joan DeJean and Nancy K. Miller (Baltimore: John Hopkins University Press, 1991), p. 164.

220 Jules and Edmond de Goncourt: Cited in Priollaud, *La Femme.*

220 Barbey d'Aurevilly: *Les Bas-Bleus,* p. 242–43.

221 "Gyp" or "Scamp": *Femmes de lettres au XIXe siècle: Autour de Louise Colet,* ed. Roger Bellet (Lyons: Presses Universitaires de Lyons, 1982), pp. 249–78.

221 *"de son patronyme":* Marie-Claude Schapira, "Peut-on encore lire *La Servante* de Louise Colet?" in Bellet, p. 73.

222 Barbey d'Aurevilly: *Les Bas-Bleus,* p. 343.

222 Frédéric Soulié: Priollaud, *La Femme,* p. 91.

222 Maxime Du Camp: Excerpts from *Souvenirs littéraires,* in *Revue des deux mondes,* August 15, 1882, p. 733.

222 Louise Colet: *Le Poème de la femme:* "La Servante" (Paris: Perrotin, 1854).

12. Fantasio and Stello

224 "come from heaven": Donnay, *Musset,* p. 18.

224 *"mon front incliné":* Alfred de Musset, "Une Promenade au Jardin des Plantes," in *Poésies postumes* (Paris: Seuil, 1963).

227 "kill George Sand. . . .": Flaubert to Colet, July 3, 1852.

227 "admiring the moon": Ibid., July 6, 1852.

227 "is insulting me": Ibid., July 12, 1852.

230 "my spirit opens": Ibid., February 23, 1853.

231 writer's 1847 seizure: See Du Camp's letter to Louise of February 16, 1847, cited in chapter 8.

231 "can enhance it": Flaubert to Colet, October 9, 1852.

231 "said of monuments": Ibid., December 16, 1852.

232 "not your glands": Ibid., April 15, 1853.

233 "would be better": Ibid., end of February 1852.

234 "been stuffed yet?": Ibid., November 29, 1853.

234 "by someone else?": Ibid., March 9, 1853.

234 named Beatrix Person: In the summer of the subsequent year (1854), several weeks after he last saw Louise, Flaubert would write Bouilhet: "The per[son] is getting out of hand, says I've blown it all, etc." The phrasing implies that the relationship had already existed for many months.

234 "our last appointment": Flaubert to Bouilhet, August 24, 1853.

234 historian Enid Starkie: Enid Starkie, *Flaubert: The Making of a Master* (London: Weidenfeld and Nicolson, 1967), p. 208.

235 "with the Muse": Flaubert to Bouilhet, December 8, 1853.

235 "her from heaven?": Ibid.

236 "my deepest depths. . . .": Flaubert to Colet, December 28, 1853.

236 "of Norman cathedrals. . . .": Ibid., December 14, 1853.

236 "fornication scene finished": Ibid., October 18, 1853.

237 *Dictionary of Accepted Ideas:* Gustave Flaubert, *Dictionary of Accepted Ideas,* translated and annotated by Jacques Barzun (New York: New Directions, 1954). The first edition of this exquisite parodic anthology of bourgeois platitudes, which Flaubert began to assemble in the 1850s, was not published until several decades after his death.

237 "turns of phrase": Flaubert to Colet, February 25, 1854.

237 "to each other": Ibid., January 9–10, 1854.

238 "of your mind": Ibid., September 1, 1852.

238 "weakness of intellect": Ibid., December 11, 1852.

238 "hen lays eggs": Ibid., December 18, 1853.

238 "in women's menses": Ibid., January 15, 1854.

239 "midst of enthusiasm": Ibid., March 27, 1853.

239 "airs, O Democracy!": Bouilhet to Flaubert, spring 1854? Cited by Jean Bruneau in footnotes, Flaubert's *Correspondance,* vol. II, p. 1246.

240 "charming daughter . . . etc.": Bouilhet to Flaubert, December 8, 1853, cited in ibid., p. 1234.

240 "out of conscience": This information comes from an obituary of Louise Colet published in *Revue brittanique,* March 1876, p. 273. Louise herself often implied that in previous years Victor Cousin had been toying with the notion of marrying her to assure Henriette a more stable future, and of setting up a 2,000-francs-a-year trust fund for Henriette, but that he had been reluctant to make any final decision until Louise broke definitively with Flaubert.

240 "refused the Philosopher. . . .": Bouilhet to Flaubert, letter of December 8, 1853, Flaubert's *Correspondance,* vol. II, p. 1234.

240 "I'll drop her": Ibid.

241 "arrange a meeting": Flaubert to Colet, October 12, 1853.

242 "only that cause. . . .": Ibid., January 13, 1854.

242 1830s, by Sainte-Beuve: The phrase occurs in Sainte-Beuve's *Pensées d'Août*: *"Et Vigny, Plus secret / Comme en sa tour d'ivoire, avant midi, rentrait."* Quoted in F.W.J. Hemmings, *Culture and Society in France, 1789–1848* (Leicester: Leicester University Press, 1987), p. 260.

243 *"feuille en feuille"*: *"Le Cor,"* in Alfred de Vigny, *Poèmes antiques et modernes* (Paris: Gallimard, Bibliothèque de la Pléiade, 1986).

243 "like a sister. . . .": Alfred de Vigny to Louise Colet, June 14, 1846.

Over 400 folio pages of Alfred de Vigny's letters to Louise Colet are preserved at the Fonds Colet, Avignon (ms. 6.414). A selection of these letters was published by Marc Varenne and Maurice Levaillant in three successive issues of *La Revue,* January 15, February 1, February 15, 1956. I have drawn my quotes from both sources.

243 "your beautiful talent!": Vigny to Colet, January 15, 1854.

244 "causes in me": Ibid., January 15, 1854.

244 "open for me. . . .": Ibid., March 16, 1854.

244 "through my hair?": Ibid., March 21, 1854.

244 "strains distract you!": Flaubert to Colet, March 1854.

244 "Empire in taste": Ibid., March 19, 1854.

244 "come after them": Ibid., April 7, 1854.

245 "that scandalize me. . . .": Ibid., April 18, 1854.

245 *"under her blanket,* etc.": Ibid., April 22, 1854.

245 "taste and chic": Ibid., April 29, 1854.

245 "Mille tendresses, G.": Bood, *Colet,* p. 167. This is the only original autograph of Flaubert's I have come across that is not included in the Pléiade edition assembled by Professor Jean Bruneau.

246 "of saluting you. G.F.": Flaubert to Colet, March 6, 1855. The missive reads thus in the original French:

Madame,

J'ai appris que vous vous étiez donné la peine de venir, hier, dans la soirée, trois fois, chez moi.

Je n'y étais pas. Et dans la crainte des avanies qu'une telle persistence de votre part, pourrait vous attirer de la mienne, le savoir-vivre m'engage a vous prévenir: que je n'y serai *jamais.*

J'ai l'honneur de vous saluer.

G.F.

247 exclaimed to Henriette: René Descharmes, *Flaubert: Sa Vie, son caractère et ses idées avant 1857* (Paris: Librairie des Amateurs, 1909), p. 409.

13. Stello and Olympio

248 "conversing with me": Journal entry of Vigny's cited in Marc Varenne and Maurice Levaillant, "Les Amours d'Alfred de Vigny et de Louise Colet," *La Revue,* February 1, 1856, p. 395.

249 "to her daughter": Fortunat Strowski, "Alfred de Vigny," in *Revue des cours et conferences* II (May 31, 1923), pp 68–69.

249 "solitary last years": Some sixty pages of letters from Victor Cousin to Henriette Colet, most of them undated, are preserved at the Fonds Colet, Avignon, ms. 6.421.

250 "of human existence": Vigny to Colet, December 19, 1854.

250 "these abysmal difficulties": Ibid., September 18 1854.

250 "she'll see there": Ibid., September 5 1854.

251 "as a game": Ibid., February 16 1855.

251 "a big hug": Ibid., April 30, 1856.

251 "pretty little novice": Ibid., Summer 1854.

251 "of your independence?": Ibid., August 12, 1854.

251 quipped about him: Varenne and Levaillant, "Les Amours," February 1, 1956, p. 395.

251 "makes me tremble": Vigny to Colet, n.d., cited in Bood, p. 156.

252 "my passionate adoration": Ibid., June 12, 1854.

252 "strokes of a hammer": "Ignotus" (F. Platel), "Une Muse," *Le Figaro,* September 14, 1882.

252 "eight hundred francs": Bouilhet to Colet, June 25, 1854, cited in Bood, p. 167.

252 "which is charming": Flaubert to Bouilhet, in ibid.

253 "feeling will last": Archives of the Bood family.

253 "change of plans": Bouilhet to Colet, September 1854.

254 "sent her packing": This undated letter of Bouilhet's to Flaubert is cited in Jackson's *Louise Colet,* p. 221. I have not been able to find it in the Pléiade edition of Flaubert's correspondence, which I've used throughout my own text.

254 "is sick, heartache": Archives of the Bood family.

254 "eight P.M. to midnight": Colet to Flaubert, March 3, 1855.

254 "was not sociable": Cited in Auriant, "Koutchouk-Hanem," p. 66.

254 Théophile Gautier reported: *Gazette anecdotique,* vol. I (1881), p. 212.

255 "a good laugh": Goncourt, *Journal,* vol. I, entry of December 8, 1862.

255 told the Goncourts: Ibid., entry of February 21, 1862.

255 "and pleasant character": Excerpts from Du Camp's *Souvenirs littéraires,* in *Revue des deux mondes,* p. 732.

255 "have no future": Ibid., p. 733.

255 " 'lack of naturalness' ": Ibid.

256 " 'Requiescat in pace!' ": Ibid., p. 735.

256 French literary critics: One cannot overestimate the harm done to Colet's reputation by the tradition of Colet-bashing that was pioneered by Maxime Du Camp and the prominent writer Barbey d'Aurevilly, and gleefully perpetuated by several generations of French literary critics.

What is most striking about their defamations of Louise, and of the French "Flaubertistes" who came to the fore in the first few decades of our century, is that they emulated that mystique of bonding, virulently exclusive of women, which had characterized Flaubert's career. The same spirit of macho cohesiveness with which Bouilhet and Du Camp helped to expunge Louise from Flaubert's life in 1848, and again in 1854, inspired several generations of French Flaubertists outrageously to minimize Louise's role in the author's existence. In a uniquely mimetic example of critical whitewashing, until midcentury Flaubert's reputation would be hygienized by vigorous denials of any genuine affection he might have had for Louise, or by distortions of her character so extreme that she lost all credibility as Flaubert's Muse.

A particularly venomous text, for instance, Gérard-Gailly's *Les Véhémences de Louise Colet,* elaborated on the totally unfounded claim, drawn exclusively on Du Camp's and Barbey d'Aurevilly's calumnies, that Louise was already on intimate terms with Victor Cousin *before* she entered her first poetry competition in 1839 and was awarded the prize only through her protector's influence. This denigration was to be aped for several more decades; as was Gérard-Gailly's contention, again based on Barbey d'Aurevilly, that she was of humble middle-class origins and had totally invented her distinguished ancestry (such attempts to deny Louise the genteel provenance that had so protected George Sand and Marie d'Agoult is an interesting comment on French elitism).

The turning point in Colet's rehabilitation occurred in Joseph Jackson's *Louise Colet et ses amis littéraires,* a severe but very fair work by a professor of French at Yale University, the first book on Louise to be graced by an index, a bibliography, copious footnotes, and every other attribute of responsible scholarship. Praising her generosity and deep loyalties, justly critical of her pushiness and hasty work habits, it refuted the numerous mistakes and injustices done to Louise by Barbey d'Aurevilly, Du Camp, and other members of Flaubert's buddy network.

This new reevaluation of Louise Colet continued full steam in the postwar years, when much of the important Flaubert studies shifted to Great Britain and the United States. Working outside the remarkably sexist prejudices of the French tradition, Enid Starkie's and Benjamin Bart's huge volumes on Flaubert, like Francis Steegmuller's two decades earlier, were considerably fairer and more appreciative of Louise than her compatriots had ever been. The Oxford don Enid Starkie, so dazzlingly portrayed in Julian Barnes's *Flaubert's Parrot* (another book most supportive of Louise), was particularly understanding of Colet's relationship with Flaubert. Stressing that the failure of this famous liaison was fully as attributable to Gustave as to Louise—"he could never have had a satisfactory relationship with any woman"—Starkie saw Louise as Gustave's "greatest emotional adventure," the only woman who "drew him into the family of human beings."

This new view of a tempestuous but eminently honorable Louise Colet was dramatically heightened in the 1970s by Jean Bruneau, the greatest Flaubertist of the past half century. In the introduction to his magisterial Pléiade edition of Flaubert's correspondence, Bruneau presents her as "a ravishing, brilliant, sentimental, ambitious woman," author of "very beautiful" verses, whose salon was, "for many years, an important focal point of Europe's progressive political movement." Attempting to explain the century of Colet-bashing that had preceded his own pioneering work, Bruneau asserted that Louise, for decades, had simply been "the victim of male caddishness."

After the publication of Bruneau's revisionist view of Colet, it was smooth sailing for our Muse. However flawed and incomplete, the biographies of Colet by Jean-Paul Clébert, and by her descendant Micheline Bood, limned with eminent fairness and compassion her complex, tormented character. The periodical press followed suit. What a *volte-face,* in the 1980s and '90s, from the previous decades of abuse! Louise was now being compared to "a Balzacian heroine," who had been the victim of "a weak, cowardly Gustave, the emotionally retarded child of a castrating mother." She was hailed as "an archetypal role model for the heyday of feminism." Even the rigorous *Le Monde* was now calling her "a phenomenon of pride and fantasy, way ahead of the demeanor and ideas of her time, who championed the eternal victims of the earth," a woman with "one of the most exemplary destinies of her century . . . a paragon for the independent, enterprising woman of the following century." As *Le Figaro* put it (1987), "her only fault was to have been born a century too early."

256 "man of genius": Excerpts from Du Camp's *Souvenirs littéraires,* in Flaubert, *Oeuvres complètes,* p. 19.

257 "come her liberation": Louise Colet, *Le Poème de la Femme,* "La Religieuse" (Paris: Perrotin, 1856).

257 *Histoire de Soldat:* Louise Colet, *Une Histoire de Soldat* (Paris: A. Cadot, 1856).

258 "her husband's death": Ibid., p. 128.

258 "kind of night?": Ibid., p. 130.

258 "thickened and clouded": Ibid., pp. 139–40.

259 "throughout the book. . . .": Hugo to Colet, August 16, 1856.

259 "Holy Family" 's residence: Maurois, *Olympio,* pp. 330–32.

260 "by the sleeve. . . .": Hugo to Colet, April 26, 1854.

261 "lose that horizon": Ibid., June 1, 1854.

261 "stifling and sullying": Ibid., November 30, 1854.

261 "to go naked": Ibid., May 24, 1856.

262 "your indignant verses!": Colet to Hugo, November 4, 1854.

262 "poor Madame Waldor": Poet Mélanie Waldor, who had been the mistress of Alphonse Karr and was one of Louise's bêtes noires.

262 "her entire life. . . .": Colet to Hugo, November 4, 1854.

262 "think they're long. . . .": Hugo to Colet, November 15, 1855.

263 "shaking their hands": Colet to Hugo, March 1856.

263 "to receiving you": Hugo to Colet, April 1, 1856.

263 "arrive on Tuesday": Ibid., July 26, 1856.

264 "Visto y tomado Julia": Maurois, *Olympio,* p. 331.

264 "in his return": Colet to Hugo, August 19, 1856.

265 "to your daughter": Adèle Hugo to Louise Colet, May 5, 1859.

265 "your beautiful verses": Vigny to Colet, January 13, 1855.

265 "drop in on me": Ibid., late March 1856.

265 "books and candy": Ibid., Summer 1856.

266 to a friend: Jackson, *Louise Colet,* p. 236.

266 "did not veil": Quoted in "Louise Colet et les Sbires du Pape," by Fleuriot de Langle, *Le Figaro,* January 21, 1933.

267 "to boot! Pouah!": Jules Troubat, *Une Amitié à la d'Arthez: Champfleury, Courbet, Max Buchon* (Paris: Lucien Duc, 1900), pp. 129–31.

267 "be that audacious": Ibid.

268 "field of poppies": Du Camp, excerpts from *Souvenirs littéraires,* in *Revue des deux mondes,* p. 734.

268 "precursive of Impressionism": G. Riat, *Gustave Courbet, peintre* (Paris: H. Fleury, 1906), pp. 172–73.

269 "has taken Rodolphe. . . .": Charles Léger, *Courbet et son temps* (Paris: Éditions Universelles, 1988) p. 62.

269 "a lover's contemplation": Lionello Venturi and F. Kimball, *Great Paintings in America* (New York: Coward-McCann, 1948), p. 172.

269 "sorrow and overwork": Colet to Hugo, December 28, 1856.

269 "still with me": Hugo to Colet, December 30, 1856.

270 "your inspired forehead": Colet to Hugo, April 1, 1857.

270 "if you're in": Vigny to Colet, Summer 1857.

271 "forgetfulness of everything": Ibid., n.d., most probably 1854, Fonds Colet.
271 "your eagle's duty": Hugo to Colet, March 17, 1857.

14. Emma and Louise

274 her financial disaster: Siler, *Mémoires de Madame Ludovica*, p. 20.
274 "refusals they made": Ibid., p. 49.
274 the 1940s wrote: Auriant, "Koutchouk-Hanem," p. 67.
274 "of his heroine": Starkie, *Flaubert*, p. 220.
275 "Paris or Mantes": Francis Steegmuller, *Flaubert and Madame Bovary*, p. 351.
275 "a funerary carriage": Sartre, *L'Idiot*, p. 1279.
276 "for Madame Bovary's": Ibid., p. 1287.
276 " 'dried up your heart' ": Flaubert to Bouilhet, June 27, 1855.
276 " 'so pure? Impossible!' ": Excerpts from Du Camp's *Souvenirs littéraires*, in Flaubert, *Oeuvres complètes*, p. 30.
277 "remained a man": Charles Baudelaire, "Madame Bovary," in *Oeuvres complètes* (Paris: Bibliothèque de la Pléiade, 1961), pp. 647–57.
278 "had slipped away": Flaubert, *Madame Bovary*, p. 315.
278 "was laughing so": Jules Troubat, "Mémoires contemporains: Madame Louise Colet," *Le Temps*, September 14, 1913.
278 "against Flaubert's disloyalty": Jules Troubat, *Notes et pensées* (Paris, 1888).
279 "fine agate seal": *Le Monde illustré*, January 29, 1859, p. 70.
279 "has deep causes": Colet to Hugo, September 16, 1857.
280 *Elle et Lui:* George Sand, *Elle et Lui* (Paris: Michel Lévy Frères, 1869).
280 *Lui et Elle:* Paul de Musset, *Lui et Elle* (Paris: Charpentier, 1871).
281 writing literary translations: All citations from Colet's *Lui* are from Marilyn Gaddis Rose's splendid English translation of the novel, *Lui: A View of Him* (Athens and London: University of Georgia Press, 1986). I'm most grateful for the brilliant insights provided by Professor Rose in her introduction to Colet's text, without which I might not have grasped the deeper feminist subtexts of the novel.
281 "grandeur and prestige": Ibid., p. 15.
282 "him in solitude": Ibid., pp. 84–85.
284 "usurping my place": Ibid., p. 133.
284 "work room again": Ibid., p. 137.
284 "profound immorality of women": Flaubert to Feydeau, August 21, 1869.
285 "of this work. . . .": Flaubert to Amélie Bosquet, November 1859.
285 "she persecuted Flaubert": Du Camp, excerpts from *Mémoires littéraires*, in *Revue des deux mondes*, p. 731.
285 "and mental habits": Spoelberch de Lovenjoul, *La Véritable Histoire de "Elle et Lui"* (Paris: Calmann-Lévy, 1897), pp. 210–11.
285 "which will endure": Sainte-Beuve to Colet, cited in Bonnerot, "A la Poursuite d'un article," p. 442.
286 *Histoire d'un scandale:* Mathurin de Lescure, *Eux et Elles: Histoire d'un scandale* (Paris: Poulet-Malassi et Débroise, 1860).
287 "Ses malheurs": Bood, *Colet*, p. 128.

15. Attending a Revolution

289 "is very eloquent": *Gazette anecdotique*, vol. I (1881), p. 269.
289 "establishing a republic": Fonds Colet.

291 written several books: Honoré Clair, *Les Monuments d'Arles, antiques et modernes* (Arles: Garcin, 1837), and *Recherches sur l'état des monuments anciens des Bouches-du-Rhône* (Arles: Garcin, 1843).

291 "had already shared": Colet, *L'Italie des Italiens,* vol. I, p. 21.

292 "today, of liberty": Ibid., p. 35.

292 "not abandon us": Ibid., pp. 107–20.

293 "who liberated us!": Ibid., p. 147.

293 "French to return!": Ibid., p. 175.

293 "here," she predicts: Ibid., p. 249.

294 "cowardice or disloyalty. . . .": Ibid., p. 159.

294 "domains whenever possible": John Parris, *The Lion of Caprera* (New York: David McKay, 1962), p. 90.

295 "their ironic light": Louise Colet, *L'Italie des Italiens,* vol. I, pp. 591–92.

296 "the renascent fatherland!": Louise Colet, *L'Italie des Italiens,* vol. II (Paris: E. Dentu, 1862), p. 5.

296 "antiquity stifles Rome": Ibid., p. 7.

297 "Thiers, Guizot, Lamoricière": Statesman Adolphe Thiers (1797–1877) was one of the most prominent leaders of the July Revolution of 1830 that had brought Louis Philippe to power; after a brief exile for having opposed Louis Napoleon's coup d'état in 1851, he was elected deputy. Two decades later, he would head the government that took power after the downfall of Napoleon III.

Henri Guizot (1787–1874), also active in the revolution of 1830, was prime minister of France in the last years of Louis Philippe's reign, and it was in good part his conservative policies that brought that government down in 1848.

Louis Juchault de Lamoricière (1806–1865) was an equally staunch supporter of Louis Philippe and became France's most popular general in the 1830s, after leading his army in the conquest of Algeria. Since the late 1850s, he served as commander in chief of the army of the Papal States, which through a pact signed earlier that decade were officially under France's "protection."

297 "of July 1830!": Colet, *L'Italie des Italiens,* vol. II, p. 8.

297 "numbing and decadence": Ibid., p. 11.

298 " 'talk to her' ": Ibid., p. 66.

299 "by the devil": Ibid., p. 223.

299 "his every move": Ibid., p. 400.

299 "of my days": Ibid., p. 402.

300 "a military ship": Ibid., p. 404.

300 "love it now": Ibid., p. 410.

301 "an entire people!": Ibid., p. 411.

301 "throughout the bay": Louise Colet, *L'Italie des Italiens,* vol. III (Paris: E. Dentu, 1863), p. 7.

16. Increasing Solitude

303 "disposition and impieties": All the letters between Sidonie Colet and Victor Cousin cited in this chapter come from the collection of Cousin's correspondence at the Bibliothèque Victor Cousin, Sorbonne, Paris, nos. 222–23.

304 "depict such turpitudes": Colet, *L'Italie des Italiens,* vol. III, p. 99.

304 " 'unworthy of you' ": Ibid., p. 71.

305 "price for it!": Ibid., pp. 132–42.

305 "a wake-up call": Cited in Jean Bruneau, "L. Colet, M. Du Camp, G. Flaubert et. . . Garibaldi," in *Mélanges offerts a la mémoire de Franco Simone* (Geneva: Éditions Slatkine, 1984), pp. 469–83.

306 "be more ridiculous": Ibid.

308 "parvenus and bankers": Colet, *L'Italie des Italiens,* vol. IV (Paris: É. Dentu, 1864), p. 38.

308 "and debauched strumpet": Ibid., p. 44.

309 " 'deny our liberation?' ": Ibid., pp. 111–14.

310 "about by violence": Ibid., pp. 430–38.

311 "a new stage. . . .": Colet, *L'Italie des Italiens,* vol. I, pp. 592–93.

311 her mother's funeral: See my essay "Mother Love: Madame de Sévigné," in *Adam and Eve and the City* (New York: Simon & Schuster, 1987).

311 a religious burial: Jean Chalon, *Chère George Sand* (Paris: Flammarion, 1991), p. 468.

312 "pleased with me": Fonds Colet, ms. 6.421, fol. 209.

312 "adorable rising dawn": Frejlich, *Les Amants de Mantes,* p. 57.

313 " 'in academic circles' ": Colet, *L'Italie des Italiens,* vol. II, p. 300.

313 "a great laugh": Ibid., p. 408.

315 "that is important . . .": Chambon, *Deux Passions,* p. 64.

316 "the last one": All the correspondence cited between Henriette and Honoré Clair in this chapter comes from the Fonds Colet, ms. 6.421, fol. 211–60. Very few of the letters are dated, so I shall not give any further footnotes.

316 "destine for her": Bood, *Colet,* p. 208.

317 "of private passions": F. Calmettes, *Leconte de Lisle et ses amis* (Paris, 1902).

317 "never leave them": Colet, *L'Italie des Italiens,* vol. IV, p. 474.

317 "the very contrary of what you should be": Flaubert to Colet, April 12, 1854. One should note that in the second-to-last sentence of that quote, the original French, which I've blandly translated as "produce detestable works," reads, "pondre *quelquefois des vers detestables."* The literal translation of *pondre* is to "lay eggs," another instance of the very frequent analogies Flaubert makes between Louise's writing and animal or ovarian functions (in this case, both).

318 "are indeed pathetic": This exchange of letters with Edma Roger des Genettes is cited in *Gazette anecdotique,* vol. I (1881), p. 277.

319 "have revived me . . .": Colet to Hugo, Summer 1864.

17. Taking on the Vatican

320 "chained my pen!": Louise Colet, *Les Derniers Abbés: Meurs religieuses d'Italie* (Paris: E. Dentu, 1868).

321 " 'a great man!' ": Ibid., p. 50.

322 "recruited among performers!": Ibid., p. 62.

323 "than divine morality": Ibid., pp. 4–12.

324 *"Voici la liberté!":* Ibid.

325 "loyally shout 'Look!' ": Ibid., p. 147.

325 "me inexhaustible serenity": Ibid. p. 98.

327 "little to give": Ibid., p. 106.

328 *"son sein maternel":* Ibid., p. 80.

330 "was finally restored": *Le Temps,* November 19, 1865.

331 is the prefect's: Louise Colet, *Les Derniers Marquis* (Paris: E. Dentu, 1866), p. iii.

334 "her mother's memory": Paul Mariéton's working notes for a projected biography of Louise Colet are part of the Fonds Louise Colet.

334 "of global interest!": "Critobule" (Eugène Vial), *Paul Mariéton d'après sa correspondance* (Paris: G. Cris, 1920).

334 "my mother's image": From Mariéton's notes for biography of Louise Colet.

334 Conard and Charpentier: Some historians have stated that Henriette Colet Bissieu sold her mother's letters to Flaubert's niece, Caroline de Commanville. But I trust the alternate version of this transaction offered by Jean Bruneau in his preface to vol. I of Flaubert's *Correspondance,* p. xviii.

335 "defame her memory": Mariéton's notes for biography of Louise Colet.

18. Dueling with Phantoms

339 "delicacy as possible": Bood, *Colet,* p. 215.

340 "dignity and decorum": *Gazette anecdotique,* March 31, 1876, p. 166.

340 famous *grande horizontale:* A Second Empire euphemism for Paris's grandest courtesans.

341 "the entire nation": Louise Colet, *Les Dévotes du grand monde* (Paris: E. Dentu, 1873), pp. 135, 125–26.

341 "burdens my conscience": *Gazette anecdotique,* March 31, 1876, p. 166.

342 *"fond du nectar":* La Satire du siècle: Paris matière, in *Les Dévotes du grand monde* (Paris: É. Dentu, 1873).

342 "most *virile* work": Article by Edmond Texier on Louise's *Paris matière,* Collection Spoelberch de Lovenjoul, Bibliothèque de L'Institut de France, Paris. Cited in Jackson, *Louise Colet,* footnote 50, p. 356.

342 "admiration and homage": Colet, *Les Dévotes du grand monde,* pp. 115–16. The original of this letter of Sainte-Beuve is at the Collection Spoelberch de Lovenjoul.

342 "to admire you": Bonnerot, "A la poursuite d'un article,"*La Muse française,* XII (October 15, 1933), p. 442.

343 "motherland and family. . . .": *Les Dévotes du grand monde,* p. 35.

344 the reading public: A characteristic entry on Louise Colet in the French press: "A passionate and intolerant woman . . . [who] played a fairly important role in the Romantic movement . . . and drew public attention by making a murder attempt on Alphonse Karr" (obituary of Louise in *Le Figaro,* March 11, 1876).

344 "has equally disappeared": Jackson, *Louise Colet,* p. 302.

345 the preceding years: Documents of the Bood family.

345 "love for me": Hugo to Colet, May 16, 1868.

345 "a single man": Louise Colet, *Les Pays lumineux. Voyage en Orient* (Paris: E. Dentu, 1876).

346 "an old man": See the brilliant study on the issue of women and aging in *Aging and Its Discontents,* ed. Kathleen Woodward (Bloomington and Indianapolis: University of Indiana Press, 1991).

346 "that of impiety": Cited in [Émile] Auriant, "Louise Colet et les Pachas," *Mercure de France,* April 15, 1934, p. 412.

347 "to a cigar": Colet, *Les Pays lumineux,* p. 27.

347 "be the wealthiest": Ibid., pp. 147–48.

348 "Egypt is Potemkinized": "Inauguration du Canal de Suez," by "Mohammed-el-Akmar," in *Le Siècle,* November 14, 1869.

348 "a tender heart": Documents of the Bood family.

349 "by my bedside. . . .": Colet, *Les Pays lumineux,* p. 205.

351 "of eternal justice": Ibid., p. 210.

352 "woman, a mother? . . .": Ibid., pp. 112–14.

352 "men or women": Documents of the Bood family.

352 "their inaccessible solitude": Louise Colet, *La Vérité sur l'anarchie des esprits en France* (Milan: F. Legros Felice Éditeur, 1873).

353 "all our woes": Flaubert to Sand, September 10, 1870.

354 "in the amphitheater": Colet, *La Vérité sur l'anarchie des esprits,* p. 107.

355 "our own generals": Ibid., p. 103ff.

355 "in a corner": Flaubert to Caroline Commanville, December 18, 1870.

356 "could disappear completely": Flaubert to Caroline, February 1, 1871.

356 her "sacrilegious discourses": Colet, *La Vérité sur l'anarchie des esprits,* p. 128, 123.

19. The Last Barricades

357 "us into barbarians": Colet, *La Vérité sur l'anarchie des esprits,* p. 43.

358 leader Gambetta declared: Jacques Rougerie, *La Commune* (Paris: Presses Universitaires de France), p. 7.

358 *"Me voici!":* Avner Ben-Amos, "Les Funérailles de Victor Hugo," in *Les Lieux de mémoire,* ed. Pierre Nora, 7 volumes: I, *La République* (Paris: Gallimard, 1984), p. 476.

359 "sake of evil": Cited in Clébert, *Louise Colet,* p. 358.

359 "ignoble and evil": Ibid.

359 "in insane asylums": Ibid.

359 "ruins of Paris": Flaubert to Sand, October 12, 1871.

359 "of immense bloodshed": Cited in Jackson, *Louise Colet,* p. 310.

360 "other as enemies": A. M. Blanchecotte, *Tablettes d'une femme pendant la commune* (Paris: Didier et Cie, 1872), p. 53.

360 "vocabulary of despair": Goncourt, *Journal,* vol. I, entry of May 19, 1871.

360 prisoners were taken: These are the figures cited in Rougerie, *La Commune.*

361 "it in history": Cited in Otto Friedrich, *Olympia: Paris in the Age of Manet* (New York: HarperCollins, 1992), p. 230.

362 "foreign to you": Colet, *La Vérité sur l'anarchie des esprits,* p. 68.

362 hearing in court: Friedrich, *Olympia,* p. 229.

363 "to await trial": Since this report was written only a few months after the carnage, and such figures are not properly calculated for years or decades to come, Louise's figures are strikingly accurate.

363 "salvation of France": Colet, *La Vérité sur l'anarchie des esprits,* pp. 165–66.

364 "a wondrous vision?": Flaubert to Edma Roger des Genettes, May 1871.

365 firebombs throughout Paris: Edith Thomas, "Y Eut-il des Pétroleuses," in *Les Pétroleuses* (Paris: Gallimard, 1963).

365 "from their jailers. . . .": Colet, *La Vérité sur l'anarchie des esprits,* pp. 73–74.

366 "burst into tears": Ibid., p. 79.

366 "of her passions": Ibid., pp. 78ff.

367 Malvina Blanchecotte commented: Blanchecotte, *Tablettes d'une femme,* pp. 348–49.

367 "judging and punishing": Ibid., p. 371.

367 "more French blood": Colet, *La Vérité sur l'anarchie des esprits*, p. 44.

367 "state of resignation": Ibid., p. 62.

367 "spreads its wares. . . .": Ibid., p. 62.

368 "of France's future": Ibid., p. 175.

368 "perfume of honesty": Colet's "Étude sur Monsieur Sainte-Beuve" was reprinted in her book *Les Dévotes du grand monde*, pp. 115–57.

369 "the following day": Colet to Hugo, November 9, 1872.

369 "will have it": Letter reprinted in *La Vérité sur l'anarchie des esprits*, p. 1, footnote.

370 "and consumes souls": Ibid., pp. 74–75.

370 "while, perhaps forever": Unpublished. Musée Paul Arbaud, Aix, Dossier 1160.A.1.

371 "the adjoining house": Louise Colet, *Edgar Quinet, L'Esprit nouveau* (Paris: Hurtau, 1876), pp. 28–29.

372 "work, I hope. . . .": Jacques Patin, "Lettres Inédites de Louise Colet," *Le Figaro*, February 7, 1931.

372 "twenty-year-old Hypatia!": The fifth-century Alexandria philosopher retained her pagan beliefs and was put to death by Christians; Colet already identified with her when she described the harassments imposed on her by Ischia's clergy (see chapter 17).

372 "indignation!" Quinet wrote: Colet, *Edgar Quinet*, p. 12.

373 "a new book": This undoubtedly refers to Louise Colet's book on Edgar Quinet.

373 "out that morning": Jules Belleudy, "La Muse provençale cinq fois couronnée: Louise Colet," in *Tablettes d'Avignon et de Provence*, August 4, 18, 1928.

374 "other great spirits. . . .": Ibid., letter of Colet to Jules Belleudy, June 22, 1875.

374 "against clerical conspiracies. . . .": Ibid.

374 Rue des Écoles: Two of Colet's biographers, Joseph Jackson and Micheline Bood, state that Louise died "in an obscure little hotel on the Rue des Écoles." Since Henriette Bissieu had a flat on the Rue des Écoles, I prefer to trust the obituary that appeared the week of her death in *Le Figaro*, which stated that "[Louise Colet] died attended by her daughter, Madame Bissieux [sic]" (March 10, 1876).

377 upon her grave: Chalon, *Chère George Sand*, p. 468.

378 "except his works": Flaubert, *Oeuvres complètes* (Paris: Club de l'Honnête Homme, 1971–1975), vol. XIII, no. 552, p. 446.

378 Louise Colet's letters: As I noted earlier, the most seductive arguments for the theory that Flaubert himself, and not his niece Caroline, destroyed Louise's letters is put forth in Hermia Oliver's wonderful book *Flaubert and an English Governess*.

379 "eager, merry faces": Goncourt, *Journal*, vol. II, entry of May 11, 1880.

380 exile in Guernsey: The only biography of Colet in which I've found this startling information is Micheline Bood's *L'Indomptable Louise Colet*. Madame Bood's biography having remained unfinished at the time of her death, her text has very few footnotes or bibliographical references, and she gave no sources for this particular data. But since she inherited most of the Colet documents owned by the author's family, she must have been privy to information not shared by other chroniclers. And the fact that Louise's daughter signed some of her correspondence "Henriette Bissieu-Colet" from 1880 on leads me to trust this interesting detail of Madame Bood's study.

381 "made everyone suffer": *Mercure de France*, May 1, 1916.

381 as "Madame X": These letters were first published in 1910 in the Charpentier et

Conard edition of Flaubert's correspondence. For a complete accounting of how the Flaubert-Colet correspondences were handled after the two writers' death, see the preface to volume I of Jean Bruneau's Pléiade edition, particularly pp. xiii–xvii.

381 letters to Gustave: Until a few years ago it was generally assumed, even by the most sophisticated Flaubertists—Francis Steegmuller, Enid Starkie, Benjamin Bart—that Caroline was responsible for the destruction of Louise's letters. But as I can not emphasize often enough, almost none of Flaubert's biographers seem to have read Maupassant's account of the letter-burning episode at Croisset. This omission, on the part of seasoned scholars, is puzzling.

382 "poses of coupling": Goncourt, *Journal,* vol. II, entry of May 17, 1871. (As with all of the Goncourts' chronicling of prominent Parisians' sexual activities, one should take this probably exaggerated report with a grain of salt.)

383 *Le Figaro* declared: Ben-Amos, "Funérailles de Victor Hugo," p. 482.

383 "humiliation of 1870": Ibid., p. 508.

383 "Mac-Mahon to speak": Ibid., p. 494.

384 "one noticed it. . . .": Excerpts from Du Camp, *Souvenirs littéraires,* in *Revue des deux mondes,* p. 735.

385 "sincerity in passion. . . .": Bood, *Colet,* p. 229.

385 "than her adversaries": Ibid.

385 "and independent spirit": Ibid.

386 "the divine laurel": de Banville, *Critiques,* p. 145.

386 "Misery on us all!": Flaubert to Edma Roger des Genettes, March 1876.

Bibliography

꧁꧂

BOOKS

Adler, Laure. *Secrets de l'alcôve: Histoire du couple de 1830 à 1930.* Paris: Hachette, 1983.

Albistur, Maïte, and Daniel Armogathe. *Histoire du féminisme français, du Moyen-Age à nos jours.* Paris: Édition des Femmes, 1977.

Ariès, Philippe, and Charles Duby, eds. *Histoire de la vie privée.* Vol. IV, *De la révolution à la Grande Guerre.* Paris: Seuil, 1985.

Aron, Jean Paul, ed. *Misérable et glorieuse: La femme au XIXe siècle.* Paris: Éditions Complexe, 1980.

Aurevilly, Barbey d'. *Les Bas-Bleus.* Paris: V. Palmé, 1878.

Auriant, Emile. *L'Envers d'une muse.* Paris: Oeuvres Nouvelles Libres, 1938.

Banville, Théodore de. *Critiques.* Edited by Victor Barrucaud. Paris: Bibliothèque Charpentier, 1917.

Barnes, Julian. *Flaubert's Parrot.* New York: Alfred A. Knopf, 1985.

Bart, Benjamin. *Flaubert.* Syracuse: Syracuse University Press, 1967.

Baudelaire, Charles. *Oeuvres complètes.* Paris: Gallimard, Bibliothèque de la Pléiade, 1976.

Les Belles Femmes de Paris et de la province. Anonymous. Paris, 1847.

Bellet, Roger, ed. *Femmes de lettres au XIXe siècle: Autour de Louise Colet.* Lyon: Presses Universitaires de Lyon, 1982.

Bernos, Marcel, Noel Coulet, et al., eds. *Histoire d'Aix en Provence.* Aix en Provence: Edisud, 1978.

Bertrand, Georges-Emile, ed. *Jours de Flaubert.* Paris: Editions du Myrte, 1947.

Blanchecotte, A. M. *Tablettes d'une femme pendant la Commune.* Paris: Librairie Academique Didier et Cie., 1872.

Bood, Micheline, and Serge Grand. *L'Indomptable Louise Colet.* Paris: Pierre Horay, 1986.

Bouilhet, Louis. *Lettres à Louise Colet.* Edited by Marie-Claude Blancquart. Paris: Presses Universitaires de France, 1973.

Brombert, Beth Archer. *Cristina: Portrait of a Princess.* New York: Alfred A. Knopf, 1977.

Burnand, Robert. *La Vie quotidienne en 1830.* Paris: Hachette, n.d.

Chalon, Jean. *Chère George Sand.* Paris: Flammarion, 1991.

Charlton, D. G. *The French Romantics.* 2 vols. Cambridge: Cambridge University Press, 1974.

Clair, Honoré. *Les Monuments d'Arles, antiques et modernes.* Arles: Garcin, 1837.

———. *Recherches sur l'état des monuments anciens des Boûches du Rhône.* Arles: Garcin, 1843.

Clark, T. J. *The Absolute Bourgeois: Artists and Politics in France, 1848–1851.* Princeton, N.J.: Princeton University Press, 1988.

Clébert, Jean-Paul. *Louise Colet, ou la muse.* Paris: Editions de la Renaissance, 1986.

Colet, Louise. *Fleurs du midi.* Paris: Dumont, 1836.

———. *Penserosa.* Paris: H-L Delloye, 1840.

———. *Charlotte Corday et Madame Roland.* Paris: Berquet et Pétion, 1842.

———. *La Jeunesse de Mirabeau.* Paris: Dumont, 1842.

———. *Coeurs brisés.* Paris: Berquet & Petion, 1843.

———. *Deux mois d'emotions.* Paris: W. Coquebert, 1843

———. *Réveil de la Pologne.* Paris: A. René, 1846.

———. *Ce qui est dans le coeur des femmes.* Paris: Librairie Nouvelle, 1852.

———. *Le Poème de la femme.* 3. vols: *La Paysanne, La Servante, La Religieuse.* Paris: Perrotin, 1853, 1854, 1856.

———. *Enfances célèbres.* Paris: L. Hachette, 1854.

———. *Poésies complètes.* Paris: Librairie de Charles Gosselin, 1854.

———. *Quatre poèmes couronnés par l'Académie Française.* Paris: Librairie Nouvelle, 1855.

———. *Une histoire de soldat.* Paris: A. Cadot, 1856.

———. *Promenades en Hollande.* Paris: L. Hachette, 1859.

———. *L'Italie des Italiens.* 4 vols. Paris: E. Dentu, 1862.

———. *Les Derniers Marquis.* Paris: E. Dentu, 1866.

———. *Les Derniers Abbés: Moeurs religieuses d'Italie.* Paris: E. Dentu, 1868.

———. *Satire du siècle. Paris-Matière.* Paris: Hurtau, 1868.

———. *Réponse aux "Guêpes" de Monsieur Alphonse Karr.* Paris: Hurtau, 1869.

———. *Ces Petits Messieurs,* Paris, E. Dentu, 1869.

———. *Les Dévotes du Grand Monde.* Paris: E. Dentu, 1873.

———. *La Vérité sur l'anarchie des esprits en France.* Milan: F. Legros Felice Editeur, 1873.

———. *Edgar Quinet: L'Esprit nouveau.* Paris: Hurtau, 1876.

———. *Les Pays Lumineux: Voyage en Orient.* Paris: E. Dentu, 1879.

———. *Lui: A View of Him.* Translated by Marilyn Gaddis Rose. Athens and London: University of Georgia Press, 1986.

———. *La Jeunesse de Goethe.* Paris: Imprimerie de Vve. Dondey-Dupré, n.d.

————, ed. *Quarante-cinq lettres de Béranger.* Paris: Librairie Nouvelle, 1857.

Colet, Louise, and M. Jay. *Jules César et la Tempête.* Traduction française. Paris: Bibliothèque Anglo-Française, 1839.

Critobule [Eugène Vial]. *Paul Mariéton d'après sa correspondance.* Paris: G. Cris, 1920.

Czyba, Luce. *La Femme dans les romans de Flaubert: Mythes et idéologie.* Lyon: Presses Universitaires de Lyon, 1983.

DeJean, Joan, and Nancy Miller, eds. *Displacements: Women, Traditions and Literatures in French.* Baltimore and London: The Johns Hopkins University Press, 1991.

Desanti, Dominique. *Daniel, ou le visage secret d'une Comtesse romantique: Marie d'Agoult.* Paris: Stock, 1980.

Descharmes, René. *Flaubert: Sa vie, son caractère et ses idées avant 1857.* Paris: Librairie des Amateurs, 1909.

Donnay, Maurice. *La Vie amoureuse d'Alfred de Musset.* Paris: Flammarion, 1926.

Douchin, Jacques-Louis. *La Vie érotique de Flaubert.* Paris: Carrère—J-J Pauvert, 1984.

Flaubert, Gustave. *L'éducation sentimentale.* Paris: Bibliothèque Charpentier, 1922.

————. *Dictionary of Accepted Ideas.* Translated by Jacques Barzun. New York: New Directions, 1954.

————. *Madame Bovary.* Paris: Garnier, 1961.

————. *Oeuvres complètes.* Edited by Bernard Masson. Paris: Seuil, 1964.

————. *Correspondance.* 3 vols. Edited by Jean Bruneau. Paris: Gallimard, Bibliothèque de la Pléiade, 1973, 1981, 1991.

————. *Bouvard et Pécuchet.* Paris: Laffont, 1981.

Frejlich, Hélène. *Les Amants de Mantes.* Paris: Sfelt, 1936.

Friedrich, Otto. *Olympia: Paris in the Age of Manet.* New York: HarperCollins, 1992.

Gérard-Gailly. *Les Véhémences de Madame Colet.* Paris: Mercure de France, 1934.

Girardin, Delphine de. *Chroniques parisiennes: 1836–1848.* Paris: Editions des Femmes, 1986.

Goncourt, Jules and Edmond de. *Journal.* 3 vols. Paris: Robert Laffont, 1989.

Gray, Francine du Plessix. *Adam & Eve and the City: Selected Essays.* New York: Simon and Schuster, 1987.

Hemmings, F. W. J. *Culture and Society in France 1789–1848.* Leicester, U.K.: Leicester University Press, 1987.

Jackson, Joseph. *Louise Colet et ses amis littéraires.* New Haven: Yale University Press, 1937.

Johnson, Paul. *The Birth of the Modern: World Society 1815–1830.* New York: HarperCollins, 1991.

Kimball, F., and L. Venturi. *Great Paintings in America.* New York: Coward McCann, 1947.

Léger, Charles. *Courbet et son temps.* Paris: Éditions Universelles, 1948.

Lescure, Marthurin de. *Eux et elles: L'Histoire d'un scandale.* Paris: Poulet-Malassi et Débroise, 1860.

Levaillant, Maurice. *The Passionate Exiles.* New York: Farrar, Straus and Cudahy, 1958.

Lottman, Herbert. *Flaubert: A Biography.* Boston: Little, Brown, 1989.

Lovenjoul, Vicomte de Spoelberch de. *La Véritable Histoire de "elle et lui."* Paris: Calmann Levy, 1897.

Marcus, Steven. *The Other Victorians.* New York: Basic Books, 1966.

Maurois, André. *Olympio, or the Life of Victor Hugo.* New York: Carroll & Graf, 1956.

Merimée, Prosper. *Lettre á une inconnue.* Paris: M. Levy, 1874.

Mestral-Combremont, J. de. *La Belle Madame Colet, une déesse des romantiques.* Paris: Fontemoing et Cie, 1913.

Mirecourt, Eugène de. *Les Contemporains, Louise Colet.* Paris: Gustave Havard, 1857.

Musset, Alfred de. *Poésies posthumes.* Paris: Seuil, 1963.

Musset, Paul de. *Lui et elle.* Paris: Charpentier, 1871.

Nabokov, Alexis, Julien Bauer, and Colombe Schneck. *Guide des auberges de campagne et hôtels de charme en France.* Paris: Rivages, 1991.

Nora, Pierre, ed. *Les Lieux de mémoire.* Paris: Gallimard, 1984, 7 volumes.

Oliver, Hermione. *Flaubert and an English Governess.* Oxford: Clarendon Press, 1980.

Parris, John. *The Lion of Caprera.* New York: David McKay Co., 1962.

Priollaud, Nicole, ed. *La Femme au XIXe siècle.* Paris: Liana Lévi et Sylvie Messinger, 1983.

Reboul, Jean. *Poésies.* New (6th) edition. Paris: H. L. Deloye, 1840.

Réval, Gabrielle. *Les Grandes Amoureuses.* Paris: Albin Michel, 1928.

Riat, G. *Gustave Courbet peintre.* Paris: H. Fleury, 1906.

Rougerie, Jacques. *La Commune.* Paris: Presses Universitaires de France, 1971.

Saarinen, Aline. *The Proud Possessors: The Lives, Times and Tastes of Some Adventurous American Art Collectors.* New York: Random House, 1958.

Sabatier, Robert. *La Poésie du XIXème siècle.* Paris: Albin Michel, 1985.

Sainte-Beuve, Charles Augustin. *Chroniques parisiennes.* Paris: Calmann-Lévy, 1876.

Sand, George. *Elle et lui.* Paris: Michel Lévy Frères, 1859.

———. *Correspondance.* Edited by Georges Lubin. Paris: Garnier, 1969.

Sartre, Jean-Paul. *L'Idiot de la famille.* Paris: Gallimard, 1971, 2 volumes.

Schell, Franck. "Une Aventurière de la littérature." In *La Femme française.* London: G. P. Putnam's Sons, 1927.

Siler, Douglas, ed. *Flaubert et Louise Pradier: Le Texte intégral des mémoires de Madame Ludovica.* Archives des Lettres Modernes, no. 145, 1973.

———. *Statues de chair; sculptures de James Pradier.* Paris: Editions de la Réunion des Musées Nationaux, 1986.

Starkie, Enid. *Flaubert: The Making of a Master.* London: Weidenfeld and Nicolson, 1967.

Steegmuller, Francis. *Flaubert and Madame Bovary.* New York: Viking Press, 1939.

———, ed. *Flaubert in Egypt.* Chicago: Academy Publishers, 1972.

Thévenot, Arsène. *Méridionales: Poésies intimes.* Arles, 1835.

Thomas, Edith. *Les Pétroleuses.* Paris: Gallimard, 1963.

Troubat, Jules. *Notes et pensées.* Paris: Librairie Générale de L. Sauvaitre, 1888.

———. *Une Amitié à la d'Arthez: Champfleury, Courbet, Max Buchon.* Paris: Lucien Duc, 1900.

Venturi, Lionello, and F. Kimball. *Great Paintings in America.* New York: Coward-McCann, 1948.

Vigny, Alfred de. *Poèmes antiques et modernes.* Paris: Gallimard, Bibliothèque de la Pléiade, 1986.

Woodward, Kathleen, ed. *Aging and Its Discontents.* Bloomington and Indianapolis: University of Indiana Press, 1991.

Zeldin, Théodore. *France 1848–1945.* 5 vols. New York and Oxford: Oxford University Press, 1980.

UNPUBLISHED DOCUMENTS AND PERIODICAL ARTICLES

Auriant, [Emile]. "Histoire de Safia, dite Koutchouk-Hanem, Almée d'Esneh." *Les Marges,* 26 June 1926.

———. "Louise Colet et les Pachas." *Mercure de France,* 15 April 1934.

———. "Madame Bovary, née Colet." *Mercure de France.* 1 June 1936.

———. "Koutchouk Hanem, l'almée de Flaubert." *Mercure de France,* 1943.

Benassis. "Essais de clinique littéraire: Les Amis de Flaubert: Louise Colet." *Les Alcoloides,* December 1950.

Bonnefon, Paul. "Lettres inédites de Béranger à Victor Cousin." *Revue Politique et Littéraire. Revue Bleue,* no. 17, 29 April–6 May 1911.

Bonnerot, J. "A la poursuite d'un article, ou trente ans de la vie de Sainte-Beuve et de la belle Madame Colet." *La Muse Française,* vol. XII, 15 October 1933.

Bruneau, Jean. "Louise Colet, Maxime du Camp, Gustave Flaubert . . . et Garibaldi." In *Mélanges offerts a la mémoire de Franco Simone.* Geneva, Editions Slatkine, 1984, pp. 469–83.

Cesare, Raffaele de. "Silvio Pellico e Louise Colet." *In Giornale Storico della Letteratura Italiana,* 1973, Turin, Loescher Editor: 1973.

Chambon, Félix. "Deux passions d'un philosophe." *Annales Romantiques. Revue d'histoire du romantisme,* vol. I, 1904.

Colet, Louise, *A Monsieur Canonge.* MS. 492, fol. 258, Bibliothèque de Nîmes.

Cousin, Victor. Correspondance. Folios. 281–282. Bibliothèque Victor Cousin, Université de la Sorbonne.

Descaves, Lucien. "La Belle Amie de Gustave Flaubert." *La Petite Histoire Littéraire,* 2 September 1936.

Documents of the Bood Family, Paris. Courtesy of Maurice Hendrik Bood and Christopher Bood.

Dorsenne, Jean. "Une Muse." *Au Jour le Jour,* 8 March 1926.

Dossier Colet 1160.A.1. Musée Paul Arbaud, Aix-en-Provence.

Doutrelkeau, Louis. "Quelques lettres inédites de Prosper Mérimée." *Études,* vol. 204, 20 September 1930.

Du Camp, Maxime. "Souvenirs littéraires." *Revue des Deux Mondes,* 15 August 1882.

DuFay, Pierre. "Champfleury, Mme Hanska et Louise Colet." *Mercure de France,* August 15, 1927.

Dumesnil, René. "Louis Bouilhet." In *Les Nouvelles Littéraires,* Page 28 Anthologiques, January 1933.

———. "Louise Colet, Champfleury et le garde-champêtre de Meudon." *Les Nouvelles Littéraires,* 8 September 1934.

Fonds Louise Colet. Bibliothèque Municipale d'Avignon.

Gazette Anecdotique, no. 6, 31 March 1876.

Gazette Anecdotique, 15 January 1881.

Gazette Anecdotique, vol I, no. 413, 1882.

Henriot, Emile. "La Femme Colet." *Le Temps,* Courrier Littéraire, 3 April 1934.

Ignotus [Baron Félix Platel]. "Une Muse." *Le Figaro,* 14 September 1882.

Jackson, Joseph. "Flaubert et Louise Colet." *Nouvelles Littéraires,* 5 November 1938.

————. "Louise Colet et ses amis littéraires." *Nouvelles Littéraires,* 28 January 1939.

Karr, Alphonse. *Les Guêpes,* May 1840 (no. 2), June 1840 (no. 2), September 1840 (no. 3).

Kempf, Roger. "Le Double Pupitre." *Cahiers du Chènevis,* October 1969.

Langle, Fleuriot de. "Louise Colet et les Sbires du Pape." *Le Figaro,* 21 January 1933.

Léger, Charles. "Un Portrait inconnu de Louise Colet par Gustave Courbet." In *Nouvelles Littéraires,* 1 Septembre 1934.

Levaillant, Maurice. "Gustave Flaubert et Louise Colet." *Le Figaro,* Supplément Littéraire, 1 May 1926.

Levaillant, Maurice, and Marc Varenne. "Les Amours d'Alfred de Vigny et de Louise Colet." *La Revue,* 15 January, 1 February, 15 February 1956.

Maynial, Edouard. "Ce qui est dans le coeur des femmes ou les confidences de la belle Madame Colet." *Revue d'Histoire Littéraire de la France. Mercure de France,* 1 May 1916.

Mohammed-el-Akmar [pseudonym for Louise Colet]. "Inauguration du canal de Suez." *Le Siècle,* 14 November 1869.

Molènes, Guy de. "Simples essais d'histoire littéraire. I. Les Femmes Poètes." *Revue des Deux Mondes,* 1 July 1842.

"La Muse et le Titan." *Le Figaro,* 22 May 1926.

"Obituaire de Louise Colet." *Le Figaro,* 11 March 1876.

"Obituaire de Louise Colet." *Revue Britannique: Chronique et Bulletin Bibliographique,* March 1876.

Pascal, Félicien. "Une Circé romantique." *Le Gaulois,* 27 March 1926.

Patin, Jacques. "Lettres inédites de Louise Colet." *Le Figaro,* 7 February 1931.

Picard, Gaston. "Le Cinquantenaire de Louise Colet à travers la *Gazette Anecdotique,*" *Le Figaro,* 13 March 1926.

Pommier, Jean, and Claude Digeon. "Du nouveau sur Flaubert et son oeuvre." *Mercure de France,* 1 May 1952.

Revue de Paris, 30 June 1839.

Revue des Deux Mondes, 1 December 1839.

Ségur, Marquis de. "Mme Louise Colet." *Conférences et Conférenciers,* 15 February 1910.

Simon, Gustave. "Victor Hugo et Louise Colet." *Revue de France,* 15 May 1926.

Strowski, Fortunat. "Alfred de Vigny." *Revue des Cours et Conférences,* 16 April–31 May 1923.

Le Temps, 19 November 1865.

Thibaudet, Albert. "Amis et amies des lettres." *Candide,* 16 June 1927.

Treich, Leon. "Louise Colet." *L'Éclair,* Courrier des Lettres, 7 March 1926.

Troubat, Jules. "Mémoires contemporains: Mme Louise Colet." *Le Temps,* 14 September 1913.

"Victime, elle?" (review of *Louise Colet ou la muse* by Jean-Paul Clébert and *L'Indomptable Louise Colet* by Micheline Bood and Serge Grand). *Le Monde,* 7 November 1986.

Wieclawik, Louise de. "Victor Cousin amoureux et critique littéraire. Lettres inédites (Juillet–Décembre 1839)." *Revue des Sciences Humaines,* vol. XXXV, no. 140, October–December 1970.

W. O. "Nécrologie." *Bulletin du Bibliophile,* 1876.

Zemmour, Eric. "La Revanche de la muse." *Le Quotidien de Paris,* 9 December 1986.

Index